CW01018767

Piracy and the State

The Politics of Intellectual Property Rights in China

China has the highest levels of copyright piracy and trademark counterfeiting in the world, even though it also provides the highest per capita volume of enforcement. In this original study of intellectual property rights (IPR) in relation to state capacity, Martin K. Dimitrov analyzes this puzzle by offering the first systematic analysis of all IPR enforcement avenues in China, across all IPR subtypes. He shows that the extremely high volume of enforcement provided for copyrights and trademarks is unfortunately of a low quality and as such serves only to perpetuate IPR violations. In the area of patents, however, he finds a low volume of high-quality enforcement.

In light of these findings, the book develops a theory of state capacity that conceptualizes the Chinese state as simultaneously weak and strong. It also demonstrates that fully rationalized enforcement of domestic and foreign IPR is emerging unevenly and, somewhat counterintuitively, chiefly in those IPR subtypes that are least subject to domestic or foreign pressure.

The book draws on extensive fieldwork in China and five other countries, as well as on ten unique IPR enforcement datasets that exploit previously unexplored sources, including case files of private investigation firms.

Martin K. Dimitrov is Assistant Professor of Government at Dartmouth College. He has also been a postdoctoral Fellow at Harvard University, in the Fairbank Center for Chinese Studies and in the Davis Center for Russian and Eurasian Studies. He received his B.A. in government and French from Franklin and Marshall College and his Ph.D. in political science from Stanford University in 2004. His publications have appeared in the *Journal of Democracy, Current History,* and *Twenty-First Century (Ershiyi shiji).* He is currently working on a book-length study of the collapse and resilience of communist regimes.

For my mother,
Zlatka Kostadinova,
and in memory of my father,
Kostadin Kostadinov

Piracy and the State

The Politics of Intellectual Property Rights in China

MARTIN K. DIMITROV
Dartmouth College

CAMBRIDGE
UNIVERSITY PRESS

CAMBRIDGE UNIVERSITY PRESS
Cambridge, New York, Melbourne, Madrid, Cape Town, Singapore,
São Paulo, Delhi, Dubai, Tokyo

Cambridge University Press
32 Avenue of the Americas, New York, NY 10013-2473, USA

www.cambridge.org
Information on this title: www.cambridge.org/9780521897310

© Martin K. Dimitrov 2009

This publication is in copyright. Subject to statutory exception
and to the provisions of relevant collective licensing agreements,
no reproduction of any part may take place without the written
permission of Cambridge University Press.

First published 2009

Printed in the United States of America

A catalog record for this publication is available from the British Library.

Library of Congress Cataloging in Publication Data
Dimitrov, Martin K., 1975–
Piracy and the state : the politics of intellectual property rights in China / Martin K. Dimitrov.
    p. cm.
Includes bibliographical references and index.
ISBN 978-0-521-89731-0 (hardback)
1. Intellectual property – China. 2. Piracy (Copyright) – China. 3. Intellectual property – Govern-
ment policy – China. 4. Trademarks – Law and legislation – China. 5. Copyright – China. 6. Patent
laws and legislation – China. 7. Product counterfeiting – China. I. Title.
KNQ1155.D54 2009
346.5104'8 – dc22   2008054787

ISBN 978-0-521-89731-0 Hardback

Cambridge University Press has no responsibility for the persistence or accuracy of URLs for
external or third-party Internet Web sites referred to in this publication and does not guarantee
that any content on such Web sites is, or will remain, accurate or appropriate.

Contents

List of Tables

List of Figures and GIS Maps

Acknowledgments

It gives me great pleasure to thank the individuals and institutions whose generous support made the writing of this book possible. At Stanford, I especially benefited from the advice of Larry Diamond, Judith Goldstein, Michael McFaul, Jean Oi, and Barry Weingast. I was fortunate to have Jean Oi as my adviser, mentor, and friend. Across the years, Jean has provided exceptional advice, good counsel, and sustained encouragement, along with a perfect sense of when I needed to move faster and when I needed to slow down. I am deeply grateful for her support.

My colleagues at Dartmouth College have enriched the past four years with their conversation, advice, and friendship. I want especially to thank John Carey and Linda Fowler, who strengthened my book through their detailed comments and generous engagement with my manuscript. I also owe much to M. Anne Sa'adah, William Wohlforth, Ned Lebow, and Allan Stam, who gave me incisive suggestions for improvements.

Many others have read my work. I am especially grateful to Margaret Levi, Melanie Manion, and Randall Peerenboom, who commented on the entire manuscript, and offered me substantial suggestions for improvement. I also thank William Alford, who provided encouragement along with extensive written and oral comments. Conversations with a number of people helped me formulate my ideas. I am grateful to Lisa Baldez, Calvin Chen, Xi Chen, Jerome Cohen, Taylor Fravel, Mary Gallagher, Andrei Hagiu, Yoshiko Herrera, Yasheng Huang, Nahomi Ichino, David Laitin, Matthew Levendusky, Peter Lorentzen, Stanley Lubman, Roderick MacFarquhar, Edmund Malesky, Isabela Mares, Nikolay Marinov, Eva Meyersson-Milgrom, Kevin O'Brien, Elena Obukhova, Elizabeth Perry, Victor Shih, Kay Shimizu, Konstantin Sonin, Hiroki Takeuchi, Jeremy Wallace, and Dali Yang.

For their stimulating questions and helpful insights, I thank the audiences of seminars held at Dartmouth College, Harvard University (the Davis Center, the Fairbank Center, the Center for the Environment, Harvard Business School, and Harvard Law School), Miami University, Middlebury College, Oxford

University, Stanford University, Tsinghua University, the University of California at San Diego, and the University of Maryland.

A number of institutions provided the financial assistance that enabled my research. I am grateful to the Department of Political Science at Stanford University; the Center for East Asian Studies at Stanford University; the Center for Russian, East European, and Eurasian Studies at Stanford University; the Social Science History Institute at Stanford University; the Graduate Research Opportunity Fund at Stanford University; the Center on Democracy, Development, and the Rule of Law at Stanford University; the Office of the Dean at Dartmouth College; the Dickey Center for International Understanding at Dartmouth College; the Rockefeller Center for Public Policy and the Social Sciences at Dartmouth College; the U.S. Department of Education (Foreign Language and Area Studies Fellowship); the Social Science Research Council (International Predissertation Fellowship Program); the China and Inner Asia Council of the Association for Asian Studies (Small Grants Program); and the Harvard University Center for the Environment. Postdoctoral fellowships from the Davis Center for Russian and Eurasian Studies at Harvard University and the Fairbank Center for Chinese Studies at Harvard University, as well as the Arthur M. Wilson and Mary Tolford Wilson Faculty Research Fellowship from Dartmouth College, gave me time to complete the project. During leave, the Davis Center at Harvard and the East Asian Legal Studies Program at Harvard Law School graciously hosted me as a research associate or visiting scholar.

This book would not have been possible without the help of the more than four hundred individuals who agreed to be interviewed in China, Russia, Taiwan, the Czech Republic, France, and the United States. Although I am not able in general to name them, several public figures have given me permission to thank them personally. In Hong Kong, Joseph Simone and the late Tony Gurka were exceptionally generous with their time, archival materials, and expertise. In Russia, Igor Pozhitkov, Tom Thomson, and Denis Voevodin shared their data and gave advice. In Taiwan, Robin Winkler and Judge Peggy Pi-hu Hsu from the Supreme Court allowed me to use their rich archives. Thanks also to Jiří Šír, Milan Šmíd, and Zbyněk Suchomel in Prague; Delphine Sarfati-Sobreira in Paris; and Michael Schlesinger and Andy Sun in Washington, DC. I owe a special debt to Diana Matthias, who gave me a new perspective on China.

A project like this depends on printed sources as well. I am grateful to various institutions and libraries for their assistance. The collections at the National Library of China, the Bibliothèque nationale de France, the East Asia Library at Stanford University, the Fung Library at Harvard University, the Harvard-Yenching Library, and the International Legal Studies Collection of the Harvard Law School Library proved especially useful. Miles Yoshimura and Nien Lin Xie help make the Baker-Berry Library at Dartmouth College the rich resource it is, and they graciously entertained my requests to purchase obscure yearbooks from China and Russia.

My students at Dartmouth have helped me think about my project and why it matters. I am particularly grateful to several who provided research assistance: Trudy Hong, Douglas Raicek, Manya Sleeper, Charlotte Taylor, Chunhua Vivienne Wei, and Jennifer Xi. Natalie Koch deserves special thanks for constructing the GIS maps used in this book.

At Cambridge University Press, I want particularly to thank Lew Bateman, who was enthusiastic about my research from an early stage and whose unfailing encouragement and judicious advice have brought the project along. I also want to thank Monica Finley, Emily Spangler, Janis Bolster, and Susan Thornton, as well as two anonymous reviewers for the Press, whose comments richly improved the manuscript. Before the book went to press, Nancy Hearst proofread the whole manuscript with an expert eye, saving me from many mistakes. Anne Holmes and Rob Rudnick prepared the index.

For a long time, my friends in many places have listened to me talk enthusiastically about arcane matters. Their support made my work easier. I want to thank Sonu Bedi, Antonia Cameron, Nahomi Ichino, Nedka Ivanova, Diana Marinova, Diana Matthias, Rebecca Matthias, Adam Rozan, Josh Rozan, Anne Sa'adah, and Kenneth Yalowitz. In Moscow, on several occasions, Zinaida Kourochkina opened her home and her city to me. Bradin Cormack brings joy to my life and at different times has made a challenging project again seem possible.

My greatest debt is to my family. My sister, Katya; my brother-in-law, Milen; and my nieces, Vasilka and Zlatka, have been constant sources of support. My father, Kostadin Kostadinov, and my mother, Zlatka Kostadinova, have loved me in all the ways parents do. They encouraged me to pursue my dreams, even the strange ones. Most of all, they have been models of integrity, tenacity, and courage. I dedicate this book to them.

List of Abbreviations

ACC	Anticounterfeiting Committee (Taiwan)
AFSSAPS	Agency on the Sanitary Security of Medical Products (Agence française de sécurité sanitaire des produits de santé) (France)
AIC	Administration for Industry and Commerce
AQSIQ	General Administration of Quality Supervision, Inspection, and Quarantine
BOFT	Board of Foreign Trade (Taiwan)
BSA	Business Software Alliance
BSMI	Bureau of Standards, Metrology, and Inspection (Taiwan)
CACC	China Anticounterfeiting Coalition
CAEFI	China Association of Enterprises with Foreign Investment
CC CCP	Central Committee of the Chinese Communist Party
CIPR	Coalition for Intellectual Property Rights (Russia)
CNTC	China National Tobacco Corporation
ČOI	Czech Commercial Inspection (Česká obchodní inspekce)
CSRC	China Securities Regulatory Commission
DCPAF	Direction centrale de la police aux frontiers (France)
DCPJ	Direction centrale de la police judiciaire (France)
DCSP	Direction centrale de la sécurité publique (France)
DGCCRF	Directorate General on Competition, Consumer Affairs, and Fraud Control (Direction générale de la concurrence, de la consommation et de la répression des fraudes)
DNRED	National Directorate on Customs Inquiries and Investigations (Direction nationale du renseignement et des enquêtes douanières)
DOH	Department of Health (Taiwan)

DOM-TOM	Overseas Departments and Territories (Départements d'outre-mer et territoires d'outre-mer) (France)
DRC	Development Research Center
EPB	Environmental Protection Bureau
FAS	Federal Antimonopoly Service (Russia)
FDA	Food and Drug Administration
FDI	foreign direct investment
FIPS	Federal Service for Intellectual Property, Patents, and Trademarks (Russia)
FSB	Federal Security Service (Federal'naia sluzhba bezopasnosti) (Russia)
FTC	Fair Trade Commission (Taiwan)
FTS	Russian Federal Customs Service (Federal'naia tamozhennaia sluzhba)
GAC	General Administration of Customs
GACEB	General Administration for Combating Embezzlement and Bribery
GAPP	General Administration of Press and Publications
IACC	International Anticounterfeiting Coalition
IETF	Integrated Enforcement Task Force (Taiwan)
IFPI	International Federation of the Phonographic Industry
IIPA	International Intellectual Property Alliance
IPO	Intellectual Property Office
IPR	intellectual property rights
IPRP	Specialized IPR Police (Taiwan)
ITC	International Trade Commission (United States)
JODE	Joint Optical Disk Enforcement Force (Taiwan)
KMT	Kuomintang
MEP	Ministry of Environmental Protection
MJIB	Ministry of Justice Investigation Bureau (Taiwan)
MOA	Ministry of Agriculture
MOC	Ministry of Culture
MOEA	Taiwanese Ministry of Economic Affairs
MOFTEC	Ministry of Foreign Trade and Economic Cooperation
MOH	Ministry of Health
MOI	Ministry of the Interior (Taiwan)
MOU	memorandum of understanding
MPA	Motion Picture Association
MPS	Ministry of Public Security

MVD	Russian Ministry of the Interior (Ministerstvo vnutrennikh del)
NAPWC	National Anti-Pornography and Anti-Piracy Working Committee
NBS	National Bureau of Standards
NCAC	National Copyright Administration of China
NPA	National Police Administration (Taiwan)
NPC	National People's Congress
OD	optical disk
OEM	original equipment manufacturer
PAP	People's Armed Police
PCA	Provincial Copyright Administration
PLA	People's Liberation Army
pmp	per million people
ppp	purchasing power parity
PRB	Patent Reexamination Board
PRC	People's Republic of China
PSB	Public Security Bureau
QBPC	Quality Brands Protection Committee
RMB	Renminbi (Chinese yuan)
R&D	research and development
SAIC	State Administration for Industry and Commerce
SARFT	State Administration of Radio, Film, and Television
SDA	State Drug Administration
SEPA	State Environmental Protection Agency
SEZ	special economic zone
SFDA	State Food and Drug Administration
SID	source identification
SIPO	State Intellectual Property Office
SNEP	Syndicat national de l'édition phonographique (France)
SPC	Supreme People's Court
SPP	Supreme People's Procuratorate
STMA	State Tobacco Monopoly Administration
SÚKL	State Institute for Drug Control (Státní ústav pro kontrolu léčiv) (Czech Republic)
SZPI	Czech Agricultural and Food Inspection Authority (Státní zemědělská a potravinářská inspekce)
TIPO	Taiwan Intellectual Property Office

TRIPS	Agreement on Trade-Related Aspects of Intellectual Property Rights
TSB	Technical Supervision Bureau
TVE	township and village enterprise
US PTO	United States Patent and Trademark Office
USTR	United States Trade Representative
WCO	World Customs Organization
WIPO	World Intellectual Property Organization
WTO	World Trade Organization

PART I

INTRODUCTION

I

Intellectual Property and the State

In 2001, I found myself in Beijing, speaking to a private investigator about cigarette counterfeiting in China. I already knew something about the scale of the problem. What I had not expected was the investigator's blunt cynicism about the raids he helped organize. "The work we do is simple," he said. "We are hired by a tobacco company to find out who is faking their cigarettes, we investigate whatever leads our paid informants give us, we find a government agency willing to enforce, and then we go along with its representatives to raid the site. Counterfeiting is so entrenched in China that we're able to raid the same place over and over, usually with success. Last year, for example, we organized more than a hundred raids in Da'ao alone." Da'ao is a nondescript village of twenty thousand inhabitants in Raoping county of Guangdong, a province that is known as a center for the production of counterfeit and pirated goods. "Did the hundred raids solve the problem?" I asked. He smiled. "You know," he said, "raids are not always effective. If we pay a bribe, the agency will conduct a raid, but that doesn't mean they seize or destroy the fake cigarettes. Sometimes, the goods disappear right before the raid. Sometimes, the goods are seized, but then sold back to the counterfeiters. It is very rare for fakes to be destroyed. So, we pay the agencies to raid the same counterfeiters again and again."

The logic eluded me. Didn't the companies want to know that the goods had been destroyed? "Companies that have to worry about their bottom line usually pay us just to organize a basic raid," the investigator said. "Destruction would involve paying an additional bribe for the enforcement agency to seize and destroy the goods." Why not go to a more reliable agency, then? "It's true," he said, "that there are a number of government agencies that can provide enforcement. But we find that you can't really go back and forth between them. They don't like being played off against one another. So once we establish a relationship with one enforcement agency, we rarely switch over to another. Our clients want enforcement, and that's what we give them, even if it is imperfect."

Piracy and the State is an attempt to understand the causes and consequences of the kind of enforcement debacle the Beijing investigator described to me. His story illustrates the pitfalls of *routine* enforcement of the laws governing intellectual property rights (IPR) in China. When right holders suffer infringement of the valuable intellectual property they own, they are indeed able to seek enforcement from a number of different government agencies. Although these agencies do respond, the enforcement they provide seems to have little or no impact on the levels of copyright piracy and trademark counterfeiting. Anyone who has visited China knows how easy it is to obtain pirated Beatles CDs or knockoff Gucci bags or fake Viagra. But this is only the tip of the problem. Da'ao village is not alone in producing counterfeits. On the contrary, ineffective enforcement has allowed counterfeiting to emerge as the main source of income for many midsized towns and, sometimes, even for entire counties.[1] The lack of effective oversight by the state has allowed whole sectors of the economy to become addicted to piracy and other IPR violations.

The central government is aware of such centers of endemic counterfeiting, but its response has been to address the problems only at the point of crisis, when radical enforcement measures have to be taken. The story of Da'ao village, which has long been known to government officials and private investigators as a major source of cigarette counterfeiting, is again instructive. Since the early 1990s, hundreds of routine small-scale raids have been conducted by various enforcement agencies here every year, without stemming the tide of counterfeiting. In 2004, the central government, eventually admitting that there was a crisis situation in Da'ao, dispatched three thousand enforcement personnel to the village, with orders to unleash a "tsunami" enforcement campaign. The result? The authorities arrested some counterfeiters and confiscated counterfeit tobacco products worth 56 million yuan (US$7 million).[2] This outcome was considered so exceptional as to merit inclusion on the list of major enforcement accomplishments of the State Tobacco Monopoly Administration (STMA), one of the many agencies with an IPR mandate in China.[3]

Was this a good use of resources or an adequate response to a systemic problem? Sending three thousand enforcement personnel to a village of twenty thousand is an example of *campaign-style* enforcement in response to a crisis situation. Campaign-style enforcement typically features more than one enforcement agency (in the case of Da'ao, enforcement was provided by the STMA and the police) and is aimed at the rapid resolution of a major problem. But the need for this kind of response to address counterfeiting in a single village underscores the state's inability to nip this problem in the bud. It is neither feasible nor in the end desirable for government agencies to expend so much energy on crisis management. In sum, Da'ao illustrates the basic enforcement problem facing the Chinese government in the area of IPR. Routine enforcement raids are ineffective; that

---

[1] There are five hierarchically organized levels of government in China: center, provinces, prefectures, counties, and townships/towns. Villages are located below the townships/towns but are not considered an official level of government.

[2] Instead of RMB, I use the more widely accepted yuan to refer to China's currency.

[3] *Zhongguo yancao nianjian 2004* (China Tobacco Yearbook 2004) (Beijing: Jingji ribao chubanshe, 2006), 160.

means that relatively small-scale problems eventually require the unleashing of enforcement campaigns. Even worse, these campaigns are not necessarily effective at resolving the problem: counterfeiting operations are merely moved to the next village or the next town, and the fakes continue to be churned out until the next crisis, in a predictable cyclical pattern, results in the next campaign.

The puzzle I have been describing is this: why, in spite of its high volume, is China's enforcement of IPR laws typically ineffective in resolving the problems of copyright piracy and trademark counterfeiting? The question requires us to turn to the state.

As a window onto state capacity, this book focuses on the full range of bureaucracies that provide enforcement of IPR laws in China. My basic premise is that a strong state is capable of enforcing laws and regulations, whereas a weak state is not. To assess state capacity in a given area, we need to know what agencies are empowered to provide enforcement and how well they do it. This book insists that both the volume and the quality of IPR enforcement are relevant for this assessment. It argues that under some conditions the Chinese state can provide high-quality enforcement of IPR laws. Most of the time, nevertheless, there is a high volume of enforcement, which, however, is of a low quality. This is characteristic of both campaign-style enforcement and most routine enforcement.

This research has three implications for our understanding of state capacity in reform-era China. The first is that any assessment of state capacity based on the volume of enforcement alone will be erroneous. We can evaluate state capacity only when we have data about both the quantity and the quality of enforcement. In other words, a state that provides a high volume of low-quality enforcement is not strong, even though it is doing a lot. A second implication is that state capacity varies by issue area. As we will see, even within IPR, one subtype (patents) benefits from high-quality enforcement, whereas other subtypes (copyrights and trademarks) are subject to ineffective enforcement of the kind that plagues Da'ao. Blanket assessments of state strength or state weakness may be misleading. A third and final implication is that reliable predictions about the direction in which the Chinese state is headed cannot be made until we have a better map of *how* the state does what it does in different issue areas. IPR is one of hundreds of issue areas regulated by the Chinese state. In most of these (as in IPR), the gaps in our knowledge are such as to require a comprehensive study of both the organization and the operation of the numerous actors who provide enforcement. Without first adequately filling in these gaps, we will not be able to assess with accuracy whether China is moving toward rationalization and the rule of law.

STATE STRENGTH AND ENFORCEMENT CAPACITY

One of the key functions of a modern state is to enforce contracts that protect property rights.[4] Property rights are enshrined in laws, and the state has

---

[4] Margaret Levi, "The State of the Study of the State," in *Political Science: The State of the Discipline*, ed. Ira Katznelson and Helen V. Milner (New York: W. W. Norton, 2002), 33–55.

responsibility for enforcing these laws. However, the state does not enforce the laws directly, but rather creates and maintains institutions to supply enforcement when necessary. In general, there are three main channels for providing enforcement within a country's territory – civil courts of law, administrative agencies, and the criminal justice system. In addition, the Customs Administration can provide border enforcement. Some types of property are protected only through a single channel. For example, disputes over land ownership are adjudicated through civil courts of law. Other types of property may be protected through multiple channels. Personal property, for example, is protected by the police and criminal courts in a case of burglary or by a civil court of law in an ownership dispute. Intellectual property (copyrights, trademarks, and patents) is one of the rare forms of property protected through all four main channels. In China, the courts of law, administrative agencies, police, and Customs Administration are all empowered to protect IPR. The breadth of IPR enforcement options therefore provides us with an unusually comprehensive lens through which we can evaluate the capacity of the state to enforce its laws and regulations.

How can we assess the enforcement capacity of states? A natural response is to look at the volume of enforcement provided, and to conclude that a higher volume of enforcement suggests a stronger enforcement capacity. A model here is the scholarship on extractive capacity that associates a higher level of tax collection with state strength. However, as this book demonstrates, a high volume of enforcement does not necessarily mean that the state has the capacity to ensure a high quality of enforcement. The tradeoff between volume and quality is nicely illustrated by the example of manufactured goods in the Soviet Union, where plan fulfillment was based on the quantity of goods produced rather than on their quality. As is well known, this led to the voluminous production of shoddy goods, hardly an indicator of state strength. This book maintains that a similar dynamic in the enforcement of laws governing IPR in China makes quality and quantity equally relevant for the measurement of state capacity.

What kind of enforcement is high-quality enforcement? This is enforcement that is consistent, transparent, and procedurally fair. More extensive definitions of these terms will be provided later in this chapter. It is sufficient here to say that consistent enforcement is predictable enforcement: it exists when similar penalties are applied to similar cases, regardless of the status of the plaintiff. Consistency is the opposite of arbitrary enforcement. Transparent enforcement is open enforcement, which may involve the holding of public trials or open administrative hearings, as well as the publication of court decisions or the issuance of written punishment decisions by administrative agencies. Transparency reduces the opportunities for corruption. Finally, procedural fairness exists when the law is justly applied and when those who feel that they have been treated unjustly have the right to appeal the decision of the court or of the administrative agency. In this book, I often refer to enforcement that is consistent, transparent, and procedurally fair as "rationalized enforcement" or "high-quality enforcement." A state with a strong enforcement capacity is a state capable of providing rationalized enforcement.

Taking a step back, we can ask how important the *enforcement* of property rights is for our account of state capacity. Of course, modern states have other responsibilities and functions: they provide defense and security for their citizens, they collect taxes, and they supply public goods like roads, education, and welfare. These areas of state activity, especially taxation and the provision of public goods, have received a great deal of scholarly attention.[5] Particularly notable is their prominence in the literature about the weaknesses of the postcommunist states in Eastern Europe and China. Scholars who focus on Eastern Europe have produced a long list of problems: regional defiance of the center,[6] a rise in crime and criminality,[7] and wholesale "capture" of the state by a handful of oligarchs able to "purchase" laws and regulations that are favorable to them.[8] All of this occurred against the background of declining tax capacity and deteriorating provision of social services.[9] Though on a smaller scale, China scholars have also identified a decline in extractive capacity,[10] which has been accompanied by increased corruption and criminality.[11] There

[5] This literature is immense. On taxation, see especially Margaret Levi, *Of Rule and Revenue* (Berkeley: University of California Press, 1988). On the rise of the welfare state in the United States, see especially Theda Skocpol, *Protecting Soldiers and Mothers: The Political Origins of Social Policy in the United States* (Cambridge, MA: Belknap Press of Harvard University Press, 1992).

[6] Kathryn Stoner-Weiss, *Resisting the State: Reform and Retrenchment in Post-Soviet Russia* (New York: Cambridge University Press, 2006).

[7] Vadim Volkov, *Violent Entrepreneurs: The Use of Force in the Making of Russian Capitalism* (Ithaca, NY: Cornell University Press, 2002).

[8] Joel Hellman, Geraint Jones, and Daniel Kaufmann, *Seize the State, Seize the Day: State Capture, Corruption, and Influence in Transition*, World Bank Policy Research Paper, no. 2444 (September 2000); Venelin Ganev, *Preying on the State: The Transformation of Bulgaria after 1989* (Ithaca, NY: Cornell University Press, 2007).

[9] On taxation in Russia, see Alexei Lavrov and Alexei Makushkin, *The Fiscal Structure of the Russian Federation: Financial Flows between the Center and the Regions* (Armonk, NY: M. E. Sharpe, 2001). For recent changes, see Gerald Easter, "Building Fiscal Capacity," in *The State after Communism: Governance in the New Russia*, ed. Timothy J. Colton and Stephen Holmes (Lanham, MD: Rowman & Littlefield, 2006), 21–52. On social services, see Linda J. Cook, *The Soviet Social Contract and Why It Failed: Welfare Policy and Workers' Politics from Brezhnev to Yeltsin* (Cambridge, MA: Harvard University Press, 1993) and Linda J. Cook, *Postcommunist Welfare States: Reform Politics in Russia and Eastern Europe* (Ithaca, NY: Cornell University Press, 2007).

[10] Shaoguang Wang and Angang Hu, *The Chinese Economy in Crisis: State Capacity and Tax Reform* (Armonk, NY: M. E. Sharpe, 2001), and Kai-Yuen Tsui and Youqiang Wang, "Between Separate Stoves and a Single Menu: Fiscal Decentralization in China," *The China Quarterly*, no. 177 (2004), 71–90.

[11] For recent studies, see Elizabeth Perry, "Crime, Corruption, and Contention," in *The Paradox of China's Post-Mao Reforms*, ed. Merle Goldman and Roderick MacFarquhar (Cambridge, MA: Harvard University Press, 1999), 308–329; Xiaobo Lü, *Cadres and Corruption: The Organizational Involution of the Communist Party* (Stanford: Stanford University Press, 2000); Yan Sun, *Corruption and Market in Contemporary China* (Ithaca, NY: Cornell University Press, 2004); Melanie Manion, *Corruption by Design: Building Clean Government in Mainland China and Hong Kong* (Cambridge, MA: Harvard University Press, 2004); Minxin Pei, *China's Trapped Transition: The Limits of Developmental Autocracy* (Cambridge, MA: Harvard University Press, 2006).

has been a vigorous and ongoing debate about the waning of the Chinese state and about the possibility of its eventual demise.[12]

As rich as the literature on the postcommunist state is, by and large it does not emphasize the degree to which the execution of state functions depends on the successful enforcement of laws and regulations. Laws structure the operation of the police, mandate proper punishments for tax evasion, and stipulate when citizens have access to social insurance benefits. But existing studies of defense, taxation, and public goods provision tend to treat enforcement in passing, rather than making it a central line of inquiry. In contrast, this study maintains that a focus on the quality of enforcement allows us to ask different and important questions about state capacity. Take tax collection, again, as an example. Focusing exclusively on the amount of taxes collected might well encourage one to associate a high level of tax collection with a high degree of extractive capacity. But if one were to examine how those taxes are collected, a different conceptualization of state capacity might emerge. Questions would have to be asked about the consistent application of the tax collection laws, about the transparency of the collection methods, and about the procedural fairness of the tax collection. Should it be discovered that tax collection is arbitrary and corrupt and that officials are extracting unreasonable or illegal taxes and levies from taxpayers, then we would be forced to conclude that although the volume of taxes collected is high, the quality of tax collection is low, and enforcement is not rationalized.[13] This, in turn, will have implications for our assessment of the extractive capacity of the state.

In short, enforcement capacity has broad significance for our understanding of state strength, most of all if we allow for the possibility that the degree of rationalization matters. A strong state is capable of providing high-quality enforcement of laws and regulations, irrespective of whether those laws protect intellectual property rights (the focus of this book) or apply in areas like tax collection and public goods provision. Although this study is geared toward explaining IPR, its arguments are methodologically and theoretically relevant to our understanding of state capacity in other areas as well.

---

[12] For arguments about decline, see Andrew Walder, ed., *The Waning of the Communist State: Economic Origins of Political Decline in China and Hungary* (Berkeley: University of California Press, 1995); Wang and Hu, *The Chinese Economy in Crisis*; and Pei, *China's Trapped Transition*. For studies emphasizing state strength, see Dali L. Yang, *Remaking the Chinese Leviathan: Market Transition and the Politics of Governance in China* (Stanford: Stanford University Press, 2004) and Barry J. Naughton and Dali L. Yang, eds., *Holding China Together: Diversity and National Integration in the Post-Deng Era* (New York: Cambridge University Press, 2004). See also Randall Peerenboom, ed., *Is China Trapped in Transition? Implications for Future Reforms* (Oxford: The Foundation for Law, Justice, and Society, 2007).

[13] For an analysis of the excesses of rural tax collection, see Thomas Bernstein and Xiaobo Lü, *Taxation without Representation in Contemporary Rural China* (New York: Cambridge University Press, 2003).

RATIONALIZED ENFORCEMENT: DEFINITION AND MEASUREMENT

There are three stages in the life cycle of a law: promulgation, institutionalization, and internalization. In the initial stage, laws are promulgated and put on the books, in the absence of institutions to enforce them. When laws exist in a general environment of lawlessness, there is little voluntary compliance. In the final stage of the life cycle, laws are internalized and self-enforcing. The rate of voluntary compliance is high because individuals feel that they have been treated fairly by those who enforce the laws.[14] Compliance is also high if individuals consider the law to be substantively fair and just. Some enforcement is necessary at this stage, of course, but for the most part laws are self-enforcing. The rule of law emerges in this final stage. But knowing the nature of the initial and final stages of legal development does not tell us how a country moves from lawlessness to voluntary compliance with the law. Institutionalization, the middle stage in the life cycle of a law during which laws come to be implemented and enforced in a predictable pattern, is crucial. The key variable during this stage is enforcement. A sustained level of consistent, transparent, and procedurally fair enforcement helps make individuals aware of the costs of noncompliance. It also strengthens the legitimacy of the law. It needs stressing that internalization is impossible without the kind of rationalized enforcement that institutionalization can deliver.[15] It is by understanding enforcement therefore that we can get leverage over the process whereby newly promulgated laws become self-enforcing.

Despite its importance, rationalized enforcement has not received extensive scholarly attention. Typically, studies of enforcement analyze its volume.[16] In contrast, as already noted, this book focuses on the relation of volume to quality of enforcement. For example, my subsequent case studies demonstrate that in spite of its high volume, enforcement in the area of trademarks in China is capricious and corrupt. In patents, by contrast, enforcement is of a low volume but is usually of a high quality. Such unevenness across the IPR subtypes is significant. When we make assessments about consistency, transparency, and fairness, we need to look at the substance of the enforcement, not just its volume. Furthermore, because each IPR subtype can be protected through

---

[14] Tom R. Tyler, *Why People Obey the Law* (New Haven: Yale University Press, 1990).

[15] Of course, enforcement is not the only necessary component for ensuring internalization. Individuals also have to become familiar with the law and decide whether it is substantively fair and just. Efforts by the government and nongovernmental organizations to publicize the law can expedite this process.

[16] A welcome exception is provided by studies on the *quality* of the implementation of the single-child policy in China. See Yanzhong Huang and Dali L. Yang, "Population Control and State Coercion in China," in *Holding China Together: Diversity and National Integration in the Post-Deng Era*, ed. Barry J. Naughton and Dali Yang (New York: Cambridge University Press, 2004), 193–225; Susan Greenhalgh and Edwin A. Winckler, *Governing China's Population: From Leninist to Neoliberal Biopolitics* (Stanford: Stanford University Press, 2005); Tyrene White, *China's Longest Campaign: Birth Planning in the People's Republic, 1949–2005* (Ithaca, NY: Cornell University Press, 2006).

different channels (civil, administrative, criminal, Customs), the consistency, transparency, and fairness of IPR protection through each of these channels will be relevant to our assessment of whether rationalized enforcement definitively exists in IPR. This technique can be applied to assess progress toward rationalization in any area of the law. The uneven or "patchy" appearance of higher- and lower-quality enforcement across those different areas may help us identify the processes through which an entire legal system may be able to move from lawlessness toward rationalization.

Measuring Consistency, Transparency, and Procedural Fairness

The consistency, transparency, and fairness of enforcement cannot be observed directly, so proxies are required. When assessing the consistency of enforcement, we are looking for evidence that laws are applied similarly in similar situations, without regard to the plaintiff's status; for that reason, our proxies relate to judicial expertise and professionalism. In the area of civil enforcement, higher-level courts and specialized courts are more likely to be consistent in their interpretations of the law because they generally have better-trained judges than lower-level courts; higher-level courts also have to produce better-reasoned decisions, because they are subject to greater scrutiny than lower-level courts.[17] Professionalism is similarly crucial for administrative enforcement. As we can observe in the area of patent enforcement (Chapter 9), agencies with better-trained personnel are more likely to provide consistent law enforcement than agencies with poorly qualified personnel.

A clearly defined enforcement jurisdiction may also contribute to the rise of consistent law enforcement, since jurisdictional ambiguities obscure responsibility for enforcement and can thus produce unpredictable enforcement. Jurisdictional ambiguity also makes it harder to appeal enforcement decisions: because an agency did not have to get involved in a case in the first place, it is difficult to sue it for abuse of discretion or for inaction. All else being equal, centralization (when it is accompanied by clearly defined enforcement mandates and by effective external supervision) may also increase consistency by limiting the opportunities for lower-level bureaucrats to use legal ambiguities as an excuse to shirk or engage in haphazard enforcement.[18]

Finally, consistency is likely to increase when judicial interpretations of decisions in key cases acquire the value of precedent. Even though China has a civil-law system, precedent is becoming very important in the area of IPR. The decisions of courts in Beijing and Shanghai are frequently cited when IPR cases

---

[17] Mei Y. Gechlik, *Protecting Intellectual Property Rights in Chinese Courts: An Analysis of Recent Patent Judgments* (Washington, DC: Carnegie Endowment for International Peace, 2007), 7–9.

[18] A growing literature details how decentralization may encourage poor provision of public goods and corruption. This literature is reviewed in Chapter 2.

are resolved in other parts of the country. In addition, judicial interpretations of the Supreme People's Court now effectively have precedential value as well. A norm of deference to precedent makes individual decisions more predictable, both for the professionals hearing the cases and for the right holder who needs to determine a legal course of action.

For transparency, our initial proxy is the frequency with which open trials (*kaiting shenli*) and open administrative hearings (*tingzheng hui*) are held, since open trials make judicial collusion and judicial bias more difficult. Another proxy for transparency is the publication of court decisions and administrative punishment decisions. Ideally, one would be able to ascertain for any court in China both what percentage of judicial decisions are published and whether these decisions contain extensive legal reasoning or just a short statement of the facts of the case. A recent empirical study of the courts in three Chinese provinces represents an important first step in this kind of scholarship, since the researchers were able to sample court records and establish what kinds of decisions were made public.[19] In relation to IPR, Gechlik's important study analyzes recent patent cases handled by two courts in Beijing and finds that a large number of the decisions in these patent disputes were made publicly available and, moreover, contained lengthy legal reasoning (lengthy legal reasoning makes it more difficult for a judge to engage in arbitrary or corrupt decision making).[20] A continuous commitment to publish judicial decisions in full is a sign of greater transparency, since published decisions make it more difficult for judges to engage in behind-the-scenes particularistic behavior in favor of one side or the other.

The concept of fairness can refer to either substantive fairness or procedural fairness. Substantive fairness exists when the laws are just, a legal and philosophical question that is beyond the scope of this project. Procedural fairness exists when the requirements for a fair trial are met. In general, these requirements include having access to legal representation and to a fair judge, the absence of intimidation during the trial, and the right of appeal. It is impossible to measure directly and systematically most indicators of procedural fairness. The rate of appeal is a useful proxy. As a matter of procedural fairness, right holders should not be prevented from appealing the outcome of a case.

The problem with this proxy is that it is difficult to establish baseline indicators of the frequency of appeal that is too low, the frequency that is normal, and the frequency that is too high. We might reasonably expect that the appeals rate would vary, depending on the professionalism of the enforcers. For example, given the widespread perception of the high professionalism of judges in IPR tribunals, and of the low professionalism of bureaucrats

---

[19] Margaret Y. K. Woo and Yaxin Wang, "Civil Justice in China: An Empirical Study of Courts in Three Provinces," *The American Journal of Comparative Law* 53:4 (2005), 911–940.
[20] Gechlik, *Protecting Intellectual Property Rights in Chinese Courts*.

supplying administrative enforcement for trademarks,[21] we would expect the decisions of IPR tribunals to be appealed less often than those of the bureaucracies that provide trademark administrative enforcement. In practice, however, the exact opposite has occurred: the appeals rate for court cases is thirty times higher than the appeals rate for the decisions of trademark administrative bureaucracies.[22] This suggests that, whereas courts seem not to discourage appeals, administrative agencies are imposing undue burdens on those who attempt to appeal. In their operation, the courts come closer than the administrative agencies to fulfilling the requirements of procedural fairness.

Two caveats about the high appeals rates of court cases are in order. Under some circumstances, high appeals rates could indicate not fairness, but judicial incompetence. This is clearly not the case for civil IPR cases, which are handled by some of the best judges in China. Second, since appeals are costly, plaintiffs may be willing to appeal only when the monetary claims in the case are relatively high. But courts in China still do not routinely issue damage awards that would justify the expense of additional litigation. In most cases, appeals are aimed at getting the infringer to stop the infringing act, not at collecting damage awards. Overall, then, the appeals rate remains the best available proxy for the degree of procedural fairness of IPR enforcement.

Kinds of Enforcement and Rationalization

There are five different kinds of enforcement in China: judicial enforcement, three kinds of routine enforcement, and campaign-style enforcement (see Table 1.1). Each of these has a different potential for developing rationalization.

Judicial enforcement is provided exclusively by courts of law in response to requests from plaintiffs. Judicial enforcement is conducted in public and concludes with a written punishment decision that can be appealed. This study demonstrates that judicial enforcement is consistent, transparent, and procedurally fair, although at the moment it is of a low volume.

There are three kinds of routine enforcement. The first subtype is quasi-judicial enforcement provided in response to a request from the right holder or some other party that has a legitimate interest in the case. In China, this enforcement is habitually provided by the patent bureaucracy (the State Intellectual Property Office [SIPO]) or by the copyright bureaucracy (the National Copyright Administration of China [NCAC]), but it does not exist in the area of

---

[21] On the low professionalism of bureaucrats engaged in trademark enforcement, see Daniel C. K. Chow, *A Primer on Foreign Investment Enterprises and Protection of Intellectual Property Rights in China* (The Hague and New York: Kluwer Law International, 2002); Loke-Khoon Tan, *Pirates in the Middle Kingdom: The Art of Trademark War* (Hong Kong: Sweet & Maxwell Asia, 2004); and Rebecca Ordish and Alan Adcock, *China Intellectual Property Challenges and Solutions: An Essential Business Guide* (Singapore: John Wiley, 2008).

[22] On average, about 30 percent of the cases handled by the IPR tribunals are appealed (see Chapter 4). On average, fewer than 1 percent of the cases handled by the administrative agencies are appealed (see Chapters 2, 5, 7, 8, and 9).

TABLE 1.1. *Kinds of IPR Enforcement in China and Their Providers*

Enforcement Kind	Provided by
Judicial	Courts of law (especially the IPR court tribunals)
Quasi-judicial administrative	SIPO and NCAC
Raids in response to complaints	SAIC (also, occasionally by Customs and the police)
Proactive administrative	All enforcers (except the courts)
Campaign-style administrative	All enforcers (except the courts)

trademark protection. Quasi-judicial enforcement features an administrative hearing and a written punishment decision, which can, in principle, be appealed. In terms of rationalization, this type of routine administrative enforcement comes close to the judicial enforcement supplied by the courts. Like judicial enforcement, quasi-judicial administrative enforcement has a limited volume. The combined SIPO/NCAC quasi-judicial caseload in 2005 was slightly smaller than the total number of IPR cases handled by the specialized IPR tribunals in China (see Chapter 4).

The second subtype of routine enforcement is a raid action organized in response to a complaint (*tousu*) from the right holder or his legal representative. Cases initiated by private investigators on behalf of right holders fall into this category. This type of enforcement is provided in the area of trademark administrative protection, but not in the area of patents or copyrights. Even in the area of trademarks, however, this type of enforcement is exceedingly rare: data from the State Administration for Industry and Commerce (SAIC), which is designated as the main provider of trademark administrative enforcement, indicate that fewer than 5 percent of the trademark enforcement cases that it handled were initiated after complaints from right holders.[23]

Several types of inconsistencies plague enforcement in response to complaints from right holders. In the first instance, the enforcement agency can simply shirk and refuse to organize a raid. The presence of multiple enforcers with poorly defined trademark enforcement mandates facilitates this strategic

[23] This is an average for the years for which we have data. For specific values, see *Zhongguo zhishi chanquan nianjian 2000* [China IPR Yearbook 2000] (Beijing: Zhishi chanquan chubanshe, 2001), 238–239; *Zhongguo zhishi chanquan nianjian 2001–2002* [China IPR Yearbook 2001–2002] (Beijing: Zhishi chanquan chubanshe, 2002), 258–259; *Zhongguo zhishi chanquan nianjian 2003* [China IPR Yearbook 2003] (Beijing: Zhishi chanquan chubanshe, 2003), 249–250; *Zhongguo zhishi chanquan nianjian 2005* [China IPR Yearbook 2005] (Beijing: Zhishi chanquan chubanshe, 2005], 297–298; *Zhongguo zhishi chanquan nianjian 2006* [China IPR Yearbook 2006] (Beijing: Zhishi chanquan chubanshe, 2006], 391–392; *Zhongguo zhishi chanquan nianjian 2007* (China IPR Yearbook 2007) (Beijing: Zhishi chanquan chubanshe, 2007), 530–531.

move, because it allows the agency to claim that another agency is better qualified to enforce. Bribing agencies has become endemic for this reason, since the alternative for the right holder is to engage in a costly and inefficient search for another agency that is willing and able to take his or her case. Another possibility is to accept the case, but to inform the counterfeiter of the impending raid, in order to receive a second bribe from the counterfeiter to match the one from the right holder. Finally, when the agency does organize a raid, it may choose not to confiscate or destroy the goods. Because enforcement is nontransparent, right holders may not be aware of any details beyond the raid's having been undertaken. This makes it possible for agency employees to suspend fines, retain rather than destroy the infringing goods, and even sell the goods back to the counterfeiters. Enforcement raids in response to complaints are not procedurally fair: bureaucrats rarely issue enforcement decisions that can be appealed by the right holders or the alleged counterfeiters.

The third subtype of routine enforcement is proactive administrative enforcement, undertaken in the absence of a complaint from a right holder or direct pressure from the central government. This enforcement exists primarily in the area of trademark administrative protection, where it has emerged as the dominant mode of enforcement. It occurs when enforcement officers inspect businesses for compliance with the various production licenses issued to them (paradoxically, most counterfeiting operations are licensed, though obviously not for the production of counterfeits). In the course of these routine inspections, enforcement officers sometimes come across cases of trademark counterfeiting. However, IPR enforcement is incidental to performing other duties: although enforcement officers typically know where counterfeiting operations are located, on average only about 1 percent of such routine inspections uncover counterfeiting cases.[24] Once a counterfeiting case is discovered, it is handled like a routine case initiated after a complaint is filed; for this reason, routine proactive enforcement is not rationalized either.

The fifth (and final) kind of enforcement is campaign-style enforcement. This enforcement features market sweeps during short periods of "concentrated enforcement," which last on average about two weeks. Campaign enforcement exists both in trademarks and in copyrights. In the last several years, there has also been campaign-style enforcement for cases in the area of patent counterfeiting and patent passing off (but not for patent examination, reexamination, and invalidation or for patent infringement disputes). Patent enforcement campaigns are conducted only by the SIPO, but trademark and copyright enforcement campaigns involve the collaboration of at least two, and sometimes many more, agencies. As it is provided in response to a crisis situation, campaign-style enforcement tends to be nonrationalized. During campaigns, the involvement of multiple agencies with overlapping enforcement

---

[24] Between July 2004 and December 2005, the SAIC inspected 7,660,747 small businesses and 319,504 commodities markets. These inspections uncovered 87,352 cases of trademark violations. *Zhongguo zhishi chanquan nianjian 2006*, 106.

portfolios leads to duplicative, uncoordinated, and inconsistent enforcement, where some infringers are raided repeatedly, whereas others are ignored. When it comes to imposing fines on the various infringers, or managing the confiscated goods, or reporting enforcement statistics, interagency conflicts emerge, which are resolved by imposing multiple fines on the same infringer or by reporting a single case several times. In the end, campaign-style enforcement almost always leads to the waste of administrative effort and delivers a high volume of low-quality enforcement.

EMPIRICAL RATIONALE

This study of state capacity, which is empirically grounded in an investigation of the enforcement of IPR laws, compares China's record with that of Russia, the Czech Republic, Taiwan, France, and the United States. Three questions are in order: why study IPR, why in China, and why adopt a comparative framework?

Why IPR?

What are intellectual property rights? IPR laws cover three broad subcategories of rights: copyrights, patents, and trademarks. Copyrights protect literary, artistic, and creative works, including books, music, motion pictures, and computer software. Patents protect new, nonobvious, and useful inventions, such as the molecule of sildenafil citrate, the active ingredient in Viagra. Trademarks (e.g., Coca-Cola) protect the brand names of goods, ranging from clothing to food to electronics. All three subtypes of IPR are subject to theft, typically through the manufacture of unauthorized copies of various products, which are then passed off to customers as genuine. One characteristic of intellectual property makes theft especially attractive: the development of the original product often takes years of investment, yet the costs of producing a perfect copy are extremely low. A genuine canvas bag with a Burberry label can retail for US$1,000, even though a convincing fake might cost only about US$10 to produce. An entrepreneurial counterfeiter aware of this huge differential can sell fake bags at a fraction of the typical retail price, thus reaping a huge profit and simultaneously diluting and eventually destroying a brand that took decades to create. The International Anticounterfeiting Coalition estimates that the global counterfeiting business is worth US$600 billion a year, or about 5 percent to 7 percent of world trade.[25] The costs of copyright piracy and trademark and patent counterfeiting include IPR infringement (which hurts individual intellectual property right holders) and tax evasion (which hurts

---

[25] http://www.iacc.org/counterfeiting/counterfeiting.php (accessed April 10, 2008). Also see Tim Phillips, *Knockoff: The Deadly Trade in Counterfeit Goods* (London: Kogan Page, 2005).

the state). In addition, substandard food, medicine, cosmetics, and electronics can pose a threat to consumer health and safety.

In most jurisdictions, piracy and counterfeiting are recognized as crimes. What differs from country to country is the way the state enforces its IPR laws. Capricious enforcement, which involves arbitrariness and corruption, presents an obstacle to the development of respect for IPR laws because it engenders distrust of the law and undermines the legitimacy of the enforcers. In contrast, rationalized enforcement can create the foundations for limiting piracy and counterfeiting and for instituting compliance with IPR laws.

IPR is perfectly suited for a cross-country investigation of enforcement capacity. A comparison of laws that are functionally identical yet differ substantively in content (e.g., two constitutions) can be misleading. We need to identify a set of laws whose content and function are identical across countries. Most suitable are laws that conform to some international standard, such as the one that is used when candidates for membership in the World Trade Organization (WTO) amend their domestic laws in exchange for WTO entry. The WTO-administered Agreement on Trade-Related Aspects of Intellectual Property Rights (TRIPS) serves as the international standard in the area of IPR protection. New entrants to the WTO must harmonize their domestic laws with TRIPS and provide at least the minimal level of protection that it specifies.[26] Since the domestic laws of all six countries examined in this book are TRIPS-compliant, differences in enforcement will not be attributable to differences in the laws themselves. This isomorphism of the laws makes IPR especially useful for a cross-national study of enforcement.

Why China?

Although the great majority of countries around the world currently have laws providing at least some IPR protection,[27] there are two main reasons for making China the chief focus of this study. First, China is one of the largest IPR pirates in the world. Available statistics on copyright piracy indicate that 88 percent of the business software (e.g., Microsoft Office) in use in China in 2005 was pirated, leading to losses of US$1.3 billion from unrealized sales. Overall,

[26] Russia is not yet a member of the WTO, but its domestic legislation is fully TRIPS-compliant. All six countries examined in this study protect pharmaceutical patents, an area where the most significant TRIPS-related controversies have emerged. See World Trade Organization, *Declaration on the TRIPS Agreement and Public Health* (Doha, November 14, 2001), which allows developing countries undergoing a public health emergency to use compulsory licensing for the manufacture of inexpensive generic drugs.

[27] According to a dataset I constructed, in 2006 the UN-sponsored World Intellectual Property Organization (WIPO) boasted 183 member-states, 96 percent of which had patent and trademark laws, and 92 percent of which had copyright laws. More importantly, 78 percent of the WIPO member-states (China among them) were also members of the WTO; that means that they had or would shortly acquire TRIPS-compliant IPR laws. The dataset was compiled from information available at http://www.wipo.int/about-ip/en/ipworldwide/country.htm (accessed April 11, 2008).

losses from all types of copyright piracy in China in 2005 amounted to US$2.4 billion.[28] In addition, an estimated US$15–$20 billion lost each year is due to trademark counterfeiting.[29] IPR violations cause serious damage both to the emerging Chinese economy and to foreign companies operating in China. Second, as revealed by a 183-country World Intellectual Property Organization (WIPO) dataset I compiled, no country in the world devotes as many resources to IPR enforcement as China does. China has not only established specialized IPR tribunals, as well as Customs and police units, but also empowered over a dozen different administrative agencies with enforcement responsibilities in this domain. Because of the large number of government agencies involved in enforcement, IPR in China presents a particularly complex case that allows us to get a deeper grasp of state capacity.

This book focuses on China also because its IPR enforcement regime is in need of a comprehensive empirical study. Despite the importance of IPR, the bulk of the existing literature, both in Chinese and in English, analyzes the substantive content of Chinese laws rather than the nitty-gritty of their enforcement on the ground.[30] Studies focusing directly on enforcement are rare and typically examine only one subtype of intellectual property rights – copyrights,[31] trademarks,[32] or patents[33] – instead of presenting a comprehensive account of the enforcement of all three IPR subtypes. An additional limitation of the existing research is that when it does attempt to analyze enforcement across all three IPR subtypes, it does not examine the interplay among civil, administrative, and criminal enforcement, nor among the different administrative actors with IPR enforcement portfolios.[34] Clearly, findings can be biased when analysis of

---

[28] http://www.iipa.com/pdf/2006SPEC301LOSS.pdf.pdf (accessed April 10, 2008). For a much higher estimate see http://w3.bsa.org/globalstudy//upload/2007-Global-Piracy-Study-EN.pdf (accessed April 10, 2008). I have used the International Intellectual Property Alliance (IIPA) figures because they have the status of an official piracy estimate that is used by the U.S. Trade Representative in its annual decisions about the progress individual countries have made in protecting IPR.

[29] *Zhijia shoujia weihai jida, yanli daji kebu ronghuan* (The Production and Sale of Counterfeits Are Extremely Harmful, Severe Crackdowns Should Start without Delay), an internally circulated report issued by the Development Research Center of the State Council in February 2000 (Chinese version on file with the author).

[30] For representative examples, see Zheng Chengsi, *Zhishi chanquan lun* (Intellectual Property Theory) (Beijing: Falü chubanshe, 1998), and Qu Sanqiang, *Copyright Law in China* (Beijing: Foreign Languages Press, 2002).

[31] Michel Oksenberg, Pitman B. Potter, and William B. Abnett, "Advancing Intellectual Property Rights: Information Technologies and the Course of Economic Development in China," *NBR Analysis* 7:4 (1996).

[32] Chow, *A Primer on Foreign Investment Enterprises*; Tan, *Pirates in the Middle Kingdom*.

[33] Xiang Wang, *Chinese Patent Law and Patent Litigation in China* (Baltimore: School of Law, University of Maryland, 1998).

[34] Andrew Mertha, *The Politics of Piracy: Intellectual Property in Contemporary China* (Ithaca, NY: Cornell University Press, 2005). See also Andrew Mertha, "Policy Enforcement Markets: How Bureaucratic Redundancy Contributes to Effective Intellectual Property Implementation in China," *Comparative Politics* 38:3 (April 2006), 295–316.

IPR enforcement is truncated in these ways. An equally serious problem with the existing literature is that it makes no use of the extensive national and regional enforcement statistics that have become available in the PRC over the last decade. Finally, with a few notable exceptions mentioned later, the literature has made no attempt to compare China's IPR enforcement record with that of other countries. In brief, a comprehensive empirical study is necessary for generating new theories about both IPR enforcement and state capacity.

Why Compare China with Other Countries?

This book is squarely focused on IPR in relation to state capacity in China, but it is also committed to the idea that we can best understand what is unique about one country through comparison with others. The study's cross-country comparisons are based on several types of data. One source is the 183-country WIPO dataset mentioned, which lists the international IPR treaties to which each country has acceded and the IPR laws the country has on its books and provides some information on the IPR enforcement arrangements in different countries.[35] In addition to the WIPO dataset, I have constructed a dataset on the criminal enforcement of copyright laws in thirty-two countries.

Of course, such cross-national datasets tell us little about what the enforcers actually do in the individual countries. When, for example, do they enforce, and how much? More fine-grained data are necessary to answer these questions. Yet, with the exception of some early research on Taiwan and a doctoral dissertation on pharmaceutical patents in Brazil, there are no in-depth empirical studies of IPR enforcement outside the Chinese case.[36] Given these limitations in the secondary literature, the only way to perform a meaningful midrange cross-country comparison was to gather data in individual countries personally. In addition to China, I conducted extensive fieldwork in Russia, Taiwan, the Czech Republic, and France, as well as more modest fieldwork in the United States. This research was geared toward gathering data specifically about who the IPR enforcers were and what were their activities.

The five countries to which China is compared were chosen according to several criteria (see Table 1.2). First, I included countries that had different levels of piracy and counterfeiting (high, medium, and low). China and Russia

---

[35] In some chapters I refer to a 176-country WIPO dataset, which I compiled using 2000 WIPO data. The 176-country dataset contains some details on enforcement options in individual countries that is not contained in the 183-country 2006 WIPO dataset.

[36] On Taiwan, see Chung Jen Cheng, "The Role of the Patent System in the Development of Technology in Taiwan" (JSD Dissertation, Stanford University School of Law, 1993); William Alford, *To Steal a Book is an Elegant Offense: Intellectual Property Law in Chinese Civilization* (Stanford: Stanford University Press, 1995); and Andy Sun, *From Pirate King to Jungle King: Transformation of Taiwan's Intellectual Property Protection* (Baltimore: School of Law, University of Maryland, 1997). On Brazil, see Andre de Mello Souza, "The Power of the Weak: Advocacy Networks, Ideational Change and the Global Politics of Pharmaceutical Patent Rights" (Ph.D. Dissertation, Department of Political Science, Stanford University, 2005).

TABLE 1.2. *Case Selection Criteria*

Country	U.S. Trade Sanctions	Regime Type	Federal State	GDP US$ (ppp)	Piracy/ Counterfeiting	Enforcement Volume
China	High threat	Authoritarian	Semi	6,572	High	High
Russia	Low threat	Authoritarian	Yes	10,897	High	Low
Taiwan	Medium	Democracy	No	21,317	Medium	Medium
Czech Republic	Low threat	Democracy	No	27,500	Medium	Medium
France	No threat	Democracy	Semi	30,120	Medium	Medium
U.S.	N/A	Democracy	Yes	41,854	Low	Low

Sources: GDP ppp (purchasing power parity) 2005 data from *World Development Indicators*. Taiwan data from https://www.cia.gov/cia/publications/factbook/geos/tw.html (accessed December 6, 2006).

have some of the highest levels of IPR violations in the world; in contrast, Taiwan, the Czech Republic, and France have medium levels of piracy and counterfeiting. The inclusion of the United States is analytically useful since it is the country with the lowest rate of piracy in the world. Second, there are countries that, like China, have been subjected to U.S. pressure to provide more enforcement, as well as countries that have not been subjected to such pressure. Third, the countries represent different outcomes in terms of their system of governance (democracy vs. authoritarianism). Fourth, I controlled for different levels of wealth and socioeconomic development, as measured by per capita income. Fifth, both federal and unitary states were included.[37] Though the six countries (China included) were by no means randomly selected, they were chosen to maximize variance.

The cross-national comparison in this study provides additional theoretical leverage over the factors that impact IPR enforcement in China. As subsequent chapters make clear, an unusually complex IPR enforcement framework has emerged in China, in contrast to the more streamlined systems in other countries. The entrenchment of these complex enforcement arrangements in China is a result of the central government's reaction to persistent foreign and domestic pressure to provide a high volume of copyright and trademark enforcement as quickly as possible. The government has responded to such pressure by drawing on a very wide array of administrative agencies in enforcement campaigns geared at providing rapid and high-volume enforcement. In some other countries, more consistent and effective enforcement frameworks have been able to develop, often in the absence of similar pressure. Overall, the cross-country comparison not only helps situate China's enforcement record but also gives us theoretical leverage over the relationship between pressure and the quality of enforcement.

EXISTING EXPLANATIONS OF IPR ENFORCEMENT

Since the 1980s, China has been notorious for its poor enforcement of IPR laws. Two studies in particular have advanced explanations for the staggering levels of piracy and counterfeiting. The first argues that cultural factors serve as a disincentive for enforcement of IPR laws, whereas the second maintains that the improvement of IPR enforcement depends on interbureaucratic competition.

Culture

Serious scholarly analysis of IPR enforcement in China began with William Alford's *To Steal a Book Is an Elegant Offense* (1995). Like other scholars

---

[37] The United States and Russia are federal states, whereas Taiwan and the Czech Republic are unitary states. Though not formally federal, China has experimented with extensive decentralization, thus giving some scholars reason to call it "de facto federal" or "quasi-federal." France has also experienced extensive decentralization since the early 1980s.

arguing that laws cannot simply be taken from one country and transplanted into another with the expectation that they will work there, Alford stresses the importance of understanding the historical and cultural contexts in which laws operate.[38]

In particular, Alford develops a theory for the persistence of piracy and counterfeiting, namely, that political culture prevents the successful enforcement of IPR laws in China. He emphasizes the role of three interrelated historical-cultural factors: the resilience of Confucian culture, which encourages learning through copying the works of others; a residual resentment of the West for forcing China to adopt both its pre-1949 IPR laws and the new IPR laws of the 1980s and 1990s; and the legacy of the Mao era, when copyrights, trademarks, and patents were virtually abolished. Since IPR laws protect private property and the free exchange of ideas, the Chinese government during the Mao era also opposed them on ideological grounds. Although China adopted a series of IPR laws after 1978, it did not take their enforcement to heart. In short, Alford argues, cultural legacies explain China's unwillingness to protect IPR. I find this historical argument convincing.

As important as cultural legacies are, I argue that the bureaucratic organization of the state may present an even greater obstacle to the emergence of effective IPR enforcement now. In the years following publication of Alford's study, two important and telling improvements in the IPR enforcement apparatus occurred. One was the creation of more than a hundred specialized IPR tribunals within the civil courts of law. The second was the emergence of the patent bureaucracy (the SIPO) as a model enforcer. Although the IPR tribunals and the SIPO provide a small volume of enforcement, this enforcement is of a high quality. What is characteristic of the IPR tribunals and the SIPO is that they were created anew, thus allowing the central government to overcome entrenched problems that diminished the effectiveness of the existing bureaucracies.

How relevant are cultural legacies for understanding the persistence of piracy and counterfeiting in China today? Although economic factors seem to be the most important (after all, commercial-scale piracy and counterfeiting are highly lucrative activities), cultural factors may indeed be among the forces limiting the efficacy of IPR enforcement. This may be especially true for Chinese reactions to demands from the United States to provide more administrative enforcement in the area of copyright protection. Although China has responded to these requests, it has done so reluctantly. Unwillingness to kowtow to the West may contribute to the relatively low quantity and quality of copyright enforcement in cases of piracy of non-Chinese copyrights. In addition, residual Marxist feelings against private property may explain in part the existence of inefficient

---

[38] Various limitations of legal transplants are highlighted by Otto Kahn-Freund, "On Uses and Misuses of Comparative Law," *The Modern Law Review* 37:1 (1974), 1–27; for a view supportive of transplants, see Alan Watson, *Legal Transplants: An Approach to Comparative Law* (Charlottesville: University of Virginia Press, 1974).

arrangements for providing trademark enforcement. Clearly, a comprehensive account of IPR enforcement requires attention to cultural-historical legacies.

Interbureaucratic Competition and the Protection of Foreign IPR in China

The second major Western study that addresses IPR enforcement is Andrew Mertha's *The Politics of Piracy* (2005), which provides a valuable and detailed account of the complex Sino-U.S. negotiations in the 1990s, culminating in the promulgation of laws protecting IPR that are still in effect today. Mertha also sets out to explain how foreign companies can protect their IPR in China. He argues that foreigners have attempted to improve IPR enforcement through exogenous pressure and lateral exogenous pressure, with different results in each case. Lateral exogenous pressure is pressure exerted by foreign businesses and private investigation firms operating in China. Mertha finds that such pressure has produced interbureaucratic competition between two trademark enforcement bureaucracies (the SAIC and the General Administration of Quality Supervision, Inspection, and Quarantine [AQSIQ]). As a result, trademark enforcement volume has increased and enforcement has become effective and "actually flourished."[39] Exogenous pressure, in contrast, is pressure applied directly by the U.S. government on the Chinese government, which in turn puts pressure on various bureaucracies to enforce. Mertha finds that this pressure existed in copyrights but did not lead to competition between the General Administration of Press and Publications (GAPP) and the Ministry of Culture (MOC). Because the volume of copyright enforcement remained low, Mertha concludes that, as a consequence of the lack of interbureaucratic competition, enforcement of copyrights was "supine and ineffective."[40] In general, Mertha argues that lateral exogenous pressure facilitates interbureaucratic competition and so brings about a high volume of enforcement, which he then equates with effective, flourishing enforcement.

Mertha's study is highly focused, but it is of limited use as a guide to understanding IPR enforcement in China more generally. First, he analyzes only administrative enforcement, without attention to Customs, courts, or the police, all of which offer insights on the overall state of IPR protection in China. Second, Mertha attends exclusively to the protection of foreign IPR in China. But most IPR in China is Chinese-owned: foreign-owned copyrights, trademarks, and patents constitute only about 10 percent of all IPR in China. Third, Mertha's theoretical argument about enforcement depends on one particular kind of enforcement. In my typology, this is raids: routine administrative enforcement organized in response to complaints by right holders or private investigators. As previously mentioned, raids organized in response to complaints account for only about 5 percent of the routine administrative enforcement undertaken in China. The vast majority of trademark enforcement,

---

[39] Mertha, *The Politics of Piracy*, 166–167.
[40] Mertha, *The Politics of Piracy*, 119.

whether for domestic or foreign cases, is proactive administrative enforcement and campaign-style enforcement, neither of which Mertha discusses.

Raids are an option for trademark administrative enforcement, but not for copyrights and patents.[41] Mertha's finding about lack of competition between the GAPP and the MOC in copyright enforcement partly reflects the fact that these enforcers engage in campaign-style enforcement following central government orders but are by and large typically unwilling to organize raids in response to complaints, even when right holders offer them bribes. This means, in effect, that there is no basis for the kind of competition in which Mertha is interested. The core of Mertha's argument about interbureaucratic competition therefore applies to the administrative protection of trademarks by the SAIC and the AQSIQ. Since the argument results in a theory for IPR protection in general, it is important to consider its terms closely.

Like Mertha, I find evidence that interbureaucratic competition exists in the area of routine trademark enforcement in response to complaints. This is not surprising, given the large number of bureaucracies that can provide this type of enforcement: when faced with an easy case, bureaucracies will be eager to take it on. The distinction between easy and hard cases is instructive. In contrast to Mertha, I find that bureaucracies may shirk when faced with hard cases, for instance, when the counterfeiters are in cahoots with the local government. So interbureaucratic competition *for* cases is only half the story. I agree with Mertha that increases in lateral exogenous pressure will lead to a higher volume of enforcement (in easy cases), but I differ radically in my interpretation of this trend. Often, such increases in pressure are simply equivalent to additional bribes, which the enforcers are only too willing to accept in exchange for organizing raids: far from producing a flourishing enforcement, this sort of activity may actually undermine good enforcement. In contrast to Mertha, I believe that increases in the volume of enforcement do not per se improve IPR protection. Given the reality of administrative enforcement on the ground in China, this means that, unlike Mertha, I do not see the encouragement of interbureaucratic competition as a sound strategy for foreign companies looking to protect their trademarks in China. In fact, for several years now, private investigators specializing in trademark protection have been advising their clients to opt for judicial enforcement instead of administrative enforcement.[42]

My own study focuses on the conditions that facilitate the rise of rationalized enforcement in China. Although I recognize that foreign intellectual property matters in China (and I examine it at length), I am concerned primarily with the protection of *Chinese* IPR in China. On the basis of a comprehensive examination of the enforcement of all IPR subtypes in China, of all enforcement

---

[41] Routine enforcement in response to complaints is in theory an option also for Customs and police enforcement. But in practice, as Chapters 3 and 6 illustrate, both agencies use this option very infrequently.

[42] China Interview 080105, with a private investigator based in Shanghai (Shanghai, by phone); China Interview 080112, with a private investigator based in Shanghai (Ji'nan).

options (Customs, court, administrative, criminal), and of all kinds of enforcement (judicial, quasi-judicial, raids organized in response to complaints, proactive routine, and campaign-style) for both domestic and foreign IPR, I find
that rationalization is most likely to emerge when the enforcement structures
are given a chance to develop outside the spotlight of either foreign or domestic
pressure.

HOW DOES RATIONALIZED ENFORCEMENT EMERGE?

Studies of state capacity typically portray the state in a dichotomous way, as
either weak or strong. However, an early insight in the literature on the state is
that state capacity varies across issue areas: states that appear strong in one area
may be weak in another.[43] This book accepts that the state is simultaneously
weak and strong, and attempts to explain the variation in state capacity. An
understanding of this variation also helps us grasp the variation in the presence
of rationalized enforcement.

Detailed Synopsis

Piracy and the State is organized in four sections. The first part (to which this
chapter belongs) develops a theoretical argument about the conditions under
which the state can provide high-quality enforcement of IPR laws. Part II
presents a map of the state, examining in depth how it is organized to provide
Customs, civil, administrative, and criminal protection of IPR. This section
helps us understand why China's IPR enforcement arrangements are so complex in comparison to those of the other countries in this study. Part III analyzes
the state in action through case studies of copyright, trademark, and patent
enforcement on the ground. This further clarifies what conditions facilitate the
emergence of rationalized enforcement. A final chapter concludes the study
by highlighting the broader implications of the argument for other issues in
Chinese politics.

Part I consists of two separate chapters that together theorize the paradox
that such a high volume of enforcement in China is so ineffective. Building on
the major distinction presented in this chapter between high-volume and high-
quality enforcement, Chapter 2 analyzes the factors that affect the quality of
IPR enforcement in China. Low-quality enforcement is unaccountable enforcement: government agencies may shirk enforcement altogether (when asked to
enforce by right holders), may provide corrupt routine enforcement, or may
engage in massive (yet usually ineffective) campaign-style crackdowns on

---

[43] Stephen Krasner, *Defending the National Interest: Raw Materials Investments and U.S. Foreign
Policy* (Princeton, NJ: Princeton University Press, 1978), 58. See also the contributions to Peter
B. Evans, Dietrich Rueschemeyer, and Theda Skocpol, eds., *Bringing the State Back In* (New
York: Cambridge University Press, 1985).

counterfeiters, all without being accountable for their action or inaction. The chapter finds that most IPR agencies operate under conditions of decentralization, which prevents effective oversight of bureaucratic discretion. Bureaucracies do react to enforcement pressures from organized foreign and domestic groups, but those pressures have increased only the quantity of enforcement, not its quality. Despite its ability to supply rapid enforcement under pressure, the state is unable to provide high-quality enforcement: in this regard, what looks like a strength may actually be a weakness.

Part II maps the bureaucratic organization of IPR enforcement in China by presenting empirical information about the operation and efficacy of all agencies with an IPR portfolio. This surprisingly complex apparatus includes the Customs Administration, which has exclusive jurisdiction at the borders, as well as the civil, administrative, and criminal enforcement entities that exist inside the borders of the state. Part II supplements its analysis of the Chinese agencies with international comparisons that allow for a more sophisticated theoretical understanding of the factors driving rationalized enforcement. Two observations are key here. First, China is unusual in terms of its keen responsiveness to foreign pressure; nevertheless, even in China, domestic considerations trump foreign pressure during enforcement. Second, rationalized enforcement has emerged in the area of civil court enforcement, which has not been subject to either domestic or foreign enforcement pressure.

Part III gives a sense of how this apparatus works, in three case studies that provide an in-depth look at copyright, trademark, and patent enforcement on the ground. These chapters focus primarily on China but are supplemented by brief case studies of trademark and copyright enforcement in Russia. The major finding in this section concerns the unevenness in the presence of rationalization across the main subtypes of IPR. Rationalized enforcement has emerged for some types of patent protection (patent examination, reexamination, and invalidation, as well as patent infringement disputes), but not for trademarks. In copyrights, there is a complex enforcement situation: although campaign-style enforcement exists and is unpredictable, the NCAC is the sole provider of routine quasi-judicial copyright enforcement; this type of copyright enforcement holds some promise of future rationalization.

The emergence of rationalization in patent protection is of great significance. Patents have been free of both foreign and domestic pressure to provide a high volume of enforcement, and this has given the state an opportunity to create from scratch a regulatory system that supplies a measured, reasonable volume of enforcement. This stands in contrast to the structures the state uses for trademark enforcement and for campaign-style copyright enforcement, since these aim to provide a high volume of enforcement. In terms of the findings about civil court and patent administrative enforcement, it appears that enforcement that occurs in the absence of pressure to enforce may be more likely to become rationalized than enforcement supplied in response to pressure.

Chapter 10 concludes the study by suggesting how its arguments about IPR enforcement can be extended to other areas as well. Environmental protection, for example, is marked by a complexity of regulation similar to that characterizing IPR. In other words, this chapter (and this book as a whole) argues that complexity of regulation needs to be recognized as a defining feature of governance in reform-era China. In that light, the chapter also provides some concluding reflections about rationalization, state capacity, and the rule of law under authoritarianism.

Theoretical Findings

This book focuses on the nitty-gritty empirical details of IPR enforcement in China. However, it is not only an empirical book. For an issue area that has been as poorly understood as the quality of IPR enforcement, no theoretical claims can emerge that are not firmly grounded in empirical knowledge about both the quantity and the quality of enforcement. For that reason, this book invests considerable energy in documenting the activities of the various IPR enforcers. On the basis of these empirical investigations, the book develops a set of theoretical arguments about state capacity.

What factors impact the quantity of IPR enforcement in China? The book finds that enforcement in China is primarily reactive, with agencies responding to foreign and domestic pressures. This finding is consistent with our basic understanding of the politics of developing countries. China, given its high absorption of foreign direct investment (FDI) and its high level of trade as a percentage of GDP, is especially responsive to foreign pressure, which is usually expressed as threats of Special 301 sanctions.[44] The argument that domestic pressures can also play a role in an authoritarian regime like China may seem counterintuitive at first, but it is supported by empirical evidence about the reaction of the Chinese government to various product-quality scandals in recent years. This responsiveness to foreign and domestic pressures helps explain the high volume of IPR enforcement in China.

Despite its high volume, IPR enforcement is typically ineffective. This book finds that when agencies operate under pressure, two dynamics may ensue. In one, agencies find themselves compelled to supply "quick and dirty" routine enforcement, without concern for the principles of consistency, transparency, and fairness. In the other, agencies are encouraged by the central government to participate in enforcement campaigns, which are not aimed at providing rationalized enforcement either. In short, enforcement under pressure, be it routine or campaign-style enforcement, is unlikely to be rationalized.

When does rationalized enforcement emerge? Our investigations of IPR enforcement suggest that rationalized enforcement exists in two areas: in civil court enforcement (for all IPR subtypes) and in some types of patent

---

[44] Various avenues for exercising foreign pressure exist. They will be discussed in Chapter 2.

administrative enforcement. Why has rationalized enforcement emerged in these areas, but not in others? Two conditions hold here. One is that these areas were free of pressure to enforce. Second, in contrast to routine enforcement of trademarks, where the enforcement responsibilities of individual enforcers are poorly specified, the mandates of the IPR tribunals and of the patent bureaucracy (the SIPO) are clearly delineated. The clarity of enforcement mandates is essential, making it more difficult to shirk enforcement; easier to ascertain when the principles of consistency, transparency, and fairness are respected; and, in cases where those principles have been violated, easier to lodge an appeal.

These empirical findings have four theoretical implications about the emergence of high-quality enforcement in China. The first implication is that pressure (both domestic and foreign) increases the volume of enforcement. Such pressure might also increase the quality of enforcement, but only if those pressing for enforcement explicitly demand high-quality enforcement. Since foreign and domestic pressure groups have both focused on high-volume enforcement, unsurprisingly the Chinese government has structured bureaucratic incentives in such a way as to deliver that volume through the various enforcement agencies. The more informed pressure groups are about the factors that promote rationalized enforcement, the better equipped they will be to supply selective pressure targeted at improving the quality of enforcement.

The second theoretical implication concerns the impact of crisis on enforcement standards. Very often, a crisis forces the government to provide campaign-style enforcement, which is usually a recipe for high volume and low quality. On rare occasions, however, a crisis may compel the government to restructure the enforcement system, for example, by attempting coordination and centralization. This can occur either when a short-term energetic response is needed (as in the case of the SARS outbreak in 2003)[45] or when the regulatory environment is relatively uncluttered (as in tax collection and smuggling).[46] However, in areas where enforcement is provided by multiple enforcement agencies with poorly defined mandates, a crisis cannot on its own resolve the problem of duplicative, uncoordinated enforcement: in IPR, neither the 2004 baby formula scandal nor the 2007 tainted antibiotics scandal led to systematic restructuring.[47] It remains

---

[45] John Wong and Zheng Yongnian, eds., *The SARS Epidemic: Challenges to China's Crisis Management* (Singapore: World Scientific, 2004). See also Patricia M. Thornton, "Crisis, 'Normal Politics' and the Pathologies of State and Society under Reform," paper presented at the conference *Reconfiguring the Party-State: The Shifting Locus of Power*, Fairbank Center for East Asian Research, Harvard University, May 19–20, 2006.

[46] For an insightful argument on the role of various crises in rationalizing the Chinese state, see Yang, *Remaking the Chinese Leviathan*.

[47] In 2004, at least thirteen babies died after being fed counterfeit formula; in 2007, tainted antibiotics approved by Zheng Xiaoyu, the head of China's State Food and Drug Administration, led to the deaths of at least ten people. On both scandals, see Ordish and Adcock, *China Intellectual Property Challenges and Solutions*, 94.

to be seen whether the 2008 melamine-tainted formula scandal, which emerged as this book went to press, will usher in rationalized enforcement.[48] Outside IPR, the mine safety and environmental protection scandals were similarly ineffective at producing radical change.[49]

The bureaucratic responses to pressure and crisis are indicative that the institutions *already in place* are not working. It is difficult to reform existing institutions by centralizing, merging, or coordinating their activities. It is considerably easier to create a new bureaucracy (as occurred in the case of patent administrative enforcement) or to carve out a new enforcer from an existing enforcer (as occurred with the creation of the specialized IPR tribunals within the existing civil courts).

This finding relates to the book's third theoretical implication: rationalization is more likely to emerge in new regulatory areas. In regulating new areas, the central government can create clearly specified enforcement mandates. A case in point is the mandate of the SIPO, which partly overlaps with the courts' mandate to accept patent cases. However, this overlap neither creates ambiguity as to who should enforce nor encourages shirking in the way that overlapping enforcement jurisdictions in copyrights and trademarks do. Clear enforcement mandates also allow for improved accountability.

The fourth and final implication for rationalization is that neither formal centralization nor exclusive jurisdictions are on their own conducive to the rise of rationalized enforcement. The Customs Administration is instructive in this regard. Customs is formally centralized and has exclusive jurisdiction over the border protection of IPR. But it has not provided rationalized enforcement. The main reason is that it has not been subject to effective oversight by the courts, the Procuratorate, or any other government agency. Decentralization and overlapping jurisdictions lower the quality of enforcement. But centralization and jurisdictional exclusivity will not improve the quality of enforcement unless they are accompanied by clearly stipulated enforcement mandates that allow individual right holders to hold government officials responsible for inaction or abuse of discretion.

---

[48] At least 54,000 Chinese babies became ill after consuming substandard melamine-tainted Sanlu formula in the summer and early fall of 2008. Although the formula was only substandard, and not both substandard and counterfeit, an improvement in quality control will inevitably also lower the level of counterfeiting: the regulations governing quality control and anticounterfeiting often overlap and China's chief quality watchdog (the AQSIQ) is also a top provider of anticounterfeiting enforcement. On the Sanlu scandal, see "Milk Scandal under Control, China Says," Reuters, September 25, 2008.

[49] On mine safety, see Fubing Su, "Centralization and Decentralization: Agency Problem and Institutional Change in China's Coal Mining," paper presented at the conference *Reconfiguring the Party-State: The Shifting Locus of Power in Reform-Era China*, Fairbank Center for East Asian Research, Harvard University, May 19–20, 2006, and Tim Wright, "State Capacity in Contemporary China: 'Closing the Pits and Reducing Coal Production,'" *Journal of Contemporary China*, no. 51 (2007), 173–194. Environmental protection will be discussed in Chapter 10.

APPENDIX: SOURCES AND METHODS

Prior research on the enforcement of IPR laws in China has relied primarily on interviews and has not made use of the enormous amount of statistical material that has become available over the last two decades. Another gap in the existing research is that it has not compared IPR enforcement in China with enforcement in other countries.[50] This project uses as wide an array of sources as possible in order to compare China to other countries systematically.

I rely on four kinds of primary sources. First, I make use of the complete runs of over twenty national and over ten provincial and county-level statistical yearbooks from China, as well as the complete runs of a smaller number of statistical yearbooks from Russia, the Czech Republic, Taiwan, France, and the United States. Second, I draw on the transcripts of 401 in-depth interviews that I conducted in China, Russia, Taiwan, the Czech Republic, France, and the United States over thirty months of fieldwork between 2000 and 2008. Third, I have used the proprietary enforcement records of a private investigation firm in China, as well as the proprietary files of an anti-piracy association in Russia. These files open up a window onto bureaucratic behavior and state capacity that remains closed if we rely only on interviews or official statistical yearbooks. Fourth, I make extensive use of newspaper reports of enforcement published in Chinese and Russian.

I used the materials collected during fieldwork and archival research to construct ten unique datasets for this project. One dataset contains statistics on the IPR enforcement options that exist in 183 countries that have joined the World Intellectual Property Organization. Another dataset provides information about copyright criminal enforcement patterns in thirty-two countries. A third dataset contains provincial-level data on the enforcement activities of three administrative agencies (the National Copyright Administration, the State Administration for Industry and Commerce, and the State Intellectual Property Office), as well as on the caseload of the specialized IPR court tribunals in China. Both the second and the third dataset contain a rich array of economic development indicators, which allowed me to conduct regression analysis that illuminated certain cross-national and subnational enforcement patterns. A fourth dataset on cigarette anticounterfeiting activity is based on data extracted from 107 case files obtained from a private investigative agency operating in China. In addition, four enforcement datasets were compiled from Chinese newspaper articles published between 1999 and 2006: one on cigarette anticounterfeiting enforcement in Guangdong province, another on cigarette anticounterfeiting enforcement in other Chinese provinces, a third on optical media anti-piracy enforcement, and a fourth on Viagra anticounterfeiting enforcement. Finally, this book makes use

---

[50] An important exception is Alford, *To Steal a Book*; Alford explicitly compares copyright protection in China and Taiwan.

of a Russian tobacco enforcement dataset (constructed from newspaper articles) and a Russian copyright enforcement dataset (extracted from the proprietary files of a right holders' association operating in Russia). Collectively, these unique datasets allow us to measure which agencies participate in enforcement, how often they participate in enforcement, why they participate in enforcement (voluntarily or because of a bribe), and what is the outcome of their participation (effective enforcement or ineffective enforcement).

Many arguments presented in this book first emerged during a series of intensive interviews. These were semistructured interviews based on convenience sampling.[51] Each interviewee was asked a general set of questions, yet I was also perfectly willing to probe any leads that interviewees provided. As my research progressed, the interview questions became more targeted and specific. My final interviews in any given country tended to be the most useful and thus are referred to more frequently in the subsequent chapters. I cite interviews by their location (China, Russia, Taiwan, Czech Republic, France, or the United States) plus the date on which they took place; when I conducted more than one interview on a given day, uppercase letters after the date (A, B, C, D, or E) are used. With a few exceptions, interviewees are not cited by name in order to protect their privacy.

I conducted 239 interviews in China. The interviews were distributed as follows: Beijing (131 interviews), Shanghai (56 interviews), Guangzhou (18 interviews), Shenzhen (1 interview), Zouping county (8 interviews), Ji'nan (1 interview), Dalian (4 interviews), Haikou (3 interviews), and Hong Kong (17 interviews). Admittedly, this distribution is skewed and omits the majority of Chinese provinces. We should emphasize, however, that Beijing, Shanghai, and Guangdong province (both Guangzhou and Shenzhen are in Guangdong province) account for a large portion of IPR enforcement in China. In 2005, with only 8.5 percent of China's population, the three provinces accounted for 17 percent of GDP, 29 percent of FDI inflows, more than half of Customs enforcement, at least one-third of the criminal IPR cases, 46 percent of the civil IPR court cases, and well over 50 percent of enforcement in cases of foreign trademark and copyright violations. Therefore, with limited time for research in China, these three provinces can provide extraordinarily high returns.[52] My interviews in other, less developed areas (Haikou) as well as in a developed coastal city that is not a provincial capital (Dalian) provided some important correctives to information gathered from the three cities where China puts on

---

[51] Given the multiplicity of IPR enforcers in China, I was mainly interested in mapping out the enforcement terrain – who enforces, when, how, how often, and why. Random sampling was neither possible nor desirable to explore these types of questions.

[52] China has 31 territorial units with provincial-level status: 22 provinces, 5 ethnic autonomous regions, and 4 municipalities. Technically, among the three units, only Guangdong is an actual province, whereas Beijing and Shanghai are provincial-level municipalities.

its best face. Finally, some of my most illuminating interviews took place in Zouping county (Shandong province) in early 2008.[53]

In terms of occupational characteristics, my China interviews were distributed as follows: 107 interviews with government officials, 20 interviews with lawyers and judges, 25 interviews with right holders' associations and NGOs, 23 interviews with managers in firms producing intellectual property, 22 interviews with private investigators, 15 interviews with foreign diplomats, 3 interviews with journalists, and 24 interviews with academics. My research strategy was to gain access to each of the more than a dozen administrative agencies sharing the IPR administrative enforcement portfolio in China, as well as to Customs, the police, and the specialized IPR tribunals in as many different parts of China as possible. I also wanted to talk to lawyers, representatives of right holders' associations, private investigators, and managers of firms that were affected by piracy and counterfeiting. Diplomats, journalists, and academics were interviewed in order to get background information on IPR enforcement or to secure contact information about bureaucrats and businesspeople who would provide more pertinent information for this project. To the extent possible, this research strategy was also used in the other countries where I conducted fieldwork.

In Russia, I conducted a total of 86 interviews, most of them in Moscow (75 interviews). The rest of the interviews took place in St. Petersburg (1 interview) and Kazan, the capital of Tatarstan (10 interviews). In terms of occupational breakdown, I conducted 27 interviews with government officials, 15 interviews with lawyers and judges, 13 interviews with right holders' associations, 12 interviews with managers of firms producing intellectual property, 2 interviews with private investigators, 3 interviews with foreign diplomats, 2 interviews with journalists, and 12 interviews with academics.

In Taiwan, I conducted 38 interviews (36 in Taipei and 2 in Hsinchu), which were distributed as follows: 10 with government officials, 11 with lawyers and judges, 7 with right holders' associations, 6 with managers of firms producing intellectual property, 2 with private investigators, and 2 with foreign diplomats. In the Czech Republic, I conducted 22 interviews (all in Prague), which were distributed as follows: 10 with government officials, 4 with lawyers and judges, 5 with right holders' associations, 1 with a manager of a firm producing intellectual property, 1 with a foreign diplomat, and 1 with an academic. In France, I conducted 12 interviews (all in Paris), 5 of which were with government officials and 7 with right holders' associations. Finally, I conducted 4 interviews in the United States (3 in Washington, DC, and 1 in Cambridge), which were distributed as follows: 1 with a former Chinese government official, 1 with a former Chinese judge, 1 with a U.S. right holders' association, and 1 with an academic.

---

[53] Foreign scholars have been conducting research in Zouping county since the 1980s. At that time Zouping's level of development was roughly equivalent to the national average, but Zouping is currently among China's richest one hundred counties, with both its rural and urban residents enjoying incomes that are well above the national averages.

My interviews were the most important initial source of information for this project. Without them I would not have obtained many of the internal circulation (*neibu*) materials that this book uses.[54] Furthermore, interviewees clarified uncertainties, frequently pointed me to printed sources, and helped me interpret them. As a research tool, however, interviews have well-known biases. For this reason, I have provided, whenever possible, a printed source (yearbook, newspaper article, or scholarly analysis) or statistical evidence to back up my interview findings. The final product is a mixed-method study, drawing on different types of evidence to elucidate the enforcement of IPR laws in China.

[54] There are no consistent rules about what materials are classified as *neibu*. Despite increased openness, many documents, such as the annual reports of various bureaucracies, remain *neibu*. In principle, a *neibu* classification makes the material inaccessible, especially to foreign researchers.

2

Regulating the Quality of Enforcement

In the United States, media outlets, business groups, and the government have all fueled the popular misconception that high rates of piracy and counterfeiting in China persist because of the lack of enforcement of IPR laws. Over the last two decades, the U.S. media have provided the public a steady stream of stories about Chinese factories that churn out pirated software and counterfeit Nike shoes.[1] The bottom line of such reports is the same: too little enforcement. Business groups similarly bemoan the insufficient enforcement of IPR laws in China.[2] In addition, the Office of the U.S. Trade Representative never fails to emphasize in its annual reports on piracy that the Chinese government should provide more enforcement of IPR laws.[3] The message is loud and clear: the easy way to fix the problem is to step up enforcement. Yet the solution is not so simple. Controlling for population, China already has the highest volume of IPR enforcement in the world. Strikingly, this enforcement has not led to an appreciable drop in piracy and counterfeiting. Why? The main problem with the current enforcement structure in China is that high-quality enforcement is the exception, whereas low-quality enforcement is still the norm.

---

[1] See, for example, "Fakes!" *Business Week*, February 7, 2005, http://www.businessweek.com/magazine/content/05_06/b3919001_mz001.htm (accessed April 21, 2008), and Daniel Schearf, "Fakes Flourish in China Despite Government Promise to Halt Piracy," *Voice of America* news report, May 4, 2006, http://www.voanews.com/english/archive/2006–05/2006–05-04-voa4.cfm? CFID=298963095&CFTOKEN=39822490 (accessed April 21, 2008).

[2] See the annual *White Paper of the American Chamber of Commerce* (available at www.amcham-china.org.cn) or the annual enforcement recommendations of the International Intellectual Property Alliance (www.iipa.com), a powerful copyright lobbying group based in Washington, DC. See also *The Business Climate in China Today: Attitudes of British, Japanese and U.S. Companies (Questionnaire and Results)* (Hanover, NH: Tuck School of Business, Center for International Business, 2005).

[3] See www.ustr.gov for the annual assessments of the Office of the U.S. Trade Representative (USTR).

Why does low-quality enforcement persist in China? This chapter develops a theoretical argument that stresses the mutually reinforcing impact of two variables: bureaucratic organization and pressure to enforce.

Two aspects of bureaucratic organization can impact enforcement: administrative decentralization and jurisdictional ambiguity. Some bureaucracies responsible for IPR enforcement are decentralized, whereas others are not. A problem arises when decentralized bureaucracies are unwilling to enforce centrally mandated laws and regulations. When bureaucracies are centralized, Beijing can wield two instruments to compel local governments to enforce laws and regulations: the carrot of budgetary allotments and the stick of administrative punishments. Administrative decentralization blunts both instruments: the center has no control over the budget and personnel allocations of grassroots bureaucracies, and its ability to monitor the behavior of local-level bureaucrats is extremely limited. The farther down the administrative hierarchy we move, the less strong the presence of the central state becomes. Under decentralization, the interests of local enforcers are aligned with those of the local state, which, far from perceiving fakes as a problem, often derives sizable financial benefits from condoning businesses that engage in the production and sale of pirated and counterfeit goods. Administrative decentralization has two consequences for enforcement: it encourages shirking (refusal to enforce in difficult cases), as well as corrupt enforcement (enforcing in exchange for bribes in easy cases). Neither outcome is conducive to the emergence of consistent, transparent, and fair enforcement.

Jurisdictional overlap creates an additional problem: it makes it more difficult to determine which agencies should enforce IPR laws. In China, ambiguous mandates seem to be the norm: in many areas, multiple agencies share (poorly defined) responsibility for enforcement. This parceling of authority in the Chinese political system is well known: the "fragmented authoritarianism" model describes how authority over policymaking in China is dispersed among multiple bureaucratic actors. The fragmentation of authority means that a protracted bargaining process precedes the formulation of all important policies in China.[4] Less well understood is that the enforcement of laws and regulations in many issue areas reflects a similar dynamic: multiple agencies share an enforcement mandate, sometimes even when they are not interested in participating in enforcement. Coordination is consequently a challenging process, and it often ends in failure. Ambiguous responsibility for enforcement creates perverse incentives for agencies to reject difficult cases and to accept easy ones. The response in Beijing has been to ensure at least some enforcement

---

[4] See Kenneth Lieberthal and Michel Oksenberg, *Policy Making in China: Leaders, Structures, and Processes* (Princeton, NJ: Princeton University Press, 1988), and Kenneth Lieberthal and David M. Lampton, eds., *Bureaucracy, Politics, and Decision-Making in Post-Mao China* (Berkeley: University of California Press, 1992). See also David Lampton, ed., *Policy Implementation in Post-Mao China* (Berkeley: University of California Press, 1987).

by requiring agencies to participate in periodic enforcement campaigns. As subsequent chapters demonstrate, these campaigns typically lead to unnecessary duplication of administrative activity, producing uncoordinated and inefficient enforcement. Jurisdictional overlap combined with administrative decentralization creates an environment that nurtures low-quality enforcement.

However, not all enforcement in China is of a low quality: certain bureaucracies and the IPR courts can supply consistent, transparent, and fair enforcement. Subsequent chapters present evidence that exclusive enforcement mandates are a key precondition for the emergence of this type of enforcement. Exclusive jurisdictions unambiguously designate which agency is responsible for enforcement. Clearly mandated exclusive jurisdictions also increase accountability, because they make it easier to determine whether an agency has shirked. Whereas centralization may also facilitate rationalization, we should stress that high-quality enforcement of IPR laws can emerge even in the absence of formally centralized bureaucratic structures. Bureaucratic reach matters more than formal centralization: decentralized bureaucracies that only penetrate down to the provincial level can supply rationalized enforcement as well, provided they have exclusive enforcement mandates (as is the case in patents). Some decentralized bureaucracies penetrate as far as the township – yet, counterintuitively, a deeper bureaucratic reach makes it more likely that these bureaucracies will succumb to the forces of local protectionism and will not provide high-quality enforcement.

In spite of its poor quality, administrative enforcement in China has emerged as the dominant avenue for providing IPR protection. Why? To understand what drives enforcement, we need to introduce an additional variable: the pressure to provide quick enforcement. Chinese IPR bureaucracies are under constant pressure to enforce more, from both foreign and domestic sources. Foreign pressure is channeled by foreign governments, which may threaten to impose trade sanctions unless enforcement increases, or by foreign companies that have already invested in China and therefore can use the threat of exit to compel the government to provide enforcement. Domestic pressure is exercised by the media and consumer groups, which raise awareness of the dangers posed by counterfeit products. Foreign pressure is directed toward the greater enforcement of copyright and trademark laws, whereas domestic pressure is directed mainly toward the enforcement of trademark laws protecting consumer goods.[5] Because the government is accountable to both domestic and foreign constituencies, it addresses both foreign and domestic concerns in the same way: by unleashing national-level campaigns in the area of copyright and

---

[5] Domestic audiences support pirated copyright items, because they are much cheaper than legitimate products and do not pose any threat to consumer health and safety. China Interview 020117, with consumer rights advocate Wang Hai (Beijing).

trademark protection.[6] These campaigns produce a very high volume of enforcement. Yet enforcement is duplicative, uncoordinated, and, at least sometimes, corrupt.

Campaign enforcement can have negative effects even when a single agency has exclusive jurisdiction over enforcement in a certain domain. Take for example the State Intellectual Property Office (SIPO). Although the SIPO has exclusive jurisdiction over enforcement in cases of patent counterfeiting and patent passing off, this enforcement is not rationalized. The reason? The SIPO has employed campaign-style enforcement in cases of patent counterfeiting and patent passing off. Contrast this with the way in which the SIPO handles patent infringement disputes, as well as patent reexamination and invalidation proceedings: enforcement is consistent, transparent, and fair. This reflects the facts that the SIPO does not use campaign-style enforcement in this area and, furthermore, that courts can also handle patent infringement and patent invalidation cases. Thus, patents demonstrate both the danger of campaign-style enforcement and the problems created by excluding the courts from participation in IPR enforcement.

The remainder of this chapter is organized as follows. First, I argue that by default, bureaucratic enforcement in China is unaccountable. Though mechanisms for bureaucratic accountability to the public and the government do exist, they are ineffective. This situation creates obstacles for the rise of rationalized enforcement. Second, I maintain that decentralization and overlapping mandates further exacerbate the enforcement problems created by inadequate bureaucratic control mechanisms. Finally, I stress that bureaucracies are responsive to pressures to enforce more: the central government has been successful in forcefully co-opting agencies to participate in several major multiyear IPR and product-quality campaigns, but I conclude that these campaigns have delivered high-volume rather than high-quality enforcement.

ESTABLISHING ACCOUNTABLE ENFORCEMENT: MECHANISMS FOR CURBING OFFICIAL DISCRETION

How can bureaucrats be held accountable for their behavior? First, citizens can curb official discretion through various channels, most generally grouped under

---

[6] A number of scholars have analyzed the role of campaigns during the Mao period. See, for example, David Zweig, "Strategies of Policy Implementation: Policy 'Winds' and Brigade Accounting in Rural China, 1968–1978," *World Politics* 37:2 (January 1985), 267–293, and Jean C. Oi, *State and Peasant in Contemporary China: The Political Economy of Village Government* (Berkeley: University of California Press, 1989). Campaigns continue to the current day, especially in the areas of anticorruption work (Melanie Manion, *Corruption by Design: Building Clean Government in Mainland China and Hong Kong* [Cambridge, MA: Harvard University Press, 2004], and Yan Sun, *Corruption and Market in Contemporary China* [Ithaca, NY: Cornell University Press, 2004]); "strike hard" (M. Scot Tanner, "State Coercion and the Balance of Awe: The 1983–1986 'Stern Blows' Anti-Crime Campaign," *The China Journal*, no. 44 [2000], 93–125); and propaganda work (Daniel C. Lynch, *After the Propaganda State: Media, Politics, and "Thought Work" in Reformed China* [Stanford, CA: Stanford University Press, 1999]).

the category of "rightful resistance":[7] protests, letters and visits,[8] administrative reconsideration (*xingzheng fuyi*), and administrative litigation (*xingzheng susong*).[9] In addition, individuals can discipline bureaucrats by successfully mobilizing media attention. Oftentimes, citizens pursue their claims simultaneously or successively through as many channels as possible.[10] Second, the government can police its bureaucrats by controlling their budgets and by punishing them for abuse of discretion and corruption.

Citizens versus Bureaucrats

Administrative reconsideration allows a citizen dissatisfied with an agency's decision to lodge a complaint with its hierarchical superiors (e.g., decisions of provincial-level agencies will be examined by the national-level agency) or with the people's government at the same level at which the agency operates. Administrative litigation, on the other hand, gives individuals the option of challenging administrative acts in court.[11] The number of administrative litigation cases in China increased from 527 first-instance cases in 1983 to 95,707 first-instance cases in 2005.[12] High as this number is, the growth of administrative litigation seems less impressive when compared to places such as Taiwan and Russia, both of which, like China, have had a relatively short

---

[7] Kevin J. O'Brien and Lianjiang Li, *Rightful Resistance in Rural China* (New York: Cambridge University Press, 2006).

[8] Xi Chen, "An Authoritarian State and a Contentious Society: The Case of China" (Ph.D. Dissertation, Department of Political Science, Columbia University, 2005); Isabelle Thireau and Linshan Hua, "One Law, Two Interpretations: Mobilizing the Labor Law in Arbitration Committees and in Letters and Visits Offices," in *Engaging the Law in China: State, Society, and Possibilities for Justice*, ed. Neil J. Diamant, Stanley B. Lubman, and Kevin J. O'Brien (Stanford, CA: Stanford University Press, 2005), 84–107.

[9] Minxin Pei, "Citizens v. Mandarins: Administrative Litigation in China," *China Quarterly*, no. 152 (1997), 832–862; Stanley B. Lubman, *Bird in a Cage: Legal Reform in China after Mao* (Stanford, CA: Stanford University Press, 1999), 204–216; Veron Mei-Ying Hung, "Administrative Litigation and Court Reform in the People's Republic of China" (J.S.D. Dissertation, Stanford University School of Law, 2001); Kevin O'Brien and Lianjiang Li, "Suing the Local State: Administrative Litigation in Rural China," in *Engaging the Law in China*, ed. Diamant, Lubman, and O'Brien, 31–53; Pierre Landry and Yanqi Tong, "Disputing the Authoritarian State in China," paper presented at the Annual Meeting of the American Political Science Association, Washington, DC, September 1–4, 2005.

[10] Landry and Tong, "Disputing the Authoritarian State," and O'Brien and Li, *Rightful Resistance*. On protest tactics, see also Xi Chen, "Between Defiance and Obedience: Protest Opportunism in China," in *Grassroots Political Reform in Contemporary China*, ed. Elizabeth J. Perry and Merle Goldman (Cambridge, MA: Harvard University Press, 2007), 253–281.

[11] In China, individuals may only challenge the application of the law rather than the legality (constitutionality) of the law itself. For a failed attempt at challenging the constitutionality of a law, see "Judge Sows Seeds of Lawmaking Dispute," *China Daily*, November 24, 2003; "Luoyang City 'Seed' Case Highlights Chinese Courts' Lack of Authority to Declare Laws Invalid," *China Law and Governance Review*, no. 2 (2004), http://www.chinareview.info/pages/case.html (accessed December 10, 2004).

[12] *Zhongguo falü nianjian* (China Law Yearbook) (Beijing: Falü chubanshe, various years).

experience of allowing citizens to sue bureaucrats.[13] Undoubtedly, the growth of administrative litigation in China has been thwarted by the rise of administrative reconsideration, which is not widely used in either Taiwan or Russia.[14]

Although individuals in principle are allowed to choose freely between administrative reconsideration and administrative litigation,[15] in practice administrative agencies use internal (*neibu*) regulations to encourage the former. Administrative reconsideration limits the number of administrative litigation cases because it adds an extra barrier (and an additional expense) to citizen use of the courts. Grassroots bureaucrats prefer reconsideration over litigation because they face a much lower chance of having their decisions overturned during the course of reconsideration proceedings. Top bureaucrats also prefer administrative reconsideration because their agencies avoid losing face by being sued in court for mistakes they made during enforcement. In addition, courts in China are reluctant to accept administrative litigation cases where the parties have not pursued administrative reconsideration first, thus slowing the rise of administrative litigation as the channel of choice for resolving administrative grievances in China.[16] Finally, and unsurprisingly, a pervasive fear of suing the government still exists, and that fear helps to limit the number of administrative litigation lawsuits.[17]

However, despite the limited access to the courts,[18] when Chinese citizens do succeed in having their administrative litigation lawsuits accepted, they can be reasonably sure that justice will be dispensed according to the principles of consistency, transparency, and fairness. Consistency in the application of the law is enhanced by the creation of specialized administrative tribunals (*xingzheng ting*). Transparency is aided by the use of open trials, media attention to sensitive cases, and the publication of judicial decisions either electronically or

---

[13] In 2004, the number of Taiwan's first-instance administrative litigation cases per million people was 5.5 times greater than that of China, whereas Russia's was 80 times greater. See *Zhongguo falü nianjian 2005*, 1064–1066 (first-instance cases); www.judicial.gov.tw (first-instance cases); www.arbitr.ru (both first-instance and appeals cases are included in the Russian statistics).

[14] Administrative litigation cases grew sharply until 1999, when the Administrative Reconsideration Law regularized administrative reconsideration (until then there were provisional administrative reconsideration regulations). In 2000, the number of administrative litigation cases fell by 14 percent when compared to the number of administrative litigation cases in 1999. As soon as administrative reconsideration was legally sanctioned, government agencies and the courts began to pressure claimants to eschew litigation. The number of administrative reconsideration cases continued to grow after 1999. By 2004, administrative agencies handled as many as 81,883 administrative reconsideration cases, whereas the courts accepted 92,613 first-instance administrative litigation cases. See *Zhongguo falü nianjian 2005*, 1079.

[15] See Article 37 of the 1989 Administrative Litigation Law.

[16] China Interview 020129A, with two judges from the No. 1 Intermediate People's Court (head of the Case Acceptance Division and vice head of the General Affairs Office) (Shanghai).

[17] China Interview 020128A, with the head of the Anticounterfeiting Office, Administration of Quality Supervision, Inspection, and Quarantine (AQSIQ) (Beijing); China Interview 020129B, with a judge from the Enforcement Division of the No. 1 Intermediate People's Court (Shanghai).

[18] Landry and Tong, "Disputing the Authoritarian State."

in printed compendia. Finally, how do we assess fairness? Pierre Landry finds that the courts provide more effective and fairer means of resolving administrative grievances than direct negotiations, letters and visits, and mediation.[19] Additional evidence to support this claim is provided by the fact that although courts upheld the initial administrative decision in 41.6 percent of the administrative litigation cases in 1989, the proportion had dropped to 17.8 percent in 2004, indicating that, over time, less political pressure is being applied on the courts to resolve cases in ways favorable to the administrative agency.[20] Similarly, rates of individual case supervision for administrative litigation cases hover around 2 percent, which is higher than the rate for criminal and civil cases but is not so high as to discourage courts from deciding on the merits of the case.[21] In addition, the high rate of appeals of first-instance administrative litigation cases (29.7 percent in 2004) indicates that individuals (and government bureaucrats) who feel they did not receive a fair trial have ample opportunities for redress.[22]

Letters and Visits

The question remains why there have been so few administrative litigation lawsuits in China, especially when compared with places like Taiwan and Russia. Apart from administrative reconsideration, perhaps the greatest culprit is the continued use of the letters and visits (*xinfang*) system as a substitute for resolving administrative grievances through the courts.[23] Citizens in China can lodge a complaint (by writing a letter or by making a visit in person) with any of a range of different agencies: the party, the government, the courts, and so on. In the early 2000s, there were about 11.5 million letters and visits per year in China,[24] which is well in excess of all first- and second-instance cases handled by the entire Chinese judicial system. The courts alone received 4.1 million letters in 2004.[25] Since most letters are merely passed back and forth between

[19] Landry and Tong, "Disputing the Authoritarian State."
[20] In 2004, agency decisions were 3.3 times more likely to be upheld in administrative reconsideration than in administrative litigation. In administrative reconsideration, the initial agency decision was upheld in 58.1 percent of the cases (see *Zhongguo falü nianjian 2005*, 1065–1066, 1080). Subnational data indicate the same trend: in Shanghai, the rate of approval of agency decisions in reconsideration cases ranged from 52 percent to 66 percent between 1995 and 1999. See Ying Songnian, *Zouxiang fazhi zhengfu: Xingzheng lilun yanjiu yu shizheng diaocha* (Towards a Government by Laws: Research and Empirical Investigation on the Theory of Administration According to Laws) (Beijing: Falü chubanshe, 2001), 519.
[21] On how individual case supervision can constrain judicial independence, see Randall Peerenboom, "Judicial Independence and Judicial Accountability: Individual Case Supervision," *The China Journal*, no. 55 (2006), 67–92.
[22] There were 27,495 second-instance administrative litigation cases in 2004. *Zhongguo falü nianjian 2005*, 1066.
[23] A *xinfang* system existed in Russia during the Soviet period as well, but it fell into disuse after the collapse of communism, when grievances against administrative agencies began to be channeled to the courts.
[24] Congressional Executive Commission on China, *2005 Annual Report*, http://www.cecc.gov/pages/annualRpt/annualRpto5/2005_5e_access.php#8b (accessed July 23, 2008).
[25] *Zhongguo falü nianjian 2005*, 1066.

the various government units sharing "competency" over the case and so are ultimately left unaddressed, writing a letter or making a visit to a government office is oftentimes not the most effective tactic for people who seek redress.[26] Letters and visits surely were an important channel of accountability in the past, when courts had no expertise in handling administrative litigation cases. However, the continued existence of the letters and visits system (which is free and supposedly less intimidating to complainants than the courts) may now serve as a disincentive for court use and may therefore perpetuate an environment where the application of the law is uncertain and arbitrary. Given the deficiencies of the letters and visits system, various prominent Chinese academics have argued that it should be abolished.[27]

How often are reconsideration, litigation, and letters and visits used in the area of IPR? There is no evidence that the letters and visits system has been used for IPR matters. When it comes to administrative reconsideration and administrative litigation, there are very few such cases brought against IPR agencies. Data presented in subsequent chapters reveal that considerably fewer than 1 percent of the copyright and trademark administrative enforcement actions carried out by IPR agencies become subject to control through administrative reconsideration and administrative litigation. This compounds the already existing problems of unaccountable enforcement and creates a vicious circle within which inconsistent, nontransparent, and unfair enforcement thrives.[28] Overall, then, reconsideration, litigation, and letters and visits are very weak tools for controlling IPR agencies.[29]

The Government versus the Bureaucrats: Strategies of Control

Bureaucrats may also be controlled by the government, which acts as their principal. Is the government more effective than the citizens in controlling its agents? Two avenues for control exist: personnel (rather than budget) allocations and institutions of horizontal accountability (e.g., anticorruption agencies).[30]

[26] Chen, "An Authoritarian State and a Contentious Society."

[27] Jianrong Yu, "Seeking Justice: Is China's Administrative Petition System Broken?" Carnegie Endowment for International Peace Seminar, April 5, 2006, summary available at http://www.carnegieendowment.org/events/index.cfm?fa=eventDetail&id=870&&prog=zch (accessed April 22, 2008).

[28] Chapter 9 reveals that patent enforcement is an exception to this rule: it is subject to high levels of reconsideration and litigation, which have further improved its already high quality.

[29] Following the promulgation of the State Compensation Law (*guojia peichang fa*) in 1996, individuals may now receive monetary compensation in addition to or instead of the remedies provided by the Administrative Litigation Law. The State Compensation Law provides for compensation in both criminal cases (e.g., illegal detention) and noncriminal cases. However, the number of state compensation cases remains very low, reaching only 3,298 in 2004 (*Zhongguo falü nianjian 2005*, 1066). There is no evidence that the State Compensation Law has been used in IPR cases in China.

[30] On horizontal accountability in general, see Andreas Schedler, Larry Diamond, and Marc F. Plattner, eds., *The Self-Restraining State: Power and Accountability in New Democracies* (Boulder, CO: Lynne Rienner, 1999).

Personnel Allocations

Personnel allocations are crucial in China: in general, the larger the agency, the more powerful it is.[31] Whereas studies of U.S. bureaucracies have focused on budget allocations,[32] the key to increasing an agency's clout in China is to secure a larger personnel allocation (*bianzhi*) from the Ministry of Personnel (Renshi bu); once the agency is allotted more personnel, it can justify a request to the Finance Ministry for a bigger budget. At the national level, the general trend after the 1998 reform has been to cut the size of most government agencies by half. Nonetheless, some IPR enforcement agencies such as the State Food and Drug Administration (SFDA) managed to gain formal independence from their ministerial hats, thus allowing them to increase their personnel allocations.[33] At the local level, personnel allocations of administrative enforcement agencies are made by the local people's governments; this system leads to significant regional variation in the relative size and power of individual agencies. As a result, both the central and the local governments can either "penalize" or "reward" an agency by changing its personnel allocation. As a secondary mechanism, the government can also increase the agency's budget allocation, typically by allowing it to keep a larger part of the proceeds collected from the various fines it is authorized to impose.

Institutions of Horizontal Accountability

The second avenue for control by the government is provided by three different institutions of horizontal accountability: the Central Discipline Inspection Commission of the CCP (Zhongjiwei), the Ministry of Supervision (Jiancha bu), and the Procuratorate (Jiancha yuan).[34] The Central Discipline Inspection Commission is the most powerful agency in China; in one body, it combines the functions of the police, the Procuratorate, and the courts. It can enter and inspect premises, summon witnesses, and seize evidence without having to obtain a search warrant. It can then adjudicate the culpability of the official under investigation and, under unusually serious circumstances, transfer cases for criminal prosecution to the Procuratorate.[35] Although in principle it is limited to investigating party members, in practice its mandate to discipline

---

[31] On the personnel allocation system more generally, see Kjeld Erik Brødsgaard, "Institutional Reform and the *Bianzhi* System in China," *The China* Quarterly, no. 170 (2002), 361–386.

[32] William A. Niskanen, *Bureaucracy and Representative Government* (Chicago: Aldine-Atherton, 1971).

[33] In the 2008 Chinese government reorganization, the State Food and Drug Administration reverted to the jurisdiction of the Ministry of Health.

[34] For other mechanisms, for instance, the General Audit Administration, see Yasheng Huang, "Administrative Monitoring in China," *The China Quarterly*, no. 143 (1995), 828–843. See also Yasheng Huang, "Managing Chinese Bureaucrats: An Institutional Economics Perspective," *Political Studies* 50:1 (2002), 61–79.

[35] China Interview 020919A, with a Central Discipline Inspection Commission employee (Beijing).

officials is extraordinarily broad because most bureaucrats in China are party members as well.

The Ministry of Supervision conducts inspections on the implementation of state laws and regulations by civil servants.[36] It also investigates cases of violations of administrative laws, regulations, and policies committed by government employees. The Ministry of Supervision has a similar role to that of the Central Discipline Inspection Commission, except that it can inspect the work of all government employees, regardless of whether or not they are party members. This should, in theory, make the Ministry of Supervision more powerful than the Central Discipline Inspection Commission. However, it is widely known that the Central Discipline Inspection Commission calls the shots.[37] The Ministry of Supervision is a weak bureaucratic actor, and below the provincial level, it is merged with the discipline inspection offices, under the principle of "one system of government offices, two nameplates" (*yige jigou, liangkuai paizi*). Effectively, this means that the Ministry of Supervision has no reach below the provincial level. As a consequence, its caseload is relatively light: annually, it investigates only fifteen to seventeen ministerial- and provincial-level officials (who have equal rank in the Chinese administrative hierarchy) for dereliction of duty. These figures do not necessarily reflect the absence of high-level bureaucratic corruption in China but rather bespeak the relative weakness of the Ministry of Supervision.

Importantly, despite the fact that the Central Discipline Inspection Commission and the Ministry of Supervision enjoy unparalleled rights of access to virtually any party member or government employee, they can only summon individuals to give testimony; they cannot impose criminal detention (*xingshi juliu*), which is the prerogative of the police and the Procuratorate. In theory, the Procuratorate can initiate investigations of corruption and bribery of public officials without relying on the police to collect evidence first. However, in practice, the rights of the anticorruption bureaus of the Procuratorate are circumscribed.

In the late 1990s, a special entity was created within the Supreme People's Procuratorate to prosecute official corruption: the General Administration for Combating Embezzlement and Bribery (GACEB) (Fan tanwu huilu zongju).[38] Despite its impressive name, the GACEB has a very low status in the Chinese bureaucratic hierarchy. Officially, it has the rank of a vice-ministry (*fu buji*), as it is only a department within a ministerial-level (*buji*) agency (the Supreme People's Procuratorate). According to Chinese

[36] Unless otherwise indicated, this and the following paragraph are based on China Interview 020919B, with two Ministry of Supervision employees (Beijing) and *Zhonghua renmin gongheguo jiancha bu jianjie* (A Brief Introduction to the Ministry of Supervision of the PRC) (Beijing: n. d. [2001]).
[37] China Interview 020206A, with a Peking University law professor (Beijing).
[38] Unless otherwise indicated, the following three paragraphs are based on China Interview 020918, with a GACEB employee (Beijing) and *Zhonghua renmin gongheguo renmin jianchayuan jianjie*.

bureaucratic practice, lower-level administrative entities cannot investigate entities at higher levels. As a result of its low bureaucratic rank, the GACEB cannot initiate investigations of officials with the rank of minister or provincial governor, since they are its administrative superiors. This greatly limits the ability of the GACEB to prosecute instances of grand corruption. Occasionally, such cases are prosecuted, but only if they are transferred to the GACEB from the Central Discipline Inspection Commission. For the entire 1989–2001 period, the GACEB prosecuted only thirty-nine ministers and provincial governors in China for corruption, averaging three prosecutions per year. In contrast, from 1998 to 2000, the Central Discipline Inspection Commission investigated 50 cases of grand corruption, an average of 13.3 cases a year.[39] Thus, only a small number of the already very few cases of grand corruption investigated by the Central Discipline Inspection Commission actually reach the GACEB and eventually result in criminal prosecution.

In addition to the difficulties facing the GACEB in the area of prosecuting grand corruption, the Procuratorate is constrained in its ability freely to prosecute the much more common cases of everyday petty bureaucratic corruption. Although it has a legal right to initiate such prosecutions, the GACEB and its territorial subdivisions work primarily on cases that are transferred to them from the Central Discipline Inspection Commission and the Ministry of Supervision. At a minimum, this means that all criminal cases are investigated twice (by the Central Discipline Inspection Commission first, and then by the Procuratorate), thus leading to unnecessary duplication of effort and a considerable waste of scarce administrative resources. A more troubling consequence is that some cases that meet the criminal liability threshold are treated by the Central Discipline Inspection Commission and the Ministry of Supervision as disciplinary or administrative cases, thus allowing corrupt officials who should be put behind bars to get away with a minor fine or warning.

A final problem with the current system is that prosecutions for dereliction of duty are not handled by the GACEB, but rather by a different entity at the Procuratorate: the Prosecutorial Department for Dereliction of Duty and Infringement of Citizens' Rights (Faji jiancha ting). This jurisdictional fragmentation has important consequences for the effectiveness of anticorruption efforts. The crimes of dereliction of duty (*duzhi zui*), abuse of power (*lanyong zhiquan*), and favoritism (*xunsi wubi*) often involve a simultaneous acceptance of bribes and other payments. For example, an official is committing acts of both corruption and abuse of power when he awards a retail license to a citizen in exchange for a bribe. What happens in cases when two different legal

---

[39] He Zengke, *Fanfu xinlu: Zhuanxingqi Zhongguo fubai wenti yanjiu* (A New Path to Combat Corruption: Research on the Issue of Corruption in Transitional China) (Beijing: Zhongyang bianyi chubanshe, 2002), 51–54.

provisions are violated? Who prosecutes them? When I posed these questions to an official at the GACEB, I was told that "the more serious crime will be prosecuted,"[40] yet the official would not clarify what specific coordination mechanisms are in place for dealing with such cases. Only a few thousand officials are prosecuted annually for dereliction of duty.

In short, the triad of the Central Discipline Inspection Commission, the Ministry of Supervision, and the GACEB is not effective in fighting corruption. The reason is simple: the three agencies have overlapping (and poorly specified) anticorruption mandates, a situation that prevents them from coordinating their activities successfully and fighting corruption effectively and efficiently. As a result, a minuscule number of bureaucrats are investigated for corruption by any of the three agencies. Furthermore, some investigations never reach the Procuratorate, which is the only agency that can actually initiate the process of imposing a criminal punishment on officials who engage in acts of corruption and bribery. On average, only 30 percent of the cases handled by the Central Discipline Inspection Commission and the Ministry of Supervision are transferred to the Procuratorate for criminal investigation.[41] In turn, around 40 percent of the corruption cases handled by the Procuratorate result in criminal conviction.[42]

The area of IPR follows the national patterns described: a very small number of bureaucrats are prosecuted for corruption each year by the Central Discipline Inspection Commission, the Ministry of Supervision, or the Procuratorate. For example, in 2000, the State Administration for Industry and Commerce (SAIC) investigated 385 of its employees for discipline violations and illegal behavior. This was less than one-tenth of 1 percent of the SAIC staff. Of those investigated, only seven individuals were transferred to the judicial authorities for prosecution, eleven were terminated or forced to retire, and four were stripped of their party membership.[43] These numbers do not mean that there is no corruption in the agencies with IPR enforcement mandates, but rather that the existing system for prosecuting government corruption, both overall and in the narrow area of IPR, is seriously flawed.

---

[40] China Interview 020918, with a GACEB employee (Beijing).

[41] China Interview 020919A, with a Central Discipline Inspection Commission employee (Beijing); China Interview 020919B, with two Ministry of Supervision employees (Beijing).

[42] Tony Saich, *Governance and Politics of China* (New York: Palgrave, 2001), 301. Saich quotes a report from the Procuratorate, stating that in 1999, 38,382 cases of official corruption were prosecuted, of which 15,748 resulted in criminal conviction. This is confirmed by He Zengke, who reports that in 2000, there were 119 investigations per million people by the Central Discipline Inspection Commission, but only 30 percent of those investigations resulted in criminal prosecution. See He Zengke, *Fanfu xinlu*, 51–52.

[43] *Zhongguo gongshang xingzheng guanli nianjian 2001* (China Industry and Commerce Yearbook 2001) (Beijing: Gongshang chubanshe, 2001), 169. No statistics on the size of the SAIC staff are available for 2000, but in 1999, the SAIC system employed a total of 508,145 people (*Zhongguo gongshang xingzheng guanli nianjian 2000*, 516). We can assume that staff size was similar in 2000.

Other Control Mechanisms

Before we turn to a discussion of how unaccountable bureaucrats operate under conditions of decentralization and jurisdictional ambiguity, we should briefly review several other mechanisms of control that have been highlighted by China scholars: appointment, promotion, and rotation of cadres;[44] the *nomenklatura* system;[45] and the annual cadre evaluations (*ganbu kaohe*) and performance contracts (*gangwei mubiao zerenzhi*).[46] Although these mechanisms may allow for effective central control over some crucial policy areas (such as inflation, investment, banking, and taxation), there is no evidence that they have been used to force the localities to implement centrally mandated laws and regulations in low-priority areas, for instance, environmental protection or IPR. When it comes to IPR, first, central leaders have no control over *nomenklatura* appointments below the national level and cannot use them to fine-tune IPR implementation. Second, performance contracts virtually never include clauses covering IPR enforcement or consumer protection.[47] The only mechanism that may impact lower-level enforcement is cadre rotation, which has been implemented in centralized bureaucracies like the General Administration of Customs, as well as in partially centralized bureaucracies like the SAIC and the AQSIQ.[48] However, it is still too early to tell whether cadre rotation will have a positive effect on the quality of IPR enforcement.

In sum, neither citizens nor the government is able to keep bureaucrats accountable for their actions. By default, bureaucrats have incentives to engage

[44] Zhiyue Bo, "The Institutionalization of Elite Management in China," in *Holding China Together: Diversity and National Integration in the Post-Deng Era*, ed. Barry J. Naughton and Dali L. Yang (New York: Cambridge University Press, 2004), 70–100; Pierre Landry, *Decentralized Authoritarianism in China: The Communist Party's Control of Local Elites in the Post-Mao Era* (New York: Cambridge University Press, 2008).

[45] Melanie Manion, "The Cadre Management System, Post-Mao: The Appointment, Promotion, Transfer, and Removal of Party and State Leaders," *The China Quarterly*, no. 102 (1985), 203–233; John Burns, "Strengthening Central CCP Control of Leadership Selection: The 1990 Nomenklatura," *The China Quarterly*, no. 138 (1994), 458–491; John Burns, "'Downsizing' the Chinese State: Government Retrenchment in the 1990s," *The China Quarterly*, no. 175 (2003), 775–802; Hon S. Chan, "Cadre Personnel Management in China: The *Nomenklatura* System, 1990–1998," *The China Quarterly*, no. 179 (2004), 703–734.

[46] Susan H. Whiting, *Power and Wealth in Rural China: The Political Economy of Institutional Change* (New York: Cambridge University Press, 2001); Maria Edin, "State Capacity and Local Agent Control in China: CCP Cadre Management from a Township Perspective," *The China Quarterly*, no. 173 (2003), 35–52; Susan H. Whiting, "The Cadre Evaluation System at the Grassroots: The Paradox of Party Rule," in *Holding China Together*, ed. Naughton and Yang, 101–119.

[47] Performance contracts need not lead to better government performance even for targets included in the contract: Lily Tsai finds that village and township leaders who sign a performance contract with their administrative superiors do not perform better (and sometimes perform worse) in terms of the provision of public goods than do leaders who do not sign these contracts. See Lily L. Tsai, *Accountability without Democracy: Solidary Groups and Public Goods Provision in China* (New York: Cambridge University Press, 2007).

[48] Below the provincial level, the Administration of Quality Supervision, Inspection, and Quarantine is known as the Technical Supervision Bureau (TSB).

in illegal behavior. These incentives are strengthened by the presence of decentralization and ambiguously defined enforcement mandates.

DECENTRALIZATION AND ENFORCEMENT

This book argues that decentralization diminishes state capacity in China and, by extension, thwarts the rise of rationalized enforcement and progress toward the rule of law. This is at odds with an extensive literature on the benefits of decentralization for economic development and improved governance. In terms of economic development, the basic intuition is that in the absence of heavy-handed central involvement, localities will be free to pursue their economic interests. In the aggregate, more growth should occur under decentralization than under centralization.[49] Similarly, in the area of governance, local officials are supposed to have better information than the central government about local needs and local preferences for the provision of public goods.[50] This standard argument has been challenged by a more recent school of thought, which notes that decentralization does not necessarily lead to improved provision of public goods.[51] In addition, new research highlights that under decentralization, poor oversight and monitoring of local officials may breed corruption and lower the quality of governance.[52]

In concert with the general decentralization literature, China studies have shifted from being overly optimistic about the benefits of decentralization to recognizing some of its shortcomings. Initially, the literature focused on how the devolution of fiscal, administrative, and legal authority empowered local

[49] This idea has a long history in economics. See Charles Tieboult, "A Pure Theory of Local Expenditures," *Journal of Public Economy* 64:5 (1956), 416–424; Richard T. Musgrave and Alan T. Peacock, *Classics in the Theory of Public Finance* (London: Macmillan, 1958); Wallace Oates, *Fiscal Federalism* (New York: Harcourt Brace Jovanovich, 1972); Jeffrey Brennan and James M. Buchanan, *The Power to Tax: Analytical Foundations of a Fiscal Constitution* (New York: Cambridge University Press, 1980); and Wallace Oates, "An Essay on Fiscal Federalism," *Journal of Economic Literature* 37:3 (1999), 1120–1149. The market-preserving federalism literature is an outgrowth of this idea: for an application to China, see Gabriella Montinola, Yingyi Qian, and Barry Weingast, "Federalism, Chinese Style: The Political Basis for Economic Success in China," *World Politics* 48:1 (1995), 50–81.
[50] Friedrich Hayek, "The Economic Conditions of Interstate Federalism," in *Individualism and Economic Order* (Chicago: University of Chicago Press, 1949 [1939]), 255–272.
[51] Peyvand Khaleghian, *Decentralization and Public Services: The Case of Immunizations*, World Bank Policy Research Paper Working Paper, no. 2989 (2003); Tsai, *Accountability without Democracy*. For a detailed account of the costs and benefits of decentralization, see Daniel Treisman, *The Architecture of Government: Rethinking Political Decentralization* (New York: Cambridge University Press, 2007).
[52] See Rémy Prud'homme, *On the Dangers of Decentralization*, World Bank Policy Research Working Paper, no. 1252 (1994); Vito Tanzi, *Corruption, Government Activities, and Markets*, International Monetary Fund Working Paper, no. 94/99 (1996); Daniel Treisman, "The Causes of Corruption: A Cross-National Study," *Journal of Public Economics* 76:3 (2000), 399–457; Conor O'Dwyer and Daniel Ziblatt, "Does Decentralization Make Government More Efficient and Effective?" *Journal of Commonwealth and Comparative Politics* 44:3 (2006), 326–343.

governments and fueled economic growth.[53] However, in the mid- to late 1990s, there was a growing awareness that decentralization might also have a negative side. The slowing down of rural growth, the explosion of several high-profile corruption scandals, and the wild interregional variations in the effectiveness of policy implementation alerted scholars to the dangers of decentralization. Over time, studies began to explore how decentralization may facilitate the rise of corruption,[54] crony capitalism,[55] and predatory taxation.[56] A related question that has received insufficient attention is how decentralization may impact the prospects for the rise of the rule of law.[57] When multiple bureaucracies share an enforcement mandate, the resulting jurisdictional ambiguities may be exploited by bureaucrats who will either refuse to enforce the law (shirk) or enforce only in exchange for a bribe. Shirking and bribery occur because of the dual subordination of decentralized bureaucracies in the Chinese political system.

Dual Bureaucratic Subordination

In China, local branches of decentralized bureaucracies are subjected to dual subordination (*shuangchong lingdao*). First, they are subordinate to agencies with

---

[53] Jean C. Oi, "Fiscal Reform and the Economic Foundations of Local State Corporatism in China," *World Politics* 45:1 (1992), 99–126; Susan Shirk, *The Political Logic of Economic Reform* (Berkeley: University of California Press, 1993); Montinola, Qian, and Weingast, "Market-Preserving Federalism"; Andrew G. Walder, ed., *Zouping in Transition: The Process of Reform in Rural North China* (Cambridge, MA: Harvard University Press, 1998); Jean C. Oi, *Rural China Takes Off: The Institutional Foundations of Economic Reform* (Berkeley: University of California Press, 1999); Jean C. Oi and Andrew G. Walder, eds., *Property Rights and Economic Reform in China* (Stanford, CA: Stanford University Press, 1999); Whiting, *Power and Wealth in Rural China*; Kellee S. Tsai, *Back-Alley Banking: Private Entrepreneurs in China* (Ithaca, NY: Cornell University Press, 2002).

[54] Xiaobo Lü, "Booty Socialism, Bureau-preneurs, and the State in Transition: Organizational Corruption in China," *Comparative Politics* 32:3 (2000), 273–294; Sun, *Corruption and Market*; Andrew Wedeman, *From Mao to Market: Rent Seeking, Local Protectionism, and Marketization in China* (New York: Cambridge University Press, 2003).

[55] David L. Wank, *Commodifying Communism: Business, Politics, and Trust in a Chinese City* (New York: Cambridge University Press, 1999); Yi-Min Lin, *Between Politics and Markets: Firms, Competition, and Institutional Change in Post-Mao China* (New York: Cambridge University Press, 2001); and Thomas Gold, Doug Guthrie, and David Wank, eds., *Social Connections in China: Institutions, Culture, and the Changing Nature of Guanxi* (New York: Cambridge University Press, 2002). For an argument on the declining role of *guanxi*, see Doug Guthrie, *Dragon in a Three-Piece Suit: The Emergence of Capitalism in China* (Princeton, NJ: Princeton University Press, 1999).

[56] Thomas Bernstein and Xiaobo Lü, *Taxation without Representation in Contemporary Rural China* (New York: Cambridge University Press, 2003).

[57] The only English-language exception is Randall Peerenboom, *China's Long March toward Rule of Law* (New York: Cambridge University Press, 2002). Several works exist in Chinese. See Tang Wei and Hua Kezhi, *Difang lifa de minzhuhua yu kexuehua gouxiang* (Proposal for Making Local Legislation Democratic and Scientific) (Beijing: Beijing daxue chubanshe, 2002) and Tian Chengyou, *Difang lifa de lilun yu shijian* (Theory and Practice of Local Legislation) (Beijing: Fazhi chubanshe, 2004). Useful statistics on local rule making can be found in Ying Songnian, *Zouxiang fazhi zhengfu*, and Cui Zhuolan, *Difang lifa shizheng yanjiu* (Empirical Investigation of Local Legislation) (Beijing: Zhishi chanquan chubanshe, 2007).

which they have a vertical bureaucratic relationship (*tiao guanxi*). For example, for a provincial-level Administration for Industry and Commerce (AIC), the vertical superior will be the central-level State Administration for Industry and Commerce in Beijing. Second, bureaucracies are horizontally subordinate to the local government at the level at which they operate. Subordination to the local government is referred to as a "horizontal relationship" (*kuai guanxi*). This dual – that is, vertical and horizontal – subordination is the chief problem that blocks the center from asserting its authority vis-à-vis the provinces.[58]

The ability of the center to control lower levels depends on whether the bureaucracy has a centralized vertical bureaucratic structure (*chuizhi jigou*) or a "local" bureaucratic structure (*shudi jigou*).[59] In a centralized structure, personnel and budget allocations for the subnational levels of a bureaucracy are made at the central level of the same bureaucracy (for instance, the allocation for Shanghai will be determined in Beijing). This stands in contrast to a local bureaucratic structure, in which the center maintains a so-called professional relationship (*yewu guanxi*) with the subordinate levels, meaning that personnel and budget allocations are determined by the local government (in this structure, allocations for Shanghai are made in Shanghai).

How does dual subordination impact enforcement? Agencies with a local bureaucratic structure are more likely to side with the local government than with the center. This limits the ability of the center to monitor local-level compliance with centrally mandated laws and regulations, and it increases the likelihood that agencies will shirk in order to protect local interests that may be opposed to the effective enforcement of IPR laws.

Significantly, prior to 1998, all agencies with an IPR mandate (except the State Tobacco Monopoly Administration [STMA]) had a local bureaucratic structure. Take, for example, the SAIC. In the 1990s, this bureaucracy had a very deep reach. Officially, it penetrated down only to the county level (*xianji gongshangju*), but in practice it also operated at the township level through a "system of subbranch offices" (*paichu jigou*).[60] Within the industry and commerce system (*xitong*), each level was responsible to the level immediately above it (province to center, prefecture to province, county to prefecture, and township to county); that meant that the lower levels below the province were not directly responsible to the highest level (the center). As a result of this structure, in practice, the central level could not inspect and punish officials at the county level without the cooperation of the prefectural level, which in turn would not cooperate with the center unless asked by the provincial level.[61]

---

[58] See Lieberthal and Oksenberg, *Policy Making in China*. Scholars sometimes refer to this as the *bumen/zhengfu* (bureaucracy/government) division.

[59] Bureaucracies with a vertical structure (*chuizhi jigou*) are often referred to as bureaucracies having "vertical management" (*chuizhi guanli*). I use the two terms interchangeably.

[60] *Zhongguo gongshang xingzheng guanli nianjian 2000*, 511.

[61] This finding, backed up by numerous interviews, differs from Huang, "Administrative Monitoring"; Huang, "Managing Chinese Bureaucrats"; and Edin, "State Capacity," who have a more optimistic view about the administrative monitoring mechanisms in the Chinese bureaucratic system.

This particular bureaucratic structure effectively limited the possibility for the uniform implementation of laws across the country, especially in decentralized bureaucracies with a deep bureaucratic reach.

Centralization and the Quality of Enforcement

How can the negative effects of decentralization be offset? One possible solution is to implement centralization, which might lead to greater transparency and predictability of enforcement. An emerging body of literature examines the politics of centralization in China.[62] Although these works are important, they leave some unanswered questions. First, why is it that only some issue areas have been centralized? Second, why have some issue areas been fully centralized from the center down to the lowest levels, whereas others have only been "softly" centralized from the province down to the prefecture/county (*sheng yixia chuizhi*)? Third, is centralization sufficient to bring about bureaucratic rationalization? I shall address these questions in turn.

An examination of the agencies that are centralized and those that are not centralized reveals a clear and unsurprising pattern: bureaucracies of strategic importance to the state have been subject to complete centralization from the center all the way down to the lowest levels. For example, the State Administration of Taxation, the National Audit Office, the General Administration of Customs (GAC), and the National Bureau of Statistics are now centralized all the way down from the center. These administrations are the fiscal and statistical sinews of the central state, and by centralizing them the state strengthens its extractive and planning capacity.

On the other hand, agencies like the SAIC, the AQSIQ, and the SFDA have been subject to only "soft" centralization since 1998.[63] These agencies deal with enforcement mainly in the area of consumer protection from shoddy, substandard, and dangerous goods. A series of scandals called these areas to the attention of the central leaders in the 1990s and early 2000s. Even if such questions were seen as less important than fiscal matters, they were still deemed serious enough by the government to justify the soft centralization of the relevant enforcement bureaucracies. Land management provides another example of soft centralization. In the early 2000s, the expansion of the illegal use of agricultural land for commercial purposes compelled Beijing municipality to introduce soft centralization within the Land and Natural Resources Bureau.[64]

---

[62] See, for example, Dali L. Yang, *Remaking the Chinese Leviathan: Market Transition and the Politics of Governance in China* (Stanford, CA: Stanford University Press, 2004).

[63] Andrew Mertha, "China's 'Soft' Centralization: Shifting *Tiao/Kuai* Authority Relations," *The China Quarterly*, no. 184 (2005), 791–810.

[64] "Tudi chuizhi guanli Beijing zhendang" (Beijing Shaken by Vertical Land Management), http://64.233.179.104/search?q=cache:hpyKDPIW79gJ:www.caijing.com.cn/mag/preview.aspx%3 FArtID%3D5625+%E5%9E%82%E7%9B%B4%E7%AE%A1%E7%90%86&;;hl=en (accessed March 30, 2005).

Why have these bureaucracies not been subject to full centralization like the fiscal and customs bureaucracies? The reason is that full centralization will be unpopular with the provincial governments.[65] Therefore, the strategy seems to be to limit full centralization only to crucial issues.[66] Less important areas are subject to partial centralization. Issues of least importance to the center are not subject to centralization (e.g., health, environmental protection, and education).

Currently, only two bureaucracies with IPR enforcement portfolios have a vertical (i.e., centralized) bureaucratic structure, the GAC and the STMA; both agencies serve as primary revenue generators for the consolidated national budget: centralization allows the central government to establish better control over the tax revenue it collects from these agencies. The SAIC, the AQSIQ, and the SFDA are partially centralized. Other bureaucracies with an IPR enforcement portfolio are fully decentralized: the Ministry of Culture (MOC), the Ministry of Agriculture (MOA), the Ministry of Health (MOH), the General Administration of Press and Publications (GAPP), the National Copyright Administration of China (NCAC), and the MPS (known as the Public Security Bureau or PSB at the local level). The SIPO, though formally decentralized, functions in practice as a quasi-centralized bureaucracy, since it only penetrates down to the provincial level, a structure that makes monitoring easier than for bureaucracies with deeper reach.

Is centralization sufficient for the emergence of bureaucratic rationalization? Even when partial centralization is implemented, the problem of lack of inter-provincial coordination *within* the bureaucracy may emerge. This was an obstacle to effective enforcement in the fake baby formula case, which affected a range of provinces in 2004. Although the Food and Drug Administration system was centralized from the province down, there was no working system for interprovincial coordination. As a consequence, the problem grew until it reached a crisis level and the center intervened with a campaign. We should stress that attempts at interprovincial coordination have historically been frustrated by the insufficient authority of Beijing vis-à-vis the provinces and by

---

[65] The following are representative articles: "Zhengming: Zhongyang chuizhi guanli bingfei youxiao 'liangyao'" (We Contend That Centralized Management Is Not an Effective "Good Medicine"), http://opinion.people.com.cn/GB/1036/3245688.html (accessed March 30, 2005); "Chuizhi guanli shi zuihou yi gen daocao?" (Is Centralized Management the Final Straw?), http://www.southcn.com/opinion/pe/200503140341.htm (accessed October 25, 2008). There is also a special Web site on the constitutionality of the centralization, http://www.jcrb.com/zyw/ccgl/ (accessed March 30, 2005).

[66] In this regard, the lack of attention to the centralization of the Ministry of Public Security is baffling. Interviewees claim that centralization has not been attempted as it is impossible to break up the nexus of local governments and the local police. Another interpretation is also possible: when it comes to public security matters, the regime is certain that the police will act in accordance with its wishes, thus making centralization unnecessary. Additional research is needed to assess the validity of those competing interpretations.

lingering local protectionism.[67] Nor can centralization resolve the challenge of successful coordination *across* bureaucracies, when multiple agencies share a mandate to enforce.

INTERBUREAUCRATIC COORDINATION: THE PROBLEM OF BUREAUCRATIC RANK

Sometimes localism and bureaucratic corruption result not only from decentralization, but also from too many bureaucracies having mandates to enforce in the same issue area. As this study amply demonstrates, a large number of agencies have overlapping enforcement jurisdictions in the area of IPR. Unnecessary duplicative enforcement is one consequence of this setup. More importantly, in the absence of meaningful coordination and oversight of their activity, these agencies can engage in shirking (failure to enforce) or enforcement in exchange for bribes. The central government has repeatedly charged various bureaucracies with coordination in this area. However, those attempts at coordination have been frustrated either by the low rank of the coordinating entity (for instance, the SIPO, tasked with coordination of the enforcement activity of all agencies with an IPR portfolio, has a vice-ministerial rank) or by the sheer complexity of coordinating the activities of numerous bureaucratic actors with diverging interests.

In particular, the bureaucratic rank system adversely affects the effectiveness of IPR enforcement. In China, agencies with a higher bureaucratic rank can issue binding orders to agencies with a lower bureaucratic rank. Successful coordination of all agencies providing IPR enforcement is more likely to occur when an agency with a high bureaucratic rank is the lead agency in charge of enforcement. The bureaucratic rank of an agency depends on its position in the administrative hierarchy. In China, the rank table is ministerial-level agencies (*guowuyuan zucheng buwei*), vice-ministries directly under the State Council (*guowuyuan zhishu jigou*), and bureau-level agencies supervised by a ministry.

In IPR, six ministerial-level agencies along with seven vice-ministerial level agencies and two bureau-level agencies share the enforcement portfolio, producing a total of fifteen agencies with primary or secondary responsibility for IPR protection.[68] The large number of ministerial-level agencies might lead us to believe that a number of high-ranking bureaucracies are involved in IPR enforcement. However, in practice these ministerial-level agencies have only a secondary responsibility for IPR enforcement in China. This means that agencies with primary IPR enforcement responsibility are either

[67] China Interview 041226A, with a senior official of the Department of Safety Supervision at the State Food and Drug Administration (Beijing).

[68] Listed according to their official ranking in the Chinese government hierarchy, these agencies are the MPS, the Ministry of Justice, the MOA, the Ministry of Commerce, the MOC, the MOH, the GAC, the SAIC, the AQSIQ, the State Administration of Radio, Film, and Television (SARFT), the GAPP, the NCAC, the SIPO, the STMA, and the SFDA (which had the status of an administration under the MOH as of 2008).

at the vice-ministerial level (e.g., the SAIC) or even at the bureau level (e.g., the STMA). Occasionally, an individual agency may seem to be at a vice-ministerial level, though in fact its true status is lower. For example, officially the NCAC is a vice-ministerial agency. However, in practice, the NCAC is a department within another vice-ministerial agency, the GAPP. As a consequence, the NCAC has the status of a bureau and cannot mobilize higher-ranked agencies to participate in enforcement.

The line of command in the Chinese bureaucratic hierarchy depends on whether an agency has a leadership relationship (*lingdao guanxi*) with another agency or only a professional relationship (*yewu guanxi*). The important point is that agencies that do not have a leadership relationship with other agencies cannot issue binding orders to them. In the Chinese context, only agencies of a superior rank can issue binding orders to lower-level agencies. In practice, this means that only the State Council can issue binding orders to central-level ministries. However, as ministerial-level agencies and provincial governments are considered to be at identical levels in the bureaucratic hierarchy, central-level bureaucracies can only issue binding orders to the provincial level of the same bureaucracy, and not to provincial governments.[69] Unfortunately, at the provincial level the dual subordination logic is already at work, and agencies might display primary loyalty to the provincial government rather than to the central-level bureaucracy. The problem is exacerbated at the prefecture, county, and township levels, because the center has limited ability to control the sub-provincial levels of the bureaucracy.

What is the specific result in the area of IPR enforcement? The SIPO is the agency supposed to coordinate the enforcement activities of all bureaucracies with an IPR enforcement mandate. However, it has the rank of a vice-ministry, which does not allow it to issue binding orders to ministerial-level agencies or to other vice-ministerial agencies with which it has only professional relations. In addition, the SIPO has established only fifty-four territorial offices in China, hardly penetrating below the provincial level. In principle, the SIPO should be coordinating the activities of all agencies with an IPR enforcement mandate, but its limited personnel and low bureaucratic rank diminish its ability to conduct any meaningful coordination. Agencies like the SAIC and the AQSIQ, which reach all the way down to the township level, have major responsibility for routine enforcement at the local levels. The reach of these agencies at such deep levels limits the possibility for central-level coordination and creates opportunities for the rise of corruption. Enforcement occurs, but it is unpredictable, uncoordinated, and often wasteful and inefficient.

Indeed, top Chinese policymakers of the rank of Premier Zhu Rongji and State Councilor Luo Gan have recognized this problem and openly called for a change. In 1998, Zhu Rongji expressed concern about issue areas plagued by

---

[69] Yasheng Huang, *Inflation and Investment Controls in China: The Political Economy of Central-Local Relations during the Reform Era* (New York: Cambridge University Press, 1996), chap. 2.

"jurisdictional overlap, lack of clear powers and responsibility, and management by multiple agencies."[70] He identified over one hundred issue areas where responsibilities had to be clarified and enforcement coordinated.[71] In his capacity as secretary of the Committee on the Operation of Government Agencies, Luo Gan has also spoken about the need to limit jurisdictional overlap and coordinate enforcement activity.[72] In 2000, Vice Premier Wu Bangguo reiterated the same two goals.[73] We should take seriously the fact that top Chinese policymakers are concerned about the impact of jurisdictional overlap on enforcement. Common sense would suggest that predictability, clarity, and consistency of enforcement are reasonable goals for any country that wants to rationalize its bureaucracies.

To sum up this part of the chapter, enforcement under decentralization can be capricious and beyond the control of the center. One way to make enforcement more predictable is to attempt to centralize the various agencies with an IPR portfolio. Although centralization may not be sufficient for the rise of regularized enforcement, it makes bureaucratic monitoring easier, thus serving as a disincentive for the capricious enforcement of laws and regulations. However, centralization alone will not eliminate interjurisdictional overlap; coordination of the activities of multiple enforcers is also necessary to resolve this problem.

The next part of the chapter will discuss how accountability works in practice, by focusing primarily on the strategies that foreign and domestic interest groups have used to nudge (and sometimes force) bureaucracies to deliver enforcement.

THE INFLUENCE OF FOREIGN PRESSURE ON ENFORCEMENT

Foreign companies operating in China have two strategies at their disposal to improve property rights protection in general, and IPR protection in particular: they can lobby their country-of-origin governments to impose trade sanctions against China, or they can use their leverage based on levels of FDI inflows to lobby directly either the central government or the local government (e.g., the Shanghai municipal government) to step up enforcement. For different reasons, neither has been effective at producing higher-quality enforcement in the area of IPR.

[70] Zhu Rongji, "Jiaqiang lingdao jingxin zuzhi he jiji jituo de shishi guowuyuan jigou 'sanding' guiding" (Strengthen Leadership, Carefully Organize, and Zealously Implement the "Three Rectifications" Regulations of the State Council), June 19, 1998, reprinted in *Zhongyang zhengfu zuzhi jigou 1998* (Central Government Organs 1998) (Beijing: Gaige chubanshe, 1998), 38–45. Citation from p. 39.

[71] Ibid., p. 39.

[72] Luo Gan's March 6, 1998, National People's Congress (NPC) speech, published in *Zhongyang zhengfu zuzhi jigou 1998*, 8–17. Relevant passages on p. 9 and p. 11.

[73] Wu Bangguo, "Common Understanding to Strengthen and Further the Efforts of the Strict Crackdown on Criminal Activities Involving the Manufacture and Sale of Fake and Shoddy Goods," October 26, 2000, televised speech, copy on file with the author.

Sanctions

Sanctions aim to send a signal to a target that it will be punished unless it changes its behavior. The two basic types of sanctions are military and economic. As military sanctions cannot enhance the protection of property rights, I will only discuss economic sanctions here. Economic sanctions are either multilateral (e.g., imposed by the UN) or unilateral (e.g., imposed by the United States alone).[74] When discussing the utility of sanctions, one has to make the distinction between the threat of the imposition of sanctions and the actual imposition of sanctions. Whereas the threat of sanctions is quite frequent, the imposition of sanctions is rare, representing a failure to send credible signals to the target through threat escalation.[75]

Turning to IPR in particular, since 1974, the United States Trade Representative has had the option of imposing special trade sanctions against countries that fail to provide adequate protection for IPR. After passage of the 1988 Omnibus Trade and Competitiveness Act, these sanctions became known as Special 301 trade sanctions, named after the relevant article in the act. In the area of IPR, threats of sanctions have been more frequent than sanctions themselves. A range of threats can be issued before the actual imposition of sanctions. Depending on the level of IPR violations observed in a particular country, the USTR can place it on one of several lists, which rank the threat posed as innocuous (Other Observation), slightly more serious (Watch List), serious (Priority Watch List), and very serious (Priority Foreign Country). According to the Omnibus Trade and Competitiveness Act, when a U.S. trading partner is designated a "priority foreign country," the USTR can launch an investigation into its trade practices and then make a final determination whether to impose sanctions. Special 301 sanctions are very rarely imposed: although about eighty countries are on one of the USTR's lists every year, for the entire 1985–2003 period, sanctions were imposed only four times: against Brazil in 1988, India in 1991, Thailand in 1991, and Ukraine in 2001.[76]

Are threats of Special 301 sanctions and actual Special 301 sanctions effective tools for improving the enforcement of IPR laws? In the first decade

---

[74] There is an additional mechanism for imposing sanctions – a case can be brought unilaterally (e.g., by the United States against China) through a multilateral body such as the WTO. This is a new mechanism that has been used infrequently to address IPR enforcement problems. My analysis of the twenty TRIPS cases brought to the WTO in the 1995–2003 period shows that only three cases concerned TRIPS enforcement, and all three were brought by the United States against developed countries (Denmark, the EU/Greece, and Sweden). Until recently, unilateral Special 301 sanctions remained the modus operandi of the U.S. government for developing countries. However, in 2007 the United States used the WTO to bring a case against China, which focused on deficiencies in IPR enforcement. Data obtained from www.wto.org.

[75] See, for example, Nikolay Marinov, "Do Economic Sanctions Destabilize Country Leaders?" *American Journal of Political Science* 49:3 (2005), 564–576.

[76] See the case histories on Brazil, Thailand, and India in Thomas Bayard and Kimberly Ann Elliott, *Retaliation and Reciprocity in U.S. Trade Policies* (Washington, DC: Institute for International Economics, 1994), as well as www.iipa.com for the Ukrainian case. Sanctions were also imposed on Taiwan for a very brief period (six days) in 1989.

following passage of the 1988 Omnibus Trade and Competitiveness Act scholars were optimistic about the power of "aggressive unilateralism" to bring about improved IPR protection around the world.[77] Two subsequent developments diminished this initial enthusiasm of the academic community. First, over time scholars came to appreciate more fully that what they had been measuring were improvements in the formal laws on the books and not the actual enforcement of these laws. Laws on the books and the modalities of their enforcement are two separate issues, and trade sanctions seem to have had no clear effect on enforcement. Related to this was a second observation: countries that were targets of threats of Special 301 sanctions came to view these threats as "cheap talk," since the actual imposition of sanctions was extremely rare. More recent studies of Special 301 sanctions therefore take a dim view of their usefulness.[78]

Large N studies often obscure important exceptions to general patterns. As this chapter shows, although the effectiveness of sanctions threats to bring about a higher volume of enforcement is diminishing globally, threats may still be successful in individual countries. There is no question that U.S. pressure on the Chinese government to enforce copyright laws has led to a higher enforcement volume. As this book argues, the efficacy of that increase is limited by the fact that the ensuing enforcement is not of a high quality.

Foreign Direct Investment

Does the influence of FDI stop at the border, or can foreign companies have an impact once they have invested in a country? Most research on FDI focuses on explaining how countries attract foreign capital.[79] Few studies analyze how

---

[77] Jagdish Bhagwati and Hugh T. Patrick, eds., *Aggressive Unilateralism: America's 301 Trade Policy and the World System* (Ann Arbor: University of Michigan Press, 1990).

[78] Susan K. Sell, *Private Power, Public Law: The Globalization of Intellectual Property Rights* (New York: Cambridge University Press, 2003).

[79] See, for example, Tim Büthe and Helen Milner, "The Politics of Foreign Direct Investment into Developing Countries: Increasing FDI through Policy Commitment via Trade Agreements and Investment Treaties?" mimeo, Duke University and Woodrow Wilson School (2005). We should stress that even studies that focus specifically on FDI and IPR do not explain whether higher FDI dependence increases the willingness of the host-country government to protect IPR. Such studies (see, for example, Lee Branstetter, Raymond Fisman, and C. Fritz Foley, "Do Stronger Intellectual Property Rights Increase International Technology Transfer? Empirical Evidence from U.S. Firm-Level Data," *Quarterly Journal of Economics* 121:1 [2006], 321–349) typically attempt to answer the opposite question – does stronger IPR protection lead to increased inflows of high-technology investments into developing countries? Willingness to transfer high-tech equipment into a host country tells us nothing about the subsequent ability of investors to motivate the host government to protect their high-tech assets.

foreign investors can protect their rights once they have committed their money to a particular country.[80]

Even China-specific research on FDI has not produced any conclusive findings about the ability of foreign companies to bargain with the central government to achieve stronger protection of property rights. Early studies describe the initial system of FDI approvals, when Beijing exercised ultimate discretion over FDI inflows and was able to target investment to a small number of select provinces or special economic zones (SEZs).[81] The system was gradually liberalized as FDI approvals were decentralized, so much so that currently central-level ministries handle only about 1 percent of the total investment inflows in the country.[82] Therefore, we might expect foreign companies to have a lot more pull with subnational governments today than they did earlier, when the ultimate power to allocate investments stayed with the center. Nevertheless, most scholars remain skeptical about the emergence of stronger property rights protection at the local level in China: they stress the cultural preference for extrajudicial means of dispute resolution;[83] obstacles to strengthening the judicial system, such as the low quality of judges;[84] the difficulty of enforcing judicial decisions;[85] and local protectionism.[86] Other scholars have challenged these views, by showing that investors may have heterogeneous preferences (non-ethnically-Chinese foreign

[80] Important exceptions include Edmund Malesky, "Straight Ahead on Red: The Mutually Reinforcing Impact of Foreign Direct Investment on Local Autonomy in Vietnam," paper presented at the Annual Meeting of the American Political Science Association, Washington, DC, September 1–4, 2005, and Nathan M. Jensen, *Nation-States and the Multinational Corporation: A Political Economy of Foreign Direct Investment* (Princeton, NJ: Princeton University Press, 2006).

[81] Margaret Pearson, *Joint Ventures in the People's Republic of China: The Control of Foreign Direct Investment under Socialism* (Princeton, NJ: Princeton University Press, 1991); Shirk, *The Political Logic of Economic Reform*; Susan Shirk, "Internationalization and China's Economic Reforms," in *Internationalization and Domestic Politics,* ed. Robert O. Keohane and Helen V. Milner (New York: Cambridge University Press, 1996), 243–258; Huang, *Inflation and Investment Controls*.

[82] In 2003, central-level ministries utilized US$600 million of FDI, accounting for 1.1 percent of the total utilized FDI. See *China Commerce Yearbook 2004* (Beijing: China Commercial Press, 2004), 665.

[83] Overseas Chinese communities in Hong Kong, Taiwan, Macau, and Singapore, as well as other culturally similar nations of Northeast and Southeast Asia, supply over 75 percent of China's FDI inflows. For an argument that foreign investors usually prefer to use kinship networks rather than the formal court system to resolve disputes, see Hongying Wang, *Weak State, Strong Networks: The Institutional Dynamics of Foreign Direct Investment in China* (Oxford: Oxford University Press, 2001).

[84] Lubman, *Bird in a Cage*; Hung, *Administrative Litigation and Court Reform*.

[85] Donald Clarke, "The Execution of Civil Judgments in China," *The China Quarterly*, no. 141 (1995), 65–81; Anthony R. Dicks, "Compartmentalized Law and Judicial Restraint: An Inductive View of Some Jurisdictional Barriers to Reform," *The China Quarterly*, no. 141 (1995), 82–109.

[86] Pitman Potter, "The Chinese Legal System: Continuing Commitment to the Primacy of State Power," *The China Quarterly*, no. 159 (1999), 673–683; Hung, *Administrative Litigation and Court Reform*.

investors, for example, may demand more secure property rights than overseas Chinese),[87] and that important positive changes in the supply of the rule of law in China are already taking place.[88]

How can we adjudicate these competing claims? China's record of absorption of FDI is impressive: over US$700 billion of FDI entered China between 1979 and 2006.[89] Over three decades, China has been transformed from a country that was closed off to foreign capital into one of the top three recipients of FDI in the world.[90] However, national-level data can obscure the level of regional dependence on FDI. Scholars have extensively described the wide regional inequalities plaguing FDI distribution in China.[91] In some coastal provinces and cities (e.g., Shanghai and Jiangsu) FDI inflows are equivalent to as much as 7 percent of the gross provincial product, whereas in central and western provinces (e.g., Qinghai and Xinjiang) they are equivalent to less than 1 percent of the gross provincial product.[92] Therefore, some Chinese provinces are much more dependent than others on FDI (see GIS Map 2.1). Not surprisingly, this uneven distribution of FDI has made some provinces more sensitive to foreign pressure to enforce IPR laws than other provinces.

As statistical data presented in subsequent chapters show, there is a very strong positive correlation between levels of FDI and foreign copyright and trademark enforcement in China (regional data on foreign patents are not available). The local governments that are most dependent on FDI do respond to the property rights concerns of foreign investors. However, there are two limitations to this response. First, enforcement in China is geographically concentrated. Provinces that receive no FDI provide no enforcement: in 2003, seventeen Chinese provinces did not handle any foreign copyright cases; in

[87] Mary Gallagher, *Contagious Capitalism: Globalization and the Politics of Labor in China* (Princeton, NJ: Princeton University Press, 2005).

[88] Katharina Pistor and Philip Wellons, *The Role of Law and Legal Institutions in Asian Economic Development 1960–1995* (Hong Kong: Oxford University Press, 1999); Peerenboom, *China's Long March*; Randall Peerenboom, *China Modernizes: Threat to the West or Model for the Rest?* (New York: Oxford University Press, 2007).

[89] See *China Commerce Yearbook 2007* (Beijing: China Commercial Press, 2007), 282.

[90] In 2005, only the United Kingdom and the United States received more FDI than China. In some years, China has been the top FDI recipient in the world. See *UNCTAD Handbook of Statistics 2006–07*, Table 7.2.1, http://www.unctad.org/en/docs/tdstat31ch7_enfr.pdf (accessed February 29, 2008).

[91] Most notably, see Huang, *Inflation and Investment Controls*; Dali L. Yang, *Beyond Beijing: Liberalization and the Regions in China* (New York: Routledge, 1997); Yasheng Huang, *Selling China: Foreign Direct Investment during the Reform Era* (New York: Cambridge University Press, 2003); and Gallagher, *Contagious Capitalism*.

[92] In 2003, FDI dependence (FDI/gross provincial product) ranged from 0 percent for Tibet to 7.22 percent for Shanghai. Guangdong ranked sixth in FDI dependence among Chinese provinces, after Shanghai, Jiangsu, Hainan, Tianjin, and Beijing. Calculations based on *Zhongguo tongji nianjian 2004* (China Statistical Yearbook 2004) (Beijing: Zhongguo tongji chubanshe, 2004), 61, 714, 735.

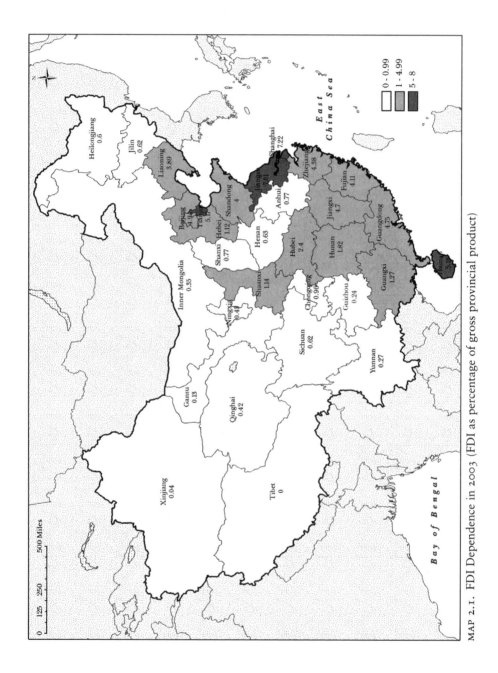

MAP 2.1. FDI Dependence in 2003 (FDI as percentage of gross provincial product)

the same year, thirteen provinces handled no trademark cases.[93] This means that although piracy and counterfeiting exist throughout the country, roughly half of China's thirty-one provinces provide no enforcement for foreign IPR. Second, although we cannot perform reliable statistical tests to confirm this, the case studies in Chapters 7 and 8 indicate that the local governments that do enforce often provide enforcement in exchange for bribes. Foreign pressure has not been conducive to the emergence of rationalization.

PRESSURE TO ENFORCE: COPYRIGHT FIRMS IN CHINA

How have foreign companies working in China sought to protect their property rights on the ground? We should note that copyright firms operating in China chose a very different strategy from that adopted by trademark firms. Whereas trademark firms established a business association and lobbied both the central and some local governments, copyright firms lobbied local governments in some regions of the country and simultaneously pressured the USTR to impose Special 301 trade sanctions against China. Importantly, although both strategies led to increases in the volume of enforcement, neither produced high-quality enforcement.

The U.S. copyright industry has historically relied on its considerable clout over the USTR (which has been very responsive to its demands), as well as on particularistic dealings with local governments in China. This had allowed U.S. copyright firms operating in China to bypass the central Chinese government, by leaving it to the U.S. government to engage Beijing. However, over time this strategy has backfired, as it alienated the central government from the concerns of the copyright industry and led only to grudgingly undertaken campaign-style enforcement.

Because of the efforts of the U.S. copyright industry, China has been designated a priority foreign country on four occasions (1989, 1991, 1994, and 1996), allowing the USTR to initiate an investigation into its trade practices.[94] One effect of the threats of Special 301 sanctions was a substantial improvement in the formal legal framework for IPR protection. At the same time, the threats alienated the central government, which felt that U.S. firms did not appreciate what it was already doing to improve the enforcement of IPR laws. The Chinese government did not welcome Special 301 threats, which they saw as serving the narrow interests of the U.S. copyright industry and not those of other foreign firms. Nonetheless, the Chinese government felt that it should do something to stave off U.S. demands for enforcement. The solution was to include copyright piracy in the already existing Anti-Pornography Campaign.

---

[93] *Zhongguo zhishi chanquan nianjian 2004* (China IPR Yearbook 2004) (Beijing: Zhishi chanquan chubanshe, 2004), 315–317.

[94] For more details on this period, see Li Mingde, *"Tebie 301 tiaokuan" yu Zhong Mei zhishi chanquan zhengduan* (Special 301 and Sino-U.S. IPR Disputes) (Beijing: Shehui kexue wenxian chubanshe, 2000), 348–351.

Chapter 8 provides further details on this campaign, so I will simply sketch its contours in the following.

The Response: The Anti-Pornography and Anti-Piracy Campaign

The Anti-Pornography Campaign was launched in 1989 in the wake of the Tiananmen Square protests. Initially, the campaign dealt only with counter-revolutionary and pornographic publications, both of which were obviously illegal. Copyright issues were added to the scope of the campaign in the mid-1990s, and in 1999 the campaign was officially renamed the Anti-Pornography and Anti-Piracy Campaign. Since its inception, the campaign has delivered high-volume enforcement. For example, between 1994 and 2004, 1.3 billion illegal publications were seized; of these, 1.15 billion were pirated and smuggled materials protected by copyright. In addition, over 200 optical disk production lines were seized between 1996 and 2004. Over time, counterrevolutionary and pornographic materials have become relatively less important to the campaign. For example, in 2003, only 37.72 million pornographic publications, 1.32 million political publications, and 5.42 million Falun Gong publications were discovered.[95] In contrast, seizures of pirated materials in the same year amounted to 177 million items (80 percent of the total). In 2004, total seizures were 229 million, 93 percent of which were pirated materials.[96]

Although the volume of enforcement provided through the campaign is significant, this enforcement is uncoordinated, inefficient, and ineffective in reducing piracy. Because participation in the campaign is considered prestigious, as many as sixteen agencies are currently officially included in it.[97] Under any conditions, coordinating so many agencies would be a challenge. It is particularly difficult in this campaign because the coordinating entity (the National Anti-Pornography and Anti-Piracy Working Committee of the PRC, or NAPWC) has a low bureaucratic rank, equivalent to that of a department within the General Administration of Press and Publications. This makes the work of coordinating the activities of agencies that are its bureaucratic superiors impossible.

Lobbying Local Governments

Some copyright companies have tried another approach, namely, directly lobbying local governments to provide personalistic enforcement. The use of

[95] *Zhongguo chuban nianjian 2004* (China Publishers' Yearbook 2004) (Beijing: Zhongguo chuban nianjian she, 2004), 54.
[96] *Zhongguo zhishi chanquan nianjian 2005* (China IPR Yearbook 2005) (Beijing: Zhishi chanquan chubanshe, 2005), 88.
[97] Quanguo saohuang dafei gongzuo xiaozu, *Saohuang dafei zai Zhongguo* (Anti-Pornography and Anti-Piracy in China) (Beijing: Xinwen chuban zongshu, 2001), 1.

connections (*guanxi*) in Chinese politics has been well documented.[98] In addition, there is a growing literature on the role of *guanxi* in Chinese business.[99] Given the difficulties of protecting copyrights, many firms will hire specific personnel simply for their connections with the relevant enforcement agencies. Contrary to popular expectations, Western firms have not shied away from using *guanxi*. I personally interviewed two highly placed employees of Top Dog Software, a foreign software company operating in China, who had been hired to manage the company's government relations precisely because they used to work for important enforcement agencies.[100] Another widespread practice requires firm employees to cultivate good relations with key bureaucrats in the relevant enforcement agencies, in order to ensure that the company's cases will be given due consideration, should the need arise. In this manner, Top Dog Software has successfully convinced the Shanghai Provincial Copyright Administration (PCA) to conduct raids on its behalf, even though the copyright administration does not, as a matter of principle, provide enforcement in response to complaints.[101]

These relations are highly variable and success in one locale does not necessarily transfer elsewhere. Top Dog Software had difficulties in forcing another PCA to conduct a raid on its behalf against a state-owned enterprise that had used infringing copies of its software in Guangdong province.[102] The company first approached the Guangdong PCA and asked it to organize a raid. As copyright administrations prefer to provide quasi-judicial enforcement (unless pressured by the central government to join a campaign-style enforcement action), the Guangdong PCA resorted to a technicality and responded that cases involving foreign companies have to be handled by the National Copyright Administration in Beijing. Top Dog duly contacted the NCAC, which replied that the Guangdong PCA had to handle the case, since the infringer was based in Guangdong. Having no success in Beijing, Top Dog returned to Guangdong,

[98] For the relevance of *guanxi* to Chinese political life, see Andrew Nathan, "A Factionalism Model for CCP Politics," *The China Quarterly*, no. 53 (1973), 34–65; Lowell Dittmer, "Chinese Informal Politics" and "Informal Politics Reconsidered," *The China Journal*, no. 34 (1995), 1–34 and 193–208; Andrew Nathan and Kellee Tsai, "Factionalism: A New Institutionalist Restatement," *The China Journal*, no. 34 (1995), 156–192; Huang Jing, *Factionalism in Chinese Communist Politics* (New York: Cambridge University Press, 2000); and Victor C. Shih, *Factions and Finance in China: Elite Conflict and Inflation* (New York: Cambridge University Press, 2008).

[99] See Frank Pieke, "Bureaucracy, Friends, and Money: The Growth of Capital Socialism in China," *Comparative Studies in Society and History* 37:3 (1995), 494–518; Wank, *Commodifying Communism*; Guthrie, *Dragon in a Three-Piece Suit*; Wang, *Weak State, Strong Networks*; and Gold, Guthrie, and Wank, eds., *Social Connections in China*.

[100] We should note that this practice is not unique to China. France is well known for its tolerance of *pantouflage*, or switching between posts in government agencies and work in private business.

[101] China Interview 010703, with an employee of a software company (Shanghai); China Interviews 010713A and 020129C, with an employee of the Shanghai Copyright Administration (Shanghai).

[102] This case took place prior to the November 2001 amendments to the Copyright Law.

but the Guangdong PCA still refused to take the case and organize a raid. After attempting for more than six months to receive administrative enforcement, in August 2001 the software company dropped the case in frustration.[103]

Top Dog's experience can be understood in two ways. On the one hand, it demonstrates the fragmentation within the NCAC enforcement system and, even more powerfully, the strength of local protectionism. In the end, it was the local Guangdong producer of pirated software that the PCA chose to protect, not the foreign software company. On the other hand, what Top Dog asked the Guangdong PCA for was to organize a raid, which went against its mandate and against established norms of bureaucratic behavior. The regulators kept emphasizing that this case should be resolved in a quasi-judicial manner through an administrative hearing (however, it was not specified where this hearing should take place). Though Top Dog did not receive the kind of enforcement it desired from the PCA (Top Dog eventually got a local AIC to organize a raid on its behalf, in exchange for a bribe), the letter of the law was respected in this case. In the end, respect for the law may help increase predictability of IPR protection in China.

Interview evidence indicates that the differing attitudes that the Shanghai and Guangdong copyright administrations took toward Top Dog simply reflected the different relationships that the Shanghai and Hong Kong offices of the company had with the local enforcement authorities. Overall, then, it may be a risky and time-consuming strategy to rely on personalistic connections with local governments and to bypass the central government altogether. The provincial-level data presented earlier in this chapter indicate that enforcement of foreign copyrights in China is highly skewed in favor of a few coastal provinces, a condition that does not bode well for the rise of rationalized enforcement throughout the country.

PRESSURE FROM THE TRADEMARK INDUSTRY

In contrast to copyright firms, the trademark industry chose to lobby the central government. The trademark companies formed an association called the Quality Brands Protection Committee (QBPC) to represent their interests and to lobby the central government. As already alluded to in previous sections, the QBPC is a very powerful and successful association. In contrast to copyright associations like the Business Software Alliance (BSA), the Motion Picture Association (MPA), and the International Federation of the Phonographic Industry (IFPI), all of which focus narrowly on single products, the QBPC is an inclusive association, representing a wide spectrum of companies whose trademark-protected goods have been counterfeited. It is divided into seven industry working groups (automotive, footwear, luxury goods, fast-moving consumer goods, batteries, pharmaceuticals, and IT) and six committees (best practices/enforcement, communications, customs, government cooperation,

---

[103] China Interview 010808, with a senior legal associate in a software company (Hong Kong).

legal, and membership services). Unlike the foreign copyright associations working in China, which represent only American companies, the QBPC has a multinational membership. At the end of 2005, it consisted of 164 companies from Europe, Japan, and the United States and thus could not be easily tied to the interests of any one country. Finally, its solid financial stake in China's future (backed up by US$50 billion in investment from major multinational corporations as of 2005) and registration through the China Association of Enterprises with Foreign Investment (CAEFI) as a *Chinese* industrial association (albeit one with no Chinese companies) ensure that its voice will be heard by the Chinese government.

The QBPC was not always as powerful as it is now. A study of its organizational evolution can be instructive about the means through which foreigners can compel the Chinese government to listen to them. The QBPC grew out of the China Anticounterfeiting Coalition (CACC), which started out in 1998 as an informal gathering of several companies that were frustrated by the failure of their individual anticounterfeiting programs to stem their losses from counterfeiting.[104] The first informal meetings took place in Guangzhou and Hong Kong, with the purpose of working together to combat counterfeiting. The U.S. commercial attaché soon decided to lend a hand and host some of the organizational meetings at the U.S. Embassy,[105] an unsurprising choice of venue considering that seven of the eight founding companies were American: S. E. Johnson, Proctor & Gamble, Gillette, Colgate, Best Foods, Coca-Cola, and Nike. The only non-U.S. company in the original group was the Anglo-Dutch Unilever.[106] The eight companies each contributed US$25,000, and the CACC was registered in Hong Kong. Its initial goal was to work cooperatively with the Chinese government to recognize that there was a trademark counterfeiting problem in China and that something needed to be done to address it.[107]

To get a sense of the scope of the counterfeiting problem and of possible remedies, in 1999 the CACC commissioned an internal report on the state of counterfeiting in China. The report was frank about the size and severity of the problem, providing case studies of how the brands of CACC member companies were being destroyed by imitation products. The main thrust of the report, however, was that it was not foreign companies but Chinese consumers who were suffering the most from unsafe counterfeits. The report outlined three problems with enforcement as it stood. First, the high burden of proof rendered proactive police involvement unlikely. Second, unwillingness of administrative enforcement agencies to transfer suspected criminal liability cases to the police further reduced police participation in the enforcement of IPR laws. Third, the association of local governments with counterfeit production operations and wholesale distribution markets for counterfeit goods further hindered effective

---

[104] China Interview 010626A, with a QBPC vice president (Beijing).
[105] China Interview 020913A, with a QBPC vice president (Beijing).
[106] China Interview 010716B, with the QBPC president (Shanghai).
[107] China Interview 010716B, with the QBPC president (Shanghai).

enforcement. The report recommended that comprehensive legislative changes, coupled with administrative reforms, would be necessary to address these inter-related enforcement problems.[108]

As the internal circulation report was being prepared, the CACC simulta-neously initiated two additional projects. First, it commissioned a second report, intended to reach the desks of China's top leadership. It also began looking for a way to legitimize itself as a serious right holders' association.

As part of its strategy to educate the Chinese leadership about the extent of counterfeiting in China and its impact on the economy, the CACC commis-sioned a special research report from the Development Research Center (DRC) of the State Council.[109] The choice of the DRC, a research and analytical division of the Chinese government with direct links to Premier Zhu Rongji, was highly strategic. The DRC assembled a special research team that produced an eight-page report outlining the effects of the production and sale of counter-feits on the national economy and suggesting appropriate countermeasures. The DRC report bore a striking resemblance to the internal CACC report, in terms of both the problems identified and the solutions proposed. It is remark-able for its clarity and focus.

The DRC report painted a grim picture of the extent of counterfeiting in China and its impact on the national economy. According to research cited by the authors, 34.8 percent of the Chinese enterprises surveyed in 1999 had experienced problems with counterfeiting. Furthermore, the estimated value of the counterfeits produced in 1998 was 132.9 billion yuan (about US$16.5 billion), a figure comparable to the 154 billion yuan (US$19 billion) worth of goods that were smuggled into China in the same year. The report posited that there were four negative effects of counterfeiting. First, the government lost tax revenue from unreported clandestine production of counterfeits: for example, the estimated loss from forgone taxes in 1998 was 24.7 billion yuan (US$3 billion). Second, counterfeiting could give China's business climate a bad rep-utation and even lead to the exit of FDI from the country. Third, Chinese producers suffered losses from forgone profits and displaced market share. Finally, consumers could suffer severe health consequences from low-quality counterfeit goods.

The report also identified several reasons for the spread of counterfeiting. Most obvious was that those engaged in the production and sale of counterfeits reaped huge profits without fear of deterrent sanctions by the law enforcement authorities. Ambiguous laws combined with lax enforcement and weak punish-ments accounted for the proliferation of counterfeiters. In addition, local

---

[108] China Anti-Counterfeiting Coalition, *Report on Counterfeiting in the People's Republic of China* (Third Draft) (May 3, 1999) (copy on file with the author).

[109] This and the following three paragraphs are based on Development Research Center of the State Council, *Zhijia shoujia weihai jida, yanli daji kebu ronghuan* (The Production and Sale of Counterfeits Are Extremely Harmful, Severe Crackdowns Should Start without Delay) (February 2000) (copy on file with the author).

protectionism made it more difficult to enforce the existing laws successfully, since local governments were benefiting from the continued existence of production and distribution centers for counterfeit goods.

The report not only identified the causes and the impact of counterfeiting, but also proposed a multipronged approach to solving the problem. It stressed that the government should step up existing anticounterfeiting measures, for the good of the economy and the consumers. Specifically, enforcement would have to be stricter, fines steeper, and the criminal liability thresholds lower. In addition, the report emphasized the importance of training enforcement authorities and educating the public about the dangers posed by counterfeits. Finally, the report made a radical recommendation. The authors felt that the already existing implementing regulations issued by the various agencies with IPR enforcement mandates should be revised in order to coordinate and unify the fines and other punishments imposed by different agencies and different localities. In addition, they advanced the crucial recommendation that jurisdictional overlap be eliminated. As a long-term goal, the report also suggested that enforcement should eventually be transferred from administrative agencies to courts of law.

In their internal report (and the DRC report they commissioned), the CACC members arrived at a consensus that both improved enforcement and legislative amendments would be necessary to stem the tide of counterfeiting. The difficult question was how this could be achieved. The CACC decided that it had to find ways to lobby the Chinese government and the legislature (the National People's Congress) directly in order to have its story heard. However, the first order of business was for the CACC to be recognized as a legitimate entity with a higher status than that of a foreign copyright association.[110] The CACC found its administrative benefactor in the China Association of Enterprises with Foreign Investment (CAEFI) under the Ministry of Foreign Trade and Economic Cooperation (MOFTEC). In March 2000, the CACC renamed itself the Quality Brands Protection Committee (QBPC) of the CAEFI. With twenty-eight member companies, the QBPC had gained the official approval of the regime. The vice president of the CAEFI, Mr. Liu Wanzhong, was appointed honorary chairman of the QBPC, thus lending the new association much-needed legitimacy. Today, the QBPC officially has the status of a Chinese industrial association, even though it represents only foreign companies operating in China.

The QBPC quickly made itself heard. The DRC report began circulating among the top Chinese leadership. There are rumors that even Premier Zhu

---

[110] Foreign copyright associations have pariah status in China. For more information on the history of foreign and domestic copyright associations in China, Russia, and Taiwan, see Martin Dimitrov, "Administrative Decentralization, Legal Fragmentation, and the Rule of Law in Transitional Economies: The Enforcement of Intellectual Property Rights Laws in China, Russia, Taiwan, and the Czech Republic" (Ph.D. Dissertation, Department of Political Science, Stanford University, 2004), chap. 3.

Rongji read it.[111] In addition, there is evidence that Zhang Xiaoji, the director-general of the Foreign Economic Relations Department of the DRC and, not coincidentally, author of the commissioned DRC report, engaged in an active QBPC promotion and awareness campaign.[112] Furthermore, the QBPC chairman, Joseph Johnson, delivered a speech on the harm of counterfeiting at the Fourth Annual Investment and Trade Fair in Xiamen on September 8, 2000.[113] State Councilor Wu Yi was present to hear the speech. Considering that Wu Yi was one of the fifteen most powerful people in China at the time, it is safe to say that the QBPC had managed to get the ear of the central government. Beijing reacted fast, yet it emphasized the tried and true tactic of campaign-style enforcement, instead of attempting to provide rationalized enforcement.

The QBPC also managed to give the government its words. On October 26, 2000, Vice Premier Wu Bangguo delivered a televised speech, "Common Understanding to Strengthen and Further the Efforts of the Strict Crackdown on Criminal Activities Involving the Manufacture and Sale of Counterfeit and Substandard Goods."[114] The speech bore a striking resemblance to the QBPC-commissioned DRC report, outlining the same problems and proposing the same solutions. This suggests that Vice Premier Wu had read the report prior to preparing his own televised remarks. The top leadership had finally understood the need to crack down on counterfeit and substandard goods, a major goal of the QBPC. On the following day, the State Council issued a "Circular on the Joint Campaign to Crack Down on Criminal Activities Involving the Production and Sale of Counterfeit and Substandard Goods," thereby demonstrating resolve to fight counterfeiting. This circular was followed by a range of significant documents that I have discussed elsewhere.[115] Overall, from the fall of 2000 onward, the Chinese government has been engaged in a trademark anticounterfeiting campaign. There is no doubt that as an inclusive, cooperative, and formally Chinese association, the QBPC was instrumental in inducing the government to act.

The example of the QBPC demonstrates that direct lobbying of the central government can be an effective strategy for ensuring a higher volume of enforcement of IPR laws. The government also introduced initiatives aimed at centralization and coordination of the various agencies sharing the IPR enforcement portfolio, but without success. These measures have not as yet led to the rise of consistent, transparent, and fair enforcement in the area of copyrights and trademarks. It needs to be stressed that the government focused

---

[111] China Interview 010626A, with a QBPC vice president (Beijing); China Interview 010716B, with the QBPC president (Shanghai).

[112] "Anti-Faking Measures Called For," *China Daily*, July 4, 2000, 1.

[113] Chairman Johnson's speech at meeting with Councilor Wu Yi (copy on file with the author).

[114] Vice Premier Wu Bangguo's speech, October, 26, 2000 (copy on file with the author).

[115] See Dimitrov, "Administrative Decentralization, Legal Fragmentation, and the Rule of Law in Transitional Economies," chap. 3.

only on campaign-style enforcement and has not yet implemented some of the more radical proposals of the DRC report.

THE INFLUENCE OF DOMESTIC PRESSURE ON ENFORCEMENT

We should not have the impression that only foreign pressure impacts the enforcement of IPR laws in China. In fact, domestic pressure matters even more, because the government is ultimately more concerned about domestic audiences than about the wishes of foreign governments. Domestic concerns can be articulated through two channels: consumer-protection groups and the media.

Although more numerous than foreign pressure groups operating in China, domestic pressure groups tend to be less well organized than their foreign counterparts. During fieldwork, I interviewed representatives of dozens of Chinese IPR associations and consumer-protection groups. Typically, most associations focused on trademark protection rather than on copyrights and patents. They were small, usually represented by one man, who either was a retired SAIC bureaucrat or was currently working for some IPR bureaucracy and represented the association on a part-time basis. These past or present connections with enforcement agencies allow the representatives of such associations to lobby effectively for enforcement on behalf of their members. These associations and consumer-protection groups typically facilitate the organization of raids that follow a complaint from the right holder. As mentioned previously, such raids are not conducive to the rise of rationalized enforcement.

What about affecting enforcement through the media? The Chinese media are becoming more independent, and the government cannot afford to ignore them.[116] Since the late 1990s, media exposure has raised a series of product-quality scandals to national prominence. In 2004, the deaths of thirteen babies who had been fed fake formula infuriated the general public and led to concerted efforts to find and prosecute those guilty of violating the relevant trademark protection and product-quality laws. Eventually, as many as ninety-seven officials complicit in the counterfeit formula scandal were punished.[117] There are many other such examples in China. The government does respond to media pressure to provide enforcement. However, the problem with this enforcement strategy is that it is focused around campaigns and can have only limited viability. What the media demand is quick action – which typically means that there will be a high volume of enforcement, but this enforcement

---

[116] Susan L. Shirk, *China: Fragile Superpower* (New York: Oxford University Press, 2007). For a less sanguine view, see Ashley W. Esarey, "Caught between State and Society: The Commercial News Media in China" (Ph.D. Dissertation, Department of Political Science, Columbia University, 2006).

[117] "China Blames 97 over Milk Scandal," *BBC News*, November 8, 2004, http://news.bbc.co.uk/go/pr/fr/-/2/hi/asia-pacific/3991335.stm (accessed April 21, 2008). See also Waikeung Tam and Dali Yang, "Food Safety and the Development of Regulatory Institutions in China," *Asian Perspective* 29:4 (2005), 5–36.

will be of a low quality. Thus, overall, neither pressure groups nor the media seem to be effective in bringing about rationalized enforcement.

CONCLUSION

Several conclusions can be drawn from the material presented in this chapter. First, the formal mechanisms of accountability to the people and to the government are not effective tools for establishing bureaucratic accountability. Second, administrative decentralization and overlapping mandates allow for the persistence of inconsistent, nontransparent, and unaccountable enforcement. Third, pressure from domestic or foreign interest groups provides an effective mechanism for forcing bureaucracies to supply a higher volume of enforcement, but it has so far been ineffective in ensuring rationalized enforcement. Fourth, central intervention aimed at transcending the problems of local protectionism and corruption has also been ineffective. The process of partial centralization of government bureaucracies (under way in China since 1998) facilitates the rise of bureaucratic rationalization and the eventual establishment of the rule of law. However, centralization must be accompanied by effective oversight and by the successful coordination of enforcement, especially in trademark and copyright protection, where multiple agencies share the enforcement portfolio. Yet it is extremely difficult to achieve effective oversight and successful coordination during campaign-style enforcement. In sum, China provides an extraordinarily high level of enforcement, which is neither efficient nor effective.

The remainder of this study sets out to accomplish two goals. First, Chapters 3–6 analyze the complexities of Customs, civil, administrative, and criminal IPR enforcement in China and five other countries. These chapters suggest where rationalization is most likely to emerge. Chapters 7–9 present case studies on the enforcement of copyright, trademark, and patent laws, further identifying the conditions under which rationalized enforcement can emerge, as indeed has happened in the highly specialized area of patents. Cumulatively, Chapters 3–9 argue that enforcement pressures of the type described in this chapter are unlikely to produce rationalization under the current IPR enforcement regime in China. Chapter 10 concludes with some reflections on the implications of IPR enforcement for our understanding of state capacity and the eventual rise of rule of law in China.

PART II

THE ORGANIZATION OF THE STATE

IPR Enforcement Options

3

Customs

Centralization without Rationalization

Until his death in 2003, Tony Gurka's name was synonymous with one aspect of IPR enforcement. Long before anybody else knew that fighting piracy would itself become a booming industry, Gurka had opened a private firm in Hong Kong focusing on IPR investigations.[1] His influence as a pioneer carries on: the majority of top investigators in Greater China today worked for him earlier in their careers. So when Tony agreed to see me in 2001, it felt as if I were being ushered into the center of things (and not just because I had to pass through six doors to get to his office).

I found Tony standing in front of a large map of China and North Korea. After briefly introducing my research, I jumped to my first question, about cigarette counterfeiting in China. "What you should know," he said, "is that these days counterfeiting of top-end foreign brands is sometimes done in North Korea, not in China. All materials are Chinese, but the final assembly takes place at a factory in North Korea, and then the containers are shipped back to a Chinese port. In fact, there is a forty-foot container full of counterfeit Marlboros en route from Nampo to Dalian right now. We won't inform Chinese Customs about it – we will let this one go. But next time, when they send in a really big shipment, we will get them."[2] A forty-foot container, I thought, is not big enough?

Tony's story highlights three key issues in IPR enforcement today. First, as is well known, the scale of counterfeiting is enormous. Second, private investigators have emerged as an important intermediary between right holders and the different enforcement agencies empowered by the state to protect IPR. Enforcement agencies will often not act on the request of the right holders

---

[1] On Tony Gurka's career, see Richard Tomkins, "Operation Counter-Fake," *Asia Magazine* (December 30, 1984), 8–9. For his obituary, see *The Correspondent* (June–July 2003), http://www.fcchk.org/correspondent/corro-juno3/gurka.htm (accessed November 16, 2006).

[2] China Interview 010802B, with Tony Gurka (Hong Kong).

unless approached by private investigators supplying them with evidence of a specific infringement. Third, counterfeiting, even for the domestic Chinese market, is now a global phenomenon, with goods often being made in one country for consumption in another.

This chapter focuses on the third issue, specifically on the role of Customs in preventing the cross-border trade in counterfeits. The remaining chapters in Part II will analyze the civil, administrative, and criminal enforcement options that exist for right holders who want to protect their IPR *within* China. But it is appropriate to start with border protection, where the regulatory framework is straightforward: in effect, Customs has exclusive jurisdiction over the border protection of IPR. This stands in marked contrast to the administrative protection of IPR, where multiple agencies have overlapping enforcement jurisdictions.

The cross-border trade in IPR-infringing goods is a serious business. In 2005, Chinese Customs prevented the importation of pirated and counterfeit goods worth 1.6 million yuan (US$210,000) and the exportation of such goods worth 98 million yuan (US$13 million). The problem is multiplied many times over on a worldwide scale.[3] Chinese Customs serves two important functions in IPR protection. First, when counterfeits are produced in China for export to another country, Customs can stop the goods from being exported abroad. Second, when fakes are imported into China from another country (as in the story that Gurka told me), Customs can prevent the importation of the goods into Chinese territory.

A comparative approach is useful for analyzing Customs enforcement, since the emphasis on border protection of IPR varies greatly from country to country and reflects the state's decisions about prioritizing policy implementation in some areas by devoting scarce bureaucratic resources to them. Comparing China (where counterfeit goods are more likely to be produced for export) with countries whose economies encourage the importation of counterfeit goods is particularly helpful for defining the differential impact of foreign and domestic pressure on enforcement. China imports few counterfeits but is a major exporter of counterfeits to other countries. Therefore, in China, most pressure for a higher volume of Customs enforcement will be external rather than domestic. In countries like the United States, where counterfeits are primarily imported, the government will find itself under strong domestic pressure to protect consumers from foreign fakes.

---

[3] See "Statistics for China Customs IPR Seizures (in 2005)," http://english.customs.gov.cn/publish/portal191/tab7039/info70268.htm (accessed September 21, 2008). To take another example, in 2005 alone, U.S. Customs prevented the importation onto American soil of pirated and counterfeit goods worth over US$93 million. See *U.S. Customs and Border Protection and U.S. Immigration and Customs Enforcement FY 2005 IPR Seizure Statistics* (U.S. Customs and Border Protection LA Strategic Trade Center, November 3, 2005), http://www.cbp.gov/xp/cgov/import/commercial_enforcement/ipr/seizure/ (accessed July 24, 2006). Typically, China is the largest single source of counterfeit exports to the United States.

The protection of IPR by the Customs Administration in China has not been the subject of extensive scholarly analysis. Existing studies by Western scholars either pass over Customs altogether or limit discussion to a brief account of the legal basis for Customs involvement in IPR protection.[4] Chinese scholarship, even that which focuses squarely on Customs, similarly uses a strictly legal approach.[5] In sum, we lack an empirically grounded analysis of what Chinese Customs does to protect IPR. Nor do we have a sense of how China's IPR border protection efforts compare to those of other countries.

This chapter has four goals. The first is to measure the volume of Customs enforcement of IPR in China, and to contrast it with Customs activity in Russia, Taiwan, the Czech Republic, France, and the United States. This comparison allows us to highlight what is distinctive about Chinese Customs and to assess how China performs relative to other countries. A second goal is to analyze why Customs enforces in the way it does. My conclusion is that, although foreign pressure can explain the initial push toward Customs enforcement and some of the enforcement patterns we observe, in the end domestic considerations limit the impact of international factors on enforcement volume. The third goal is to assess whether enforcement is effective. The effectiveness of enforcement is measured as its deterrent capability, and deterrence increases with both the frequency and the severity of enforcement. I conclude that neither in China nor in Russia is either of these deterrence conditions met. The chapter's fourth goal is to shed light on whether Customs enforcement of IPR is rationalized. Although data limitations make my answer to this question provisional, in the Chinese case indications are that the requirements for consistency, transparency, and fairness are not fully met. This is striking, considering that Chinese Customs is centralized and has exclusive jurisdiction over the border protection of IPR. The implication is that centralization and exclusive jurisdictions are insufficient on their own for high-quality enforcement to emerge. It is also necessary to have rules that clearly specify the modalities of enforcement and establish proper punishments (by the courts or the police) for bureaucratic inaction or abuse of discretion.

A study of Customs activity is useful for our understanding of IPR enforcement and, more generally, in relation to state capacity. The state must make a

---

[4] Loke Khoon Tan, *Pirates in the Middle Kingdom: The Art of Trademark War* (Hong Kong: Sweet & Maxwell Asia, 2004); Paul Ranjard, Huang Hui, and Benoît Misonne, *The Legislation Protecting Intellectual Property Rights and Its Enforcement in the European Union and the People's Republic of China* (Beijing: European Commission EU-China Trade Project, December 2005); Andrew Mertha, *The Politics of Piracy: Intellectual Property in Contemporary China* (Ithaca, NY: Cornell University Press, 2005).

[5] Notable exceptions include Li Qunying, "Woguo haiguan dui zhishi chanquan de baohu" (IPR Customs Protection in China), in *Zhongguo zhishi chanquan ershi nian 1978–1998* (Twenty Years of IPR in China 1978–1998), ed. Liu Chuntian (Beijing: Zhuanli wenxian chubanshe, 1998), 210–220, and Zhu Qiuyuan, *Zhishi chanquan bianjing baohu zhidu lilun yu shiwu* (Theory and Actual Practice of IPR Border Protection) (Shanghai: Shanghai caizheng daxue chubanshe, 2006).

number of choices with respect to IPR protection. It has to decide whether to invest resources to create and adequately staff specialized IPR units in the Customs Administration. Second, it must decide whether these units should focus more on the importation of counterfeits into the country or on their exportation for consumption abroad. Above all, the state must decide whether to nurture high-quality enforcement and how to do so. All of these decisions are interactive and reflect the influence of other factors, most notably domestic and foreign pressures. This chapter highlights how these decisions are made in China and concludes with reflections on conceptualizing state capacity.

THE VOLUME, EFFECTIVENESS, AND QUALITY OF CUSTOMS ENFORCEMENT OF IPR

When we assess Customs enforcement of IPR, we should seek to answer three questions. Is enforcement volume high (and why)? Is enforcement deterrent? And, finally, is enforcement rationalized?

Both foreign and domestic pressures affect the volume of Customs IPR enforcement in China. Foreign pressure can be applied directly by other governments (the U.S. government has been the most important player here) as top-down pressure, or by foreign trade associations working in China as lateral pressure.[6] Although foreign pressure matters enormously, the key explanatory variable for variation in enforcement across countries is domestic interests. In certain cases, like Taiwan and the Czech Republic, we observe high-volume enforcement without foreign pressure; in others, like China and Russia, foreign pressure exists but leads to no significant change in enforcement volume. Both scenarios suggest that domestic interests have stronger explanatory force for enforcement behavior than foreign pressure. As this chapter demonstrates, in the absence of domestic interests in favor of stronger enforcement, foreign pressure applied on Chinese Customs does not translate into high-volume (or high-quality) enforcement. When foreign pressure aligns with domestic interests, we can expect to see significant increases in the volume of enforcement.

Both the frequency and the severity of Customs IPR enforcement increase its deterrence, and thus its efficacy. Those who violate IPR will be less likely to do so when punishment is either certain or predictably severe.[7] Frequency is measured as Customs seizures per million people (pmp), whereas severity is measured in terms of the size of the average fine and the proportion of cases transferred from the Customs Administration to the police and the Procuratorate for

---

[6] See Mertha, *The Politics of Piracy*, as well as Ka Zeng, *Trade Threats, Trade Wars: Bargaining, Retaliation, and American Coercive Diplomacy* (Ann Arbor: University of Michigan Press, 2004).

[7] An extensive academic debate exists regarding whether the frequency or the severity of punishment has a greater impact on the deterrence of enforcement. The seminal piece remains Gary Becker, "Crime and Punishment: An Economic Approach," *The Journal of Political Economy* 72:2 (1968), 169–217.

criminal prosecution. Countries with low frequency and low severity of Customs enforcement of IPR are understood as not having deterrent enforcement.

When is enforcement rationalized? As laid out in Chapters 1 and 2, rationalized enforcement (high-quality enforcement) emerges when the requirements for consistency, transparency, and procedural fairness are fulfilled. Despite some progress, China has not been able to develop rationalized Customs enforcement. Data limitations do not allow us to assess whether Customs enforcement is rationalized in the other countries analyzed in this book.

CUSTOMS PROTECTION OF IPR: GLOBAL PERSPECTIVES

We have two sources of data from which to gauge the attention that individual countries pay to Customs enforcement of IPR laws: country profiles in the World Intellectual Property Organization's (WIPO) *Guide to Intellectual Property Worldwide* and the membership list of the World Customs Organization's (WCO) IPR Strategic Group. I use these data to compile two datasets: a WIPO dataset and a WCO dataset. In 2000, the Customs administrations in 50 of the 176 WIPO member-states showed some type of specialization in the area of IPR enforcement: a special IPR unit, an anticounterfeiting unit, or at least an IPR liaison employee.[8] In 2006, the WCO IPR Strategic Group had fifty-eight members.[9] The contents of the two datasets are not identical: only twenty-seven countries that are on the WIPO IPR list can also be found on the WCO list. In total, as many as eighty-one countries worldwide have some type of Customs specialization in IPR. These numbers are significant. By comparison, we should note that according to the WIPO dataset, ten countries in the world have specialized IPR courts, thirty-seven have specialized police units, and thirty-three have specialized administrative agencies.[10] Therefore, countries are more likely to invest resources in Customs than in any other entity with a specialized IPR enforcement portfolio. For the most part, this attention to Customs reflects the extensive border measure requirements imposed on members of the WTO through the TRIPS Agreement. As more countries join the WTO, the protection of IPR by Customs becomes that much more common.

Knowing that a country has some type of Customs specialization in the area of IPR does not tell us what Customs does. As this chapter will demonstrate, the precise type of Customs specialization does not seem to be linked with the volume of Customs activity. For example, we will see that a country that has a specialized IPR unit (Russia) may do much less than a country that has only liaison officers with part-time responsibility for IPR (the Czech Republic). The WIPO and the WCO do not compile or disseminate empirical data about the specific IPR enforcement efforts of individual countries. In order to obtain this

---

[8] WIPO, *Guide to Intellectual Property Worldwide* (Geneva: WIPO, 2000).
[9] http://www.wcoipr.org/wcoipr/Menu_CustomContacts.htm (accessed October 1, 2006).
[10] WIPO, *Guide to Intellectual Property Worldwide.*

TABLE 3.1. Cross-National Customs IPR Enforcement Efforts in 2004

Country	Piracy Rate	Customs Seizures (per million people)	Enforcement Effort	Foreign Pressure	Domestic Pressure
China	High	0.8	Low	Low/ medium	Negligible
Russia	High	1.1	Low	Low	Negligible
Taiwan	Medium	14.7	Medium	Low	Medium
Czech Republic	Medium	51.9	Medium/ High	Medium	Medium
France	Medium	106.6	High	Negligible	High
U.S.	Low	24.8	Medium	Negligible	High

Source: Compiled by the author, based on individual country Customs statistics.

kind of data, I rely on country-specific Customs yearbooks and on interviews with Customs officials.

Using such data, Table 3.1 employs a standardized metric (Customs seizures pmp) to assess China's enforcement effort in comparison with that of five other countries. There is an inverse relation between the level of IPR violations in a given country (measured by the rate of piracy) and the response by Customs (measured by seizures pmp): countries with high rates of piracy (China and Russia) have very low levels of Customs enforcement. Another pattern revealed in Table 3.1 is that enforcement volume is very strongly influenced by domestic pressure. The two patterns are related. Countries with low levels of IPR violations tend to import counterfeits. In such countries, Customs is subject to strong domestic pressure to increase the volume of enforcement. In contrast, countries with high levels of IPR violations tend to export counterfeits. Customs in such countries is subject to correspondingly low levels of domestic pressure and high levels of external pressure. The next section will focus on China, where the state *is* providing recourse to right holders via Customs, but where volume remains low as a result of a lack of domestic pressure.

THE ORGANIZATION OF CHINESE CUSTOMS

Chinese Customs is a ministerial-level entity directly under the State Council. It is hierarchically organized, with the General Administration of Customs (Haiguan zongshu) (GAC) at the top, followed by a middle tier composed of the Guangdong Subadministration of the GAC (Haiguan zongshu Guangdong fenshu),[11] two supervisory offices (in Tianjin and Shanghai), and forty-one Customs regions. At the lowest tier of the system, there are 562 Customs houses and offices. Although there are only 251 central-level staff, collectively the

[11] The Guangdong Subadministration of Customs incorporates seven Customs regions.

Customs Administration and its affiliated units employ over 48,000 people across China.[12] Since the 1998 centralization, Customs regions no longer report to their respective local governments and instead have established direct vertical reporting relationships with the GAC in Beijing.

Traditionally, the mission of Customs has been to combat tax fraud and smuggling. In the 1990s, as a result of foreign pressure, Customs acquired the new mandate of IPR protection. The mandate developed in stages. At first, Article 5 of the 1992 Sino-U.S. Memorandum of Understanding (MOU) stated in general terms that China should provide effective Customs procedures to prevent IPR infringement. In July 1994, the State Council "Decision on Further Strengthening the Enforcement of IPR" stressed that Customs was responsible for stopping the importation and exportation of IPR-infringing goods. In September 1994 and May 1995, Customs issued its own notices (*gonggao*), stipulating that it could seize and destroy IPR-infringing goods. Further details on the role of Customs in fighting counterfeiting were provided by the February 1995 IPR Action Plan. Most notably, the Action Plan specified that Customs would establish a recordation (*bei'an*) system for IPR and investigate IPR violations, both at the request of right holders and, in the absence of such a request, proactively on an ex officio basis. Importantly, Customs would not initiate an action to detain goods unless the right holder posted a bond that could be used to defray potential damages to the consignor or consignee. Right holders would also be held responsible for warehousing and destruction costs. In July 1995, the State Council issued the Regulation on the Customs Protection of IPR, which further clarified the mandate of Customs in this area.[13]

The main legislative changes after 1995 include the explicit enumeration of IPR violations in the 2000 Customs Law (Articles 44 and 91), the clarification of fine thresholds,[14] and the stipulation that Customs can enforce property preservation rulings and decisions to stop an infringing act handed down by the People's Court.[15] In addition, there have been regulations on the transfer of suspected criminal cases to the Public Security Bureau (PSB).[16] It is important to stress that all these changes have occurred in response to foreign pressure; domestic pressure to step up Customs enforcement has been virtually absent.

---

[12] *Zhongyang zhengfu zuzhi jigou 1998* (Central Government Organs 1998) (Beijing: Gaige chubanshe, 1998), 363.

[13] This paragraph is based on Li Qunying, "Woguo haiguan," 213–216.

[14] See Article 25 of the 2004 Regulations Governing Customs Penalties of the People's Republic of China, http://www.customs.gov.cn/YWStaticPage/7021/a54c5683.htm (accessed April 29, 2008). Article 25 specifies that IPR-infringing goods imported into and exported from China can be seized and a fine amounting to 30 percent of their value can be imposed.

[15] See the 2003 Regulations of the People's Republic of China on Customs Protection of Intellectual Property Rights, http://www.customs.gov.cn/YWStaticPage/7021/ffafb2ee.htm (accessed April 29, 2008).

[16] See *Gong'an bu haiguan zongshu guanyu jiaqiang zhishi chanquan zhifa xiezuo de zanxing guiding* (Temporary Provisions of the Ministry of Public Security and General Administration of Customs on Strengthening Coordination in IPR Enforcement) (March 24, 2006), http://www.customs.gov.cn/YWStaticPage/419/1293407f.htm (accessed April 29, 2008).

Despite the abundance of new laws and regulations, the administrative resources devoted to Customs enforcement of IPR in China have been relatively modest. Few Customs branches have established an IPR unit, and the IPR units that do exist tend to be very small. For example, the GAC in Beijing employs only four people in its IPR division, and the Customs units in Shanghai and Guangzhou employ between two and three.[17] Regional Customs administrations often do not have any full-time employees handling IPR matters: normally, the person responsible for IPR works in the Legal Department and deals with IPR on a part-time basis. This staff shortage in the IPR units reflects the fact that Customs still does not see enforcement of IPR laws as one of its core priorities.

CUSTOMS ENFORCEMENT OPTIONS

Right holders can obtain redress in two ways. The first option is to make a request to Customs to detain a shipment of infringing goods (this is equivalent to requesting an enforcement raid from a trademark bureaucracy). Customs will not act unless the right holder supplies all the necessary documentation and pays the mandatory bond. In addition, if Customs receives a statement from a People's Court within twenty days of detaining the goods, it can assist the right holder in taking further actions, such as property preservation or cessation of the infringing act (this is equivalent to a situation in trademark enforcement when bureaucrats themselves discover acts of counterfeiting in the course of performing other duties). In the second option Customs engages in proactive ex officio actions to protect IPR goods that have already been subject to recordation in the Customs database.[18] When border control agents discover goods suspected of infringing a recorded right, they may give the right holder the option of making a request to detain the goods. If the right holder decides to make the request, then the goods will be detained upon payment of a bond or a bank guaranty. Customs can also confiscate the goods after it determines that they are infringing. Both options allow for the eventual destruction of the infringing goods.

We have no national-level data on how often each procedure is used. However, we know that between January 2003 and February 2004, Guangzhou Customs carried out ninety-nine seizures of suspected infringing goods, and only one of these seizures was conducted at the request of a right holder, the

---

[17] China Interview 010828, with Customs official (Guangzhou); China Interview 010906A, with Customs official (Guangzhou); China Interview 010720B, with Customs official (Shanghai); and China Interview 020115, with the head of the Customs IPR unit of the GAC (Beijing).

[18] In China ex officio actions are available only for goods that have been recorded with Customs. See the 2004 Rules of the Customs of the People's Republic of China on Implementing the Regulations of the People's Republic of China on Customs Protection of Intellectual Property Rights, http://www.customs.gov.cn/YWStaticPage/7021/3f632061.htm (accessed April 29, 2008).

rest being ex officio actions.[19] Similarly, a Pudong Customs employee stated that twenty-three of the thirty IPR seizures carried out in Shanghai in 1999 were done ex officio.[20] By 2005, 87 percent of Customs enforcement in Shanghai consisted of ex officio actions.[21] This suggests that Customs is similar to trademark enforcement bureaucracies, which also prefer to perform ex officio actions rather than to organize raids at the request of right holders.

THE PATTERN OF CUSTOMS SEIZURES IN CHINA

What is the pattern of Customs seizures in China? One aspect of China's record of IPR protection by Customs should be noted at the outset. Although China protects both IPR imports and exports, it gives disproportionate weight to export monitoring. For example, imported goods accounted for only 4 percent of seizures in 2005, and export seizures for the remaining 96 percent.[22] This is unusual because most countries use Customs to protect themselves from the inflow of counterfeits. In contrast, China has used its Customs resources chiefly to protect *other* countries, by stopping the exportation of counterfeits. This situation reflects the differential impact of domestic and foreign pressures on enforcement. Although Chinese commentators have urged that more efforts be directed toward imports,[23] the reality is that Customs determines its enforcement priorities mainly in reaction to pressure, and domestic pressure to focus on imports has been absent. Currently, the IPR activity of Chinese Customs disproportionately benefits foreigners who put continual pressure on the Chinese government to step up export-oriented enforcement.

Time-series data on Customs activity between 1996 and 2005 reinforce the significance of this basic pattern. The data presented in Table 3.2 reveal several intriguing trends. First, the number of cases handled by Customs has waxed and waned, depending on how much pressure the United States has put on the Chinese government. The caseload was high in 1996, then dropped in the late 1990s, but increased again after 2000, reaching a peak of 1,210 cases in 2005. This pattern is fully consistent with the annual assessments of China's IPR record made by the U.S. Trade Representative (USTR): the caseload grew in years when the USTR stressed that Customs should provide more enforcement. Another reason for the sharp increase in Customs acitivity in the early 2000s is that the Quality Brands Protection Committee (QBPC) applied pressure on the Chinese government to step up enforcement as well. The QBPC even created a special Customs Committee, which developed a detailed strategy for increasing

[19] Zhu Qiuyuan, *Zhishi chanquan bianjing baohu*, 210.
[20] China Interview 010720B, with Customs employee (Shanghai).
[21] *Status of Intellectual Property Rights Protection in Shanghai in 2005*, http://www.sipa.gov.cn/chan_eng/Information2_detail.asp?id=169 (accessed November 16, 2006).
[22] There were 51 import cases and 1,159 export cases in 2005. This pattern is consistent with 2000, when there were 7 import cases and 288 export cases. *Statistics for China Customs IPR Seizures (1996–2005)*, http://english.customs.gov.cn (accessed October 28, 2008).
[23] Zhu Qiuyuan, *Zhishi chanquan bianjing baohu*, 209–210.

TABLE 3.2. *IPR Cases Handled by Chinese Customs, 1996–2005*

Year	Value (million yuan)	Total Seizures	Average Value (yuan)	Trademarks	Copyrights	Patents
1996	15.8	705	22,411	38	659	8
1997	32.2	193	166,839	92	85	16
1998	52.7	233	226,180	139	67	27
1999	92	225	408,888	178	42	5
2000	56.7	295	192,203	235	3	57
2001	134.9	330	408,788	308	1	21
2002	95.6	573	166,841	557	2	14
2003	68	756	89,947	741	1	14
2004	84.2	1,051	80,114	1,009	16	26
2005	99.8	1,210	82,479	1,106	67	37

Source: *Statistics for China Customs IPR Seizures (1996–2005)*, http://english.customs.gov.cn (accessed April 29, 2008).

the volume and effectiveness of Customs enforcement and engaged in training seminars with Customs officials.[24]

The differences in the volume of Customs activity across IPR subtypes (as represented in Table 3.2) also reflect the role of foreign pressure. Since 1996, the number of copyright cases has been very small in comparison to the number of trademark cases. This is explained by the fact that Customs entered IPR as a result of the 1995 IPR Action Plan, which heavily favored copyright protection. The spike in copyright enforcement in 1996 reflects that pressure. However, as U.S. pressure on China to enforce copyright laws diminished after 1996, there was a drop in the number of copyright cases. The volume of copyright seizures remained low through 2005.[25] Correspondingly, pressure slowly shifted toward trademarks and became especially intense after the creation of the QBPC in 1999–2000.

We also have data on the kinds of goods that are typically seized by Customs. These include apparel, light industry products, and electronics, but not software, pharmaceuticals, or cigarettes.[26] The data do not disaggregate export

[24] China Interview 010713B, with the head of the QBPC Customs Committee (Shanghai).

[25] It is possible that official statistics underestimate the value of copyright seizures, because in the late 1990s, Customs began to classify both pirated and smuggled goods simply as smuggled. Smuggling is attractive for Customs because it is easier to prove than piracy and because it is subject to higher fines than IPR violations. China Interview 020103, with an EU diplomat and former foreign copyright association representative (Beijing), and China Interview 020115, with the head of the Customs IPR unit of the GAC (Beijing).

[26] *Statistics for China Customs IPR Seizures (1996–2005)*, http://english.customs.gov.cn (accessed October 28, 2008) and *1996–2004 nian zhishi chanquan anjian tongji biao* (Statistics of China Customs IPR Cases 1996–2004), http://www.customs.gov.cn (accessed October 28, 2008). Pharmaceuticals accounted for 0.76 percent of the caseload in 2004 and for 0.91 percent in 2005.

seizures from import seizures, but we can safely assume that most of the seized goods would have been destined for export. The emphasis on apparel, light industry products, and electronics is easily understood: these goods are exported and foreign governments want to shield consumers from such counterfeits. When it comes to software, pharmaceuticals, and cigarettes, they are either produced domestically for domestic consumption or (in the case of cigarettes) sometimes imported into China from abroad. Customs has no mandate to serve as a quality watchdog for goods produced domestically. In the case of cigarettes manufactured abroad and imported into China, domestic pressure for Customs enforcement is absent, because counterfeit brands generally pose no greater threat to health than do regular brands: consumers are happy to get the chance to purchase a cheap product, regardless of whether it is counterfeit.

REGIONAL VARIATION IN CUSTOMS IPR PROTECTION ACTIVITY

Any statement about policy implementation in China has to be qualified by taking into account patterns of regional variation. Other chapters of this book provide detailed analysis of the factors accounting for interprovincial differences by enforcement avenues (civil, criminal, and administrative) and by IPR subtypes (trademarks, copyrights, and patents). Unfortunately, we lack comprehensive data on regional variation in Customs IPR protection. Nevertheless, it is possible to obtain information about Guangdong province and Shanghai, which jointly account for more than half of Customs activity in China.

Guangdong is the only Chinese province that has a subadministration (*fenshu*) of the GAC. This elevated status reflects Guangdong's role as the principal region for import-export trade in China.[27] In terms of IPR enforcement, Guangdong accounted for 459 seizures in 2004 (43.3 percent of the total for all of China), with a value of 37.97 million yuan (45.1 percent of the total).[28] Consistent with national trends, most of the enforcement effort was aimed at trademarks (441 cases), followed by patents (17 cases, 2 of which simultaneously infringed trademarks) and, last, by copyrights (3 cases). In terms of goods seized, most detained shipments consisted of apparel, shoes, spare parts, tobacco, and food. Export cases heavily dominated imports, and most cases involved foreign right holders rather than domestic Chinese companies.[29] In short, the Guangdong data and the national data are consistent.

[27] The value of Guangdong province's imports and exports stood at US$357.133 billion in 2004 (30.9 percent of the total for all of China). *China Commercial Yearbook 2005* (Beijing: China Commercial Press, 2005), 305, 619.

[28] This is a significant increase when compared to 2001, when Guangdong had seventy-two seizures (22 percent of China's total) valued at 50.3 million yuan (37 percent of the total). *Guangdong zhishi chanquan nianjian 2002* (Guangdong IPR Yearbook 2002) (Guangzhou: Huacheng chubanshe, 2002), 54.

[29] All 2004 Guangdong IPR data are from *Guangdong zhishi chanquan nianjian 2005* (Guangdong IPR Yearbook 2005) (Guangzhou: Guangdong jingji chubanshe, 2005), 84–87.

Shanghai has also promoted Customs IPR protection. According to interview evidence and published sources, Shanghai Customs handled 30 IPR cases in 1999 (13.3 percent of the national total), 97 cases in 2000 (32.9 percent of the total), and 150 cases in 2005 (12.4 percent of the total).[30] These figures are not surprising, given that Shanghai is often at the forefront of enforcement efforts for virtually all IPR subtypes. Unfortunately, we do not know how the Shanghai seizures break down by IPR subtype.

When more complete subnational statistics become available, we can further analyze the factors that drive regional variation in enforcement. For the time being, we can safely assume that most Customs activity in relation to IPR takes place in the developed coastal provinces, since it is there that the bulk of China's foreign trade is conducted.

IS CUSTOMS ENFORCEMENT DETERRENT?

We can assess the deterrence of Customs enforcement indirectly, by examining its frequency and severity. The time-series data presented in Table 3.2 indicate that the frequency of enforcement has been increasing since the early 2000s but remains very low in comparison to that in places like Taiwan, the Czech Republic, France, and the United States (see Table 3.1). The low frequency of Customs enforcement is explained by the limited efficacy of foreign pressure in the absence of strong domestic constituencies that also favor enforcement.

Ideally we would use the average value of fines imposed to assess the severity of Customs enforcement – the higher the fine, the greater the severity of enforcement. Unfortunately, these statistics are lacking. However, we do have data on the average value of each seizure, which we can use as a proxy for the severity of enforcement (larger seizures lead to greater losses for the counterfeiters, regardless of the value of the fine imposed). In 2005, the value of the average Customs seizure in China was higher than that of the average seizure in the Czech Republic and lower than that of the average seizure in France and the United States. We should stress that although the absolute number of Chinese Customs seizures continued to increase in the early 2000s, the average value of each seizure fell sharply (by 80 percent) between 2001 and 2005 (see Table 3.2). Customs is working to increase the frequency of seizures, but this increase seems to have decreased their severity. A broader reach has resulted in lower average yield.

Another indicator of the severity of enforcement is the proportion of cases that are transferred to the police and the Procuratorate for criminal prosecution. In China, criminal sanctions have a higher deterrent effect than

---

[30] *2000 nian Shanghai zhishi chanquan baohu zhuangkuang* (Report on the Protection of IPR in Shanghai in 2000) (Shanghai: Shanghai Intellectual Property Administration, 2001), 11; China Interview 010820B, with Customs employee (Shanghai). For 2005 data, see *Status of Intellectual Property Rights Protection in Shanghai in 2005*, http://www.sipa.gov.cn/chan_eng/Information2_detail.asp?id=169 (accessed November 16, 2006).

administrative punishments like fines or seizures of goods. Unfortunately, Customs has not been successfully integrated among the agencies responsible for prosecuting criminal IPR violations. Although Customs can in theory transfer cases to the police when criminal liability thresholds are met,[31] Customs employees openly admit that in practice they are unaware of any successful case transfers.[32] This is striking, because data indicate that many cases do meet the transfer threshold. For example, the average value of a Customs seizure in 2005 was 82,479 yuan, meaning that most cases met or surpassed the 50,000-yuan threshold for transfer to the PSB. When asked to explain the apparent inconsistency (or administrative oversight), Customs employees usually point out that, because the 1997 Criminal Law does not explicitly include a crime of importing or exporting IPR-infringing goods, there is no legal basis for transferring such cases to the police.

To address this gap, a special regulation on strengthening the cooperation between Customs and the PSB was passed in March 2006.[33] Unfortunately, this regulation did not clarify when and how cases should be transferred to the PSB; nor did it include provisions for procuratorial supervision over case transfer. In effect, the regulation is a paper tiger. It reveals the unwillingness of Customs and the PSB to become involved in the prosecution of IPR-related import-export crimes. As we will see in Chapters 5 and 6 on administrative and criminal enforcement options, coordination problems with the PSB are not unique to Customs: all agencies with an IPR mandate suffer from such problems. The effectiveness of IPR enforcement is greatly diminished by the reluctance of the administrative agencies to transfer cases to the PSB, and by the unwillingness of the PSB to accept them. In short, in terms of the indicators examined here, Customs enforcement in China does not seem to have a strong deterrent effect.

IS CUSTOMS ENFORCEMENT RATIONALIZED?

We lack reliable data to directly assess the consistency, transparency, and fairness of enforcement by Customs. Nevertheless, certain indirect indicators do suggest that the overall quality of enforcement by Customs is improving. One such indicator is the centralization of Customs in 1998, a development that tightened discipline and reduced opportunities for corruption.[34] This improvement in consistency should, presumably, also apply to IPR enforcement, especially since Customs has exclusive jurisdiction over the border

---

[31] See Article 91 of the 2000 Customs Law. Also see Article 44, which gives Customs an IPR mandate.

[32] China Interview 010828, with Customs employee (Guangzhou); China Interview 010906A, with Customs employee (Guangzhou); and China Interview 010720B, with Customs employee (Shanghai).

[33] See *Gong'an bu haiguan zongshu guanyu jiaqiang zhishi chanquan zhifa xiezuo de zanxing guiding*.

[34] On Customs reform, see Dali L. Yang, *Remaking the Chinese Leviathan: Market Transition and the Politics of Governance in China* (Stanford, CA: Stanford University Press, 2004), 122–124.

protection of IPR and as such is already exempt from the pressure of coordinating with other enforcers. A second sign that progress is at least possible is that more than half of Customs enforcement takes place in Guangdong and Shanghai, which are known as places that respect the rule of law more than less-developed parts of China. The concentration of enforcement in these two provinces may help raise overall consistency. Finally, Web sites maintained by the GAC, and by a handful of regional Customs offices, make laws and regulations available to the public and even publish enforcement statistics. So there is some attempt at improving Customs activity.

The absence, on these Web sites and elsewhere, of public data about appeals procedures and appeals frequency raises an alarm bell, however. It is possible that those data have simply not been compiled, and that enforcement by Chinese Customs is procedurally fair. It is equally likely that the missing appeals data would indicate that legal ambiguities and onerous administrative procedures discourage individuals from appealing Customs decisions. If this indeed turns out to be the case, it would be consistent (as we will see in Chapters 7–8) with the behavior of most administrative agencies with an IPR enforcement portfolio, which use various methods to prevent right holders from appealing their decisions.

Another worrying sign is the low number of cases that are transferred to the police and the Procuratorate for criminal investigation. Transfers provide an indirect instrument of bureaucratic accountability, because they allow other government agencies to receive information about what is happening inside Customs. Therefore, a low transfer rate would suggest that enforcement by Customs has low transparency. For similar reasons, the absence of published punishment decisions also raises doubts about the overall quality of IPR enforcement by Chinese Customs.

To sum up the main findings about China, Customs IPR activity has been guided by foreign pressure, which was important for changing the legal basis for handling IPR violations. Foreign pressure also governed the introduction of IPR as a protected subject matter in the Customs Code, the sanctioning of ex officio seizures, and the heavy emphasis on export monitoring rather than import control.

Although the Chinese state has invested resources to set up specialized Customs IPR enforcement units, the volume of enforcement provided by these units is strikingly low. This is mainly due to the negligible domestic pressure in favor of IPR enforcement by Customs. In the end, domestic interests are the main variable that helps us understand the volume of Customs enforcement. In terms of currently available indicators, enforcement is most likely also low in quality and deterrence. Quality may be improved if steps are taken to increase transparency and fairness.

COMPARATIVE PERSPECTIVES ON CUSTOMS

A comparison of China with five countries with equivalent or higher volumes of enforcement substantiates the finding that domestic pressure is central to the development of a robust Customs IPR-protection regime.

Russia

In Russia, as in China, Customs has only recently become involved in IPR protection.[35] Both countries provide a relatively low volume of Customs enforcement, and in both enforcement has been driven primarily by foreign pressure.

The Russian Federal Customs Service (Federal'naia tamozhennaia sluzhba) (FTS) is a hierarchical organization with 7 regional directorates, 150 Customs houses, and 600 Customs posts, which collectively employ well over 50,000 people. Despite this abundance of personnel, there are no specialized Customs units tasked with IPR protection. At the central level, within the Directorate General of Tariff and Nontariff Regulation, there is a Department for Control of the Circulation of Intellectual Property and Information Technology Goods, which has seven employees whose job description includes handling IPR, among other matters. At the regional level, however, each of the seven Customs directorates has only one or two people handling IPR as part of their professional responsibilities. Lower-level Customs houses and Customs posts have no personnel involved in IPR enforcement, even on a part-time basis.

Like most other countries, Russia maintains a Customs IPR registry, which included 676 trademarks in 2006.[36] Under Russian law, Customs seizures can be made only in response to a formal complaint from a right holder; in contrast to China, no ex officio actions are allowed in Russia.[37] This will change, however, once Russia accedes to the WTO and has to comply with the requirements of Article 58 of the TRIPS Agreement.[38] Currently, seizures are conducted only after a complaint has been received and Customs has verified that the goods have been entered into the IPR registry. As in other countries (with the exception of France), right holders must post a bond before Customs initiates a seizure.

Customs activity in relation to IPR in Russia is very low. Prior to the May 2003 revision of the relevant articles of the Customs Code, there were so few IPR cases that no record was kept of the exact number. After 2003, statistics

---

[35] Unless otherwise noted, this discussion of Russian Customs is based on Russia Interview 020516, with the deputy chief of the Department for Control of the Circulation of Intellectual Property and Information Technology Goods of the Russian State Customs Committee (GTK) (Moscow).

[36] See FTS *na zashchite prav intellektual'noi sobstvennosti* (IPR Protection by the Federal Customs Service), http://www.customs.ru/ru/press/index.php?&date286=200606&;id286=10736 (accessed October 28, 2008).

[37] The absence of ex officio provisions in the Customs Code has been a sore point for right holders. See the April 9, 2003, Coalition for Intellectual Property Rights (CIPR) letter to Customs, at http://www.cipr.org/activities/advocacy/cipr_letter040503.htm and the official May 23, 2003 Customs response to the CIPR, at http://www.cipr.org/coalition/rfcustoms_ru.htm (both accessed October 28, 2008). The response claims that the inclusion of ex officio powers in the Customs Code would increase opportunities for corruption.

[38] Russia's accession to the WTO is slated for 2009–2010.

began to be compiled, revealing in 2004 a mere 154 seizures, and in 2005 only 390, still a low number.[39] On a per capita basis, the record of Russian Customs in 2004 was comparable to that of Chinese Customs, standing at 1.1 cases pmp. Although by 2005 the caseload in Russia had risen to 2.7 cases pmp, it still remains low in comparison to international standards. Countries like France and the United States, which have much less serious IPR infringement problems, report Customs activity that is considerably higher than that in Russia. What explains this? Russian Customs enforces in response to foreign pressure, and such pressure was not seriously applied until the early 2000s. If pressure continues to be exerted, enforcement volume should increase further. Indeed, in light of Russia's candidacy for accession to the WTO, which requires evidence of strong IPR protection, the central government has already shown signs of putting pressure on Customs to increase enforcement. Should domestic pressure to enforce emerge as well, we can expect enforcement volume to increase even more rapidly. As in China, this will depend on whether the importation of counterfeit goods is perceived as undesirable by domestic interest groups.

Enforcement in Russia is not yet deterrent, because enforcement frequency and severity are both low. In relation to severity, we have no data on the size of the average fine (or on the value of the average seizure), but we do know that very few cases are transferred by Customs to the police and the Procuratorate for criminal investigation. This is puzzling, given that Article 411 of the Russian Customs Code mandates the transfer of cases that meet the criminal liability threshold to the police or the Procuratorate for further prosecution. But by transferring a case, Customs loses the opportunity to impose lucrative fines and receive public recognition for its enforcement effort. The response of Customs has been to avoid transferring major IPR cases that meet the criminal liability threshold to the police. What makes matters worse is that the police and the Procuratorate are not interested in accepting the few cases that Customs does attempt to transfer. This appears to result from differences in bureaucratic culture. In the words of one IPR expert, the police think that "killing an old lady with an ax is a crime, but IPR violations are not" and on those grounds refuse to take on IPR cases.[40] This attitude explains why only about 1 percent of Customs cases are eventually transferred to the police.[41] Overall, then, as in China, Customs enforcement in Russia is not deterrent. Unfortunately, we have

---

[39] *FTS na zashchite prav intellektual'noi sobstvennosti.*

[40] Russia Interview 020516, with the deputy chief of the Department for Control of the Circulation of Intellectual Property and Information Technology Goods of the Russian State Customs Committee (GTK) (Moscow).

[41] In the first half of 2006, Customs handled 520 IPR cases, only 7 of which were transferred to the police. See *Itogi zaderzhaniia kontrafaktnoi produktsii v pervom polugodii 2006 goda* (Summary of Seizures of Counterfeits in the First Half of 2006) (August 9, 2006), http://www.customs.ru/ru/right_def/fight_with_contraband/index.php?id286=11128 (accessed October 28, 2008).

insufficient data to evaluate the quality of the IPR enforcement provided by Russian Customs.

Taiwan

Taiwanese Customs is a three-tier entity: the Ministry of Finance Directorate General of Customs (Caizhengbu guanshui zongju) is at the top, followed by four Customs offices located in Keelung, Taipei, Taichung, and Kaohsiung, which are subdivided into eight branches (*fenju*) and four suboffices (*zhiju*).[42]

Since the 1980s, Taiwan has gradually deployed an unusually wide array of Customs measures aimed at stemming both the importation of IPR-infringing goods and their exportation overseas. Without exception, all export measures have been introduced as a result of foreign pressure, usually from the United States.[43] Currently, copyright is protected through the following specialized border controls: Optical Disk (OD) Manufacturing Implement [SIC] and Border Inspection Measures, Source Identification (SID) Code Export Inspection System, Inspection for Exports of Audio-Visual Copyrighted Works and Original Equipment Manufacturer (OEM) Audio CDs, Export Monitoring System for Computer Program Related Products, and Border Control for Read-Only Memory Chips. Trademarks are protected by the Trademark Export Monitoring System. In addition, to show its resolve to combat the export of IPR-infringing goods, Taiwanese Customs established a specialized IPR task force in March 2003.[44]

As the data in Table 3.3 indicate, unlike Chinese Customs, which favors exports over imports, in Taiwan the share of export cases has been declining, with more and more attention focused on preventing the importation of pirated

TABLE 3.3. *IPR Cases Handled by Taiwanese Customs, 2002–2005*

Year	Total Cases	Export Cases	Total Import Cases	Copyright Import Cases	Trademark Import Cases
2002		328			
2003	140	45	95	27	68
2004	339	44	295	87	208
2005	265	15	250	76	174

Source: http://eweb.customs.gov.tw/lp.asp?ctNode=6501&CtUnit=730&;BaseDSD=7 (accessed July 24, 2006).

[42] http://web.customs.gov.tw (accessed September 29, 2006).
[43] For many years Taiwan was the leading source of imports of IPR-infringing goods into the United States.
[44] *Performance Report on Intellectual Property Rights Protection in Taiwan 2003: Towards Developing Adequate and Effective IP Protection Environment* (Taipei: Intellectual Property Office, 2004), 23–25.

and counterfeit goods.[45] For example, in 2005, export cases accounted for 6 percent of the IPR-infringement cases handled by Customs.[46] This makes sense in light of interview evidence that many more counterfeits are now being imported than exported.[47] The sharp decrease in the number of export cases between 2002 and 2003 also reflects an easing of foreign pressure for more enforcement, as a consequence of the great advances in IPR protection made by Taiwan in the late 1990s and early 2000s. Along with the decline in foreign pressure, there was a rise in domestic pressure to protect Taiwanese consumers from unsafe counterfeit and substandard goods, as reflected in the increase of import cases in the early 2000s.

As in China, trademark cases account for the bulk of Customs activity in Taiwan. We lack reliable data on the frequency of case transfers to the police and the Procuratorate, but we do know that such transfers occur, although sometimes cases are first transmitted to the Anticounterfeiting Committee, which then turns them over to the police.[48]

In Taiwan, as in China, right holders can seek protection from Customs in two ways. One option is to make a request to Customs to suspend the release of the suspected infringing goods. After the posting of a bond and a court order, Customs can detain and eventually destroy the infringing goods. Customs can also conduct a proactive ex officio action in the absence of a request from the right holder. After Taiwan's accession to the WTO, the relevant laws were amended to include this provision in order to conform to Article 58 of TRIPS. Unfortunately, Customs does not publish data on the percentage of its IPR caseload that is composed of ex officio seizures. However, as in China, the provision for ex officio actions allows for a more proactive attitude toward IPR protection on the part of Customs.

International comparisons reveal a relatively strong Customs response to the problem of counterfeiting in Taiwan. When piracy was high in the 1990s, Customs mounted an energetic enforcement effort. Given that the frequency of piracy and counterfeiting is currently low, enforcement activity by Customs has dropped in recent years as well. Nevertheless, Taiwan's 11.5 cases per million people in 2005 compare favorably with those of the United States (25 cases pmp in 2005) and are considerably higher than the enforcement

---

[45] The importation of IPR-infringing goods is prohibited by the Copyright Act (Article 90.1), the Trademark Act (Articles 65–68), the Customs Act (Article 15), and other relevant laws and regulations.

[46] Taiwan regards the low number of export cases as evidence that its efforts at stemming the export of infringing goods are successful. In the first half of fiscal year 2004, only US$60,000 worth of Taiwan-originating goods were seized by U.S. Customs. See *Performance Report on Intellectual Property Rights Protection in Taiwan 2004: Towards Developing Adequate and Effective IP Protection Environment* (Taipei: Intellectual Property Office, 2005), 23.

[47] Taiwan Interview 060327C and Taiwan Interview 060331, both with private investigators (Taipei).

[48] The Anticounterfeiting Committee was abolished in January 2006.

volume in Russia and China. Like Russia, Taiwan does not publish statistics on the value of its Customs seizures.

The Czech Republic

As in Taiwan, the Czech Customs Administration is subordinate to the Ministry of Finance.[49] It has a Directorate General (Generální ředitelství cel), eight regional directorates (*celní ředitelství*), and fifty-four Customs houses (*celní úřady*). Although any Customs office can in theory handle IPR cases, in practice, the Directorate General does not involve itself in such matters. Prior to 2002, the eight regional directorates only accepted IPR complaints and delegated enforcement to the Customs houses. This decentralized system where the lowest and least competent tier of Customs was entrusted with enforcement in a complex area resulted in a very light IPR caseload, which stood at forty-two cases in 1997 and had expanded to only eighty cases by 2001 (see Table 3.4).[50]

In order to improve the coordination of enforcement activity, in 2002 the Hradec Králové regional directorate was designated as the main Customs point for interacting with right holders seeking border protection for their intellectual property.[51] In 2005, five employees at the Hradec Králové regional directorate worked on distributing IPR directives from the EU to the other regional directorates and on compiling enforcement statistics. This represented an attempt to integrate the middle-tier regional directorates in enforcement, instead of placing the burden entirely on the bottom-tier Customs houses. These structural changes, along with the EU pre- and postaccession requirements for stronger Customs enforcement, led to an appreciable increase in the IPR caseload. In 2005, Czech Customs handled 519 cases of IPR infringement. Altogether, 770,980 pieces of counterfeit goods were seized, with a value of 515 million Czech crowns (about US$21 million). Most of the goods were trademark counterfeits, with a total value of 496 million Czech crowns. Seizures of pirated copyrighted goods amounted to only 3 million Czech crowns. Overall, the Czech case shows that foreign pressure can be a powerful tool for increasing the volume of enforcement by Customs. In this regard, the Czech Republic is similar to China, Russia, and Taiwan. In addition, there is domestic pressure in the Czech Republic (as in Taiwan) to protect Czech consumers from the importation of counterfeit goods and substandard goods dangerous to human health from places such as China and Turkey.[52]

---

[49] Unless otherwise indicated, this discussion is based on correspondence with Mr. Petr Jirák, Dept. 40 – IP Protection, Customs Directorate Hradec Králové, Czech Republic, August 3, 2006, and August 11, 2006.

[50] Czech Interview 020703, with the deputy director of the Investigation Division, General Directorate of Customs, Ministry of Finance of the Czech Republic (Prague).

[51] Hradec Králové has a population of about 95,000 and is located close to the Polish border (about fifty miles east of Prague).

[52] Czech Interview 020703, with the deputy director of the Investigation Division, General Directorate of Customs, Ministry of Finance of the Czech Republic (Prague).

TABLE 3.4. *IPR Cases Handled by Czech Customs, Selected Years*

Year	Customs IPR Cases
1997	42
1998	45
1999	56
2000	67
2001	80
2005	519

Sources: Comments by the Czech Republic on IIPA Report – Special 301 List for 2002 (2002) (internal circulation report on file with the author); Czech Interview 020703, with deputy director of the Investigation Division, General Directorate of Customs, Ministry of Finance of the Czech Republic (Prague); correspondence between Mr. Petr Jirák, Dept. 40 – IP Protection, Customs Directorate Hradec Králové, Czech Republic, and the author, August 3, 2006, and August 11, 2006.

In terms of international comparisons, the Czech Republic has the second most active Customs service (after France) among the six countries analyzed in this book, with fifty seizures per million people in 2005.[53] Nonetheless, the average value of each seizure in the Czech Republic stands at US$3,969, which puts it in last place after France, the United States, and China.[54] It appears that the Czechs have decided to pursue a higher volume of seizures rather than an increased average value, with the hope that a higher likelihood of detection will deter individuals from smuggling pirated and counterfeit goods in and out of the country. Available data do not allow us to assess whether enforcement by Customs is deterrent and rationalized.

France

In France, the Directorate General of Customs and Indirect Rights (Direction générale des douanes et droits indirects) is an entity under the Ministry of the Economy, Finance, and Industry (Ministère de l'économie, des finances et de l'industrie). It is hierarchically organized, with the national administration of Customs and five national directorates at the top. The middle level consists of ten interregional offices, forty regional directorates in continental France, and

---

[53] As in China, enforcement figures may underrepresent true enforcement activity because they do not include smuggling cases (e.g., most counterfeit cigarettes are processed as smuggling cases, since the penalties are higher for smuggling than for trademark counterfeiting) or the work of the mobile inspection groups (*skupiny mobilního dohledu*), which, like their counterparts in France, can seize goods on the entire territory of the Czech Republic on grounds of tax evasion and IPR violations. For example, in 2005, the mobile groups seized 501,000 pieces of copyright-infringing goods, while Customs officers at points of entry and exit seized 208,798 pieces. Correspondence with Mr. Petr Jirák, August 3, 2006.

[54] As already indicated, Russia and Taiwan do not publish data on the value of their Customs seizures.

three directorates and two services in the overseas territories (*départements d'outre-mer et territoires d'outre-mer*) (DOM-TOM). The lowest level is composed of 275 Customs bureaus and 302 surveillance teams (*brigades de surveillance*). Collectively, Customs employs more than 20,000 people.[55] There are IPR specialists at both the national and regional levels. Nationally, IPR matters are handled by the Counterfeiting Section of Bureau E4 at the Directorate General, as well as by the antifraud squad known as "the flying Customs" (*la douane volante*), whose official appellation is the National Directorate on Customs Inquiries and Investigations (Direction nationale du renseignement et des enquêtes douanières) (DNRED). DNRED's plainclothes employees have national jurisdiction and can conduct seizures of counterfeit goods anywhere on French territory,[56] unlike their colleagues in many other countries, who are limited to operating only at Customs points of entry and exit. At the subnational level, regional directorates and Customs bureaus have at least one specialist, who usually works part-time on anticounterfeiting matters.[57]

Both EU and French law give Customs an extraordinarily broad mandate that covers counterfeit goods that are imported, exported, reexported, and transshipped through French territory. Without the posting of a bond, at the written request of a right holder (*demande d'intervention*), Customs can retain counterfeits for up to ten working days, thus giving the right holder time to obtain a court order to preserve the goods.[58] In addition, Customs can act on its own initiative and seize trademark counterfeits both at the border and inside the entire territory of France, including commercial and residential properties.[59] These broad powers of French Customs have led to a very high number of seizures of counterfeit goods. In 2005, over 5.6 million counterfeit items were seized, with a total value of €314 million. The number of seizures grew from 2,598 in 2003 to 11,419 in 2005.[60] In 2005, the value of the average Customs seizure was €27,489. Most seizures consisted of trademark goods rather than copyrights, a difference that can be explained by the low number

---

[55] www.douane.gouv.fr (accessed September 29, 2006).

[56] France Interview 020418A, with the spokesperson of the trademark association Union des Fabricants (Paris).

[57] France Interview 020419A, with the section chief of Bureau E4, Customs and Excise Headquarters (Paris).

[58] Right holders can be held responsible for paying warehousing and destruction fees (*frais du stockage et de la destruction*) after the goods are retained by Customs. France Interview 020419A, with the section chief of Bureau E4, Customs and Excise Headquarters (Paris).

[59] *La Douane et la lutte contre la contrefaçon* (Customs and Anticounterfeiting) (Paris: Direction générale des douanes et des droits indirects, 2000). See also "La rôle de l'administration des Douanes dans la lutte contre les contrefaçons" (The Role of Customs in Anticounterfeiting), in *La lutte contre la contrefaçon: Enjeux, nouveaux moyens d'action, guide pratique* (Anticounterfeiting: Stakes, New Means of Action, Practical Guide) (Paris: Ministère de l'Économie et Ministère du Budget, 1994), 167–175.

[60] *La Douane en 2005* (Customs in 2005) (Paris: Direction générale des douanes et des droits indirects, 2006), 9–12.

of valuable domestic copyrights in comparison to the trademarks associated with France's leading position as a luxury brand producer.[61]

France comes out on top among the six countries analyzed in this book, both in terms of seizures per million people (106.6 in 2004 and 190 in 2005) and in terms of the value of the average seizure. We have no data on the frequency of case transfer to the police for criminal investigation, but the Customs Web page features a notice warning individuals that they may be fined up to €300,000 and be imprisoned for up to three years for importing or exporting counterfeits.[62] Along with the other data presented in this chapter, this public announcement demonstrates that the French state takes Customs enforcement very seriously, despite the relatively low levels of counterfeiting. The resolve to limit the flow of counterfeit goods into French territory is driven by a domestic concern to protect French producers from unfair competition, as well as by the mandatory implementation of stringent EU border measures, which, not surprisingly, were adopted by the EU largely as a result of advocacy by France.

The United States

U.S. border controls are carried out by two agencies, U.S. Customs and Border Protection and U.S. Immigration and Customs Enforcement, both of which have been part of the Department of Homeland Security since 2002. Hierarchically organized, the two agencies collectively employ over 44,000 people. Like Customs in most other countries, U.S. Customs maintains a registry of copyrights and trademarks and usually enforces in response to a request from a right holder, although ex officio actions in the absence of such a request are also possible. The most important difference between the United States and the rest of the world is that the United States conducts IPR inspections only on goods imported into U.S. territory, with no attention whatsoever to exports. This reflects the fact that few counterfeits are produced in the United States, and that the United States is consequently exempt from foreign pressure to enforce. At the same time, domestic consumer groups have been actively pressuring the federal government to stop the importation of counterfeit and substandard goods produced abroad.

In the 1980s, counterfeit imports originated mainly in Taiwan; by the 1990s, China had supplanted Taiwan as the main source of IPR-infringing goods destined for the United States. Among the kinds of merchandise confiscated by U.S. Customs, apparel, cigarettes, footwear, and handbags take the lead.[63] We have no data on how often Customs and Immigration transfer cases to the FBI or the district attorneys for criminal prosecution.

---

[61] France Interview 020418B, with the spokesperson of an *haute couture* association (Paris).

[62] http://www.douane.gouv.fr/page.asp?id=40 (accessed September 30, 2006).

[63] *U.S. Customs and Border Protection and U.S. Immigration and Customs Enforcement FY 2005 IPR Seizure Statistics.*

TABLE 3.5. *IPR Seizures by U.S. Customs and Border Protection and U.S. Immigration and Customs Enforcement, 2001–2005*

Fiscal Year	Total Seizures	Seizures (per million people)	Total Value of Seized Goods, US$	Average Value, US$
2001	3,586	12.6	57,438,680	16,017
2002	5,793	20.3	98,990,341	17,088
2003	6,500	22.5	94,019,227	14,464
2004	7,255	24.8	138,767,885	19,127
2005	8,022	27.2	93,234,510	11,622

Source: U.S. Customs and Border Protection and U.S. Immigration and Customs Enforcement FY 2005 IPR Seizure Statistics.

The combined seizure statistics of Customs and Immigration are presented in Table 3.5. We can see that there has been a strong upward trend, with the number of seizures more than doubling between 2001 and 2005. However, as in China, this rise has been accomplished somewhat at the expense of the average value of each seizure, which dropped from US$16,017 in 2001 to US$11,622 in 2005. International comparisons demonstrate that U.S. Customs has fewer seizures per million people than France (190 in France vs. 27.2 in the United States in 2005). In addition, the average value of each seizure is lower in the United States (€27,489 vs. US$11,622 in 2005). The U.S. enforcement record compares favorably with those of Taiwan and the Czech Republic and far surpasses those of China and Russia.

SUMMARY AND DISCUSSION: CUSTOMS ENFORCEMENT AND STATE CAPACITY

The main finding of this chapter is that enforcement volume is sensitive to both domestic and foreign pressure, but that domestic considerations have a primary impact on the overall volume of enforcement. In countries like China and Russia, domestic pressure for Customs enforcement is negligible, with enforcement coming about primarily as a result of foreign pressure. Although the state provides some enforcement, it is of a low volume, has no deterrent effect, and is not rationalized. In Taiwan and the Czech Republic, enforcement occurs under moderate domestic pressure and low-to-moderate foreign pressure. Both provide a much greater volume of Customs IPR enforcement than either China or Russia, a reflection of the limited impact that foreign pressure can have on total enforcement volume in the absence of domestic pressure. In France and the United States, where foreign pressure to enforce is virtually absent, enforcement volume is the highest. This can reflect the general public's opposition to the importation of counterfeits for reasons of health and safety, or the state's interest in nurturing and maintaining a powerful domestic industry (as in the case of France's protection of its luxury brands).

This chapter also presents findings about the deterrence and quality of Customs IPR enforcement. In both China and Russia, the low certainty and low severity of enforcement diminish its deterrence. The chief obstacle to increasing the severity of enforcement is the unwillingness of Customs to transfer cases that meet the criminal liability threshold to the police and the Procuratorate, which, in turn, are also unwilling to accept IPR cases. This double bind has major implications for the further rationalization of Customs activity in the area of IPR.

In terms of the consistency, transparency, and fairness of enforcement, we can draw some preliminary conclusions only about China. Although important progress has been made, this chapter has discussed several patterns that raise doubts about the quality of Customs enforcement in China: the absence of written punishment decisions, the difficulty of appeal, and the low rate of case transfer to the police and the Procuratorate. Although these signs are worrying, Customs nevertheless has a good potential to increase the quality of the enforcement it provides, both because it has a centralized structure (which makes shirking less likely) and because in effect it has exclusive jurisdiction over Customs enforcement cases (thus eliminating the problem of coordinating with other agencies with IPR enforcement portfolios). What is needed is more personnel, a greater will to enforce, and, above all, clearer rules and institutionalized norms for appeals and case transfers.

What conclusions about state capacity emerge from this study of Customs? China presents a case in which the state has the capacity to provide more and better Customs IPR enforcement but does not fully exploit that capacity. The state has taken several important steps to create the foundation for solid Customs IPR enforcement: it has promulgated a number of laws and regulations, it has created specialized IPR units, and it has centralized Customs (though the impetus for centralization was smuggling, not IPR violations). On the other hand, the state has neither clarified legal ambiguities on case transfers, nor increased Customs personnel to deal with the rapidly changing nature of Customs violations, nor encouraged Customs itself to engage in more transparent and procedurally fair IPR enforcement. Like Customs, the state is fundamentally reactive: it does only as much as it has to do. In the case of enforcing IPR along China's borders, an understandably negligible amount of domestic pressure has been combined with a still relatively modest amount of foreign pressure to allow the state to provide only minimal enforcement with neither high deterrent value nor an evidently high quality.

4

Courts

The Emergence of Rationalization

The previous chapter analyzed Customs enforcement as one facet of state capacity to protect IPR. The remaining chapters of Part II describe the civil court, administrative, and criminal enforcement options available to right holders seeking to protect their IPR within China's borders. I start by examining the operation of a key enforcer that also holds the greatest promise for facilitating the emergence of a fully rationalized system of enforcement: the courts of law.

The common wisdom regarding the civil courts is that they matter in industrialized countries but are inconsequential in emerging-market economies such as China. Let us suppose that Proctor & Gamble has suffered from trademark counterfeiting and is now seeking redress. In the United States a layperson would immediately suppose that P&G should initiate a civil lawsuit in a court of law. Legal scholars working on IPR in developed countries similarly focus on the courts, more or less to the exclusion of other enforcement options. This orientation has been strengthened by the professional training offered in U.S. law schools, where courses on American and international intellectual property law rarely mention the possibility of nonjudicial redress through Customs, administrative agencies, or the police. But what should Proctor & Gamble do if the violation has happened in, say, China? In contrast to the shared optimism about the role of courts in developed countries, journalists and scholars alike hold a pessimistic view of the capacity or willingness of Chinese courts to offer redress. In the Chinese case, furthermore, the marginal role of the courts is taken as representative of an overall absence of the rule of law.

The lack of confidence in and attention to the courts can be attributed to two factors: unrealistic and even naïve expectations of what the courts should do and lack of familiarity with empirical trends in the enforcement of IPR laws through the civil courts, as revealed by cross-country and within-country time-series data. In relation to the first, there is a widespread belief, for example, that foreign firms have been wronged whenever they lose in a Chinese court. Individual high-profile cases are often cited as evidence of the absence of rule of law in China, without subjecting them to a detailed examination: the premise is that foreigners should not lose in Chinese courts, and when they do the conclusion is that the loss was inevitable, given the state of the courts. Yet foreign entities are often negligent with their intellectual property, failing, for example, to register their trademarks in China but still expecting automatic protection. In fact, the great majority of cases heard by the specialized courts are resolved in an impartial manner. There is a mismatch between foreign perception of these courts and their actual operation. If there is a single problem with the civil courts in relation to IPR, it is not the quality of the decisions, but the relatively limited volume of cases heard.

This chapter argues that courts provide a key mechanism for enforcing IPR laws. Nonetheless, we should not assume that courts are or should always be the main enforcers of IPR laws. As this chapter demonstrates, there is wide cross-national variation in the importance of courts. The United States, where the courts have emerged as the main avenue for addressing IPR violations, is the exception. In other countries, courts are overshadowed by nonjudicial means of dispute resolution. This chapter describes the implications of this cross-country variation for enforcement.

Variation within countries is also a reality. In China, there is geographical variation in court use, as well as sectoral differences in the importance of the courts for different subtypes of IPR. This chapter explains why some Chinese provinces have higher rates of litigation than others and describes the emergence of the courts as the dominant enforcers for some subtypes of IPR (patents), but not for others (trademarks).

BACKGROUND: COURTS AND THE ABSENCE OF RULE OF LAW IN CHINA

One of the main governance issues in China today is the lack of rule of law, with an attendant pervasiveness of corruption.[1] Most scholars take a dim view of Chinese legal reform, focusing on the numerous obstacles facing the courts: low professionalism, local protectionism, and lack of independence from the

---

[1] Ting Gong, *The Politics of Corruption in Contemporary China* (Westport, CT: Praeger, 1994); Julia Kwong, *The Political Economy of Corruption in China* (Armonk, NY: M. E. Sharpe, 1997); Xiaobo Lü; *Cadres and Corruption: The Organizational Involution of the Communist Party* (Stanford, CA: Stanford University Press, 2000); Xiaobo Lü, "Booty Socialism, Bureau-preneurs, and the State in Transition: Organizational Corruption in China," *Comparative Politics* 32:3 (2000), 273–294; Melanie Manion, *Corruption by Design: Building Clean Government in Mainland China and Hong Kong* (Cambridge, MA: Harvard University Press, 2004); Yan Sun, *Corruption and Market in Contemporary China* (Ithaca, NY: Cornell University Press, 2004); Andrew Wedeman, "The Intensification of Corruption in China," *The China Quarterly*, no. 180 (2004), 895–921; Minxin Pei, *China's Trapped Transition: The Limits of Developmental Autocracy* (Cambridge, MA: Harvard University Press, 2006).

Communist Party.[2] Although many areas of the Chinese legal system suffer from a lack of the rule of law, intellectual property rights have often been singled out as the quintessential example of the generalized lack of respect for property rights that exists in China.[3] The situation has changed, however. Although intellectual property may indeed have been plagued by lawlessness and corruption in the past, today it is an area in which consistent, transparent, and fair enforcement is beginning to emerge. The IPR courts are an important phenomenon in themselves and a model for how courts in general might develop through focused state intervention.

The Chinese Court System

Before we discuss the role of the courts in enforcing IPR laws, we need to look briefly at some general patterns in the evolution of the Chinese court system. Scholars have discussed the structure of the system at some length, so I will review it only briefly here.[4] China has a five-tier court system, with the Supreme People's Court (Zuigao renmin fayuan) at the top. The high people's courts (*gaoji renmin fayuan*) are located a step lower in the judicial hierarchy. There are thirty-one such courts in China, one for each province, autonomous region, or municipality directly under the central government. The intermediate people's courts (*zhongji renmin fayuan*) are more numerous: as of 2001, there were 346 such courts in China. The basic people's courts (*jiceng renmin fayuan*) are located at the county level (or, within cities, at the level of the district). In 2001, there were 3,135 basic people's courts. People's tribunals (*renmin fating*) are located at the level of townships and towns. As of 2001, there were 11,000

[2] William Alford, "Tasseled Loafers for Barefoot Lawyers: Transformation and Tension in the World of Chinese Legal Workers," *The China Quarterly*, no. 141 (1995), 22–38; Donald Clarke, "The Execution of Civil Judgments in China," *The China Quarterly*, no. 141 (1995), 65–81; Anthony R. Dicks, "Compartmentalized Law and Judicial Restraint: An Inductive View of Some Jurisdictional Barriers to Reform," *The China Quarterly*, no. 141 (1995), 82–109; Stanley B. Lubman, *Bird in a Cage: Legal Reform in China after Mao* (Stanford, CA: Stanford University Press, 1999); William Alford, "The More Law, the More...? Measuring Legal Reform in the People's Republic of China," in *How Far across the River? Chinese Policy Reform at the Millennium*, ed. Nicholas C. Hope, Dennis Tao Yang, and Mu Yang Li (Stanford, CA: Stanford University Press, 2003), 122–149; William Alford, "Of Lawyers Lost and Found: Searching for Legal Professionalism in the People's Republic of China," in *East Asian Law: Universal Norms and Local Cultures*, ed. Arthur Rosett, Lucie Cheng, and Margaret Y. K. Woo (London: Routledge Curzon, 2003), 181–203; Pei, *China's Trapped Transition*.
[3] William Alford, *To Steal a Book Is an Elegant Offense: Intellectual Property Law in Chinese Civilization* (Stanford, CA: Stanford University Press, 1995); Michel Oksenberg, Pitman B. Potter, and William B. Abnett, "Advancing Intellectual Property Rights: Information Technologies and the Course of Economic Development in China," *NBR Analysis* 7:4 (1996); Andrew Mertha, *The Politics of Piracy: Intellectual Property in Contemporary China* (Ithaca, NY: Cornell University Press, 2005).
[4] See, for example, Stanley B. Lubman, *Bird in a Cage*, and Randall Peerenboom, *China's Long March toward Rule of Law* (New York: Cambridge University Press, 2002).

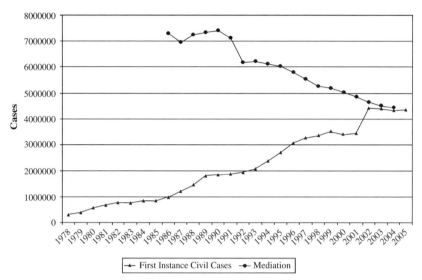

FIGURE 4.1.   The Rise of Civil Litigation in China, 1978–2005. *Source: Zhongguo falü nianjian* (China Law Yearbook) (Beijing: Zhongguo falü nianjianshe), all years between 1987 and 2006.

people's tribunals, a reduction from 1994, when there were as many as 20,000.[5] The courts at the two lowest levels of the hierarchy (the basic people's courts and people's tribunals) are at greatest risk of having unqualified judges.

General Trends in Litigation and Legal Professionalism in China

Because we now have access to almost three decades of judicial statistics from the reform period, we are able to make some generalizations about overall trends in court use in China since 1978. Three developments are especially significant: the rise of litigation, the expansion of the bar and the bench, and the decline of the use of individual case supervision.

Litigation grew twelvefold between 1978 and 2005.[6] Most importantly, despite a well-documented cultural preference for extrajudicial dispute resolution, judicial statistics reveal two related trends: a declining use of extrajudicial mediation and an increasing reliance on the courts to resolve civil disputes (see

---

[5] Data for 2001 from Jiang Zhipei, "Zhonghua renmin gongheguo renmin fayuan he zhuanmen renmin fayuan" (People's Courts and Specialized People's Courts of the PRC), http://www.chi naiprlaw.com/spjg/spjg6.htm (accessed January 9, 2004). Data for 1994 from Jiang Zhipei, "The Organization, Function and Powers of the People's Courts," http://www.chinaiprlaw. com/english/courts/court1.htm (accessed January 9, 2004).

[6] There were 447,755 first-instance court cases in 1978 and 5,139,888 first-instance court cases in 2005. *Zhongguo tongji nianjian 2004* (China Statistical Yearbook 2004) (Beijing: Zhongguo tongji chubanshe, 2004), 886; *Zhongguo falü nianjian 2006* (China Law Yearbook 2006) (Beijing: Zhongguo falü nianjianshe, 2006), 988.

Figure 4.1).[7] Although we should note that the decline in mediation (which is free) means that economically disadvantaged groups may have diminished access to law,[8] the increased reliance on the courts is in general a welcome step toward the rise of a more transparent and predictable system of dispute resolution in China.[9]

The increased caseload of the Chinese courts has been made possible by an expanded bar and bench. According to publicly available statistics, in 2004 there were 145,196 lawyers (*lüshi gongzuo renyuan*), of whom 100,875 worked as full-time lawyers (*zhuanzhi lüshi*).[10] The continued growth of the bar is ensured by the popularity of law as both an undergraduate and a graduate major in China and by the presence of 328 universities that offer specialized training in law.[11] Although they are not as qualified as their American counterparts, in 2003, 95.5 percent of China's lawyers and 40 percent of its judges (across all courts) had at least a degree from a two-year college (*dazhuan*).[12] Importantly, only 26 percent of lawyers were members of the Communist Party.[13] The number of judges has grown as well, reaching 220,000 in 2004, a marked increase from 70,000 in 1998.[14] Although doubts about the educational level of these judges are surely well founded,[15] the 2001 introduction of special exams for lawyers and judges does point to an ongoing state commitment to raise the quality of the bar and the bench in China.

The third trend has been the sharp decline in the number of cases subject to individual case supervision (*ge'an jiandu*) by the court adjudication committees (*shenpan weiyuanhui*), to retrial (*zaishen*) ordered by higher-level courts, and to

[7] In 1986, there were only 989,409 first-instance civil cases and 7,307,049 cases of mediation, whereas in 2004 there were 4,332,727 first-instance civil court cases and 4,414,233 cases of mediation. See *Zhongguo falü nianjian 2005* (China Law Yearbook 2005) (Beijing: Zhongguo falü nianjianshe, 2005), 1064.

[8] Alford, "The More Law"; Alford, "Of Lawyers Lost and Found"; Benjamin Liebman, "Legal Aid and Public Interest Law in China," *Texas International Law Journal*, no. 34 (1999), 211–286.

[9] For a less sanguine view, see Stanley B. Lubman, "Chinese Courts and Law Reform in Post-Mao China," in *East Asian Law*, ed. Rosett, Cheng, and Woo, 205–232.

[10] *Zhongguo tongji nianjian 2005* (China Statistical Yearbook 2005) (Beijing: Zhongguo tongji chubanshe, 2005), 779. The increase in the number of lawyers has been accompanied by a sharp drop in the number of people's mediators – from 8.8 million in 1999 to 5.1 million in 2004 (ibid.).

[11] *2002 Zhongguo daxue faxue zongpaiming* (2002 Ranking of Law Programs in China), http://www.people.com.cn/GB/kejiao/230/6034/8079/20021009/838516.html (accessed November 14, 2003). These numbers should not be taken at face value, as under their definition "law" includes law, Marxist theory, sociology, political science, and criminology.

[12] See *Zhongguo lüshi nianjian 2001–2003* (China Lawyers' Yearbook 2001–2003) (Beijing: Renmin fayuan chubanshe, 2005), 520. On lawyers' qualifications, see Pei, *China's Trapped Transition*, 67.

[13] *Zhongguo lüshi nianjian 2001–2003*, 520.

[14] Jean-Pierre Cabestan, "The Political and Practical Obstacles to the Reform of the Judiciary and the Establishment of a Rule of Law in China," *Journal of Chinese Political Science* 10:1 (2005), 43–64.

[15] Alford, "Tasseled Loafers"; Lubman, *Bird in a Cage*; Lubman, "Chinese Courts and Law Reform."

procuratorial protests (*kangsu*).[16] It is not straightforward how this trend should be interpreted. Some argue that individual case supervision is necessary to ensure a high degree of legal professionalism and to guard against local protectionism in adjudication, especially in remote and underdeveloped areas. Others stress that with the overall rise in the qualifications of both lawyers and judges, the need for individual case supervision has declined, and that consequently the continued existence of the system serves more as a curb on judicial independence than as a mechanism for ensuring judicial accountability.[17] The latter interpretation is closer to describing the place of supervision in intellectual property cases. IPR cases are decided by specialized courts located in developed parts of China and at higher levels within the judicial hierarchy. These are courts that are less likely to need high levels of supervision as insurance against low professionalism. The decline in supervision in relation to IPR is therefore better seen as encouraging independence.

Major Weaknesses of the Chinese Judicial System

Although these three general trends reveal some welcome developments in the Chinese judiciary (higher litigiousness, higher legal professionalism, and higher judicial independence), there are substantial reasons for continued concern. The chief obstacles facing the further development of legal institutions are of two kinds: technical and political.

The technical difficulties facing the Chinese legal system are manifold. In the area of lawmaking, China needs newer and clearer laws and regulations that can be made available to the public without delay. Areas such as criminal law seem to be particularly in need of reform; numerous civil and administrative laws have to be revised as well. When it comes to the bench and the bar, China needs more judges and lawyers (with better training), especially in rural and underdeveloped areas. As even the best laws remain meaningless unless they are well enforced, Chinese courts and administrative agencies must discover ways to build their enforcement capacity and engage in consistent, transparent, and fair enforcement. Finally, some way to limit judicial corruption has to be found, probably through a combination of positive incentives (higher pay) and negative incentives (stiffer penalties for those who engage in corruption).

Political difficulties are also plentiful. The Chinese Communist Party (CCP) hinders the rise of the rule of law in two ways. First, it limits judicial independence. Both internal court institutions (adjudication committees) and external institutions (political-legal committees) help to ensure that judges toe the party

---

[16] See *Zhongguo falü nianjian* (all years beginning in 1987). The number of criminal cases subject to supervision dropped by a factor of 134 between 1986 and 2004 (on the implications of this development, see Congressional-Executive Commission on China, *Annual Report 2005* [Washington, DC], 32); supervision in ordinary civil cases dropped by a factor of 25 between 1986 and 2004.

[17] Randall Peerenboom, "Judicial Independence and Judicial Accountability: Individual Case Supervision," *The China Journal*, no. 55 (2006), 67–92.

line on politically sensitive issues. Second, as detailed in Chapter 2, by having a parallel party system of justice (the Discipline and Inspection Commission system), the CCP puts party members above the law.

The continuing presence of technical and political difficulties presents obstacles to the universal spread of rule of law in China. In the foreseeable future, legal reforms are unlikely to serve as the "Trojan horse" that will introduce wide-ranging political reforms into China's walls.[18] In this general context, it is all the more significant that China has begun to introduce geographically limited and issue-specific rationalized judicial enforcement. It is important to understand how rationalized enforcement has emerged in certain issue areas and to recognize the obstacles to its future spread. The operation of the specialized IPR tribunals is a lens onto this general dynamic. IPR is of interest also as an unusually "clean" area, which is not plagued by the typical problems of the Chinese judicial system.

A BRIGHT LIGHT: THE SPECIALIZED IPR TRIBUNALS

The creation of the specialized IPR court tribunals is a relatively new development in the Chinese court system, which has not been analyzed extensively.[19] It should be stressed that specialized IPR courts or tribunals are very rare throughout the world. In 2000, only 6 percent of the 176 member-states of the WIPO had established such courts. Furthermore, in most countries these courts have only appellate jurisdiction over IPR cases. Most impressive is the fact that China is the only country in the world to have specialized tribunals that accept first-instance civil IPR cases. One reason for this, of course, is that more developed countries do not need the specialized tribunals to supplement the regular courts, which function well in general, as well as in technical areas like IPR. In this light, China's creation of specialized tribunals is indicative of the state's resolve to invest scarce resources in an area of the law whose importance is on the rise, and to do so by adjusting the court system in ways that allow for the institutionalization of rationalized enforcement.

The IPR tribunals first emerged in the most developed cities in China. After passage of the Trademark Law in 1982, the Patent Law in 1984, and the Copyright Law in 1990, the first two specialized IPR tribunals (*zhishi chanquan fating*) were set up in the Beijing High People's Court and the Beijing Intermediate People's Court in 1993. The IPR division of the Supreme People's Court was established in 1996. The organizational hierarchy of the specialized IPR tribunals mirrors that of the general courts, because the IPR tribunals are located at ordinary courts but are staffed by judges with specialized training.

---

[18] Matthew Stephenson, "A Trojan Horse in China?" in *Promoting the Rule of Law Abroad: In Search of Knowledge*, ed. Thomas Carothers (Washington, DC: Carnegie Endowment for International Peace, 2006), 191–215.

[19] In the specialized IPR literature, the Chinese term *zhishi chanquan ting* is translated as "IPR tribunal" or "IPR division of the court." I mainly use the first translation.

TABLE 4.1. *Number of Subnational IPR Tribunals in China in 2000 (by location and type of court)*

Province	High Court	Intermediate Court	Basic Court
Beijing	1	2	2 (Haidian, Chaoyang)
Tianjin	1	2	
Hebei	1	4 (Shijiazhuang, Qinhuangdao, Baoding, Xingtai)	
Shanxi		1 (Taiyuan)	
Heilongjiang	1	1 (Harbin)	
Shanghai	1	2	2 (Pudong, Huangpu)
Jiangsu	1	2 (Nanjing, Yancheng)	
Zhejiang	1		
Anhui	1	2 (Hefei, Chuzhou)	
Fujian	1	2 (Fuzhou, Xiamen)	
Jiangxi		1 (Jingdezhen)	
Shandong		3 (Ji'nan, Yantai, Qingdao)	
Henan	1	1 (Anyang)	
Hubei		1 (Wuhan)	
Guangdong	1	4 (Guangzhou, Shenzhen, Foshan, Shantou)	
Hainan	1	1 (Haikou)	
Chongqing	1		
Sichuan	1	1 (Chengdu)	
TOTAL	14	30	4

Source: Zhongguo zhishi chanquan nianjian 2000 (China IPR Yearbook 2000) (Beijing: Zhishi chanquan chubanshe, 2001), 69, 413.

Therefore, the IPR division of the Supreme People's Court is at the top of the system. One step down are the tribunals at the high people's courts, followed by those located within the intermediate people's courts. At the bottom of the ladder are the IPR tribunals at the basic people's courts. As of 2000, the high people's courts in ten provinces and the four provincial-level municipalities (Beijing, Tianjin, Shanghai, and Chongqing) had established IPR tribunals. In addition, thirty intermediate people's courts had IPR tribunals. At the lowest level of the judicial hierarchy, four basic people's courts had created IPR tribunals: Haidian and Chaoyang (in Beijing) and Pudong and Huangpu (in Shanghai). Table 4.1 summarizes the geographical distribution of IPR tribunals in China in 2000.

As Table 4.1 demonstrates, in 2000 thirteen Chinese provinces had no specialized IPR tribunals at any level of the judicial system. These provinces were Inner Mongolia, Liaoning, Jilin, Hunan, Guangxi, Guizhou, Yunnan, Tibet,

Shaanxi, Gansu, Qinghai, Ningxia, and Xinjiang. Most of these provinces are underdeveloped inland areas with economies that are primarily agriculture-based. Some (e.g., Liaoning and Jilin) form part of China's rust belt, where the inefficient heavy industrial enterprises are located. Historically, none of these provinces attracted significant foreign direct investment; as a result, the authorities are reluctant to invest in setting up specialized IPR tribunals. The IPR cases that do arise in these provinces can be heard by the ordinary courts, but these courts are also much more likely than the specialized IPR tribunals to have unqualified judges (including, for example, demobilized soldiers from the People's Liberation Army with no legal training, let alone knowledge of IPR matters) or to fall prey to local protectionism.

After China's accession to the WTO, the number of courts with IPR specialization exploded. By 2006, as many as 172 courts had established specialized IPR tribunals. Another 140 courts had specialized IPR collegiate benches (*heyi ting*), composed of a panel of judges or a judge and two people's assessors. Altogether, in 2006 China had 1,667 judges specialized in hearing civil IPR cases.[20] No data about the regional distribution of these tribunals, collegiate panels, and judges have been released.

It bears stressing that the judges serving on IPR tribunals have very high qualifications.[21] In contrast to judges in ordinary courts, IPR judges have specialized training in law, not infrequently including a master's or even doctoral degree in law.[22] Most relevant, these judges are typically trained in the arcane details of IPR law. Second, IPR judges often speak English and frequently go on study trips abroad; this gives them an opportunity to keep up with important new developments in IPR law outside China. Ultimately, judges with foreign experience and expertise are more likely to understand and respect the principles of transparency. Third, IPR judges are typically young. They are eager to learn and may be less ideological and dogmatic in their interpretations of the law than their older, less qualified colleagues sitting in the ordinary courts of law.

Caseload of the IPR Tribunals

The IPR tribunals in China only handle civil IPR cases. Criminal IPR cases are handled by the criminal divisions of the regular courts and are heard by judges who are unlikely to have a specialization in IPR (see Chapter 6).

Civil IPR court cases were very unevenly distributed among Chinese provinces in 2004.[23] When we normalize the number of court cases by dividing it by

---

[20] *Zhongguo zhishi chanquan nianjian 2007* (China IPR Yearbook 2007) (Beijing: Zhishi chanquan chubanshe, 2007), 98.

[21] This paragraph is based on personal observations made during visits to IPR tribunals in China, as well as on interviews with Chinese IPR judges and with Chinese and Western lawyers.

[22] Law is an undergraduate major in China. Most Chinese lawyers and judges have a B.A. in law, rather than an advanced degree.

[23] This is the only year for which we have systematic data on the IPR caseload in each Chinese province.

TABLE 4.2. *Determinants of IPR Court Cases per Province in China in 2004*

	Model 1	Model 2	Model 3	Model 4	Model 5
Gross provincial product (billion yuan)	.77 (.15)***	–	–	–	–
IPR tribunals	–	86.88 (20.26)***	–	–	–
Patent infringement cases 2004	–	–	5.82 (.64)***	–	–
Patent counterfeiting cases 2004	–	–	−.23 (.41)	–	–
Patents granted 2004	–	–	–	.07 (.004)***	–
Trademarks granted 2004	–	–	–	–	.47 (.004)***
Copyright registrations 2004	–	–	–	–	.47 (.027)*
Constant	−107.52 (105.59)	14.88 (97.53)	35.43 (58.08)	−39.43 (32.1)	−35.7 (43.2)
R^2	.46	.39	.75	.92	.85
N	31	31	31	31	31

* = significant at the .1 level; ** = significant at the .05 level; *** = significant at the .01 level.
Source: *Zhongguo zhishi chanquan nianjian 2005*, 260–310.

the population of each province, we find that twenty-six Chinese provinces handled fewer than ten cases per million people, whereas five provinces (Zhejiang, Tianjin, Guangdong, Shanghai, and Beijing) handled more than ten cases. The variable has a minimal value of 0.4 (Tibet) and a maximal value of 74.4 (Beijing). The mean is 8.6 cases per million people and the standard deviation 14.8. Bivariate regression analysis reveals that the number of court cases is very strongly correlated with the presence of specialized IPR tribunals, gross provincial product, and the number of patent infringement disputes accepted by the State Intellectual Property Office (SIPO) in 2004. The strongest correlation is with the number of patents granted in 2004. In addition, the number of trademarks granted in each province and the number of registered copyright contracts also have a statistically significant impact on the volume of IPR cases handled by the courts. Because many of the independent variables are very highly correlated, multivariate analysis was not always possible. I have listed the results of a series of bivariate and multivariate tests in Table 4.2.

The results of the statistical analysis are not surprising. Provinces with more abundant resources, as reflected in the number of specialized IPR tribunals in the province and the size of the gross provincial product, have more IPR court cases. The total number of patents granted in each province similarly influences the number of court cases, since the number of patents granted indicates the overall level of inventiveness of the province. All else being equal, we would expect provinces with a higher level of inventive activity to have more patent disputes. For the same reason, provinces with more trademarks granted and copyrights registered should

TABLE 4.3. *First- and Second-Instance Civil IPR Cases Accepted by Chinese Courts, 1985–2005*

Year	Copyright	Patent	Trademark	Other	Total First Instance	Second Instance
1985		6	24	317	347	
1986	100	10	23	551	684	
1987	106	46	28	666	846	
1988	171	79	41	1,210	1,501	
1989	147	130	46	1,659	1,982	
1990	112	178	51	1,261	1,602	
1991	153	330	67	1,264	1,814	
1992	143	503	150	1,698	2,494	
1993	236	680	206	1,821	2,943	
1994	326	833	204	1,941	3,204	
1995	385	1,051	311	2,009	3,756	
1996	436	1,184	320	1,921	3,861	
1997	411	1,045	338	1,850	3.644	
1998	571	1,162	527	1,833	4,093	
1999	750	1,485	460	1,587	4,282	
2000	963	1,595	393	1,860	4,811	
2001	1,117	1,597	482	2,069	5,265	
2002	1,824	2,081	707	1,589	6,201	
2003	2,493	2,110	926	1,454	6,983	2,237
2004	4,264	2,549	1,325	1,185	9,323	2,842
2005	6,096	2,947	1,782	2,999	13,424	3,114

Note: As of 2004, statistics on unfair competition cases began to be published. There were 1,331 unfair competition cases in 2004 and 1,303 in 2005.

Sources: Zhongguo zhishi chanquan nianjian 2004, 336; Zhongguo falü nianjian 2005, 155–156; Zhongguo zhishi chanquan nianjian 2005, 305–310; Zhongguo zhishi chanquan nianjian 2006, 110–115, 405–406.

have a higher level of court disputes. In sum, court cases follow a logical pattern: rich localities with high levels of inventive activity have higher rates of litigation.

Increased Caseload of the IPR Tribunals

Overall, the number of IPR cases handled by Chinese courts has increased steadily over the last twenty years. Whereas in 1985 the courts accepted only 347 IPR cases, in 2005 they accepted 13,424 first-instance cases, representing a thirty-nine-fold increase. Additional statistics on the number of first-instance and appeals cases handled by the IPR tribunals are provided in Table 4.3. The overall trend toward greater reliance on the courts for IPR dispute resolution is clear.[24] The question remains whether the courts provide justice that approximates rule-of-law principles. In the following sections, I will assess the degree of consistency, transparency, and fairness in the operation of the Chinese IPR tribunals.

[24] See "850,000 Lawsuits in the Making," *The Economist* (April 12, 2008), 74.

Measuring Rationalized Civil Enforcement: Consistency

The consistent application of the law is more likely when judges have specialized knowledge and training. In China, judicial specialization and efficiency are enhanced by the fact that typically only intermediate and high people's courts serve as courts of first instance for IPR cases.[25] When an intermediate court is the court of first instance, the appeal will be heard by the high people's court. Similarly, if the high people's court is the court of first instance, the appeals court will be the Supreme People's Court.[26] As a consequence, plaintiffs in IPR cases have access to the highest quality of judicial review that is currently available in China. Also important is the fact that, as one moves up toward the apex of the judicial hierarchy, it becomes correspondingly more difficult for local governments to pressure courts to reach particular decisions on specific cases.[27] The consistency of implementation of judicial decisions is further enhanced by the attention given to IPR by the Supreme People's Court, which regularly deliberates on IPR matters. Finally, training courses for judges, organized by the Supreme People's Court or by foreign entities like the Quality Brands Protection Committee (QBPC), help increase the technical competency of lawyers and judges handling IPR cases, making it more likely that they will hand down consistent decisions.

Transparency: Open Trials and Published Court Decisions

It is impossible to measure transparency directly, but open trials and published court decisions can serve as useful proxies. Open trials increase transparency, as they subject the work of the courts to public scrutiny and make it less likely that judges will engage in corrupt private deals with one or another party to the case. Available data indicate that in 2003, Chinese courts concluded 2,064 second-instance (appeals) IPR cases. Of these, 802 cases (38.8 percent) ended with a court judgment (*panjue*), which was announced in an open court hearing (*kaiting shenli*).[28] Although we currently do not have data on the exact proportion of first-instance IPR cases that feature open court hearings, there is no reason to doubt that most first-instance cases are subject to open court hearings.[29] I was personally able to gain access to the courts (to interview judges)

---

[25] A court of first instance is the court that has original jurisdiction over a case. A second-instance court is the court that handles the first appeal of a case (it has appellate jurisdiction over the case). A cassation court (court of final appeal) handles the second appeal of a case (not all IPR cases can be appealed twice).

[26] In China, the Supreme People's Court functions primarily as the highest appellate court rather than as a constitutional court.

[27] See Mei Y. Gechlik, *Protecting Intellectual Property Rights in Chinese Courts: An Analysis of Recent Patent Judgments*, Carnegie Paper No. 78 (Washington, DC: Carnegie Endowment for International Peace, 2007), 7.

[28] *Zhongguo zhishi chanquan nianjian 2004*, 335. The majority of the remaining cases were either withdrawn or settled before they reached trial.

[29] In principle, only cases involving state secrets and the rights of minors should be heard behind closed doors.

and received permission to be present at three different case hearings (two in Shanghai and one in Guangzhou) simply by showing my passport.

In addition to holding open court hearings, the IPR tribunals have raised the transparency of their work by publishing judicial decisions, either on their Web sites or as part of the numerous compilations of court cases that are readily available in Chinese bookstores. Some tribunals have been held up as examples of transparency to be followed by other courts around the country (e.g., the IPR tribunal at the basic people's court in Pudong). In addition to raising transparency, the publication of court decisions can increase consistency in the application of laws. There is some indication that judicial precedent is becoming more important, especially in new legal areas where it is especially unclear how the law should be applied. Compilations of IPR cases (usually issued by the Beijing and Shanghai IPR tribunals), along with the Supreme People's Court interpretations of various IPR laws (typically included in the *Supreme People's Court Gazette*), serve to solidify the consistency and predictability of the decisions of the IPR tribunals in China.

Procedural Fairness

As it is impossible to measure procedural fairness directly, we rely on the rate of appeal as a useful proxy. The use of this proxy is driven by the assumption that, as a matter of procedural fairness, right holders should not be prevented from appealing the outcome of a case. The statistics on appeals of IPR cases are encouraging. Appeals rates seem to have an inverse relationship with the quality of the judges: ordinary courts, staffed by judges with relatively poor qualifications, have an appeals rate that is three times lower than that of the IPR tribunals, where the judges are highly qualified. More specifically, whereas the average appeals rate for all first-instance cases in 2003 was 9.6 percent, the appeals rate for IPR cases was 32.6 percent (2,237 second-instance cases were accepted).[30] This healthy appeals rate indexes the above-average fairness of the IPR tribunals and the trust that right holders place in them.

Similarly, the gradual emergence of the courts of law as the main enforcers for certain subtypes of IPR can be seen as further evidence that right holders trust them to resolve their disputes fairly. In all subtypes of IPR, right holders have a choice between the courts and at least one administrative enforcer. The courts have emerged as the main enforcers for patent infringement disputes and are becoming increasingly more important in routine copyright enforcement. This development, which is discussed further in Chapters 8–9, holds important promise for the emergence of rationalized IPR enforcement.

Doubtless because of their position in the judicial hierarchy (located mostly at the level of the intermediate and high people's courts) and because of their concentration in the more developed coastal provinces, which have an interest

[30] In 2003, 2,929 first-instance cases ended with a judgment. See *Zhongguo zhishi chanquan nianjian 2004*, 334–335.

in protecting IPR, the specialized IPR tribunals emerge as a bright spot in China's IPR enforcement structure. Recent testimony on the quality of these tribunals comes from an unlikely and telling source, the International Intellectual Property Alliance (IIPA), a U.S. industry lobbying group, which historically has been a leading critic of China's IPR enforcement record. In its 2006 Special 301 submission to the U.S. Trade Representative, the IIPA declared, "The record of China's development of a cadre of well-trained IPR judges to sit on specialized tribunals at the intermediate level courts in China to hear civil cases has been a success."[31]

China's record of IPR protection indicates that the state can create a pocket of rationalized court enforcement, even when the court system is in general plagued by numerous problems. This is a remarkable achievement, especially when we keep in mind that China has no tradition of the rule of law. It also suggests a model for how the state might continue to rationalize the Chinese court system.

What is especially noteworthy is that the United States did not press China to create these tribunals, since it placed no confidence in their potential to enforce IPR; furthermore, the United States demanded measures like campaigns, which would quickly deliver a high volume of enforcement. The evolution of the IPR tribunals suggests that pressure and crisis may be counterproductive for the development of rationalized enforcement.

COMPARATIVE PERSPECTIVES ON COURTS

As part of this book's systematic comparison of China's IPR enforcement record with that of five other countries, this section discusses the record of court protection of IPR in Russia, Taiwan, and the United States; unfortunately, I was unable to find a source that reports the number of civil IPR cases in the Czech Republic or France. Table 4.4 presents statistics on the number of civil IPR cases handled by the courts in China, Russia, Taiwan, and the United States in 2004.

TABLE 4.4. *Cross-National Statistics on First-Instance Civil IPR Cases Terminated in 2004 (per million people)*

Country	Piracy Rate	Civil Court Cases (first instance)	Noncourt Enforcement	Noncourt Enforcement: Civil Court Cases Ratio
China	High	7.2	904	128.1
Russia	High	5.2	24.5	2.8
Taiwan	Medium	16.5	260.9	15.7
U.S.	Low	32.5	26	0.8

Source: Yearbooks.

---

[31] *International Intellectual Property Alliance 2006 Special 301 Report*, 111, www.iipa.com (accessed March 20, 2006).

Russia

There are three types of courts in Russia: courts of general jurisdiction (*sudy obshchei iurisdiktsii*) that handle disputes between natural persons, specialized commercial courts (*arbitrazhnye sudy*) that have jurisdiction over disputes between juridical persons, and justice-of-the-peace courts (*treteiskie sudy*) that accept small claims. The courts of general jurisdiction and justice-of-the-peace courts are plagued by local protectionism and suffer the well-documented burden of poorly qualified and corrupt judges,[32] whereas the *arbitrazh* (commercial) courts are more professional and less corrupt.[33] As most IPR cases involve disputes between two business entities, they are accepted by the *arbitrazh* courts.[34] There are four tiers in the *arbitrazh* court system: eighty-one *arbitrazh* courts for the subjects of the federation,[35] twenty appellate *arbitrazh* courts, ten cassation *arbitrazh* courts, and one Supreme Arbitrazh Court.

What is the volume of IPR cases in Russia? Available statistics reveal that the number of first-instance cases increased eight times between 1997 and 2005, indicating a steadily growing reliance on the courts for resolving IPR disputes.[36] In 2005, Russia made an earnest bid to join the WTO, and the government consequently placed an emphasis on IPR protection. This new attention to IPR was reflected in the judicial caseload statistics as well: between 2005 and 2007, there was an 83 percent increase in the IPR cases handled by the *arbitrazh* courts (see Table 4.5). Historically, Russia had a lower caseload than China, but the 2006–2007 increases in litigation now put the two countries on a par.

Although we do not have detailed statistics on the types of IPR cases handled by Russian courts prior to 2006, we know that in the first half of 2006 copyright cases accounted for 65.1 percent of the caseload, patent cases for 3.7 percent, and trade names and trademark cases for 27.7 percent.[37] We similarly lack systematic data on the regional variation of the IPR caseload, but interview

---

[32] Peter H. Solomon and Todd S. Foglesong, *Courts and Transition in Russia: The Challenge of Judicial Reform* (Boulder, CO: Westview Press, 2000); Pamela Jordan, *Defending Rights in Russia: Lawyers, the State, and Legal Reform in the Post-Soviet Era* (Vancouver: UBC Press, 2005).

[33] Kathryn Hendley, "Temporal and Regional Patterns of Commercial Litigation in Post-Soviet Russia," *Post-Soviet Geography and Economics* 39:7 (1998), 379–398; Kathryn Hendley, "Enforcing Judgments in Russian Economic Courts," *Post-Soviet Affairs* 20:1 (2004), 46–82; Kathryn Hendley, "Accelerated Process in the Russian *Arbitrazh* Courts," *Problems of Post-Communism* 52:6 (2005), 21–31.

[34] Courts of general jurisdiction have jurisdiction over IPR cases involving natural persons (nonbusiness entities). However, no statistics have been compiled about these cases. Available evidence indicates that such cases are very rare and that *arbitrazh* courts account for the bulk of IPR judicial activity in Russia.

[35] A subject of the federation in Russia is equivalent to a state in the United States. Russia had eighty-three subjects of the federation in 2008.

[36] We have no data about the IPR caseload of the *arbitrazh* courts prior to 1997.

[37] *Otchët o rabote arbitrazhnykh sudov sub"ektov Rossiiskoi Federatsii (svodnyi)* (Consolidated Report on the Activity of *Arbitrazh* Courts in the Russian Federation), http://www.arbitr.ru/news/totals/index.htm (accessed November 7, 2006), 3. The remaining 3.5 percent of the IPR caseload is made up of "other" IPR cases.

TABLE 4.5. *First-Instance IPR Cases Handled by Russian* Arbitrazh *Courts, 1997–2007*

Year	First-Instance Cases
1997	121
1998	202
1999	ND
2000	289
2001	271
2002	376
2003	466
2004	751
2005	999
2006	1,455
2007	1,831

Sources: www.arbitr.ru/news/total/97–98/move.htm (1997–1998 data); www.arbitr.ru/news/totals/2000/1inst/2-detail.htm (2000 data); and www.arbitr.ru/news/totals/2001/1inst/2-detail.htm (2001 data); www.arbitr.ru (2002–2005 data) (all accessed July 5, 2006); http://www.arbitr.ru/_upimg/0B0FA167A2880E62B12BDCE80B1C4C08_осн_показатели_2007.pdf (accessed May 1, 2008).

evidence suggests that Moscow receives the lion's share of *arbitrazh* cases.[38] This should be no surprise: IPR caseloads are very sensitive to levels of wealth and FDI, and Moscow is the largest recipient of FDI in Russia, as well as one of the wealthiest regions in the country.[39]

Are IPR cases adjudicated consistently, transparently, and fairly? Judicial specialization can enhance consistency, but Russia has no judges who specialize in IPR, let alone separate IPR tribunals within its *arbitrazh* courts. This means that luck of the draw usually determines which judge will decide on the complex matters arising in IPR litigation. Unfortunately, as my interviewees indicate, even among the relatively well-qualified judges staffing the *arbitrazh* courts there are widely varying degrees of legal knowledge and willingness to extract or accept bribes. Corruption and the lack of judicial specialization present significant impediments to the rise of consistent adjudication.

It is difficult to assess transparency because there are no statistics on the number of IPR cases that are subject to open trials. Under Russian law, access to court hearings is in theory open to anyone, with the final judgment to be made publicly available. In practice, however, court access is greatly circumscribed. My own efforts to be admitted to a hearing at the Moscow *arbitrazh* court proved futile. In contrast to China, Russian courts maintain no Web sites

[38] Russia Interviews 020524B, 020527A, 020527B, 020527C, and 020610, all with IPR lawyers (Moscow).

[39] In any given year, Moscow receives at least 50 percent of the FDI entering Russia. See, for example, *Rossiiskii statisticheskii yezhegodnik 2005* (Russian Statistical Yearbook 2005) (Moskva: Goskomstat Rossii, 2005).

containing decisions on IPR cases and publish few IPR compendia. In sum, the level of transparency in Russia is lower than in China.

What do appeals statistics tell us about the fairness of adjudication? In Russia, there are three stages of appeal: an initial appeal handled by the twenty appellate *arbitrazh* courts, cassation (second-stage appeal) handled by the ten cassation courts, and final appeal handled by the Supreme *Arbitrazh* Court. Available statistics indicate that in the first half of 2006, the appellate courts handled ninety-four IPR cases (12.8 percent of the first-instance cases handled during the same period), and the cassation courts handled ninety-three cases, suggesting that virtually every case that was appealed once also went through a second appeal.[40] No data are available on the number of cases handled by the Supreme *Arbitrazh* Court. The appeals rate for IPR cases is slightly higher than the overall appeals rate for other types of *arbitrazh* cases.[41] Interviewees have not indicated that appeals are constrained. Therefore, we can provisionally conclude that the *arbitrazh* courts meet some of the requirements for procedural fairness. However, the presence of at least some corrupt *arbitrazh* court judges, who maintain a "price list" for favorable decisions in different types of cases, prevents us from concluding that procedural fairness is fully developed.[42] In addition, doubts about the consistency and transparency of adjudication call into question the overall quality of civil IPR enforcement in Russia.

Taiwan

Taiwan's judiciary is organized into twenty-two district courts (*difang fayuan*), the Taiwan High Court (Taiwan gaodeng fayuan), and the Supreme Court (Zuigao fayuan).[43] IPR protection is a priority in Taiwan, as revealed by the very high volume of Customs, administrative, and criminal enforcement. Nevertheless, until recently, Taiwan had no specialized IPR court, even though judicial experts and practitioners had been discussing the creation of such a court since the late 1990s. Disagreements on jurisdictional questions have impeded decisive action: the Ministry of Justice felt that the court should have islandwide jurisdiction over all criminal cases, a proposal rejected by the

---

[40] *Otchët o rabote arbitrazhnykh apelliatsionnykh sudov* (Report on the Activity of the Appellate *Arbitrazh* Courts), http://www.arbitr.ru/news/totals/index.htm (accessed November 8, 2006); *Otchët o rabote federal'nykh arbitrazhnykh sudov okrugov* (Report on the Activity of the Federal *Okrug Arbitrazh* Courts), http://www.arbitr.ru/news/totals/index.htm (accessed November 8, 2006).

[41] The appeals rate has fallen in recent years. In 2001, first-instance *arbitrazh* courts handled 271 IPR cases, 105 of which (38.7 percent) were appealed, www.arbitr.ru/news/totals/2001/1inst/2-detail.htm and www.arbitr.ru/news/totals/2001/1inst/3-detail.htm(accessed November 8, 2006).

[42] Higher bribes are required for cases with larger potential damage awards. Russia Interview 060113B, with an IPR lawyer (Moscow).

[43] The Taiwan High Court has branches in Taichung, Tainan, Kaohsiung, and Hualien. In addition, although there is no Fukien High Court, Taiwan has created the Fukien High Court Kinmen Branch Court. There is a separate system of appellate administrative courts (three administrative high courts and a Supreme Administrative Court). See www.judicial.gov.tw (accessed November 7, 2006).

TABLE 4.6. *Civil IPR Cases Terminated in Taiwanese Courts in 2004*

Court Level	Copyright Cases	Patent Cases	Trademark Cases	Total
District court	125	168	87	380
High court	22	30	25	77
Supreme court	2	13	10	25
Total	149	211	122	482
Total (per million people)	5.4	9.2	5.3	20.9

Note: Population 23 million.
Source: Sifa tongji nianbao 2004 (Taiwan Judicial Statistics Yearbook 2004) (Taipei: Sifa tongji chu, 2005), 3.14, 6.19, 8.32.

Judicial Yuan on the grounds that this would require taking all criminal suspects to Taipei to be arraigned, in violation of their civil rights.[44] In 2006, the two sides seemed to have reached a compromise that the IPR court would have appellate jurisdiction over criminal cases and full jurisdiction over all civil cases.[45] The court eventually opened doors in July 2008, after passage of the relevant legislation by the Legislative Yuan.[46] This court will doubtlessly increase legal professionalism and raise the consistency of adjudication in IPR cases.

Table 4.6 presents statistics on civil IPR cases terminated in 2004 at all levels of the Taiwanese judicial system. Cross-national comparisons cast Taiwan's record in a positive light. Although Taiwanese courts handle fewer IPR cases per million people than U.S. courts, they are more active than their counterparts in both China and Russia. Another important achievement is evidenced by the fact that 60.5 percent of the first-instance civil IPR cases reached trial in Taiwan, a rate that is almost thirty times higher than the proportion of IPR cases reaching trial in U.S. courts and 50 percent higher than the proportion of second-instance IPR cases that were concluded with a court judgment in China.[47] For a place like Taiwan, where there has been a traditional emphasis on mediation and out-of-court settlement, the high ratio of cases heard by panels of judges is indicative of the growing importance of the courts and of a significant movement toward transparent enforcement.

Is court protection of IPR in Taiwan of a high quality? We lack specific data on appeals, but we can impute them from the data presented in Table 4.6. We know that the Taiwan High Court and the Supreme Court almost never serve as

[44] Taiwan Interview 060330, with an IPR lawyer (Taipei).
[45] Taiwan Interview 060327A, with an employee of the American Institute in Taiwan (Taipei).
[46] Thibault Worth, "Taiwan Established IPR Court" (July 2, 2008), http://www.billboard.biz/bbbiz/content_display/industry/e3ib9d450805b496f0eca77d5cbfe3e2e0b (accessed October 24, 2008).
[47] *Sifa tongji nianbao* 2004 (Taiwan Judicial Statistics Yearbook 2004) (Taipei: Sifa tongji chu, 2005), 8.32. As mentioned earlier, we lack statistics on the proportion of first-instance IPR cases concluded with a court trial in China.

courts of first instance. Therefore, we can assume that virtually all High Court and Supreme Court cases will be second- and third-instance cases, thus producing appeals rates of 20 percent (for first-instance cases) and 30 percent (for second-instance cases), respectively. In order to determine whether this rate is low, normal, or high, we would have to compare it with the appeals rate for other civil cases, which is not available. However, interview evidence suggests that clients worry not about the consistency, transparency, or fairness of judicial decisions in Taiwan, but rather about the slow movement of their cases through the system.[48] Overall, the high caliber of IPR enforcement in Taiwanese courts represents a major achievement for a place that has had no longstanding tradition of rule of law, and that until a few decades ago was known as the major IPR pirate in Asia.[49]

The United States

The case of the U.S. courts helps frame our analysis of the Chinese case. What is the volume of civil IPR cases handled by U.S. courts? In line with general litigiousness trends, the United States has the highest IPR caseload of any of the four places for which we have data. The actual number of civil IPR cases handled by the courts may be even higher, since we possess systematic data only for the caseload of the federal courts, even though both federal and state courts have jurisdiction over IPR.[50] Typically, most copyright, trademark, and patent disputes fall under the jurisdiction of federal courts. However, state courts do handle some trademark-related matters, like unfair competition and passing off nontrademark goods as trademark goods. Although state court cases are relatively rare, the data in Table 4.7 probably understate somewhat the rate of IPR litigation in the United States. Nevertheless, the volume of litigation is very high, especially when compared with that in China, Taiwan, or Russia.

What about the quality of civil enforcement? Although we lack for the U.S. courts the kinds of data that help us measure consistency, transparency, and fairness of IPR enforcement in developing countries, it is common knowledge that U.S. courts are dispensing high-quality justice. In this regard, it bears mentioning that in the United States civil litigation is by far the preferred method of IPR dispute resolution: as we will discover in subsequent chapters, right holders in the United States only very rarely look to administrative or criminal enforcement for redress. The United States is also important because of its potential to serve as a model of IPR protection for China. Although China did not decide to establish its IPR tribunals under U.S. pressure, Chinese legal

---

[48] Taiwan Interviews 000629B, 000703, and 060330, all with IPR lawyers (Taipei).

[49] Andy Sun, *From Pirate King to Jungle King: Transformation of Taiwan's Intellectual Property Protection* (Baltimore: School of Law, University of Maryland, 1997). For an illuminating account of the processes that led to the emergence of the courts as more active players in Taiwan, see Alford, *To Steal a Book Is an Elegant Offense*, 95–111.

[50] New York, doubtless as a consequence of the high rate of IPR litigation there, is one state that has recently begun to compile systematic data on IPR cases.

TABLE 4.7. *U.S. Civil IPR Cases (April 1, 2004–March 31, 2005)*

	Cases Commenced	Cases Terminated	Cases Reaching Court Trial (number)	Cases Reaching Court Trial (%)
Copyright	2,653	3,319	40	1.2
Patent	2,978	2,804	107	3.8
Trademark	3,706	3,509	48	1.4
TOTAL	10,932	9,632	195	2
TOTAL (per million people)	37	32.5	0.6	

Note: 2005 statistics apply to the 12-month period prior to March 31, 2005. The U.S. population for 2005 is estimated at 296 million, http://www.census.gov/popest/states/NST-ann-est.html (accessed October 23, 2006).

Source: Federal Judicial Caseload Statistics 2005, http://www.uscourts.gov/caseload2005/contents.html (accessed October 23, 2006).

scholars do pay close attention to the role of the courts in protecting IPR in the United States.

CONCLUSION

The recent emergence of the courts as an important avenue for IPR protection in China is significant, both in relation to other countries (such as Russia) and in relation to China's own legal development. In the 1980s and the early 1990s, Chinese courts had poorly qualified judges, who handed down arbitrary judgments that were not made public and could not be appealed. The government's decision in the mid-1990s to create specialized IPR tribunals within the existing court system and to staff them with the best and the brightest among China's judges represents a major step toward high-quality enforcement. To be sure, these IPR tribunals today handle a relatively small caseload, but they are providing enforcement that is consistent, transparent, and fair. China's experience with these tribunals illustrates how the state can play a decisive role in nurturing institutions capable of supplying rationalized enforcement.

What can we learn from China's modest success in judicial protection of IPR? As we look ahead to the next chapter, we should note that it is of course easier for the state to carve out a pocket of model enforcement within an already existing system, or even to create an altogether new administrative agency, than to coordinate the enforcement activities of established bureaucracies with overlapping jurisdictions. Bureaucratic expansion is usually welcomed, whereas the successful coordination of multiple enforcers with overlapping mandates is unpopular with bureaucrats because it entails a curtailing of bureaucratic powers and a corresponding reduction of personnel and budgets. This caveat is not meant to detract from China's successful protection of IPR through the specialized tribunals, but rather to suggest that the state's regulatory innovations will be most effective if they are taken up as a model that is replicated in other parts of the enforcement regime.

5

Administrative Enforcement

The Complex State

Administrative agencies play a much larger role in IPR enforcement in China than do the civil courts discussed in the previous chapter. In Chapter 3, we analyzed the activity of Customs, an administrative agency that has a relatively clear enforcement portfolio because of its focus on the border protection of IPR. The enforcement situation is much more complex for IPR administrative protection *internally* within individual countries. In China, more than a dozen agencies have general or specialized jurisdiction over the administrative protection of IPR. This chapter introduces these agencies, provides data about the volume of their enforcement activity, and compares them with similar agencies in the other five countries analyzed in this book. For reasons of clarity, I note that when I refer to *administrative enforcement*, I mean enforcement provided by these agencies. *Nonadministrative enforcement* refers to the enforcement supplied by the courts, by the police, and, at the border, by Customs.[1]

Table 5.1 presents a snapshot of cross-national administrative enforcement efforts in 2004. It provides aggregate statistics on the work of the courts, Customs, the police, and all administrative agencies with an IPR enforcement portfolio. The enforcement effort of these agencies is measured as enforcement cases per million people. Several patterns are immediately apparent. In most countries there is relative parity between administrative and nonadministrative enforcement. There are two exceptions to this rule. In the United States, administrative agencies are virtually never used to provide enforcement, as reflected in the 1:585 ratio of administrative to nonadministrative enforcement. The other exception is China, where the ratio is reversed, with cases of administrative enforcement outnumbering cases of nonadministrative enforcement by a hundredfold. Two related points from the table are especially relevant for

---

[1] Technically, Chinese Customs is an administrative enforcer. However, its exclusive jurisdiction over one type of IPR enforcement (border protection) sets it apart from the administrative agencies responsible for internal IPR protection. These agencies tend to share their enforcement portfolios with other agencies, as well as with the courts and the police.

TABLE 5.1. *Cross-National Administrative Enforcement Efforts in 2004*

Country	Piracy Rate	Administrative Enforcement (per million people)	Ratio of Administrative to Nonadministrative Enforcement	Number of Enforcement Agencies
China	High	939	106.7:1	12
Russia	High	10	1:2	5
Taiwan	Medium	63.2	1:3.4	4
Czech	Medium	201.5	1.4:1	3
France	Medium	45.2	1:3.2	2
USA	Low	0.1	1:585	1

Note: The absence of civil court enforcement data from the Czech Republic and France skews the ratio in favor of administrative enforcement.
Source: Yearbooks.

understanding the organization of administrative enforcement in China. Among the six countries China has the most "saturated" IPR portfolio, with at least twelve different agencies having IPR enforcement responsibilities. Second, China's administrative enforcement rate is the highest in the group of six, standing at 939 cases per million people in 2004. Entrenched myths about the unwillingness of the Chinese government to enforce IPR laws do not stand up to empirical scrutiny.

This chapter begins with an examination of the IPR enforcement agencies in China, grouped by subtypes (patents, trademarks, and copyrights). Thereafter, China's record is compared with those of Russia, Taiwan, the Czech Republic, France, and the United States. The chapter concludes with reflections on the interplay between administrative and nonadministrative enforcement in the six countries examined in this study.

ADMINISTRATIVE ENFORCEMENT OPTIONS IN CHINA

What agencies provide administrative enforcement of IPR laws in China? Existing research identifies only a handful of bureaucracies. In contrast, this chapter demonstrates that a range of administrative agencies have IPR responsibilities. Table 5.2 presents 2004 national-level enforcement statistics for nine of these agencies.

One characteristic of administrative enforcement should be mentioned at the outset. With the exception of patent administrative enforcement, which falls exclusively in the domain of the State Intellectual Property Office, IPR administrative enforcement in China is marked by significant jurisdictional overlap. Six agencies have responsibilities for enforcement in the area of trademarks, and five agencies share the copyright enforcement portfolio. This overlap presents significant problems for coordination of the work of the enforcers and for the emergence of predictable, rationalized enforcement. In this chapter,

TABLE 5.2. *Administrative Enforcement in China in 2004*

Agency	Total Cases
State Intellectual Property Office	3,734
State Administration for Industry and Commerce	51,851
Administration of Quality Supervision, Inspection, and Quarantine	315,683
Ministry of Health	74,521
State Food and Drug Administration	415,000
State Tobacco Monopoly Administration	269,000
Ministry of Agriculture	50,000
National Copyright Administration of China	9,497
General Administration of Press and Publications	Unknown
Ministry of Culture	Unknown
State Administration of Radio, Film, and Television	Unknown
Anti-Pornography and Anti-Piracy Office	31,862
TOTAL	1,221,148
Enforcement cases per million people	939

Note: Agencies with "unknown" caseload only disclose the total value of their seizures of pirated goods, not the number of discrete enforcement cases they handled in 2004.
Source: Yearbooks.

I describe the complex organization of IPR enforcement by presenting select material on the evolution of individual agencies with an IPR portfolio. Chapters 7–9 provide case studies of the operation of this complex enforcement apparatus on the ground.

PATENT ADMINISTRATIVE ENFORCEMENT

Unlike the trademark and copyright enforcement portfolios, which are shared by a number of agencies, the technical complexity of patent protection has served as a barrier to the entry of multiple bureaucracies in this enforcement domain. For that reason, the State Intellectual Property Office (SIPO) is the only administrative agency with jurisdiction over patent matters in China today. The SIPO (Guojia zhishi chanquan ju) grew out of the State Patent Office (Zhongguo zhuanli ju), which was created in 1980.[2] When the State Patent Office was renamed the State Intellectual Property Office in 1998, it was simultaneously elevated to vice-ministerial rank as an "organization directly subordinate to the State Council" (*Guowuyuan zhishu jigou*). The SIPO is a small bureaucracy: in 1998, it was allotted only eighty central-level staff in Beijing.[3]

[2] *Zhonghua renmin gongheguo zhengfu jigou wushi nian* (Government Organizations of the PRC over Fifty Years) (Beijing: Dangjian duwu chubanshe and Guojia xingzheng xueyuan chubanshe, 2000), 156–157.
[3] *Zhongyang zhengfu zuzhi jigou 1998* (Central Government Organs 1998) (Beijing: Gaige chubanshe, 2000), 435.

Officially, the SIPO is responsible for the administration of all subtypes of IPR. However, this is not what happens in practice. Although the SIPO represents China in international meetings of patent and trademark offices, within China its enforcement responsibilities are limited to patent protection.[4] It handles applications for patent approval, reexamination, and invalidation. In addition, it is responsible for enforcement in cases of patent infringement disputes, patent counterfeiting, and patent passing off. As will be demonstrated in Chapter 9, the SIPO has concentrated its enforcement activity in areas where it has exclusive jurisdiction (patent counterfeiting and patent passing off) and has deemphasized enforcement in cases of patent infringement, where the courts have jurisdiction as well and have emerged as the dominant providers of enforcement. A clear division of responsibilities between the courts and the SIPO (enshrined in law) has created a predictable patent enforcement environment.

In addition to its patent enforcement responsibilities, the SIPO has begun establishing IPR Protection and Assistance Centers. As of 2008, there were plans to open a total of forty-two such centers in provincial capitals and large cities.[5] These centers would function as complaint clearinghouses, which would supplement (and overlap with) the fifty IPR complaint centers (*zhishi chanquan jubao tousu zhongxin*) established by the Market Order Rectification and Standardization Offices (MOROs) of the Ministry of Commerce.[6]

TRADEMARK ADMINISTRATIVE ENFORCEMENT

In contrast to the SIPO's exclusive jurisdiction over certain types of patent administrative enforcement, trademark enforcement is not the exclusive domain of any enforcement bureaucracy. At least six agencies share the trademark portfolio: the State Administration for Industry and Commerce (SAIC); the General Administration of Quality Supervision, Inspection, and Quarantine (AQSIQ); the Ministry of Health (MOH); the State Food and Drug Administration (SFDA); the State Tobacco Monopoly Administration (STMA); and the Ministry of Agriculture (MOA).[7] The SAIC and the AQSIQ are generalist agencies, which can handle any trademark counterfeiting case. The other agencies have more specialized mandates: the MOH and the SFDA focus on food, pharmaceuticals, and cosmetics; the STMA deals only with counterfeit tobacco products; and the MOA focuses on counterfeit agricultural inputs.

---

[4] In some places like Shenzhen, the intellectual property office has been merged with the copyright office and enforces in both patents and copyrights. However, even in Shenzhen trademark enforcement is not within the purview of the intellectual property office.

[5] U.S. Department of Commerce and International Trade Administration, *China IPR News for U.S. Industry*, October 8, 2008, 2.

[6] Ibid.

[7] Several additional agencies have only peripheral responsibility for trademark enforcement. They are discussed in Chapter 7.

The State Administration for Industry and Commerce and the General Administration of Quality Supervision, Inspection, and Quarantine

Historically, the SAIC (Guojia gongshang xingzheng guanli ju) and the AQSIQ (Guojia zhiliang jiandu jianyan jianyi zongju) were given primary responsibility for trademark anticounterfeiting. The SAIC has existed since 1954, when it was established to manage private enterprises.[8] Currently, it has a wide regulatory mandate, ranging from enterprise registration and supervision to trademark registration, fair trade, consumer protection, and the regulation of advertising. It participates in anticounterfeiting on three grounds. First, trademark infringement and counterfeiting constitute unfair competition. Second, counterfeits lead to consumer confusion and deception, in addition to having a negative impact on consumer health and safety. Finally, counterfeits are often sold through false or misleading advertising. On these grounds, a total of four different departments within the SAIC have overlapping mandates over counterfeiting matters: the Fair Trade Department, the Consumer Protection Department, the Advertisement Supervision Department, and the Enforcement Team. Although it is a relatively small entity with only 260 personnel at the central level, the SAIC penetrates all the way down to the township level.[9]

Like the SAIC, the AQSIQ has existed in some form since 1954, when the State Metrology Administration (Guojia jiliang ju) was established. Over the course of a single year, the portfolio of the administration expanded by adding both standards and quality certification and supervision to its original mandate. By 1988, it had been transformed into the Administration of Technical Supervision (Guojia jishu jiandu ju), which addressed counterfeiting issues by virtue of its quality-supervision mandate.[10] The 1998 round of government reform led to its restructuring as the Administration of Quality and Technical Supervision (Guojia zhiliang jishu jiandu ju), which was allotted 180 personnel.[11] In an attempt to resolve the problem of overlap, the State Council limited the administration's IPR mandate to supervision over goods during the production and transportation stages. Once goods entered the stream of commerce, supervision was reserved for the SAIC (as we will see in subsequent chapters, the two administrations do not abide by this official division of responsibility).[12] The final step in the institutional evolution of the administration occurred in 2001, when it was merged with the Administration for Entry-Exit Inspection and Quarantine (Guojia churujing jianyan jianyi ju), which at that time was a part

---

[8] *Zhonghua renmin gongheguo zhengfu jigou wushi nian*, 147–148.
[9] *Zhongyang zhengfu zuzhi jigou 1998*, 405; China Interview 080103, with an employee of the Zouping Administration for Industry and Commerce (Zouping).
[10] *Zhonghua renmin gongheguo zhengfu jigou wushi nian*, 152–155.
[11] *Zhongyang zhengfu zuzhi jigou 1998*, 426.
[12] *Zhongyang zhengfu zuzhi jigou 1998*, 406, 426.

of the General Administration of Customs (GAC).[13] After the merger, the administration acquired its current name (the AQSIQ).

Three departments within the AQSIQ presently have jurisdiction over cases of counterfeiting: the Quality, Standardization, and Metrology Department, the Anticounterfeiting Office (Dajia ban), and the Enforcement Team. A lot of hope was placed in the anticounterfeiting offices, which were created in 2001, in the aftermath of a series of consumer protection scandals. These offices, which were housed within the AQSIQ at every level of its administrative hierarchy, were supposed to help rationalize trademark enforcement. The offices had the task of coordinating the enforcement activities of the large number of bureaucracies with IPR portfolios, including the AQSIQ itself. However, the anticounterfeiting offices had a bureaucratic rank no higher than that of a department within the AQSIQ. Not surprisingly, therefore, they were unable to coordinate the work of agencies that outranked them. Today, many of those offices have been abolished or else exist only as ghost bureaucratic entities. Their activities have been partly assumed by the MOROs under the Ministry of Commerce.

Although the SAIC is officially designated as the chief enforcer in cases of counterfeiting, statistics I have gathered indicate that in practice the AQSIQ provides a volume of enforcement several times higher than that supplied by the SAIC. For example, in 2004, the SAIC handled 51,851 cases of trademark counterfeiting[14] and seized counterfeit goods with a value of 1.2 billion yuan.[15] In the same year, the AQSIQ handled 315,683 cases of counterfeit and substandard goods and seized counterfeits worth 3.067 billion yuan.[16] The performance of the AQSIQ is especially impressive in the area of foodstuffs and liquor (over 80,000 cases investigated in 2004), as well as in the area of agricultural inputs (almost 50,000 cases accepted for investigation).[17]

The Ministry of Health and the State Food and Drug Administration

The MOH (Weisheng bu) and the SFDA (Guojia shipin yaopin jiandu guanli ju) are intimately linked entities that share a common organizational history. The

---

[13] The Administration for Entry-Exit Inspection and Quarantine was responsible for substandard goods entering or leaving the country (substandard goods can be IPR-infringing goods as well). The administration was a relatively large bureaucracy with 180 central-level staff (*Zhongyang zhengfu zuzhi jigou 1998*, 368). Currently, entry-exit personnel are found only at the central and provincial levels and have no presence at the prefectural and county levels (China Interview 080107B, with employees of the Zouping Technical Supervision Bureau [Zouping]).

[14] *Zhongguo zhishi chanquan nianjian 2005* (China IPR Yearbook 2005) (Beijing: Zhishi chanquan chubanshe, 2005), 297–298.

[15] *2005 nian quanguo chachu shangbiao weifa anjian jiben qingkuang* (Basic Situation of Trademark Counterfeiting Investigations in 2005) (April 27, 2006), http://www.saic.gov.cn/ggl/zwgg_detail.asp?newsid=396 (accessed November 10, 2006).

[16] *Zhongguo zhiliang jiandu jianyan jianyi nianjian 2005* (Yearbook of the General Administration of Quality Supervision, Inspection, and Quarantine of the People's Republic of China) (Beijing: Zhongguo biaozhun chubanshe, 2005), 192–193.

[17] *Zhongguo zhiliang jiandu jianyan jianyi nianjian 2005*, 192–193.

MOH was created in 1949 and subsequently went through several rounds of reorganization, the most important of which dealt with its mandate to regulate frequently counterfeited items such as pharmaceuticals, traditional Chinese medicines, medical devices, food, medical food, and cosmetics.[18] A significant change occurred in 1998, when the approval, registration, and safety supervision of pharmaceuticals, traditional Chinese medicines, and medical devices were transferred to the newly created State Drug Administration (SDA), a vice-ministerial agency directly subordinate to the State Council.[19] In 2003, responsibility for supervision over the quality and safety of food, health food, and cosmetics was removed from the MOH and given to the SDA, which had just been renamed the State Food and Drug Administration. Thereafter, the SFDA had responsibility for enforcement in cases of food, health food, cosmetics, pharmaceuticals, and medical-device counterfeiting. Nevertheless, the MOH continued to provide enforcement for all of those product groups as well. This overlap existed until 2008, when the two agencies were merged into an expanded MOH. As a result of data limitations, my discussion of enforcement does not cover the period after this merger.

Prior to the 2008 merger, the MOH was a ministerial-level agency, whereas the SFDA was a vice-ministerial-level agency. The MOH had a central-level staff of 225, and the SFDA a central-level staff of 120.[20] The two agencies had the same reach (down to the county level), although the MOH had a decentralized structure, whereas the SFDA, in principle, had established a system of vertical management from the province down to the county, similar to that of the SAIC and the AQSIQ.[21] Both the MOH and the SFDA had enforcement teams that handled counterfeiting cases, among other matters.

The regulation of pharmaceuticals is one area where the enforcement mandates of the MOH and the SFDA overlapped. In 2004, the SFDA investigated 285,000 cases of pharmaceutical and medical-device counterfeiting with a total value of 446 million yuan. Enforcement actions led to the confiscation of counterfeits worth 152 million yuan, as well as the revocation of licenses and destruction of underground production facilities.[22] Officially, no data were reported on the enforcement activity of the MOH in the area of pharmaceutical counterfeiting. However, data on Viagra counterfeiting presented in Chapter 9

[18] *Zhonghua renmin gongheguo zhengfu jigou wushi nian*, 129–130.
[19] In 1978, a predecessor to the SFDA called the General Administration on Medicines (Guojia yiyao guanli zongju) was created. This entity was directly subordinate to the State Council, but the MOH managed it on behalf of the State Council (*daiguan*). The General Administration on Medicines was in charge of regulating the production and use of Western and traditional Chinese medicines, as well as medical appliances. Although in 1982 it was formally integrated into the MOH hierarchy, in 1998 it again was split off from it.
[20] *Zhongyang zhengfu zuzhi jigou 1998*, 329, 421.
[21] China Interview 020130D, with the head of the Foreign and Legal Affairs Department of the Shanghai Municipal Drug Administration (Shanghai).
[22] *Zhongguo shipin yaopin jiandu guanli nianjian 2005* (State Food and Drug Administration Yearbook 2005) (Beijing: Huaxue gongye chubanshe, 2005), 213.

reveal that the MOH continued to be involved with pharmaceuticals, as were several other bureaucracies apart from the SFDA.[23]

A similar overlap can be observed in the case of traditional Chinese medicines. Technically, the Administration for Traditional Chinese Medicine (Guojia zhongyiyao guanli ju), a subsidiary organization of the MOH, was supposed to have responsibility for enforcement in this domain.[24] However, the SFDA handled the registration, approval, and safety of traditional Chinese medicines, whereas the National Development and Reform Commission had responsibility for the overall management of the traditional Chinese medicines industry. In essence, all three agencies regulated this industry, and two (the MOH and the SFDA) had enforcement responsibility as well. The same kind of regulatory and enforcement overlap existed in the area of cosmetics counterfeiting, where both the SFDA and the MOH have enforcement responsibility.

Another important area where the responsibilities of the MOH and the SFDA overlapped is food regulation. In 2004, MOH authorities conducted 74,521 food checks and confiscated and destroyed 207 tons of expired, adulterated, and substandard food. Administrative punishments were levied against 74,521 businesses, and fines in the amount of 927,490 yuan were imposed.[25] In the same year, inspectors from the SFDA conducted 391,509 checks of illegal food activities with a total value of 1.47 billion yuan (US$200 million). As a result of these checks, 130,000 cases of food counterfeiting were accepted for investigation (*li'an chachu*).[26]

Such overlap between agencies makes the coordination of enforcement difficult and leads to ambiguity as to who should enforce. Ambiguity can facilitate foot dragging and shirking of responsibility, as illustrated by the 2004 Fuyang baby formula case, in which the negligence of the multiple enforcers led to the deaths of at least twelve babies.[27] In the wake of the scandal, a series of coordination meetings were held in an attempt to iron out the respective responsibilities of the various agencies with an enforcement portfolio over food (the MOH, the SFDA, the SAIC, the AQSIQ, Customs, and the police). The

---

[23] Aggregate data also reveal the continued involvement of the MOH in food and pharmaceuticals anticounterfeiting because the MOH and SFDA structures were still merged at the county levels (though they should have been separate after 1998), thus resulting in a double counting of enforcement activity.

[24] The Administration for Traditional Chinese Medicine is a small bureaucratic entity with 71 central-level staff. This decentralized bureaucracy has formal penetration only to the provincial level. It is usually located at the provincial Health Department, rather than having independent offices. *Zhongyang zhengfu zuzhi jigou 1998*, 334. See also http://www.satcm.gov.cn/ (accessed November 11, 2006).

[25] *Zhongguo weisheng nianjian 2005* (China Health Yearbook 2005) (Beijing: Renmin weisheng chubanshe, 2005), 245.

[26] *Zhongguo shipin yaopin jiandu guanli nianjian 2005*, 102; *Zhongguo weisheng tongji nianjian 2005* (China Health Statistics Yearbook 2005) (Beijing: Zhongguo xiehe yike daxue chubanshe, 2005), 315.

[27] Waikeung Tam and Dali Yang, "Food Safety and the Development of Regulatory Institutions in China," *Asian Perspective* 29:4 (2005), 5–36.

meetings also focused on the prevention of both shirking and duplicative enforcement. With enforcement in the area of food safety by at least six distinct bureaucracies, successful coordination has proven impossible to achieve thus far.[28] In this light, the 2008 merger of the SFDA into the MOH is almost certainly a step in the right direction, although it is worrying that it may put an end to the SFDA's partially centralized management of its offices from the provincial down to the county level.

The State Tobacco Monopoly Administration

The STMA (Guojia yancao zhuanmai ju) is essentially a major corporation that also wears the hat of a regulatory agency. In principle, the STMA is supposed to exercise management supervision over the China National Tobacco Corporation (CNTC) (Zhongguo yancao zonggongsi). Yet in practice the CNTC and the STMA share the same offices and personnel and function as one and the same entity. Prior to the 1980s, the tobacco industry consisted of dispersed companies that held regional monopolies and impeded the creation of an integrated national cigarette market. In order to introduce the benefits of economies of scale, the State Council established the CNTC in 1982. In 1984, the CNTC was reorganized into the STMA, a bureau-level agency supervised by the National Development and Reform Commission. In 1998, the STMA was allotted 210 personnel at the central level.[29]

With a centralized structure that reaches down to the county level, provincial-, prefecture-, and county-level tobacco monopoly administrations are under the dual leadership of the STMA and their respective local governments, with the STMA assuming primary leadership responsibilities.[30] The STMA has a broad mandate, which includes monopoly administration of the production, sale, importation, and exportation of tobacco leaf and tobacco products, as well as the regulation of the use of tobacco machines. The IPR mandate of the STMA is based on both trademark and consumer protection laws, as well as on a series of special laws and regulations on the production and sale of tobacco and tobacco products. The STMA has the right to impose hefty fines on counterfeiters. In addition, it can confiscate and destroy both counterfeit tobacco products and unauthorized cigarette production machines.[31]

One obstacle to effective enforcement is the fact that the CNTC/STMA is often complicit in cases of counterfeiting, for example, by approving the purchase of the tobacco, packaging materials, and machines that are eventually used to produce counterfeits. The conflict of interest is obvious: the STMA is

[28] China Interview 041226A, with a senior official of the Department of Safety Supervision at the State Food and Drug Administration (Beijing).
[29] *Zhongyang zhengfu zuzhi jigou 1998*, 172.
[30] Article 4 of the PRC Law on Tobacco Monopoly (1992).
[31] China Interview 020108, with an employee of the Monopoly Supervision and Management Department at the STMA (Beijing).

supposed to investigate cases of cigarette counterfeiting, in which its own officials are often implicated.

Enforcement in cases of cigarette counterfeiting is conducted by monopoly investigation teams (*zhuanmai jicha duiwu*) located at the central, provincial, prefecture, and county levels. The personnel of these investigation teams began to increase rapidly in the late 1990s, reaching 38,717 officers by 2001.[32] Whereas in the 1980s the STMA was handling 10,000–20,000 cases of violation of the tobacco monopoly laws (including counterfeiting) each year,[33] in 2003 it investigated 220,000 cases of production and sale of counterfeit tobacco products, destroyed 2,575 underground production facilities, and seized 1,531 cigarette production machines. Furthermore, in 2003 as many as 3,569 counterfeiters were detained, 956 received criminal punishment, and another 263 were subject to reeducation through labor.[34]

Two factors explain this significant rise in enforcement activity. First, STMA officers are eligible to receive rewards of up to 300,000 yuan for locating underground cigarette production facilities.[35] A second factor is that investigation team members readily secure police (public security bureau [PSB]) assistance during enforcement.[36] As we will see in Chapter 7, tobacco anticounterfeiting work is unusually dangerous, so being able to count on the PSB is essential if STMA employees are to participate regularly in raids. Whatever state pressure the police are under to assist in the raids, the high level of PSB support certainly also reflects a commonsense prioritization of resources toward important enforcement activities.

The Ministry of Agriculture

The MOA (Zhonghua renmin gongheguo nongye bu) was established in 1949 and since then has been subject to several rounds of restructuring.[37] In 1998, it was allotted a central-level staff of 483 personnel, making it one of the bigger ministries in China. Currently, its decentralized structure reaches down to the county level.[38] The MOA has a wide mandate ranging from control over agriculture, forestry, livestock production, and fisheries to the regulation of

[32] *Zhongguo yancao nianjian 2001* (China Tobacco Yearbook 2001) (Beijing: Jingji ribao chubanshe, 2003), 36.

[33] *Zhongguo yancao nianjian 1981–1990* (China Tobacco Yearbook 1981–1990) (Beijing: Jingji ribao chubanshe, 1991), 33–34.

[34] *Zhongguo yancao nianjian 2003* (China Tobacco Yearbook 2003) (Beijing: Jingji ribao chubanshe, 2005), 81.

[35] China Interview 010829, with the vice head of the Enforcement Team of the Guangdong Provincial Tobacco Monopoly Administration (Guangzhou); China Interview 020121, with the Beijing representative of a major Chinese tobacco manufacturing company (Beijing).

[36] China Interview 020109A, with an employee of the Policy Statute and Restructuring Department of the STMA (Beijing); China Interview 010723B, with an employee of the Legal Department of a tobacco company (Shanghai).

[37] *Zhonghua renmin gongheguo zhengfu jigou wushi nian,* 121–122.

[38] *Zhongyang zhengfu zuzhi jigou 1998,* 303.

agricultural markets and township and village enterprises (TVEs).[39] Its IPR enforcement responsibilities are broad as well. The ministry's IPR enforcement mandate derives from general laws on quality, quantity, consumer protection, unfair competition, and trademarks, and from more specialized laws and regulations on, for example, seeds, seedlings, pesticides, fertilizers, fodder, veterinary medicines, and fisheries.[40] In relation to IPR, the ministry mainly handles cases of counterfeit agricultural inputs, an umbrella category that includes everything from seeds and veterinary medicines to spare parts for agricultural machines.

The MOA was not actively involved in IPR protection prior to the promulgation of the landmark 2000–2001 State Council decisions on fighting the production and sale of counterfeit and substandard goods and on rectifying market order. These decisions explicitly identified the counterfeiting of agricultural inputs as an area of concern for the government and charged the MOA with enforcement in this domain.[41] The results are striking. Promptly in 2001, the MOA created the Leading Small Group for Rectification of Market Order (Nongyebu zhengdun he guifan shichang jingji chengxu gongzuo lingdao xiaozu) at the central level. At the same time, it began to establish comprehensive enforcement teams (*zonghe zhifa dui*) at the provincial, prefecture, and county levels.[42] By 2004, 30 provinces, 137 cities and prefectures, as well as 1,388 counties were carrying out comprehensive enforcement activities, which included anticounterfeiting.[43] In 2004, anticounterfeiting specialists working

---

[39] http://www.agri.gov.cn (accessed October 15, 2006).

[40] For a list of the related laws and regulations, see Office of the Ministry of Agriculture Leading Small Group for Rectifying Market Order and the Ministry of Agriculture Department on Market and Economic Information, *Nongzi dajia gongzuo falü fagui huibian* (Compilation of Laws and Regulations Concerning Agricultural Materials Anticounterfeiting) (Beijing: Zhongguo nongye keji chubanshe, 2002).

[41] See *Guowuyuan guanyu kaizhan yanli daji zhishou jiamao weilie shangpin weifa fanzui huodong lianhe xingdong de tongzhi* (State Council Notice on Launching a United "Strike Hard" Campaign against the Illegal Activities and Crimes of Production and Sale of Counterfeit and Substandard Goods) (Guofa [2000] 32 hao), as well as *Guowuyuan guanyu zhengdun he guifan shichang jingji chengxu de jueding* (Decision of the State Council Regarding the Rectification of Market Order) (Guofa [2001] 11 hao), and *Guowuyuan bangongting guanyu jixu shenru kaizhan yanli daji zhishou jiamao weilie shangpin weifa fanzui huodong lianhe xingdong de tongzhi* (Notice of the Office of the State Council Regarding the Continuing and Deepening of the Launch of a United "Strike Hard" Campaign against the Illegal Activities and Crimes of Production and Sale of Counterfeit and Substandard Goods) (Guobanfa [2001] 32 hao).

[42] China Interview 020906A, with the president of the Crop Protection Association of China (Beijing); China Interview 020906B, with the head of the Plant Products Industry Department at the Ministry of Agriculture (Beijing); China Interview 020906C, with an employee of the Anticounterfeiting Department at the Ministry of Agriculture (Beijing); China Interview 020910A, with a vice director of the Division of Supervision at the Institute for the Control of Chemicals (attached to the Ministry of Agriculture) (Beijing).

[43] *Zhongguo nongye nianjian 2005* (China Agriculture Yearbook 2005) (Beijing: Zhongguo nongye chubanshe, 2005), 81.

at different levels of the MOA seized 9,900 tons of pesticides, 15,800 tons of seeds, 79,000 tons of fertilizers, 459 tons of veterinary and aquaculture medicines, 2,100 tons of fodder, and 187,000 agricultural machines and spare parts.[44]

In 2005, the MOA accepted for investigation over 120,000 cases of production and sale of fake and substandard agricultural inputs, thus helping avert potential losses of 2.2 billion yuan (about US$280 million).[45] Unfortunately, MOA statistics do not separate cases of counterfeiting from cases of substandard agricultural inputs. However, even if only half of the cases handled by the ministry in 2005 were counterfeiting cases, this would mean that it was a more active IPR enforcer than the SAIC, which handled 51,851 cases of trademark infringement and counterfeiting in the same year![46] This finding is striking, since it contradicts widely held assumptions that the SAIC is the main administrative enforcer in China.[47] In practice, the statistics simply reflect the underlying demographics of IPR enforcement. The SAIC is largely urban, and the MOA largely rural. The relative importance of the MOA as an IPR enforcer will seem less surprising if we take into account that over 700 million Chinese still officially reside in rural areas and use agricultural inputs on a daily basis, thus creating massive demand for agricultural counterfeits and giving MOA employees ample opportunity to engage in anticounterfeiting enforcement activities.[48]

COPYRIGHT ADMINISTRATIVE ENFORCEMENT

Like trademark anticounterfeiting, the copyright enforcement portfolio is shared by several bureaucracies: the National Copyright Administration of China (NCAC), the General Administration of Press and Publications (GAPP), the Ministry of Culture (MOC), and the State Administration of Radio, Film, and Television (SARFT). In addition, the Anti-Pornography and Anticounterfeiting Office, although not formally a stand-alone agency, plays a role in coordinating enforcement in this domain as well.

---

[44] Ibid., 110.

[45] *2005 nian quanguo nongzi dajia chengxiao xianzhu, wei nongmin wanhui sunshi 22 yi duo yuan* (Remarkable Achievements of Agricultural Materials Anticounterfeiting Work in 2005: Peasant Losses of More Than 2.2 Billion Yuan Recovered) (January 11, 2006), available at http:// zgb.agri.gov.cn/content/text/show.asp?id=327 (accessed October 16, 2006).

[46] For official government assessments of the SAIC, see *China's Intellectual Property Protection in 2005* (June 12, 2006), http://www.ipr.gov.cn/ipr/en/info/Article.jsp?a_no=5835&col_no=102&; dir=200606 (accessed October 29, 2008).

[47] Neither official Chinese IPR publications nor academic treatises in Chinese or English discuss the anticounterfeiting activities of the MOA, creating the impression that the ministry is not involved in IPR enforcement.

[48] In 2006, China had 737 million rural residents (56.1 percent of the total population). See *Zhongguo tongji nianjian 2007* (China Statistical Yearbook 2007) (Beijing: Zhongguo tongji chubanshe, 2007), 105.

The General Administration of Press and Publications and the National Copyright Administration of China

The main copyright enforcer is the General Administration of Press and Publications (Zhonghua renmin gongheguo xinwen chuban zongshu), which was established as early as 1949.[49] In 1998, the GAPP was allotted 145 personnel at the central level. Currently, its decentralized structure does not extend below the provincial and major-city levels.[50] At the county level, copyright matters fall instead within the jurisdiction of the culture authorities.[51]

The National Copyright Administration of China (Guojia banquan ju) has the status of a department within the GAPP, where it is known internally as the Copyright Management Department (Banquan guanli si). Because of its low bureaucratic standing, the NCAC does not have access to its own dedicated enforcement resources and is unable to set enforcement priorities without consultation with the GAPP. This also explains why the NCAC is unwilling to organize enforcement raids but prefers instead to conduct quasi-judicial enforcement. In 2005, the NCAC accepted 9,644 copyright infringement and piracy cases for investigation, following official requests from the right holders.[52] In contrast to enforcement raids organized in the area of trademarks, copyright cases handled by the NCAC often feature administrative hearings and are typically concluded with a written punishment decision. They provide an example of quasi-judicial administrative enforcement and will be discussed further in Chapter 8.

Several other departments within the GAPP have responsibility for piracy: the Book Publications Management Department, the Periodical Publications Management Department, the Audiovisual and Electronic Publications Management Department, the Print Circulation Management Department (which often doubles as the Anti-Pornography and Anticounterfeiting Office), and the Printing Management Department.[53] These GAPP departments do not provide quasi-judicial copyright enforcement of the kind supplied by the NCAC. They participate only in campaign-style enforcement. Importantly, in 2004, the GAPP uncovered 107 million pieces of pirated products during the Anti-Pornography Campaign. Specifically, it seized 19.08 million books, 1.14 million periodicals,

---

[49] *Zhonghua renmin gongheguo zhengfu jigou wushi nian,* 148–150.

[50] *Zhongyang zhengfu zuzhi jigou 1998,* 413. Even some major cities such as Dalian (which enjoys the status of *fushengji chengshi,* or subprovincial level city) do not have independent Press and Publications Administrations. In Dalian (Liaoning province), press and publications matters (including copyright protection) are handled by the Culture Bureau. China Interview 041224A, with the head of the Copyright Distribution Management Department of the Dalian City Culture Bureau/Press and Publications Bureau (Dalian).

[51] In some places, such as Zouping county in Shandong province, there is a Culture and Sports Bureau (Wenhua tiyu ju), rather than a Culture Bureau. See *Zouping nianjian 1999–2003* (Zouping Yearbook 1999–2003) (Ji'nan: Shandong xinhua yinshuachang, 2004), 431–440.

[52] *China's Intellectual Property Protection in 2005,* www.ipr.gov.cn (accessed June 26, 2006).

[53] *Zhongyang zhengfu zuzhi jigou 1998,* 409–412.

65.87 million audiovisual products, 13.01 million electronic publications, 7.74 million software applications, and 90,000 other pirated products.[54]

The Ministry of Culture

Created in 1949 but briefly abolished between 1970 and 1975,[55] the Ministry of Culture (Wenhua bu) is a major actor in copyright protection in China. In 1998, the MOC was allotted a central-level staff of 275. Currently, its decentralized administrative structure penetrates down to the county level.[56] The Ministry of Culture has been involved in the Anti-Pornography and Anti-Piracy Campaign since its inception in 1989 and has also gradually acquired the audiovisual media management portfolio from the GAPP.[57] The Cultural Market Department (Wenhua shichang si) is directly responsible for supervision of the wholesale, retail, and rental trade in audiovisual products, thus assuming a major role in fighting copyright piracy. The Ministry of Culture has been expanding its cultural market enforcement teams, which numbered 1,249 in 1998 and grew to 1,672 in 2004.[58] As of 2004, only fourteen of these teams were located at the provincial level, with the rest being distributed between the prefecture and the county levels. The enforcement teams had a total of 11,429 employees. We should stress that, even with this kind of attention to IPR, as many as 77 percent of China's prefectures, cities, and counties remained without cultural market enforcement teams as of 2004.[59]

Although we have indicators about the activities of the cultural market enforcement teams going back to the 1990s, inconsistencies in data reporting from year to year prevent us from constructing a reliable time-series panel.[60] Nonetheless, even the fragmented data we have clearly show that there has been an upward trend in the volume of seized and destroyed pirated audiovisual media, as well as in the number of confiscated illegal production lines.

---

[54] www.ncac.gov.cn (accessed November 28, 2006).

[55] The Ministry of Culture was known as the "Culture Group" (Wenhua zu) between 1970 and 1975. See *Zhonghua renmin gongheguo zhengfu jigou wushi nian*, 127–128.

[56] *Zhongyang zhengfu zuzhi jigou 1998*, 318.

[57] It would have made sense for the entire optical-disk portfolio to be transferred to the Ministry of Culture. However, software continues to be managed by the General Administration of Press and Publications. This setup has not led to streamlined enforcement, because the GAPP continues to work on audiovisual media despite the transfer of this portfolio to the MOC. In 2008, a proposal was made to transfer the entire media portfolio to the GAPP.

[58] *Zhongguo wenhua wenwu tongji nianjian 1999* (China Culture and Cultural Relics Yearbook 1999) (Beijing: Jingshi tushuguan chubanshe, 1999), 347; *Zhongguo wenhua wenwu tongji nianjian 2005* (China Culture and Cultural Relics Yearbook 2005) (Beijing: Jingshi tushuguan chubanshe, 2005), 122–123.

[59] *Zhongguo wenhua nianjian 2004* (China Culture Yearbook 2004) (Beijing: Xinhua chubanshe, 2005), 127.

[60] Enforcement data are contained in the *White Paper on Intellectual Property Rights Protection in China* series (www.ipr.gov.cn), as well as in *Zhongguo wenhua nianjian* (various years).

Recent statistics indicate that in 2004 the enforcement teams inspected 555,368 audiovisual businesses and seized 154 million illegal audiovisual product items.[61] In 2005, the Ministry of Culture seized 136 million pirated audiovisual products, 66.21 million of which were destroyed.[62] This means that, overall, the Ministry of Culture emerges as the main copyright enforcer in the area of pirated goods, enforcing more than the GAPP/NCAC, even though these are officially designated as the leading anti-piracy bureaucracies.

The State Administration of Radio, Film, and Television

The SARFT (Guojia guangbo dianying dianshi zongju) has existed in various forms since the founding of the PRC. Initially, it was known as the Radio Administration (Guangbo shiye ju). In 1982, when the management of TV broadcasts was added to its mandate, it was renamed the Ministry of Radio and Television (Guangbo dianshi bu). In 1986, that ministry became the Ministry of Radio, Film, and Television (Guangbo dianying dianshi bu), the better to reflect a newly added film management portfolio.[63] The most recent change occurred in 1998, when it was downgraded one level to vice-ministerial status and assumed its present name. As of 1998, the SARFT had a central-level staff of 223.[64] Its decentralized bureaucratic structure reaches down to the county level.[65] It is responsible for monitoring all radio and television broadcasts, as well as movie screenings. This mandate allows it to track down copyright law violations by radio stations, TV stations, and movie theaters. However, we have no data indicating how often the SARFT has involved itself in actual enforcement in cases of broadcasting or screening of pirated content.

Office of the National Anti-Pornography and Anti-Piracy Working Committee (NAPWC)

The Office of the NAPWC (Quanguo saohuang dafei gongzuo xiaozu bangongshi) is similar to a bureaucratic parasite, since it is not included in the official organization charts of the Chinese government and does not have its own personnel or enforcement resources. Known simply as the Anti-Pornography Office (Saohuang ban), it is always housed within another bureaucracy (see Chapter 8). The Anti-Pornography Office is usually small (up to a dozen employees), and it is mainly responsible for setting up and coordinating regular meetings of the dozen or more government agencies that participate in the

---

[61] *White Paper on the Intellectual Property Rights Protection in China in 2004*, www.ipr.gov.cn (accessed July 1, 2005).

[62] *China's Intellectual Property Protection in 2005*, www.ipr.gov.cn (accessed June 26, 2006).

[63] *Zhonghua renmin gongheguo zhengfu jigou wushi nian*, 143–144.

[64] *Zhongyang zhengfu zuzhi jigou 1998*, 392.

[65] See, for example, *Zouping nianjian 1999–2003*, 419–427. Zouping has a Radio and Television Bureau.

Anti-Pornography and Anti-Piracy Campaign.[66] Though it has no independent enforcement capabilities, the office is sometimes credited with enforcement successes. However, reports of this type are misleading. Even when enforcement is carried out as part of the annual anti-pornography campaign sweeps, credit should be awarded to the bureaucratic unit that houses the Anti-Pornography Office, not to the office itself.

In sum, the administrative infrastructure for IPR regulation in China is impressive in scale, scope, and degree of specialization according to subtypes of IPR. Taken cumulatively, the twelve agencies just described offer a significant volume of enforcement. Too much, perhaps. Because of conflict and overlap between agencies, this high volume of enforcement lacks the kind of coordination that would make it genuinely high-quality and effective. The foregoing analysis suggests that this absence reflects not so much the state's unwillingness to enforce as its relative incapacity to overcome the historically entrenched mandates of the respective bureaucracies that have assumed IPR enforcement responsibilities as part of their general regulatory and enforcement portfolios.

COMPARATIVE PERSPECTIVES

Cross-national comparison helps us gauge the specific successes and challenges China faces in providing administrative protection of IPR. In the following section, we follow the fate of administrative agencies that are functional equivalents to the various Chinese agencies with an IPR portfolio. As the case of China suggests, successful administrative enforcement follows bureaucratic specialization, centralization, and coordination.

Russia

Russia has fewer IPR agencies and a smaller volume of enforcement than China. In the area of patents, Russia, unlike China, has no specialized patent enforcement agency. The Russian counterpart to the SIPO is Rospatent (Russia Patent [Office]), which both grants and invalidates patents.[67] However, unlike the SIPO, Rospatent has no mandate to provide enforcement in cases of patent counterfeiting or patent passing off: it is simply an agency that handles patent applications.[68] Rospatent also handles trademark applications, but it has no administrative enforcement jurisdiction over cases of trademark counterfeiting.

---

[66] China Interview 020123 and China Interview 020913B, with the secretary of the Office of the NAPWC (Beijing).

[67] In 2004, Rospatent was renamed the Federal Service for Intellectual Property, Patents, and Trademarks (FIPS) and was integrated into the bureaucratic hierarchy of the Ministry of Education and Science.

[68] www.fips.ru (accessed October 15, 2006); Russia Interview 000904A, with the director general, Russian Patent and Trademark Agency (Rospatent) (Moscow).

Copyright Protection

Two entities under the Ministry of Culture share responsibility for enforcement in cases of copyright piracy. The first is the Federal Service for Supervision over the Implementation of Mass Media Laws and the Protection of Cultural Patrimony, which is simply known as Rosokhrankul'tury (Russia Culture Protection [Office]). The mandate of Rosokhrankul'tury is to issue, suspend, and revoke audiovideo production licenses. In addition, Rosokhrankul'tury can issue warnings to TV and radio stations that violate copyright laws by broadcasting pirated audiovisual material. Rosokhrankul'tury has twenty regional directorates that give it some reach throughout the country, as well as the potential to play a serious anti-piracy role. Despite the potential scope of its mandate, however, Rosokhrankul'tury is not actively pursuing pirates. For example, between January and August 2006, it conducted only nineteen inspections of licensees and suspended only three licenses.[69] In terms of broadcast supervision, Rosokhrankul'tury issued only three warnings in 2005 and none in the first half of 2006.[70]

The second entity is the Federal Agency on Print and Mass Media, which is known simply as Rospechat' (Russia Print [Office]). The Law Enforcement and Registration Department of Rospechat' is responsible for, among other things, control over the production and distribution of audio and video products.[71] The jurisdictional overlap between Rospechat' and Rosokhrankul'tury is longstanding. In 2002, employees at both agencies indicated to me, moreover, that the overlap had encouraged a degree of inactivity and shirking of enforcement responsibility.[72] As of 2006, Rospechat' had no regional subdivisions and did not publish enforcement data, circumstances that suggest, in fact, that it has come to play no practical role in anti-piracy enforcement in Russia. In practice, Rosokhrankul'tury is the sole, and inefficient, provider of administrative enforcement in cases of copyright piracy.

Trademark Protection

Russia appears to take trademarks more seriously than copyrights, but even here its record is mixed. Trademark counterfeiting is within the purview of several agencies. First and foremost is the Russian State Trade Inspectorate

[69] *Za deiatel'nost'iu po proizvodstvu (izgotovleniiu ekzempliarov) audiovizual'nykh proizvedenii i fonogramm* (On Activities Regarding the Manufacture [Making of Copies] of Audiovisual Products and Phonograms), http://new.rosohrancult.ru/controls/controls/copy/ (accessed October 13, 2006).

[70] http://new.rosohrancult.ru/controls/controls/smi/2005/ (accessed October 13, 2006); http://new.rosohrancult.ru/controls/controls/smi/2006/ (accessed October 13, 2006).

[71] http://www.fapmc.ru/about/structure/ (accessed April 28, 2008).

[72] Russia Interview 020605A, with the chief of the Mass Media Division of the Audiovisual Department of the Ministry for Press, TV, and Radio Broadcasting and Means of Mass Communication (Moscow); Russia Interview 020604, with the chief of the Licensing and Registration Department of the Ministry for Press, TV, and Radio Broadcasting and Means of Mass Communication (Moscow). The first entity was transformed into Rosokhrankul'tury and the second into Rospechat'.

(Gostorginspektsiia), which is equivalent to China's SAIC. Until 2005, the Trade Inspectorate was a centralized bureaucracy with a personnel allocation of 2,100 employees, spread throughout the Russian Federation. Impressively, in contrast to other bureaucracies, whose territorial divisions had to fend for themselves, Moscow sent money down to every one of the eighty-four trade inspectorates located in the subjects of the federation. The inspectors had relatively wide powers, including forbidding the sale of goods, ordering confiscation (*iz"iatie*) of goods, and imposing fines. In addition, trade inspectors could confiscate and destroy goods after a court order.[73]

The Trade Inspectorate was responsible for monitoring whether goods sold in Russian retail outlets and restaurants conformed to labeling and quality standards. As mislabeled and substandard goods were also often counterfeit, the Trade Inspectorate, if it so desired, could become involved in trademark anticounterfeiting. With the explosion of counterfeiting that followed the 1998 devaluation of the ruble, the Trade Inspectorate aggressively entered this domain as well, almost certainly because IPR enforcement provided a potential source of rents and justified personnel expansion. In 2001, the Trade Inspectorate claimed to have handled as many as 10,000 counterfeiting cases.[74] By 2003, it had created mobile enforcement groups staffed by its employees and police officers.[75] This growth in anticounterfeiting activity halted in 2005, when the Trade Inspectorate was absorbed by a subsidiary agency of the Ministry of Health, the newly formed Federal Service for Supervision of Consumer Protection and Human Well-Being, known simply as Rospotrebnadzor (Russia Consumer Supervision [Office]). This new Federal Service was created by adding a relatively small number of Trade Inspectorate employees to the already existing personnel of the Sanitary-Epidemiological Inspectorate. Most of the Trade Inspectorate employees were laid off, and its original status was downgraded to that of a division (*otdel*) within the Consumer Protection Department of Rospotrebnadzor.[76] Unsurprisingly, after the merger, the Trade Inspectorate ceased to work on counterfeiting, as result of a lack of interest in IPR matters on the part of Rospotrebnadzor.[77] What lesson about overlap can we draw from this case? Although it is true that the functions of the Trade Inspectorate and of Rospotrebnadzor did overlap prior to their merger (both

---

[73] Russia Interviews 020521 and 060112A, with the former head of Gostorginspektsiia (Moscow).

[74] Department of State Inspection, Internal Trade, and Public Eating Establishments at the Ministry of Economic Development and Trade of the Russian Federation, *Obzor kachestva tovarov narodnogo potrebleniia v Rossiiskoi Federatsii za 2001 god* (Overview of Merchandise Quality in the Russian Federation in 2001) (Moscow: Ministry of Economic Development and Trade, 2002), 1–3.

[75] Russia Interview 060112A, with the former head of Gostorginspektsiia (Moscow).

[76] www.rospotrebnadzor.ru (accessed October 14, 2006); Russia Interview 060112A, with the former head of Gostorginspektsiia (Moscow).

[77] Russia Interview 060119 and Russia Interview 060120B, with presidents of brand owners' associations (Moscow).

regulated the quality of goods sold in the consumer market), the total elimination of enforcement functions is not a solution to the problem of bureaucratic duplication.

Another agency that can become involved in trademark counterfeiting is the Federal Service on Technical Regulation and Metrology (Gosstandart), which is subordinate to the Ministry of Industry and Energy. Gosstandart (State Standards [Office]), like China's AQSIQ, can become involved in trademark counterfeiting on quality standards grounds. Unlike the AQSIQ, however, it has no explicit interest in IPR enforcement.[78] This is not unusual: of the six countries analyzed in this book, only China has empowered its quality supervision agency with responsibility for IPR enforcement, a reflection of the high priority the state puts on the administrative protection of IPR.

Technically, the Federal Antimonopoly Service (FAS) (Federal'naia antimonopol'naia sluzhba) can also enforce in cases of trademark counterfeiting and copyright piracy.[79] Its functions, which are equivalent to those of the Fair Trade Department and the Advertising Department of the SAIC in China, include ensuring the competitiveness of financial and physical goods markets, as well as the regulation of natural monopolies, government procurement contracts, and advertising. IPR issues are handled by the Division on Unfair Competition and the Division on Advertising, each with five to six employees.[80] Although the FAS has seventy-four territorial units throughout the Russian Federation, no employees at the regional level are engaged in full-time IPR work.

In relation to IPR, the FAS is in practice a weak administrative entity that does not issue deterrent sanctions to violators. Enforcement through the FAS is a multistage process, which, at best, culminates with a toothless "recommendation" (*predpisanie*) to the violator to stop engaging in anticompetitive practices like selling counterfeit goods. In 2001, which is the last year for which we have data, as few as fifteen IPR cases were concluded with a recommendation for some action to redress the violation.[81]

This number presents a puzzle. Given the complexity of the complaint process, and the improbability that an FAS case will end with a deterrent punishment, why would right holders resort to the FAS at all? The answer involves a provision in Article 14 of the Law on Competition, which allows right holders to use FAS

[78] www.gost.ru (accessed October 15, 2006); Russia Interview 020606, with the head and the deputy head of the Department for Control, Inspection, and Regional Affairs at Gosstandart (Moscow). In the late 1990s, Gosstandart engaged in episodic IPR enforcement when participating in market sweeps at the request of another agency, but by the early 2000s it had gradually withdrawn from this issue area.

[79] See Article 14 of the Law on Competition (2006).

[80] www.fas.gov.ru (accessed October 14, 2006), as well as Russia Interview 000831B, Russia Interview 020606B, Russia Interview 020611B, and Russia Interview 020617A, with high-level Antimonopoly Ministry personnel (Moscow). The Antimonopoly Ministry was transformed into the FAS in 2004.

[81] MAP Rossii, *Doklad o konkurentnoi politike v Rossiiskoi Federatsii (1999–2001)* (Report on Competition Policy in the Russian Federation 1999–2001) (Moskva: MAP, 2002), 10–12.

decisions as grounds for disputing bad faith registrations of their marks through Rospatent (which, as noted, regulates both trademark and patent registration).[82] In addition, some right holders have indicated that they used FAS decisions as evidence of infringement in criminal and civil court cases.[83] This quasi-evidentiary role seems to have been the FAS's primary function in relation to IPR protection. The 2004 government reorganization further limited the mandate of the FAS by transferring its consumer protection responsibilities to Rospotrebnadzor. As of 2006, the FAS had stopped publishing data about IPR enforcement, a signal that it has probably fully abandoned enforcement in this domain.

The last agency with jurisdiction over trademark protection is the Pharmaceutical Inspection Directorate (Upravlenie farmatsevticheskoi inspektsii), which is known simply as Farminspektsiia (Pharmaceutical Inspection). Although it has jurisdiction over pharmaceutical counterfeiting, Farminspektsiia is a ghost entity within the Federal Service on Supervision of Health Care and Social Development (Federal'naia sluzhba po nadzoru v sfere zdravookhraneniia i sotsial'nogo razvitiia), which is itself subordinate to the Ministry of Health and Social Development. There were discussions about creating Farminspektsiia as early as the 1990s, but the agency was officially established only in 2002. The directorate is responsible for issuing approvals and certificates for the production and distribution of pharmaceuticals as well as for conducting market checks for counterfeit medicines. Counterfeiters oftentimes operate with an officially issued pharmaceutical production license, which points to a serious conflict of interest within Farminspektsiia between licensing and enforcement (one not dissimilar to that potentially at work in China's tobacco industry, where, as we have seen, the STMA enforces against counterfeiters who often have licenses issued by the STMA itself).[84] In Russia, Farminspektsiia provides a very small amount of anticounterfeiting enforcement. In 2002, it had only ten personnel who were working on anticounterfeiting at the central level, and there was no one available to conduct inspections across the country.[85] Available data reveal that Farminspektsiia conducted 411 anticounterfeiting inspections in 2003.[86] However, interview evidence and the absence of officially published statistics after 2003 suggest that currently Farminspektsiia does not conduct market checks for counterfeit medicines.[87]

[82] Russia Interview 060113B, Russia Interview 060118A, and Russia Interview 060120A, with Russian lawyers (Moscow).

[83] Russia Interview 060116A, with a representative of a foreign copyright association (Moscow).

[84] For fascinating details on other conflicts of interest within Farminspektsiia, see Alexandra Vacroux, "Formal and Informal Institutional Change: Evolution of Pharmaceutical Regulation in Russia, 1991–2004" (Ph.D. Dissertation, Department of Government, Harvard University, 2005).

[85] Russia Interview 020613C, with senior expert, Pharmaceutical Inspection Directorate (Moscow).

[86] *Itogi 2003* (2003 Summary), http://www.regmed.ru/etap.asp?EtapNx=59 (accessed October 13, 2006).

[87] Russia Interview 060126A, with two representatives of an international pharmaceutical manufacturers' association (Moscow).

China-Russia Comparison

Although China and Russia have similarly high levels of piracy and counterfeiting, they have chosen to deploy different IPR protection strategies. China has emphasized administrative enforcement at the expense of Customs, criminal, and civil enforcement through the specialized IPR courts. Although this book takes issue with its overinvestment in administrative enforcement, China certainly cannot be accused of neglect of IPR. By contrast, in Russia we witness very low levels of administrative activity, with no compensatory enforcement by Customs, the *arbitrazh* courts, or (as we will see in the next chapter) the police. In sum, until recently, the Russian state assigned a much lower priority to IPR than the Chinese state and did not dedicate resources to enforcement in this important area. This reflected the absence of both domestic and foreign pressure to enforce IPR laws. The situation is changing. In 2004, in response to increasing pressure from the United States, Russia established an interministerial IPR commission chaired by Vice Premier Medvedkov, a step that effectively resuscitated a commission that had been in place since 2000 but was moribund.[88] The Medvedkov commission did not initially take meaningful steps to ensure that government agencies become truly invested in IPR protection. The volume of IPR enforcement began to increase only after 2006, when Russia decided to make a serious bid for WTO entry. Since then, Russia has put a greater emphasis on criminal IPR enforcement, which will be discussed in the following chapter.

Taiwan

Traditionally, Taiwan has been a hotbed of piracy and counterfeiting.[89] We might expect that, like China, it would possess a wide spectrum of bureaucracies engaged in fighting counterfeiting. However, because Taiwan has prioritized other kinds of enforcement, it has a relatively limited number of IPR bureaucracies, which provide a surprisingly modest volume of administrative enforcement, as illustrated in Table 5.3. In spite of these differences, the activities of Taiwan's administrative enforcement agencies do shed light on the Chinese case, highlighting in particular the importance of clearly defined enforcement mandates.

Until recently, the Anticounterfeiting Committee (ACC) (Chajin fangmao shangpin xiaozu) was entrusted with the coordination of IPR administrative enforcement in Taiwan. Created in 1981, the ACC was initially responsible only for patent and trademark enforcement coordination. Copyright

---

[88] http://www.government.ru/government/coordinatingauthority/medvedev/intelektualnaja_sobstvennost/ index.htm (accessed October 15, 2006). The Medvedkov commission succeeded the IPR commission chaired by ex-premier Kasyanov, which existed from 2000 to 2004. The Kasyanov commission did not take any meaningful measures to protect IPR.

[89] See Andy Sun, *From Pirate King to Jungle King: Transformation of Taiwan's Intellectual Property Protection* (Baltimore: School of Law, University of Maryland, 1997).

TABLE 5.3. *Administrative Enforcement in Taiwan in 2004*

Agency	Cases Handled	Enforcement Cases (per million people)
Anticounterfeiting Committee (ACC)	289	12.6
Joint Optical Disk Enforcement Force (JODE)	1067	46.4
Fair Trade Commission (FTC)	26	1.1
Department of Health (DOH)	72	3.1
TOTAL	1,454	63.2

Sources: http://www.tipo.gov.tw/eng/prosecution/acc.asp (accessed July 31, 2006); http://www.tipo.gov.tw/eng/prosecution/jode.asp (accessed April 29, 2008); *FTC Yearbook 2005*, http://www.ftc.gov.tw/EnglishWeb/English%E5%85%AC%E5%B9%B3%E6%9C%83.html (accessed July 25, 2006); *Quarterly Report on Taiwan's Intellectual Property Rights Protection (October–December 2005)* (Taipei: TIPO, 2006), 2.

enforcement was the prerogative of the Coordination Subcommittee for the Elimination of Copyright Infringement, which was located within the Ministry of the Interior. This fragmented structure lowered the efficiency of enforcement and led to the decision to merge the subcommittee with the ACC in 1999.[90] With ten personnel, in 1999 the restructured ACC was installed within the newly formed Taiwan Intellectual Property Office (TIPO), which had already acquired the patent and trademark examination functions of the National Bureau of Standards (NBS). The TIPO therefore emerged as the central regulator of all IPR in Taiwan.

After the TIPO was entrusted with the anticounterfeiting portfolio in 1998–1999, an ambitious plan to reduce piracy was put into place. The ACC inaugurated a series of ex officio market sweeps conducted by mobile teams composed of police, prosecutors, and ACC employees. The unfolding of the Anti-Piracy Action Plan over 2000–2001 led to an appreciable drop in piracy by 2002. For example, software piracy was as high as 72 percent in 1994 but as a result of the more vigorous, streamlined, and coordinated enforcement dropped to 43 percent by 2002.[91] After 2002, the activity of the ACC began to decline, because it no longer participated in interagency market sweeps. In addition, it received progressively fewer piracy and counterfeiting tip-offs each year, reaching a low of 360 in 2005.[92] Not surprisingly, given this trend, the ACC was abolished in January 2006 at the initiative of the TIPO, which argued that it had outgrown its role as a liaison between right holders and the relevant

[90] Taiwan Interview 000802B, with bureaucrats working for the Intellectual Property Office of the Taiwanese Ministry of Economic Affairs (MOEA) (Taipei).
[91] *Global Software Piracy Study 2006* and *Global Software Piracy Study 2004*, http://w3.bsa.org/globalstudy/2006study.cfm (accessed April 29, 2008).
[92] http://www.tipo.gov.tw/eng/prosecution/acc.asp (accessed July 29, 2006).

enforcement authorities.[93] Right holders, the TIPO claimed, could now directly approach the enforcement authorities. Notably, the TIPO did preserve the ACC's mandate of giving out cash rewards to enforcers and of encouraging the macrolevel interagency coordination of anticounterfeiting action plans.[94]

The abolition of the ACC makes sense for several reasons. First, its low bureaucratic rank as a small department (*ke*) within the Intellectual Property Office made it difficult for it to compel other government agencies to act on the anticounterfeiting cases it transferred to them.[95] Second, accepting, recording, and then transferring cases to the relevant enforcement authorities complicated and lengthened the enforcement process. Finally, ACC employees had no real interest in participating ex officio in proactive, interagency market sweeps and factory checks, since they had no real enforcement powers and the laurels went to the police and the prosecutors, who were ultimately credited with the seizures and prosecutions.[96] After the creation of the Joint Optical Disk Enforcement Task Force (JODE) in 2002, there was even less of a need for direct involvement by the ACC in market sweeps. Given these developments, the abolition of the ACC should be seen in a positive light, because it resolved the problem of duplicative enforcement and raised administrative efficiency. Right holders, who never shy away from protesting perceived inadequacies in the enforcement of IPR in Taiwan, have not spoken out against the abolition of the ACC.[97]

The JODE has emerged as a key player in enforcement. It was established by the Industrial Development Bureau; the Board of Foreign Trade; the Bureau of Standards, Metrology, and Inspection; and the Taiwan Intellectual Property Office, all of which exist under the umbrella of the Ministry of Economic Affairs. The JODE was originally staffed by military recruits doing alternative military service (*tidaiyi*) and by a few full-time personnel drawn from the four agencies that founded it. It was tasked with enforcing the 2001 Optical Disk Law and the related Source Identification (SID) Code Regulations. Specifically, it was responsible for conducting inspections of factories producing blank optical disks and prerecorded disks. As of December 2003, there were eighty-eight optical disk factories on the island, twenty-three of which were known to have engaged in IPR violations.[98] Although the initial plan was to

---

[93] Taiwan Interview 060404, with the director of the TIPO International Affairs and Planning Division, MOEA (Taipei).

[94] In 2004 alone, NT$27.6 million (US$900,000) was given to police officers who had uncovered 955 counterfeiting cases. *TIPO 2004 Annual Report* (Taipei: TIPO, 2005), 45.

[95] Taiwan Interview 060404, with the director of the TIPO International Affairs and Planning Division, MOEA (Taipei); Taiwan Interview 060329, with the commander of the IPR Police (Taipei).

[96] Taiwan Interview 000803B, with a bureaucrat from the ACC (Taipei).

[97] Taiwan Interview 060327B, with representative of the Business Software Alliance; Taiwan Interview 060328, with representative of the International Federation of the Phonographic Industry; and Taiwan Interview 060401A, with former president of the Motion Picture Association (all in Taipei).

[98] *Performance Report on Intellectual Property Rights Protection in Taiwan 2003* (Taipei: TIPO, 2004), 20.

station JODE personnel physically at the disk factories, the factories understandably opposed this.[99] Instead, factories are now subject to both scheduled and unannounced inspections. Should JODE employees discover cases of piracy, they can request the assistance of the IPR Police, but typically inspections are conducted by the JODE alone.[100]

The JODE was put in place to raise the costs of counterfeiting by increasing the rate of detection of unlicensed plants and plants that do not stamp the mandatory SID code on their disks.[101] In other words, the JODE's success has depended on its interrupting the flow of pirated disks at the source. Unauthorized disks can be seized by the JODE, and the responsible person in the enterprise that manufactured them can be ordered to suspend production or else face a stiff fine or even imprisonment.[102] The JODE's broad powers have led to some impressive results. The JODE conducted over 3,500 optical disk factory inspections between 2002 and the end of 2005. As a result of these inspections, production was suspended in thirty-seven factories, twenty-four cases were prosecuted, and twenty-seven machines were seized.[103] There were other tangible results as well. Business software piracy declined from 51 percent in 2001 to 43 percent in 2002 and remained at that level through the end of 2005.[104] Record piracy and entertainment software piracy have similarly declined since 2001.[105] The JODE has been so successful that it has forced the factories working in violation of the law either to close down or to switch to small-scale disk-burning operations in private homes.

Another entity with an IPR mandate is the Fair Trade Commission (FTC) (Xingzhengyuan gongping jiaoyi weiyuanhui). Created in January 1992 to enforce the 1991 Fair Trade Act, the FTC is a large agency with 217 personnel.[106] The Fair Trade Act charges the commission, on the grounds of unfair competition, to act against companies that create consumer confusion by counterfeiting commodities or trademarks.[107] Although it has jurisdiction over trademark anticounterfeiting, both interview data and published statistics indicate that the FTC has no interest in expanding its role in this area. The

---

[99] Taiwan Interview 060401A, with former Motion Picture Association president (Taipei).

[100] Taiwan Interview 060329, with the commander of the IPR Police (Taipei).

[101] The SID code allows tracking and identification of the producer of each optical disk.

[102] See Articles 15–23, Optical Disk Law. The "responsible person" (*fuzeren*) is typically the firm manager, who can be held legally liable on behalf of the firm.

[103] See http://www.tipo.gov.tw/eng/prosecution/jode.asp (accessed April 29, 2008).

[104] Business Software Alliance, *Global Piracy Study 2002*; Business Software Alliance and IDC, *Third Annual BSA and IDC Global Software Piracy Study Global Piracy Study 2006*, http://www.bsa.org/country/Research%20and%20Statistics/~/media/03BBAC39E2BF4D5BA8870 E2F81CFFCC2.ashx (accessed July 28, 2008).

[105] *IIPA 2006 Special 301 Report*, http://www.iipa.com/countryreports.html (accessed July 28, 2006), 399.

[106] www.ftc.gov.tw (accessed July 25, 2006).

[107] See Article 20 of the Fair Trade Act (1991; amended 1999, 2000, and 2002). We should note that the Fair Trade Act mainly regulates relations between enterprises; a physical person is liable only in his or her capacity as a representative of an enterprise.

commission is able to respond to public complaints and to self-initiate investigations in the absence of a complaint.[108] On average, however, it handled only about twenty complaints per year between 1999 and 2005 and self-initiated only one counterfeiting investigation during the same period.[109] There is no specialized anticounterfeiting department within the commission. Instead, the Third Department is responsible for, among other things, cases of trademark counterfeiting.

What explains the low activity of the FTC? Mainly, the provisions of Article 20 of the Fair Trade Act are very close to the penal provisions of Articles 81–82 of the Trademark Law. This conflict of laws blurs the respective enforcement responsibilities of the FTC and of criminal enforcers. In addition, the remedies outlined in the Fair Trade Act are relatively weak. The FTC can order the cessation of the infringing conduct, impose fines, and, under the most unusual circumstances, even suspend the operation of a business or close it down entirely. But it cannot seize and destroy goods; nor can it impose damage awards in the absence of a court decision. Although the Fair Trade Act stipulates criminal sanctions as well, they can be imposed only by a court of law; in cases transferred from the FTC, the courts have tended to find the defendants not guilty.[110] To sum up, the inability of the FTC to impose deterrent sanctions, along with the conflict between the administrative punishment provisions of the Fair Trade Act and the criminal sanctions specified in the Trademark Law, jointly account for the lack of demand by right holders for FTC services and the FTC's unwillingness proactively to identify cases of trademark counterfeiting.

The last agency with jurisdiction over IPR in Taiwan is the Department of Health (DOH) (Weisheng shu), which has an exclusive mandate to conduct inspections in cases of counterfeit drugs, misbranded drugs, prohibited drugs, and defective medical devices.[111] When such products are found, both administrative and criminal penalties apply. The DOH can confiscate and destroy the counterfeit drugs, as well as revoke the permits for the manufacture, importation, or sale of these drugs.[112] When the use of counterfeit drugs leads to serious harm, criminal penalties ranging from a fine to life imprisonment may be imposed.[113] The DOH has offices throughout the island, allowing it to mount vigorous pharmacovigilance campaigns.

---

[108] See Article 26 of the Fair Trade Act.
[109] *FTC Yearbook 2001, FTC Yearbook 2002,* and *FTC Yearbook 2005,* all available at www.ftc.gov.tw (accessed October 29, 2008).
[110] In 2001, fourteen defendants were charged by the district criminal courts with violating Article 20 of the Fair Trade Act but none of them was found guilty. In 2002, only one of the four charged defendants was found guilty. Similarly, seven defendants were charged in 2005, and only two were found guilty. See *FTC Yearbook 2001, FTC Yearbook 2002,* and *FTC Yearbook 2005,* all available at www.ftc.gov.tw (accessed April 29, 2008).
[111] Articles 20–23, Pharmaceutical Affairs Act (2005). The law does not clearly distinguish between counterfeit and misbranded drugs.
[112] Articles 77–79, Pharmaceutical Affairs Act (2005).
[113] Articles 82–83, Pharmaceutical Affairs Act (2005).

Historically, the DOH has not been interested in exercising its drug anti-counterfeiting mandate. In 2003, however, the DOH took a more active stand and formed the Drug Anticounterfeiting Interagency Group, composed of representatives from the Ministry of Justice, the Prosecutor's Office, the Investigation Bureau, the National Police Administration, Customs, and the Directorate General of Telecommunications. The interagency group meets twice a year to discuss cooperative drug anticounterfeiting activities.[114] In addition to inter-agency cooperation, the DOH has engaged in efforts to increase public awareness of fake drugs and to give ordinary citizens incentives to report cases of counterfeiting. The rising number of cases handled by the DOH (from 57 in 2003 to 72 in 2004 and 109 in 2005) testifies to the increased attention that the DOH is paying to enforcement.[115]

Overall, Taiwan's IPR enforcement is well coordinated and efficient. This is a result of Taiwan's small size, which makes coordination easier, and of the relative clarity of the laws limiting overlap among the mandates of different enforcers. As the case of the FTC demonstrates, where mandates are poorly defined, one of the agencies tends to shy away from enforcement. Thus, clarity and restraint in cases where overlap exists have helped raise the predictability of enforcement in Taiwan. It should also be emphasized that Taiwan has dedicated most of its resources to criminal enforcement. Administrative enforcement in Taiwan may work as well as it does in part because it is not the primary avenue for right holders seeking redress. In Taiwan, low volume means high quality.

The Czech Republic

The Czech Republic has three administrative enforcers with jurisdiction over IPR. The Czech Commercial Inspection (Česká obchodní inspekce, or ČOI) is responsible for counterfeiting in all areas, except pharmaceuticals, tobacco, alcohol, and foodstuffs.[116] The Czech Agriculture and Food Inspection Authority (Státní zemědělská a potravinářská inspekce, or SZPI) has jurisdiction over cases of counterfeiting in the areas of tobacco, alcohol, and foodstuffs.[117] The State Institute for Drug Control (Státní ústav pro kontrolu léčiv, or SÚKL) is responsible for counterfeit pharmaceuticals.[118] The ČOI and the SÚKL are

---

[114] *Quarterly Report on Taiwan's Intellectual Property Rights Protection (January–March 2006)* (Taipei: TIPO, 2006), 1.

[115] *Quarterly Report on Taiwan's Intellectual Property Rights Protection (October–December 2005)* (Taipei: TIPO, 2006), 2.

[116] Czech Trade Inspectorate Act (64/1986 Coll.) and Product Safety Act (102/2001 Coll.). See Articles 3 (e) and 4 (d) for the foodstuff and tobacco exceptions.

[117] Act on the Czech Agricultural and Food Inspection Authority (146/2002 Coll., amended by Act 309/2002 Coll.).

[118] Czech Interview 020712A, with the director general of the State Institute for Drug Control (Prague).

headquartered in Prague, and the SZPI is headquartered in Brno.[119] The ČOI has seven regional inspectorates, whereas the SÚKL and the SZPI each have eight.

Although the mandate of each agency is well defined, enforcement statistics show that the ČOI has been handling cigarette counterfeiting, which is technically under the jurisdiction of the SZPI. When I interviewed the director general of the ČOI, he claimed that "we will never enforce in cigarette cases, because they are the exclusive enforcement domain of the SZPI."[120] A bureaucrat working for the SZPI similarly maintained that the SZPI is the only enforcer in cases of trademark-infringing tobacco products.[121] But data on the enforcement activities of the ČOI in 2002 indicate that the value of tobacco products seized and destroyed by the inspection was about one-quarter of the value of all counterfeits seized and destroyed (71 million Czech crowns or US$2 million for tobacco versus 298 million Czech crowns or US$8.5 million for all counterfeits).[122] Despite its mandate, there is no evidence that the SZPI provides any enforcement in cases of counterfeit food, alcohol, or cigarettes. This appears to have opened a niche that was then taken over by the ČOI, despite the fact that these areas do not formally fall under its jurisdiction.

In this context, we can ask why the ČOI has not intruded in pharmaceutical counterfeiting as well but instead has allowed the entire regulatory and enforcement mandate in this area to be retained by the SÚKL. The likely reason is that the ČOI lacks the technical sophistication necessary for detecting cases of mislabeled, substandard, or counterfeit pharmaceuticals. The potentially small volume is also possibly a factor that deterred the ČOI. When I interviewed the director general of the SÚKL in 2002, he claimed that the SÚKL did not handle cases of pharmaceutical counterfeiting simply because it was not "aware of the existence of any such cases on the territory of the Czech Republic."[123] Statistics indicate that by 2005 the SÚKL had begun to accept a few cases of pharmaceutical counterfeiting per year (see Table 5.4). Interview data and annual statistics consistently show the lack of any ČOI involvement in this area.

Apart from pharmaceuticals, the ČOI has emerged as the exclusive administrative enforcer in cases of counterfeiting in the Czech Republic. In recent years, it has intensified its enforcement activity, culminating with the handling

[119] Brno is the second largest city in the Czech Republic after Prague. The Czech Constitutional Court, Supreme Court, Supreme Administrative Court, and Supreme Procuratorate are all located there.

[120] Czech Interview 020702B, with the director general of the Czech Commercial Inspection (Prague).

[121] Czech Interview 020710C, with an employee of the Czech Agriculture and Food Inspection Authority (Prague).

[122] *Kontrola v číslech: Srovnání základních údajů o kontrolní činnosti ČOI v letech 1998–2002* (Enforcement Statistics: Comparative Baseline Indicators of the Enforcement Activity of the Czech Commercial Inspection in the Years 1998–2002), www.ČOI.cz (accessed September 21, 2003).

[123] Czech Interview 020712A, with the director general of the State Institute for Drug Control (Prague).

TABLE 5.4. *Administrative Enforcement in the Czech Republic, 1997–2005*

Year	Commercial Inspection	Institute for Drug Control	Total	Enforcement Cases (per million people)
1997	160			
1998	230			
1999	522			
2000	1,019			
2001	1,301			
2002	1,216			
2003	1,342			
2004	2,007	8	2,015	201.5
2005	n.a.	5		

Sources: *Kontrola v číslech: Srovnání základních údajů o kontrolní činnosti ČOI v letech 1998–2002*, www.ČOI.cz (accessed September 21, 2003); *Srovnání základních údajů o kontrolní činnosti ČOI v letech 1998–2005* (Comparative Baseline Indicators of the Enforcement Activity of the Czech Commercial Inspection 1998–2004), www.ČOI.cz (accessed August 15, 2006); *Zpráva o činnosti SÚKL v roce 2004* (SÚKL Annual Report 2004), 29; *Zpráva o činnosti SÚKL v roce 2005* (SÚKL Annual Report 2005), 25, www.sukl.cz (accessed October 23, 2006).

of 2,007 cases in 2004 (see Table 5.4). Because of the relative domination of administrative enforcement activity by the ČOI, enforcement is predictable and regularized. The ČOI has also provided a very high volume of enforcement, which has allowed the Czech Republic to emerge as the second most active administrative enforcer among the six countries examined in this book.

France

In France, there are only two agencies that supply IPR administrative enforcement: the Directorate General on Competition, Consumer Affairs, and Fraud Control (Direction générale de la concurrence, de la consommation et de la répression des fraudes, or DGCCRF) and the French Agency on the Sanitary Security of Medical Products (Agence française de sécurité sanitaire des produits de santé, or AFSSAPS).

The DGCCRF is a large agency under the Ministry of the Economy, Finance, and Industry with a century-long history of consumer protection and combating fraud.[124] Its 3,716 employees work at its headquarters and at its 23 regional and 101 *département* offices.[125] The DGCCRF can conduct market checks for counterfeit goods either at the request of a right holder or on its own initiative. It can take samples of goods that are suspected of being counterfeit, but, unlike

[124] The DGCCRF was established as mandated by the Law on Fraud Control, August 1, 1905.
[125] See *Rapport d'activité 2005* (Annual Report 2005) (Paris: DGCCRF, 2006). A French *région* is loosely equivalent to a province in China, whereas a *département* is equivalent to a Chinese county.

Customs and the police, it cannot seize such goods.[126] When the DGCCRF suspects foul play, it can alert the right holder or transfer evidence to the courts and the Procuratorate. In recent years, there has been an impressive rise in the number of control checks, which grew from 923 to 5,032 between 2003 and 2005.[127]

Created in March 1999 with 2,900 personnel under the Ministry of Health and Social Security (Ministère de la santé et des solidarités), the AFSSAPS has a broad mandate covering market approval and surveillance over medicines, medical devices, and cosmetics.[128] The AFSSAPS has the powers of a sanitary police (*police sanitaire*), which broadly means that it can suspend, temporarily or in perpetuity, the manufacture, importation, and sale of products that violate the French Public Health Code. Therefore, in theory, the AFSSAPS can play an important role in pharmaceutical anticounterfeiting. However, despite its mandate, the AFSSAPS becomes involved in cases of counterfeiting episodically and usually reacts only when alerted to the presence of counterfeits in the market. It believes that the DGCCRF and the Procuratorate (*le parquet*), along with Customs, should be the lead enforcers in cases of pharmaceutical counterfeiting. Although it has handled a case of counterfeit contact lenses, the AFSSAPS reports that no cases of counterfeit pharmaceuticals have reached it yet.

The United States

In contrast to China, no U.S. administrative agency self-initiates investigations in cases of IPR piracy and counterfeiting. The only administrative enforcer, the U.S. International Trade Commission (ITC), puts the burden of initial evidence gathering on the right holders, who must present it with sufficient evidence to start an investigation. After filings from the public, the commission can conduct Section 337 investigations into unfair trade practices, such as the importation of patent- and trademark-infringing goods into the United States.[129] These investigations culminate with quasi-judicial proceedings that produce cease-and-desist letters or exclusion orders, which can then be used to stop the importation of infringing items into the United States. The ITC does not organize enforcement raids. The ITC handled 591 cases between 1976 and 2006, approximately 19 cases per year.[130] In 2004, the ITC accepted 0.1 case per million people, thus placing the United States last among the six countries analyzed in this book in terms of the volume of administrative enforcement.

---

[126] France Interview 020417C, with DGCCRF expert (Paris).

[127] See *Rapport d'activité 2004* (Paris: DGCCRF, 2005), 16; *Rapport d'activité 2005*, 27.

[128] This paragraph is based on *Rapport annuel 2005* (Annual Report 2005) (Paris: AFSSAPS, 2006), http://afssaps.sante.fr/htm/5/ra2005.htm (accessed April 29, 2008).

[129] See Section 337 of the 1930 Tariff Act (19 U.S.C. §1337). Although several agencies other than the ITC can also handle IPR matters (the Food and Drug Administration, the Fair Trade Commission, and the Bureau on Alcohol, Tobacco, and Firearms), we have no evidence that they do so.

[130] For a full list of the cases, see www.usitc.gov (accessed November 18, 2006).

Given the extremely high demand for court enforcement by right holders, this figure is not surprising.

The United States also has a Patent and Trademark Office (U.S. PTO), which houses the Board of Patent Appeals and Interferences, as well as a Trademark Trial and Appeal Board, both of which conduct in-house quasi-judicial proceedings on patent appeals, oppositions, and interferences.[131] However, unlike the SIPO and the SAIC in China, the U.S. PTO does not engage in any on-the-ground anticounterfeiting enforcement. In this regard, the United States is similar to Russia, Taiwan, the Czech Republic, and France, whose patent and trademark offices do not have direct enforcement responsibilities for IPR.

CONCLUSION

Several aspects of administrative IPR enforcement in China are distinctive. No other country has as many administrative agencies sharing the IPR enforcement portfolio. Nor does any other country have an administrative-to-nonadministrative enforcement ratio that is so skewed in favor of administrative enforcement. Two questions arise. Why has China been able to deliver such a high volume of administrative enforcement? Second, is that enforcement rationalized? These questions will be answered more fully in Chapters 7, 8, and 9, but we can sketch out some preliminary explanations here.

Countries like China and Russia, where piracy is high, deliver enforcement under foreign or domestic pressure. Russia's low overall enforcement volume can be explained by the lack of both foreign and domestic pressure to enforce, and by the consequent withering of the specialized IPR bureaucracies. In China, by contrast, foreign pressure has been applied in the area of copyrights, whereas trademarks have been subject to both domestic pressure (after product quality scandals, for example) and foreign pressure (through Quality Brands Protection Committee [QBPC] lobbying). These pressures have led to a high level of enforcement in these two IPR subtypes. Conversely, there has been no pressure in patents, and in consequence the volume of enforcement is relatively small.

A large quantity of administrative enforcement does not mean that enforcement will be rationalized. When enforcement is delivered by agencies with poorly defined portfolios that are operating under conditions of decentralization, enforcement is likely to be inconsistent, nontransparent, and unfair. The cause is the difficulty of holding bureaucratic actors accountable for their behavior when the rules about what they should be doing are unclear. In addition, decentralization creates obstacles to effective monitoring of local-level bureaucrats by the center.

Some caveats are in order. Neither jurisdictional overlap nor decentralization must on its own lead to unpredictable enforcement. The experiences of Taiwan, the Czech Republic, and France show that centralization can counteract the negative impact of overlap. Russia constitutes something of an outlier,

---

[131] www.uspto.gov (accessed November 18, 2006).

since it presents a situation of overlapping mandates and decentralization, with virtually no enforcement at all. In light of the cross-national comparison, it seems clear that certain peculiarities of the Chinese administrative enforcement structure best explain why the administrative enforcement for trademarks and copyrights remains arbitrary, even where there is will on the part of the state to generate a high volume of enforcement.

The fact that enforcement for some subtypes of IPR (copyrights and trademarks) is characterized by overlap and decentralization and for others (patents) by relative predictability points us back to the bureaucratic complexities of the state, which ultimately is responsible for deciding how enforcement will be organized. Certainly, it is easier to create a transparent enforcement framework in new areas like patents. But it is also possible to rationalize enforcement in domains where bureaucracies have a longer and more complicated history. Why has the state allowed so many agencies to enforce in copyrights and trademarks, when that produces an inefficient result? At times of real or imagined crises, the state often needed to provide a high volume of campaign-style enforcement quickly, a pattern that led to the creation and entrenchment of an apparently comprehensive, but actually ineffective system for enforcement. And then there is the lure of volume itself. Administrative enforcement in China is remarkable both for being the highest in the world in terms of volume and for being so low in quality. Plowing CDs into the earth makes for good copy and even good foreign relations, but it is not the way to get rationalization. What matters is whether the state can refine the mundane operations of an intricately complex enforcement apparatus.

6

Criminal Enforcement

The Failure of Coordination

In China the criminal protection of IPR is heavily overshadowed by the administrative enforcement discussed in Chapter 5. Criminal enforcement could be an effective method of IPR protection, if only because the possibility of serving prison time has a highly deterrent effect on potential counterfeiters. Furthermore, the criminal justice system in China is extremely adept at producing guilty verdicts in the cases that do reach trial. In theory, criminal enforcement should be a viable option for serious cases of IPR infringement. However, according to data discussed in the present chapter, criminal IPR cases equaled one-tenth of 1 percent of the administrative IPR cases handled in 2004. This then raises the question why criminal enforcement is used so rarely in China.

The major obstacle to criminal enforcement in IPR is that so few cases are placed on the docket. The underlying cause is that criminal enforcement is a bureaucratically complex, multistep process. Most often a case reaches the police through an administrative agency that must be willing to consider transferring the matter to the police in the first place. The police must then decide to accept the case and, thereafter, to transfer it to the Procuratorate, which, in turn, must decide whether to pursue the matter by arresting the suspect and introducing the case in court. Finally, the courts themselves have the option either to reject or to accept the case. Eventually, after a guilty verdict, the suspect may be sentenced to a fixed term of imprisonment. Although many of the cases handled by administrative agencies are indeed serious enough to merit being transferred to the police for criminal prosecution, negative incentives at each stage of the criminal enforcement process limit the number of cases that are prosecuted and ultimately reach the courts.

In brief, this chapter argues that the low volume of criminal enforcement in China is a consequence of poor coordination among the criminal divisions of the courts and the other four key actors: the administrative agencies, the police, the Procuratorate, and the central government. Administrative agencies are loath to initiate a transfer, not just because transfers are time-consuming, but also because a successful transfer forces the agency to forgo imposing a lucrative fine. In turn, the police accept only a portion of the small number of cases that the administrative agencies do attempt to transfer to them and only rarely engage in proactive IPR investigations (even though this is in theory subsumed under their mandate). The police do not see IPR as part of their core mission, and to date they lack a reason to change that view. IPR enforcement seems also to be a low priority for the Procuratorate, which does not pressure the police departments to increase their IPR caseload. The criminal divisions of the courts may themselves have an interest in limiting criminal cases to those in which a guilty verdict is likely.

Finally, the central government has until recently been reluctant to allocate scarce police resources to the prosecution of IPR crimes and so has been unwilling to pressure the administrative agencies, the police, and the Procuratorate to cooperate on making criminal prosecution a more effective enforcement option. A key variable contributing to this position of the central government has been the absence of either foreign or domestic pressure to step up criminal enforcement. The absence of foreign pressure is easily understood, given Western conceptions of the Chinese police. Since the 1989 Tiananmen Square protests, it has not been desirable or politically viable for the United States to encourage police involvement in any type of policy implementation. For its part, the China-based Quality Brands Protection Committee has also until recently been skeptical that it is possible to motivate the police to enforce in IPR cases. Domestic consumer-protection associations have also regarded criminal enforcement as a last resort and have not put pressure on the state to provide it.

This confluence of factors has worked to limit severely the number of criminal IPR cases that reach the courts. Controlling for population, China has the absolute lowest volume of criminal IPR enforcement among the six countries examined in this book, as demonstrated by Table 6.1.

This chapter analyzes the obstacles to effective criminal IPR enforcement in China, at each of the steps through which a case culminates in a court trial. It then suggests the importance of well-coordinated enforcement for the institutionalization of high-quality IPR protection by comparing China's record with those of Russia, Taiwan, the Czech Republic, France, and the United States.

CRIMINAL IPR ENFORCEMENT IN CHINA

There are three ways in which a criminal case can be initiated in China. Right holders may bypass the police altogether and take the criminal matter directly to court through private prosecution. For reasons discussed later, this option is in practice extremely rarely used. The other two options involve the police.[1] The police can accept a case transferred to them from an administrative agency or, as a third option, proactively self-initiate a case. We should note here that

---

[1] At the central level, the police are known as the Ministry of Public Security (MPS), and at the local level as the Public Security Bureau (PSB).

TABLE 6.1. *Cross-National Police Enforcement Efforts in 2004 (per million people)*

Country	Piracy Rate	Police Enforcement	Non-Police Enforcement	Ratio of Non-Police to Police Enforcement
China	High	0.8	947	1,184:1
Russia	High	13.4	16.3	1.2:1
Taiwan	Medium	183	94.4	0.5:1
Czech	Medium	88.3	253.4	3:1
France	Medium	36.9	151.8	4:1
U.S.	Low	1.2	57.4	48:1

Sources: Zhongguo zhishi chanquan nianjian 2005 (China IPR Yearbook 2005) (Beijing: Zhishi chanquan chubanshe, 2005), 306, 309; MVD RF, *Obshchie svedeniia o sostoianii prestupnosti v 2004 g.* (General Information on Criminality in 2004), www.mvdinform.ru (accessed June 30, 2006); *Performance Report on Intellectual Property Protection in Taiwan 2004* (Taiwan: TIPO, 2005), 13, 16–17, 24–27; *Statistický výkaz č. 1 – kriminalita za období od 1.1.2004 do 31.12.2004* (Statistical Report Part I: Criminality for the Period from January 1, 2004, to December 31, 2004) (Praha: Policejní prezidium ČR, 2005); *Aspects de la criminalité et de la délinquance constatées en France en 2004*, tome 1 (Paris: La Documentation française, 2005), 38, 52; *Progress Report of the Department of Justice's Task Force* (Washington, DC, June 2006), 23.

the police do not organize enforcement raids in response to complaints from right holders. In addition, the police rarely participate in enforcement campaigns on their own; typically, they join campaigns only to support administrative enforcement agencies.

As already mentioned, the low number of criminal IPR cases in China reflects the unwillingness of administrative agencies to initiate the transfer of suspected criminal matters to the police, the lack of enthusiasm among police officers to accept transfers, the reluctance of the police to initiate investigations of piracy and counterfeiting on its own, and the lack of pressure from the Procuratorate to increase police activity. The Chinese government has attempted to address this lack of coordination by issuing various regulations clarifying criminal-liability and case-transfer ambiguities. Because they lack "teeth," however, none of those regulations has been successful at making the police a more proactive enforcer or at increasing the volume of reactive IPR enforcement they provide.

IPR Criminal Liability Statutory Basis

Criminal punishments for IPR violations were available in China as early as 1979, but they were rarely used. The 1979 Criminal Law stipulated that trademark infringement is a crime: Article 127 mandated a maximum of three years imprisonment for "employees of commercial and industrial enterprises directly responsible for counterfeiting the registered trademarks of other enterprises." Article 40 of the 1982 Trademark Law also allowed for criminal punishment of trademark counterfeiting. In 1985, 1988, 1992, and 1993, six additional resolutions attempting (unsuccessfully) to clarify the criminal liability threshold for copyright piracy and trademark counterfeiting were issued by the Standing Committee of the National People's Congress, the Supreme People's Court (SPC), and the Supreme People's Procuratorate (SPP). Patents received significantly less attention from lawmakers. Although a 1985 SPC explanation and Article 63 of the revised 1992 Patent Law mandated that patent counterfeiting can be prosecuted under Article 127 of the 1979 Criminal Law, it was only after the 1997 amendment to the Criminal Law that patent counterfeiting formally became a criminal offense.

The 1997 amendment was important for moving toward stricter sentencing standards, as well. Prior to 1997, copyright piracy was punishable by up to only three years imprisonment, on the basis of a 1994 decision of the Standing Committee of the NPC and a 1995 SPC judicial explanation, among others.[2] The section on IPR crimes of the 1997 Criminal Law (Articles 213–220) supplemented and unified these numerous conflicting decisions and explanations. The maximal punishment for copyright piracy and trademark counterfeiting was raised to seven years imprisonment. Patent infringement was accorded a lower, but still serious, maximal punishment of three years imprisonment.

The 1997 Criminal Law also contains a section on crimes of manufacturing and marketing of fake and substandard commodities (Articles 140–150). This section is important because, despite multiple judicial interpretations and scholarly debate, the boundary between a "fake product" (which is classified as a substandard commodity) and an IPR-infringing product "bearing a counterfeit trademark or patent" remains very unclear. The problem is in part lexical. In Chinese "fake" is *jia*, whereas "counterfeit" is *jiamao*, and "fake and substandard" is *jiamao weilie*. Because the words have the same root and can be used synonymously to a certain degree, the law has not adequately distinguished between them; oftentimes, a product that infringes IPR (*qinfan zhishi chanquan*) may also be considered a fake and substandard product. This in turn makes it unclear how law enforcement officers should prosecute a given offense, whether as an IPR violation or as a case involving fake and substandard commodities. The practical consequences of this confusion are considerable, since substandard commodities crimes can result in heavier penalties than IPR crimes. The death penalty is available as the maximal punishment for the manufacturing and marketing of substandard medicines and foodstuffs that have led to serious harm to human health (Articles 141 and 144 of the 1997 Criminal Law). Moreover, for most crimes of manufacturing and marketing of fake and substandard commodities, the usual punishment is ten years imprisonment, as compared to three years imprisonment for a typical IPR crime. An especially important difference is that the criminal liability threshold for crimes involving fake and substandard commodities is much lower than that for IPR crimes. The high penalties and low liability thresholds explain why the police

---

[2] Zheng Liping, "Woguo xingshi falü dui zhishi chanquan de baohu" (Criminal IPR Protection in China), in *Zhongguo zhishi chanquan ershi nian 1978–1998* (Twenty Years of IPR in China 1978–1998), ed. Liu Chuntian (Beijing: Zhuanli wenxian chubanshe, 1998), 221–234. References to laws and regulations in this section are based on this source.

handle a heavier criminal caseload for substandard goods than for IPR counterfeiting and piracy.

IPR Criminal Liability Thresholds

The 1997 Criminal Law does not clearly specify the threshold above which IPR violations constitute a crime. The law implicitly sets a threshold of "serious circumstances" for applying lighter criminal penalties and "especially serious circumstances" for applying heavier penalties, but it does not spell out the meaning of these terms. A number of judicial interpretations have attempted to provide clarification. In 1998, an interpretation on the trial of criminal cases of illegal publications was issued by the SPC, specifying that in order for the "serious circumstances" threshold to be met, the suspect had to have made an illegal profit of 50,000 yuan.[3] Trademark interpretations were not revised until 2001, when the criminal threshold for large-scale trademark counterfeiting by individuals was set at 100,000 yuan of illegal business volume.[4] But these specifications did not satisfy right holders on their own, mainly because it remained unclear how the illegal business volume (*feifa jingying shu'e*) and illegal profit (*weifa suode shu'e*) should be calculated. Criminal liability thresholds are not useful unless it is known how the price of the goods will be determined.

This problem was addressed in 2004. Unlike previous interpretations that fragmented IPR crimes, a 2004 SPC/SPP judicial explanation offered an integrated interpretation of all IPR violations from trademark and patent counterfeiting to copyright piracy.[5] Criminal thresholds for individuals were lowered to an illegal business volume of 50,000 yuan or illegal profits of 30,000 yuan. In addition, the 2004 interpretation established three different methods for calculating the price of the counterfeits. For goods that had already been sold, the sales price would be used. For goods that were labeled but not yet sold, the labeled price would be used. For unlabeled (and unsold) goods, the middle market price would be used. The 2004 interpretation represents a serious attempt on the part of the courts to fill large gaps in the Criminal Law and thereby facilitate the prosecution of IPR crimes. However, the 2004 interpretation has not yet led to a significant rise in the number of criminal

---

[3] "Zuigao renmin fayuan guanyu shenli feifa chubanwu xingshi anjian juti yingyong falü ruogan wenti de jieshi" (Explanation by the Supreme People's Court on Some Questions Regarding the Use of Specific Laws in the Trial of Criminal Cases of Illegal Publications) (Fashi [1998] 30 hao).

[4] Under Chinese law, crimes may be committed either by individuals (*geren*) or by units (*danwei*), with different thresholds and penalties. See "Zuigao renmin jianchayuan gong'an bu guanyu jingji fanzui anjian zhuisu biaozhun de guiding" (Provisions by the Supreme People's Procuratorate and the Ministry of Public Security on the Prosecution Standard for Economic Crime Cases) (April 18, 2001), Articles 61–65.

[5] "Zuigao renmin fayuan, Zuigao renmin jianchayuan guanyu banli qinfan zhishi chanquan xingshi anjian juti yingyong falü ruogan wenti de jieshi" (Explanation by the Supreme People's Court and the Supreme People's Procuratorate on Some Questions Regarding the Use of Specific Laws in Handling Criminal IPR Infringement Cases) (Fashi [2000] 19 hao).

prosecutions, mainly because it left unresolved the knotty issue of case-transfer rules (which I consider later in this chapter).

One further detail is relevant. In contrast to IPR crimes, the lower liability thresholds for most crimes of manufacturing and marketing of fake and sub-standard commodities are specified in the law itself (Article 140 of the Criminal Law) and do not require the enactment of any additional judicial explanations. Even where such specifications are absent, moreover, the thresholds are simpler to ascertain (e.g., death or serious harm to human health).[6] Understandably, this makes the prosecution of these crimes easier than the prosecution of IPR crimes. As a result, the police may sometimes exploit the ambiguity between the two areas and prosecute IPR crimes as substandard commodities crimes.

Case-Transfer Rules

The frequency of criminal enforcement would increase if the administrative agencies that dominate IPR enforcement had incentives to transfer to the police more of the cases that meet the criminal liability thresholds. In the absence of clearer rules, case transfers will not rise, since the system now in place has evolved to allow administrative agencies to retain full control of virtually all cases of piracy and counterfeiting that they investigate. The first attempt to increase case transfers was made in 2001, when the State Council issued the "Regulation on the Transfer of Suspected Criminal Cases by Administrative Enforcement Agencies."[7] The regulation specified in great detail the procedures and deadlines for the prompt transfer of suspected criminal cases from administrative agencies to the public security bureaus (PSBs).

Given the potential volume of cases, in theory the 2001 regulation should have led to a sharp rise in the number of cases transferred to the PSBs. For example, in 2005 alone, the State Administration for Industry and Commerce (SAIC) handled at least 6,332 cases of trademark counterfeiting in which the value of the seized goods was over 50,000 yuan, thus meeting and exceeding the 2004 criminal liability threshold. In 2005, however, the SAIC transferred only 236 cases to the PSB (3.7 percent of the above-threshold cases).[8] Furthermore, this figure from 2005 represents a high point in the transfer of cases from the SAIC to the PSB: the average transfer rate for the entire period from 1999 to 2005 stands at well under 1 percent of the total SAIC caseload.[9] The SAIC and

---

[6] Nonetheless, such judicial explanations have been promulgated even for the manufacturing and marketing of fake and substandard commodities.

[7] Decree No. 310 of the PRC State Council, "Xingzheng zhifa jiguan yisong shexian fanzui anjian de guiding" (Provisions on the Transfer of Suspected Criminal Cases by the Administrative Enforcement Organs) (July 9, 2001).

[8] *2005 nian quanguo chachu shangbiao weifa anjian jiben qingkuang* (Basic Situation of Trademark Counterfeiting Investigations in 2005) (April 27, 2006), http://www.saic.gov.cn/ggl/zwgg_detail.asp?newsid=396 (accessed November 10, 2006).

[9] *Zhongguo zhishi chanquan nianjian* (China IPR Yearbook), all years between 2000 and 2006.

other agencies retained the lion's share of cases that met the requirements for transfer to the PSB.

Why has the 2001 regulation not had its intended effect? The chief incentive for an administrative agency to hold on to a case is that by transferring it to the PSB it forgoes the opportunity to impose a fine on the violator. For fiscally strapped administrative agencies, fines are an unusually important source of extrabudgetary income. In 2005, for example, the SAIC collected 342 million yuan (about US$42 million) in fines imposed in cases of trademark counterfeiting.[10] A second and equally important explanation for the low transfer rate is the lack of negative incentives for the administrative agency to coordinate with the criminal authorities: administrative officials are rarely punished for failure to follow the official rules stipulating prompt and regular transfer of cases.

Administrative reluctance is only one part of the story, however. Even when an administrative agency has initiated a transfer, the PSB itself can refuse to accept the case. The police do not publish data on the percentage of criminal cases accepted through transfers, but statistics from administrative agencies highlight the basic trends. For example, in 2003 the Administration of Quality Supervision, Inspection, and Quarantine (AQSIQ) initiated the transfer of 355 counterfeiting cases to the PSB, but the PSB accepted only 140 of them (40 percent).[11] In 2004, the PSB accepted about half of the 182 cases that the AQSIQ attempted to transfer. This entrenched reluctance has a predictable effect. Specific data on the number of IPR cases successfully transferred from certain administrative agencies to the police in 2004 are presented in Table 6.2, which shows that, for most agencies with an IPR portfolio, the transfer rate is usually equivalent to less than 1 percent of their total IPR caseload.

In an apparent attempt to address the low transfer rate, the central government issued the new "Opinion on the Prompt Transfer of Suspected Criminal Cases Uncovered during Administrative Enforcement" (*Guanyu zai xingzheng zhifa zhong jishi yisong shexian fanzui anjian de yijian*) on March 2, 2006. Collectively issued by the Supreme People's Procuratorate, the Market Order Rectification Office, the Ministry of Public Security (MPS), and the Ministry of Supervision, the Opinion largely restates and reaffirms the 2001 State Council case-transfer regulations. The most important innovative provision of the Opinion is the inclusion of the Procuratorate as a supervisory entity in the case-transfer process. As soon as an administrative agency transfers a case to the PSB, the Procuratorate is to receive a copy of the case-transfer documentation, presumably as a way to facilitate its supervision of the case. This initiative

[10] Technically, fines are not retained by the agency but are remitted to the Finance Bureau. However, in 2008, interviewees claimed that up to 90 percent of the fines they collect are returned to them as part of their official budgetary allocations. China Interview 080107B, with a TSB official (Zouping).

[11] *Zhongguo zhiliang jiandu jianyan jianyi nianjian 2004* (China AQSIQ Yearbook 2004) (Beijing: Zhongguo biaozhun chubanshe, 2004), 157; *Zhongguo zhiliang jiandu jianyan jianyi nianjian 2005* (China AQSIQ Yearbook 2005) (Beijing: Zhongguo biaozhun chubanshe, 2005), 193.

TABLE 6.2. *Administrative Case-Transfer Rates for Selected Chinese Agencies in 2004*

Agency	Enforcement Cases	Cases Transferred to the PSB	Transfers as % of All Enforcement Cases
National Copyright Administration	9,497	101	1.1
State Intellectual Property Office	4,121	15 (2005 data)	0.4
State Administration for Industry and Commerce	51,851	96	0.2
Administration of Quality Supervision, Inspection, and Quarantine	198,722	182 (attempted); 83 successful transfers	0.05
Food and Drug Administration	376,000	1,792	0.5
Ministry of Agriculture	50,000	750	1.5
Anti-Pornography and Anti-Piracy Office	35,379	1,014	2.9

Sources: Zhongguo zhishi chanquan nianjian 2005, 88, 260–310; *Zhongguo zhiliang jiandu jianyan jianyi nianjian 2005*, 192–193; *Zhongguo shipin yaopin jiandu guanli nianjian 2005* (China SFDA Yearbook 2005) (Beijing: Huaxue gongye chubanshe, 2005), 6, 102, 213; *Zhongguo weisheng nianjian 2005* (China Health Yearbook 2005) (Beijing: Renmin weisheng chubanshe, 2005), 245; *Zhongguo nongye nianjian 2005* (China Agriculture Yearbook 2005) (Beijing: Nongye chubanshe, 2005), 110.

may potentially improve and standardize the investigation of IPR cases that reach the police.

But what about the frequency of transfer itself? Here, the Opinion seems to lack bite. The Opinion does empower the public to inform on the unwillingness of administrative agencies to transfer cases and on the PSB's reluctance to accept them. But it does nothing to increase the penalties that can be imposed on employees of administrative agencies or PSB officers who fail to transfer or accept cases meeting the liability thresholds. These are serious limitations to the central government's efforts. Although the March 2, 2006, Opinion appears promising by pushing against an entrenched problem, we will have to wait and see whether it has any significant effect on the volume of case transfers.[12]

[12] The Opinion was followed by three different regulations that the Ministry of Public Security issued separately with the General Administration of Customs, the State Administration for Industry and Commerce, and the National Copyright Administration of China. Surprisingly, none of these regulations mentions the duty of the Procuratorate to supervise case transfers, the role of the citizenry in informing on public servants who refuse to initiate or accept case transfers, and the penalties that will be imposed on officials who obstruct case transfers. These bilateral regulations might easily sabotage the intended effect of the Opinion.

Self-Initiated Police Cases

Although the police can proactively self-initiate investigations of IPR infringement, they have traditionally been averse to doing so. A major reason is that IPR violations are perceived as less serious than murder or armed robbery.[13] The punishments for IPR crimes under Chinese law are relatively light (a maximal imprisonment of seven years), reinforcing the PSB's sense of the low status of IPR in the hierarchy of crimes.[14]

Another negative factor is the organization of the police itself. Internal divisions within the PSB make it even more difficult to have a robust response to IPR infringement. Internally, the IPR portfolio is divided between the Social Order Unit (*zhi'an jingcha dadui*) and the Economic Crimes Investigation Unit (*jingji fanzui zhencha dadui*). Social Order handles anti-pornography, anti-piracy, and product quality, while Economic Crimes handles trademarks and patents.[15] A problem arises when counterfeit items simultaneously infringe both product quality and trademark laws, since the case can be handled by either of the two units. If the case is easy, the overlap engenders unnecessary competition between the units; if the case is complex, it tends to be passed back and forth between the two units, with each claiming that the other's expertise is more relevant.[16] (This competition for easy cases and shirking when faced with difficult ones replicate a problem that exists whenever multiple bureaucracies have overlapping jurisdictions; what is interesting here is that such overlap also exists *within* the PSB, a phenomenon that, as illustrated in Chapter 5, can be found in some of the administrative agencies with an IPR portfolio as well.)

What is the solution? To be sure, a centralized IPR unit within the PSB would counter this fragmentation of authority, but currently only the Shenzhen PSB has established such a unit.[17] This is not likely to change soon. As one policeman put it, "I don't think we can ever have specially designated police personnel concentrating entirely on IPR enforcement; this is just too expensive; it also doesn't make sense for the PSB to allot personnel to IPR enforcement, considering all the other responsibilities it has."[18] A relevant case here is that of Zouping county in Shandong province. Despite its population of 700,000, Zouping does not have a

---

[13] China Interview 080111, with an employee of the PSB Economic Crimes Investigation Unit (Zouping).

[14] Maximal punishments for IPR crimes in China are comparable to those in the other countries examined in this chapter. In some, the criminal prosecution rate is very high despite the low maximal punishment. Therefore, we cannot attribute the unwillingness of the Chinese police to deal with these matters only to the low maximal punishments.

[15] China Interview 020913A, with an IPR lawyer (Beijing); China Interview 020916B, with an employee of the PSB Economic Crimes Investigation Unit (Beijing).

[16] China Interview 080105 (Shanghai, by phone) and China Interview 080112 (Ji'nan), both with a private investigator.

[17] Presentation by the head of the Social Order Department of the Shenzhen PSB, People's University, November 15, 2001 (Beijing).

[18] China Interview 020916B, with an employee of the PSB Economic Crimes Investigation Unit (Beijing).

single police officer with full-time or even part-time responsibility for IPR enforcement.[19] Personnel shortages aside, the Chinese government has taken measures to increase the direct participation of the police in anticounterfeiting work, with initiatives such as the 2004–2005 "Mountain Eagle" campaign and other special police-sponsored anti-piracy activities. Unfortunately, these efforts have not led to an appreciable rise in the number of cases handled by the police.

Foreign pressure could in theory encourage the central government to increase police activity, but until recently countries like the United States have been unwilling to press China to provide more criminal enforcement. There are excellent reasons for this reluctance. Western analysts have long been aware of the shortcomings of the Chinese criminal justice system.[20] Human rights concerns were elevated in the 1980s, when the police engaged in the brutal suppression of dissent during the "strike hard" (*yanda*) campaign of 1983–1986.[21] After the Tiananmen Square protests in 1989, foreign governments found criminal enforcement even less palatable as a solution to any kind of problem in China. U.S. scholars correctly pointed out that in general the Chinese police had developed a work style that violated basic principles of due process and often led to severe perversions of justice.[22] And for IPR in particular, experts rightly worried that an emphasis on criminal IPR enforcement might justify an increase in the number of executions.[23]

Such concerns remained valid across the 1990s, but since then the Chinese criminal justice system has developed in promising ways. Although policing is still plagued by problems,[24] economic crimes are less likely than political dissent to produce a perversion of justice. The U.S. government indirectly acknowledged this in 2007, when it initiated a WTO dispute settlement procedure against China: the United States Trade Representative (USTR) had a long list of complaints about the criminal protection of IPR in China, but it targeted mainly the high (and poorly defined) criminal liability thresholds. Tellingly, the USTR also pressed for more police enforcement.[25] There was no

[19] China Interview 080111, with a PSB officer (Zouping).

[20] Jerome A. Cohen, *The Criminal Process in the People's Republic of China, 1949–1963: An Introduction* (Cambridge, MA: Harvard University Press, 1968).

[21] Murray Scot Tanner, "State Coercion and the Balance of Awe: The 1983–1986 'Stern Blows' Anti-Crime Campaign," *The China Journal*, no. 44 (2000), 93–125.

[22] Donald Clarke and James Feinerman, "Antagonistic Contradictions: Criminal Law and Human Rights in China," in *China's Legal Reforms*, ed. Stanley Lubman (Oxford: Oxford University Press, 1996), 135–154.

[23] William Alford, "Making the World Safe for What? Intellectual Property Rights, Human Rights, and Foreign Economic Policy in the Post-European Cold War World," in *Chinese Intellectual Property Law and Practice*, ed. Mark A. Cohen, A. Elizabeth Bang, and Stephanie Mitchell (The Hague: Kluwer Law International, 1999), 147–163. See esp. p. 155.

[24] For overviews, see Michael Dutton, *Policing Chinese Politics: A History* (Durham, NC: Duke University Press, 2005), 247–316; Børge Bakken, ed., *Crime, Punishment, and Policing in China* (Lanham, MD: Rowman & Littlefield, 2005).

[25] On the background to this case, see USTR, "Trade Delivers," April 9, 2007, http://www.ustr.gov/assets/Document_Library/Fact_Sheets/2007/asset_upload_file908_11061.pdf (accessed May 26, 2008).

suggestion here that stronger police enforcement would either endanger the rights of individuals suspected of IPR violations or be used by the central government for political purposes. A critic might surmise that the United States simply let its economic interests override its commitment to safeguarding human rights in China. But this is to overlook the fact that the volume of IPR prosecutions has been kept deliberately low: the high thresholds for criminal prosecution and the highly technical nature of IPR offenses already give us some confidence that these cases are not being used for the random targeting of political opponents of the Chinese regime. In one interpretation, the PSB, the Procuratorate, and the courts are avoiding criminal IPR cases precisely because of the high evidentiary requirements and the consequent difficulties in obtaining convictions.[26] An equally likely explanation is that the evidentiary standards are themselves a way for the criminal justice organs to limit court scrutiny to those important cases in which a guilty verdict is likely. In other words, questions of bureaucratic efficiency are intertwined with questions of bureaucratic prestige: the system makes the courts look efficacious by restricting the scope of their surveillance to a very few high-profile cases.

A recent and suggestive development in the area of criminal enforcement is that the People's Armed Police (PAP), a branch of the People's Liberation Army (PLA) under the dual command of the PLA and the MPS, has shown interest in the enforcement of IPR. The State Intellectual Property Office has started organizing training sessions for PAP officers.[27] This development, which legitimates the emergence of yet another authorized enforcer, may reflect the state's ongoing commitment to bureaucratic duplication as a way of addressing a complex regulatory problem. However, it is more likely that the PAP has been authorized to enter the IPR enforcement domain because enterprises, warehouses, and transportation vehicles either owned by or connected to the PLA have historically been used for counterfeiting.[28] Counterfeiters have been tempted to use PLA facilities by the virtual immunity of the PLA from the ordinary courts of law (the PLA has its own system of courts and corruption investigation bodies).[29] Data on IPR enforcement by the PAP so far remain unavailable. The addition of yet another enforcer is the standard way through which the Chinese state attempts to solve knotty enforcement problems. It remains to be seen whether the PAP will have any positive impact on IPR protection either in its own jurisdiction or more generally.

Regional Variation in Police Enforcement

Because the MPS in China has a decentralized structure, the budget and personnel of individual PSBs are determined by the local governments. This basic

---

[26] Presentation by Professor Zhao Bingzhi, People's University, November 15, 2001 (Beijing).
[27] http://211.152.13.116/sipo_english/gftx_e/200205140001.htm (accessed on February 23, 2003).
[28] China Interview 010802B, with a private investigator (Hong Kong).
[29] China Interview 010731B, with a private investigator (Hong Kong); China Interview 020913B, with a journalist working on corruption in the PLA (Beijing).

structure results in considerable regional variation in the criminal enforcement of IPR laws across China. Police action tends to follow local economic interests. On the one hand, there are many villages, and sometimes, entire cities, plagued by local protectionism, where counterfeiting is the main source of income for the local government. Here, predictably, the police are often unwilling to prosecute counterfeiters, who in fact are the mainstay of the local economy. In contrast, some developed coastal cities take IPR enforcement very seriously. When in November 2005 the Ministry of Public Security reported the successful completion of ten IPR investigations "involving great value and causing great detriment," developed coastal provinces were primarily involved: Fujian, Guangdong, and Sichuan each claimed two cases, whereas Shanghai, Tianjin, Henan, Jiangsu, and Anhui each had one case.[30] A similar pattern underlies the distribution of awards by the Quality Brands Protection Committee (QBPC) since 2003 to local government agencies that handle the IPR infringement cases with the largest value. The awards for criminal cases have gone disproportionately to PSBs in Guangdong, Fujian, and Zhejiang provinces.[31] These are provinces whose local economies depend on protecting intellectual property rights, not on getting proceeds from counterfeiting. The character of the local economy therefore allows us to predict the volume of IPR protection.

Although we lack comprehensive data on police enforcement in all Chinese provinces, we have relatively complete statistics from Beijing, Shanghai, Guangdong, and Zhejiang provinces. The numbers show that enforcement volume in these provinces is much higher than we would expect given their proportional share of China's population. In 2003 alone, the Economic Crimes Investigation Unit of the Beijing PSB accepted for investigation twenty-two IPR cases with a total value of over 22.7 million yuan. In addition, the Beijing PSB uncovered (*pohuo*) sixteen "big and important cases" (*da'an yao'an*). In the same year, 2,039 cases of crimes of upsetting market order (*raoluan shichang chengxu zui*) with a value of 860 million yuan were accepted, with 1,896 cases being uncovered by the police themselves.[32] In 2005, the Shanghai PSB investigated 154 criminal IPR cases involving 247 suspects.[33] In 2004, police forces in Guangdong province investigated 512 cases of IPR infringement and manufacturing and marketing of fake and substandard commodities; 399 of the cases with a value of 386 million yuan were solved, and 1,514 suspects were detained.[34] In

---

[30] "MPS Announced Latest Progress on the Investigation of Ten IPR Infringement Cases in China," November 15, 2005, www.china.org.cn (accessed June 28, 2006). One of the ten cases was handled by two provinces (Tianjin and Guangdong), thus raising the province/case count to eleven.

[31] Reference Area, *10 Best Cases*, www.qbpc.org.cn (accessed July 9, 2006).

[32] *Beijing gong'an nianjian 2004* (Beijing Police Yearbook 2004) (Beijing: Guojia dang'an chubanshe, 2004), 161.

[33] *Status of Intellectual Property Rights Protection in Shanghai in 2005*, http://www.sipa.gov.cn/ chan_eng/Information2_detail.asp?id=169 (accessed November 16, 2006).

[34] *Guangdong zhishi chanquan nianjian 2005* (Guangdong IPR Yearbook 2005) (Guangzhou: Jingji chubanshe, 2005), 80.

Zhejiang, the Economic Crimes Investigation Unit accepted 162 IPR cases in 2004 (down from 164 in 2003); of these, 144 cases were solved (*po'an*); 219 suspects were investigated, and economic losses of 18.65 million yuan were averted. In addition, 1,225 crimes of upsetting market order were accepted (up from 1,065 the previous year), of which 1,048 were solved; 1,031 suspects were investigated and economic losses of 245.18 million yuan were avoided.[35] The Social Order Unit focused on investigating cases of production of substandard baby formula, wine, beverages, and cigarette machines.[36]

In the absence of more complete data, we cannot make definitive statements about the regional variation in enforcement in China. Nevertheless, it does appear that criminal IPR enforcement is regionally skewed, similar to Customs, civil court, and administrative enforcement, with most of the cases concentrated in the coastal provinces.

The Procuratorate

Before a criminal case reaches a court of law, it must pass through the Procuratorate, whose chief responsibility is the criminal indictment of the suspects. The Procuratorate approves the official arrest of the suspects (who are held in detention prior to their arrest), introduces the case in court, and represents the state against the accused. We do not have systematic statistics on how many of the IPR cases that are transferred to the Procuratorate from the PSB are eventually submitted to the courts. Data gathered during fieldwork in China indicate that, of the 901 cases of trademark counterfeiting handled by the PSB in 2000, 347 were transferred to the Procuratorate. In turn, the Procuratorate submitted 262 cases to the Case Handling Division of the People's Court, 173 of which were accepted.[37] Thus, the Procuratorate transfers a sizable portion of the cases it receives from the PSB to the courts. Nevertheless, because of the serial attrition of cases across the different stages of transfer, only about one-sixth of the already small number of cases handled by the PSB reach the courts.

Private Prosecution Cases (*Zisu Anjian*)

Individuals can bypass the PSB and the Procuratorate by lodging criminal cases directly with the court, through a private prosecution procedure.[38] The only requirement is that the victim have evidence proving a minor criminal case is at issue: major cases cannot be brought forward directly, but only through the PSB and the Procuratorate.[39] According to a 1998 SPC judicial interpretation, private

[35] *Zhejiang gong'an nianjian 2005* (Zhejiang Police Yearbook 2005) (Hangzhou: Zhejiang daxue chubanshe, 2005), 103.
[36] *Zhejiang gong'an nianjian 2005*, 110.
[37] Presentation by Jiang Wei, chief prosecutor, Supreme People's Procuratorate, People's University, November 16, 2001 (Beijing).
[38] Article 170 of the 1997 Criminal Procedure Law.
[39] Article 170.2 of the 1997 Criminal Procedure Law.

prosecution is formally allowed for both IPR crimes and crimes involving the manufacturing and marketing of fake and substandard commodities that do not seriously harm public order or the interests of the state.[40] But interview evidence and scholarly research both suggest that, although possible, private prosecution cases are exceedingly rare.[41] The main obstacle for private prosecution is not political, but procedural, namely, the unwillingness of the courts to impose a criminal penalty based on evidence collected by the victims themselves, rather than by the public security organs. For similar reasons, but also because of bureaucratic self-interest, the People's Procuratorate is loath to let cases that escaped its supervision reach the courts. Unless the incentives for the courts, police, and Procuratorate are systematically restructured, we should expect the current dominance of public prosecution over private prosecution to persist.

The Courts

As the complicated process of case transfer would suggest, the number of criminal IPR cases handled by the Chinese courts is low. Although this figure increased by 60 percent between 1992 and 2005 (see Table 6.3), that rate of increase was sixteen times smaller than the rate of increase for civil IPR cases handled by the specialized IPR tribunals during the same period (see Chapter 4).[42] Most of the cases adjudicated were trademark cases, followed by copyrights and, then, patent cases. Unlike civil IPR cases, there are no specialized tribunals for criminal IPR cases in China. This is not unusual; no country in the world has a specialized criminal IPR tribunal.

Once a criminal matter reaches the docket in China, there is a 99 percent chance of conviction, as data presented in Table 6.4 show (in 2004, only 1 percent of suspects were found either not guilty or exempt from criminal prosecution). This figure is best understood comparatively. China's conviction rate is the highest among the six countries examined in this book. Rather than pointing to any necessary bias in the courts, however, the number may reflect a process of selective enforcement aimed at guaranteeing conviction in the cases that are heard: the system is working to generate convictions, not volume. Rates of incarceration in China are also high: at close to 50 percent of all convictions, the figure is comparable only to the incarceration rate in the United States (see Table 6.6), where, as an effect of the low level of piracy, the rate of incarceration relative to convictions reflects the seriousness of the few cases made

---

[40] "Zuigao renmin fayuan guanyu zhixing 'Zhonghua renmin gongheguo xingshi susong fa' ruogan wenti de jieshi" (Explanation by the Supreme People's Court on Some Questions Regarding the Enforcement of the PRC Criminal Procedure Law), excerpted in Gong Peihua, *Qinfan zhishi chanquan fanzui goucheng yu zhengming* (Composition and Proof of the Crime of IPR Infringement) (Beijing: Falü chubanshe, 2004), 386–387.

[41] Gong Peihua, *Qinfan zhishi chanquan fanzui*, 149–151.

[42] The number of civil IPR cases increased 7.9 times between 1992 and 2005 (from 1,698 to 13,393 cases).

TABLE 6.3. *Number of Criminal IPR Cases Handled by Chinese Courts, 1992–2005*

Year	Total Number of Cases Accepted	Total Number of Cases Concluded	Patent Cases Concluded	Copyright Cases Concluded	Trademark and Trade-Secret Cases Concluded	Total Number of People Sentenced
1992	327					
1993	417					
1994	401					
1995	235					
1996	244					
1997	135					
1998	131	128	0	23	105	213
1999	174	175	2	15	158	301
2000	255	248	6	11	231	379
2001	319	314	6	17	285	509
2002	409	408	2	25	381	702
2003	401	399	1	18	380	551
2004	387	385	1	15	369	528
2005	524	505				741

Sources: Zhongguo zhishi chanquan nianjian 2003 (China IPR Yearbook 2003) (Beijing: Zhishi chanquan chubanshe, 2003), 276; *Zhongguo zhishi chanquan nianjian 2004* (China IPR Yearbook 2004) (Beijing: Zhishi chanquan chubanshe, 2004), 333; *Zhongguo zhishi chanquan nianjian 2005*, 306, 309; 2005 data from *China's Intellectual Property Protection in 2005*, www.ipr.gov.cn (accessed June 26, 2006).

TABLE 6.4. *Verdicts and Sentences Imposed for IPR Crimes in China,* *2003–2004*

Court Finding	2003 Total	2004 Total	2004 Trademark	2004 Copyright	2004 Patent
Verdict of not guilty	6	1	1	0	0
Exemption from criminal sentence	12	5	5	0	0
Imposition of fine only	57	41	41	0	0
Surveillance	4	6	6	0	0
Suspended sentence	174	206	204	2	0
Short detention	33	51	51	0	0
Imprisonment of less than 5 years	253	213	207	5	1
Imprisonment of more than 5 years	12	5	4	1	0
Total number of people sentenced	551	528	519	8	1
Acquittal rate	1.1	0.2	0.19	0	0
Incarceration rate	48.1	41.3	40.6	62.5	100

Sources: Zhongguo zhishi chanquan nianjian 2004, 333; Zhongguo zhishi chanquan nianjian 2005, 306.

subject to criminal prosecution. In Taiwan, by contrast, most criminal sentences are commutable to a fine. Together with the fact that Taiwanese law allows for two rounds of appeal of criminal sentences, this explains why in Taiwan, where the number of convictions per million people is much higher than in China, only 3.5 percent of those found guilty of committing an IPR crime will do jail time.

We lack comprehensive statistics on the number of criminal IPR cases accepted by the subnational courts in China. Nevertheless, we have some data on Shanghai and Guangdong, which together account for about one-third of the criminal IPR caseload in China. In 2003, the Shanghai courts handled 12.8 percent of the national total (51 cases), and in 2005 they handled 11.2 percent (59 cases); we do not know how these cases were distributed across IPR subtypes.[43] In 2004, the courts in Guangdong province accepted 82 first-instance criminal IPR cases (21 percent of the national total). In keeping with national trends, the bulk of these cases consisted of trademark disputes (85 percent), the remainder being copyright cases.[44] There is no evidence that the Guangdong courts adjudicated on any criminal patent matters.

---

[43] *Zhongguo zhishi chanquan nianjian 2004*, 96 (2003 data); *Status of Intellectual Property Rights Protection in Shanghai in 2005*, http://www.sipa.gov.cn/chan_eng/Information2_detail.asp?id=169 (accessed November 16, 2006).

[44] *Guangdong zhishi chanquan nianjian 2005*, 77.

TABLE 6.5. *Criminal Cases of Manufacturing and Marketing of Fake and Substandard Commodities and of Illegal Business Activity in China, 2004–2005*

	2004	2005
False and inferior commodities cases	932 (1,961 people sentenced)	1,121 (1,942 people sentenced)
Illegal business activity	1,434 (2,526 people sentenced)	1,903 (2,653 people sentenced)

Sources: Zhongguo zhishi chanquan nianjian 2005, 98; China's Intellectual Property Protection in 2005, www.ipr.gov.cn (accessed June 26, 2006).

Crimes of Manufacturing and Marketing of Fake and Substandard Commodities

For technical reasons, official statistics can be misleading about the true number of criminal IPR cases handled by Chinese courts. Most importantly, a percentage of cases prosecuted as crimes of manufacturing and marketing of fake and substandard commodities (*shengchan xiaoshou weilie shangpin zui*) and crimes of illegal business activity (*feifa jingying zui*), both of which fall under the umbrella category of crimes upsetting market order, include cases of IPR infringement. Where a case can be prosecuted either as an IPR crime or as a substandard commodities crime, the lower and clearer criminal liability thresholds, along with the higher maximal punishment, make the latter option more attractive to the police and courts: in consequence, many IPR cases are prosecuted as substandard commodities crimes. Similarly, piracy and counterfeiting activities may meet only the (lower) requirements for illegal business activity and so will be prosecuted as crimes of illegal business activity, rather than as IPR crimes. Statistics on these two categories of criminal cases handled by the courts in 2004 and 2005 are presented in Table 6.5.

Is Criminal Enforcement Rationalized?

The rationalization of criminal enforcement is a function both of the procedures for introducing cases to the courts, and of the courts' adjudication of the cases brought before them. Among the three indicators of rationalized enforcement, assessing the consistency or predictability of enforcement turns out to be the most complicated. On the one hand, the courts do offer highly predictable enforcement in the cases they adjudicate. The reason for this is that the whole system is geared toward selecting only "rock solid" cases for criminal prosecution.[45] This caution on the part of the PSB derives in part from the fact that the Procuratorate supervises police work and will not proceed with cases that do not meet the criminal liability thresholds or the strict evidentiary requirements stipulated by the law. What about the trial stage? Although the courts are

---

[45] China Interview 040824, with a private investigator (Shanghai).

known to abuse due process in human rights and death penalty cases, apolitical matters such as IPR are less likely to be subject to the perversions of justice that characterize politically explosive issues such as religious freedom or the right of assembly. As disturbing as the potential for abuse in the criminal enforcement of IPR might be, an equally worrying feature of the system as it currently stands is the restriction of court enforcement to a narrow range of high-profile cases with high probability of a guilty verdict. The U.S. Trade Representative's recent emphasis on criminal enforcement can be interpreted as an attempt to extend the courts' reach over less "certain" cases and to impose a clearer sense of what the courts' enforcement standards should be.

We have no data to assess the transparency of criminal enforcement. As a matter of principle, criminal IPR cases are heard in open trials (*kaiting shenli*), but it is nevertheless more difficult to gain access to them relative to civil cases. Most importantly, the punishment decisions in these cases are rarely published in legal compendia. Although some high-profile criminal cases, such as the Guthrie case, are publicized by the media, the overall level of transparency seems to be lower than that for civil IPR cases.[46]

Is criminal enforcement fair? We can approach this question indirectly by examining the rates of appeal. Although we lack data on the appeals of criminal IPR cases, we have statistics on all criminal cases handled by Chinese courts in 2005. The overall appeals rate for first-instance criminal cases in 2005 was 14.2 percent. This rate is somewhat higher than the appeals rate for first-instance civil cases, which stood at 9 percent in 2005.[47] Thus, there is no reason to think that courts unduly constrain the appeal of criminal cases, especially for areas like IPR, which do not touch directly on politically sensitive matters. Another favorable, though general, indicator is that on January 1, 2007, in an attempt to raise the professionalism of criminal adjudication, the Supreme People's Court began reviewing all death sentences imposed by lower-level courts.[48] It remains to be seen whether this kind of judicial scrutiny will filter down through the system and increase the procedural fairness of ordinary criminal adjudication in China, even in areas like IPR, where the death penalty is not used.

---

[46] Randolph Hobson Guthrie III was found guilty by a Chinese court in 2005 for selling US$840,000 worth of pirated DVDs out of his Shanghai penthouse to clients located mostly in the United States. Guthrie received a 30-month jail sentence and was fined RMB 500,000 (US$60,000). For more details, see Joshua Davis, "The Decline and Fall of Randolph Hobson Guthrie III," *Wired* 13.10 (October 2005), http://www.wired.com/wired/archive/13.10/guthrie.html (accessed May 27, 2008) and Rebecca Ordish and Alan Adcock, *China Intellectual Property Challenges and Solutions: An Essential Business Guide* (Singapore: John Wiley, 2008), 202.

[47] *Zhongguo falü nianjian 2006* (China Law Yearbook 2006) (Beijing: Falü chubanshe, 2006), 988, 990. There were 684,897 first-instance and 97,573 second-instance (appealed) criminal cases in 2005. In the same year, there were 4,380,085 first-instance civil cases and 394,629 second-instance civil cases.

[48] "Supreme Court to 'Strictly Control' Death Penalty," http://www.chinadaily.com.cn/china/2006-12/28/content_770205.htm (accessed December 30, 2006).

TABLE 6.6. *Criminal Sentences and Incarcerations in Six Countries in 2004 (per million people)*

Country	Copyright Piracy Rate	Guilty Sentences (per million people)	Incarcerations (per million people)	Incarceration Rate (% of those sentenced subject to incarceration)
China	High	0.4	0.17	41.3
Russia	High	1.3	ND	ND
Taiwan	Medium	115.3	4	3.5
Czech Republic	Medium	34	0.5	1.5
France	Medium	25.4	1.2	4.7
U.S.	Low	0.46	0.2	49.2

Note: Russian data are for copyright cases only; for other countries, copyright, trademark, and patent cases are combined.

Sources: China: *Zhongguo zhishi chanquan nianjian 2005*, 306, 309; Russia: *Metodika rassledovaniia prestuplenii predusmotrennykh st. 146 UK RF* (Methods of Investigating Crimes Specified in Article 146 of the Criminal Code of the Russian Federation) (Sankt Peterburg: Iuridicheskii tsentr press, 2004), 4; Taiwan: *Sifa tongji nianbao 2004* (Taiwan Judicial Statistics Yearbook 2004) (Taipei: Sifa tongji chu, 2005), 3.14, 6.19, 8.32; Czech Republic: *Statistická ročenka kriminality* (Crime Yearbook) (Praha: Ministerstvo spravedlnosti České republiky, 2005), 28–31; France: *Aspects de la criminalité et de la délinquance constatées en France en 2004*, tome 1 (2005), 38, 52; U.S.: *Intellectual Property Report*, United States Attorney's Office, FY 2005, Appendix C, http://www.usdoj.gov/criminal/cybercrime/ippolicy.html (accessed June 27, 2006).

Despite some promising signs of the procedural regularization of court adjudication, it is premature to draw any definitive conclusions about rationalization across the criminal enforcement system as a whole. The data are incomplete, thus making it difficult to reach a definitive assessment of the consistency, transparency, and fairness of criminal IPR enforcement in China.

COMPARATIVE PERSPECTIVES ON CRIMINAL IPR ENFORCEMENT

In comparison with the other five countries examined in this study, China has an extremely low rate of criminal enforcement, along with high conviction and incarceration rates. My comparative data cumulatively suggest that the development of a fully deterrent system of criminal IPR enforcement depends on the systematic coordination of the courts with the police and the various administrative actors.

Deterrence: A Comparative Perspective

There is uncertainty in the literature whether deterrence depends on the frequency or the severity of criminal punishment. Table 6.6 gives us a snapshot of enforcement across the six countries analyzed in this book. It suggests that neither variable on its own is determinative. For example, China and the United

States both have the same type of enforcement, which features low frequency and high severity. However, in China this kind of enforcement has no effect on piracy, whereas in the United States it is deterrent. The effects of frequency and severity may therefore be country-specific.

Russia

The police (popularly known as *militsiia*) are the mainstay of criminal enforcement in Russia. There are two types of *militsiia*: criminal police (*kriminal'naia militsiia*) and public safety police (*militsiia obshchestvennoi bezopasnosti*). These divisions of the police differ in status, responsibility, and – when it comes to IPR – functional specialization. The criminal police are an elite corps responsible for handling more serious, high-impact crimes requiring preliminary investigation (*predvaritel'noe sledstvie*).[49] The public safety police are responsible for maintaining public order, protecting the safety and property of individuals, as well as elucidating administrative violations and crimes that do not require preliminary investigation.[50] In the area of IPR, crimes of copyright and patent infringement require a preliminary investigation and therefore fall within the jurisdiction of the criminal police,[51] whereas crimes of trademark counterfeiting do not require a preliminary investigation and are thus handled by the public safety police. This fragmentation of the IPR enforcement portfolio is justified by certain provisions of the Criminal Code, which specify that the criminal police should investigate "moderately serious" and "serious" crimes (copyright and patent infringement are considered "moderately serious"), whereas the public safety police should handle petty crimes and misdemeanors (trademarks fall under this category).[52]

How do the Russian police enforce IPR laws? We should point out that official police reports contain no data on trademark and patent counterfeiting.[53] As can be seen in Table 6.7, the number of copyright cases subject to criminal prosecution grew tenfold between 1997 and 2005. During this period, suspects were convicted in approximately 50 percent of the cases, and 20–25 percent of the convicted received criminal sentences. This is significantly lower than the sentencing rate in China, where the Procuratorate brings forward to the courts only cases that will result in a sentence and eventual incarceration.

---

[49] Federal Law N-68-FZ (March 31, 1999), *On Amending the RSFSR Police Law*, Article 8.
[50] Federal Law N-68-FZ (March 31, 1999), *On Amending the RSFSR Police Law*, Article 9.
[51] *Criminal Procedure Code*, Article 151.2 (a).
[52] Definitions of the seriousness of different types of crimes can be found in *Criminal Code of the Russian Federation*, Article 15.
[53] In 2002, I was able to obtain unpublished reports from the Ministry of the Interior (MVD), indicating that until 1996, more trademark cases than copyright cases had been handled. After the raising of the maximal punishment for copyright infringement to five years imprisonment in 1996, copyright enforcement quickly assumed dominance over trademark enforcement. In 2002, trademark counterfeiting penalties were also raised to five years imprisonment, but we lack evidence whether this reversed the trend of copyright dominance.

TABLE 6.7. *Number of Criminal Copyright Cases Investigated in Russia,*
1997–2005

Year	Number of Crimes Registered	Number of Suspects Criminally Charged	Number of People Sentenced
1997	302	84	0
1998	607	210	29
1999	606	296	65
2000	875	543	87
2001	810	398	96
2002	949	509	138
2003	1,229	672	181
2004	1,917	989	n.a.
2005	2,924	1,450	n.a.

Sources: Metodika rassledovaniia prestuplenii predusmotrennykh st. 146 UK RF, 4; Sostoianie
prestupnosti v Rossiiskoi Federatsii za ianvar'–dekabr' 2004 g. (Crime in the Russian Federation
January–December 2004), www.mvdinform.ru/stats (accessed December 1, 2006); Sostoianie
prestupnosti v Rossiiskoi Federatsii za ianvar'–dekabr' 2005 g. (Crime in the Russian Federation
January–December 2005), www.mvdinform.ru/stats (accessed December 1, 2006).

The neglect of patents and trademarks reflects a deliberate preference for
copyright enforcement among the police, who often have very close relations
with copyright associations such as the Russian Anti-Piracy Organization,
which is staffed by former police officers who "facilitate" the organization of
police raids.[54] Such raids are not done for free, since those who want assistance
have to contribute to a special "extrabudgetary support fund" set up by the
police.[55] Furthermore, police employees often act as unofficial "consultants" to
foreign firms seeking their services.[56] Transparent enforcement is not on the
horizon yet.

In addition to the *militsiia*, there are two other important enforcers in Russia: the FSB (the Federal Security Service, a successor to the KGB) and the Tax
Police. I have not been able to locate any public source with comprehensive
national or subnational statistics on the IPR enforcement activities of the FSB or
the Tax Police. Chapter 8 does, however, discuss FSB involvement in IPR

[54] Russia Interview 000831A, with an IPR attorney (Moscow); Russia Interview 000901A and
Russia Interview 020529, with the Russia coordinator of a foreign copyright association (Moscow); Russia Interview 000904C, with the president of a Russian copyright association (Moscow); and Russia Interview 000905A, with the vice president of a Russian anti-piracy
association (Moscow).

[55] Russia Interview 020603, with an IPR lawyer (Moscow).

[56] For example, a senior manager at a multinational company told me that after many frustrating
attempts to get the police to accept their case, a police officer suggested that the case would be
accepted provided that the multinational hired a specific investigation firm that had "experience
cooperating with the police on such matters." The multinational knew that this investigation
firm was staffed with former police, and that the police officer was outsourcing work to them as
a way of bestowing "favors" on his friends. Russia Interview 020515A, with the head of
External Corporate Affairs of a foreign food manufacturing company (Moscow).

matters, based on information gleaned from a proprietary enforcement database I obtained in Moscow in 2006. In addition, I gathered information about these two agencies through lawyers and private investigators who indicated that both the FSB and the Tax Police were important but nontransparent enforcers, who would not entertain requests for assistance but would instead approach right holders directly when they had evidence that piracy or counterfeiting had occurred. This limited openness to communication means that right holders cannot rely on these agencies for consistent enforcement.

In comparison with China, Russia offers a high volume of criminal enforcement in cases of IPR violations. In 2004, Russia provided seventeen times more enforcement per million people than China (13.4 IPR crimes detected pmp versus 0.8 IPR crimes detected pmp). In response to escalating U.S. pressure after 2004, Russia stepped up its enforcement even further. In 2007, the police detected as many as fifty-five IPR crimes per million people.[57] This was an impressive fourfold increase over the number of IPR crimes handled in 2004. Provided that Russia is able to maintain this vigorous growth of IPR enforcement, it will quickly catch up with places like the Czech Republic and Taiwan. That said, concerns about the consistency, transparency, and fairness of criminal enforcement prevent naïve optimism about rapid improvement in the quality of IPR protection in Russia.

Taiwan

Taiwan presents a particularly interesting comparison with China. Unlike in China, criminal enforcement has, under foreign pressure, emerged there as a major deterrent of IPR crimes, to the detriment of the kind of administrative avenues that in China, also as a result of foreign pressure, produce a high volume of low-quality enforcement.

Patterns of Case Transfer

As in China, right holders in theory have two options for criminal enforcement in Taiwan: private prosecution and public prosecution. Private prosecution allows individuals to lodge a criminal case directly with a court of law. But Taiwanese courts, like their counterparts in mainland China, are reluctant to accept IPR cases for private prosecution. Therefore, most IPR cases are subject to public prosecution. In public prosecution, an individual first has to draw the attention of an agency with criminal jurisdiction; if the agency initiates a criminal investigation, and if the case is deemed to meet the criminal liability threshold, it will eventually reach a court of law.

Prior to 2006, four different agencies had jurisdiction over criminal enforcement in Taiwan: the Anticounterfeiting Committee (ACC), the National Police

---

[57] *Sostoianie prestupnosti v Rossiiskoi Federatsii za ianvar'–dekabr' 2007 g.* (Crime in the Russian Federation January–December 2007), http://www.mvd.ru/files/u281KzbmtHplrXo.pdf (accessed May 28, 2008).

Administration (NPA), the Ministry of Justice Investigation Bureau (MJIB), and the Prosecutor's Office. The now-defunct ACC served as a liaison office until the end of 2005, transferring the cases it received to one of the other three enforcers. Both the NPA and the MJIB could initiate investigations at the request of the Prosecutor's Office, at the request of the ACC, or directly at the request of right holders. However, regardless of how an investigation would start, it could not proceed without formal approval by the Prosecutor's Office. In addition to overseeing the investigation of cases by the NPA and the MJIB, the Prosecutor's Office could conduct investigations into criminal matters on its own, usually after receiving a complaint from the public.[58] After a case reached the Prosecutor's Office, the case would be introduced in court if the prosecutor found sufficient evidence that a crime had been committed. A change in the system occurred in 2006, when the abolition of the ACC improved coordination and centralization.

The National Police Administration

In Taiwan, multiple police forces under the umbrella of the National Police Administration have jurisdiction over IPR crimes.[59] Most important are the specialized IPR Police (IPRP) (Baohu zhihui caichanquan jingcha dadui). Officially created on November 1, 2004, the IPRP succeeded the Integrated Enforcement Task Force (IETF), which had been formed in February 2003. The IETF was staffed by police officers on a short-term rotation. In contrast, the IPRP enjoys the stability that results from having permanent personnel, who numbered 220 in 2006. The IPRP is headquartered in Taipei and has squads in Taipei, Taoyuan, Taichung, Chiayi, Kaohsiung, and Hualien/Pingtung. IPRP staff salaries are paid directly by the Ministry of the Interior, but the Ministry of Economic Affairs covers certain operating expenses and pays out cash rewards to officers for handling IPR cases.[60] Although the IPRP is a specialized police force, there is further specialization across its subdivisions: it has a special case team (for organized and computer crime), an optical disk team, and a false advertisement team.

The creation of such a specialized police force is remarkable, and a sign of real progress. Nevertheless, the IPRP officers cannot single-handedly address the problem of piracy on the island.[61] In consequence, the Taiwanese government has adopted strategies to encourage other specialized units and the ordinary police to participate actively in piracy and counterfeiting investigations.

---

[58] Interviews with IPR attorneys in Taipei, June–August 2000; oral remarks by IPR attorney Christina Chao at a Quality Brands Protection Committee meeting in Beijing, October 25, 2001.

[59] Unless otherwise indicated, the discussion on the NPA is based on Taiwan Interview 060329, with the commander of the IPR Police (Taipei).

[60] Taiwan Interview 060404, with the director of the International Affairs and Planning Division, TIPO (Taipei).

[61] Available data indicate that in 2005 the IPR Police accounted for only 31 percent of the IPR cases handled by the Taiwanese police. See *Quarterly Report on Taiwan's Intellectual Property Rights Protection October–December 2005* (Taipei: TIPO, 2006), 4–5.

Negative and positive incentives are both used. One strategy has been to issue a circular containing data on the IPR enforcement activity of each of the twenty-five county- and city-level police stations (*jingcha fenju*) in Taiwan. This is issued and distributed to all stations every six months, with the express purpose of shaming stations that fail to reach their enforcement quotas.[62] The performance of special kinds of police, such as the criminal investigation police (Xingshi jingcha ju), the air police (Hangkong jingcha ju), the border protection police (known internally as Bao'an jingcha disan zongdui), and the coast guard police (Gangwu jingcha ju) is also reflected in this circular.[63] The government also emphasizes positive incentives. At the most basic level, officers who have performed well are eligible to receive cash rewards from the Taiwan Intellectual Property Office (TIPO). Taiwan has also worked to make IPR laws more "police-friendly" as a way to encourage a higher volume of enforcement. Not all such measures have had the intended effect, however. For example, foreign right holders hoped that the 2003 Copyright Law amendments, which declared the unauthorized reproduction and distribution of optical disks a "public crime" (*gongsu zui*), would increase the copyright caseload of the police.[64] Yet available data indicate that the amendment had no effect: although piracy stayed flat between 2002 and the end of 2005, the number of copyright cases handled by the police actually fell by 40 percent (see Table 6.8).

Although the Taiwanese police certainly could provide even more enforcement, they are already doing an enormous amount when compared to police in the other countries analyzed in this book. One indicator that the system is working is client satisfaction. In contrast to right holders in China, right holders in Taiwan do not complain about corruption or shirking of responsibility. As one interviewee put it, "in Taiwan, if the police refuse to take your case, this doesn't mean they want to extract a bribe from you; they are just overburdened."[65] If the police do turn away a right holder, he or she can then approach a district court prosecutor or the MJIB or even go to another branch of the police to seek enforcement. Right holders have trust in the police and in the IPR protection system overall.

---

[62] The performance of each police station is evaluated through a point system, with points awarded depending on the value of the goods seized and the number of suspects detained and arrested. Each station is given a quota of a certain number of points it must reach every six months. An internal circulation document on file with the author indicates that in the second half of 2005, only ten of the twenty-five county- and city-level police stations reached or exceeded their quotas, and fifteen stations underperformed.

[63] The document referenced in the preceding footnote reveals that the coast guard is the only special police force that underperformed in the second half of 2005.

[64] See Article 100 of the Copyright Law. Prior to 2003, most IPR crimes were prosecuted only upon complaint (*gaosu nailun*), thus limiting the ability of the police to provide proactive enforcement. Under Taiwanese law, public crimes may be prosecuted proactively in the absence of a complaint from the right holder.

[65] Taiwan Interview 060401A, with a former president of the Motion Picture Association (Taipei).

TABLE 6.8. *Criminal IPR Matters Handled in Taiwan, 2001–2005*

Year	Total Police Cases	Copyright Police Cases	Trademark Police Cases	IPRP Cases as % of Police Cases	Cases Investigated by Prosecutors	Persons Indicted in Court	Persons Sentenced to over 6 months
2001	5,134	4,511	623		6,151	3,238	534
2002	4,988	4,032	956		5,627	2,636	433
2003	4,631	2,617	2,014	2,017 (43)	6,567	3,552	586
2004	4,209	2,358	1,851	1,219 (29)	4,906	2,798	355
2005	4,648	2,404	2,244	1,428 (31)	5,414	2,605	363

Sources: Performance Report on Intellectual Property Protection in Taiwan 2003 (Taipei: TIPO, 2004), 28–33; *Performance Report on Intellectual Property Protection in Taiwan 2004*, 13, 16–17, 24–27; *Quarterly Report on Taiwan's Intellectual Property Rights Protection October–December 2005*, 4–5.

Non-Police Enforcers: The ACC, the MJIB, and the Prosecutor's Office

In addition to the police, the ACC, the MJIB, and the Prosecutor's Office also have criminal IPR enforcement portfolios. The ACC was used much more often in the 1990s, when IPR was still relatively new and right holders had not established good working relationships with the police. At that time, ACC transfers accounted for about 10 percent of the IPR caseload of the police. In 2001, the ACC halted transferring cases to the police; as mentioned, the ACC was finally abolished in 2006.[66] We lack reliable statistics on the MJIB caseload, but interviewees indicate that it handles fewer than 100 IPR cases in any given year, which would constitute 2–3 percent of the total criminal IPR caseload.[67] The small number of cases is not surprising, given that the MJIB (which is equivalent to the U.S. FBI) is an elite police force that becomes involved only in very serious cases.

The Prosecutor's Office rarely initiates IPR cases on its own either. Rather, it decides whether to proceed with cases transferred to it by other agencies with a criminal enforcement mandate. Table 6.8 reports the cumulative number of cases handled by the Prosecutor's Office between 2001 and 2005. These numbers include all police, MJIB, and ACC cases that have reached the Prosecutor's Office.

Agency Overlap

With so many enforcers sharing the criminal IPR protection portfolio, it is inevitable that problems of overlapping jurisdiction will arise. But this is less of an issue in Taiwan than in China, where overlap leads to confusion. One reason is the dominance of the police and the consequent coordination of the

---

[66] Taiwan Interview 060404, with the director of the International Affairs and Planning Division, TIPO (Taipei).

[67] Taiwan Interview 060403, with a former prosecutor (Taipei).

other agencies to provide enforcement subsidiary to police efforts. Equally important is the question of scale. As one interviewee put it: "China is much bigger – it is very hard to coordinate and you can easily get lost in the administrative maze there. In Taiwan, you can go to the wrong entity, but after one or two tries, you will find the right agency. Scale matters and we all know each other here."[68]

Criminal Court Activity and Incarceration Rates

In order to assess the effectiveness of enforcement, we need to know what percentage of cases concluded by the Prosecutor's Office eventually enter the courts and, in turn, what percentage of those found guilty are incarcerated. Statistics presented in Table 6.8 indicate that, in all years between 2001 and 2005, about half of the cases investigated by the prosecutors ended in a court indictment. However, not every indictment resulted in a guilty verdict, and not everyone who was found guilty was incarcerated. In Taiwan, sentences of less than six months imprisonment are routinely commuted to a fine.[69] Only individuals sentenced to more than six months imprisonment stand a chance of being incarcerated, since these sentences are not commutable. But even sentences over six months can be suspended, and they sometimes are. Interestingly, Taiwan does not seem to be interested in incarceration as a deterrent. Cumulatively, the tendency to commute or suspend sentences leads to a very low incarceration rate: in 2004, only 6.5 percent of those indicted for copyright crimes and 0.9 percent of those indicted for trademark crimes were put behind bars.[70] In 2004, the overall IPR incarceration rate in Taiwan was 3.5 percent, comparable to that in the Czech Republic (1.5 percent) and France (4.7 percent), but considerably lower than that in China (41.3 percent) and the United States (49.2 percent).

If we looked only at Taiwan's low incarceration rate, we might conclude that it does not impose deterrent criminal sentences. But since the incarceration rate tells us only the proportion of those found guilty of a crime who end up behind bars, it has limited predictive value. Consider a system in which a very small number of people are found guilty, yet all of them are imprisoned. Here, we would find a very high incarceration rate, but such a low frequency of incarceration as to have no deterrent effect. So it is important to know the number of incarcerations per million people, as a guide to the likelihood that someone from the general population will end up in prison for IPR piracy or counterfeiting. In this regard, Taiwan is at the top among our six cases. With 4 incarcerations per million people in 2004 (see Table 6.9), Taiwan is well ahead of

---

[68] Taiwan Interview 060403, with a former prosecutor (Taipei).

[69] This provision of Taiwanese law has been a sore point for the United States since the 1980s. Virtually every year, American industry complains to the USTR about commutation problems. For an early example, see *Presentation to the United States Trade Representative: Intellectual Property Problems in Taiwan* (International Anticounterfeiting Coalition, May 1992), 15.

[70] These statistics are calculated by the author after subtracting the commuted and suspended sentences from the total number of guilty verdicts in 2004. See *Sifa tongji nianbao 2004*.

TABLE 6.9. *Taiwan Criminal Enforcement Rates in 2004*

	Total Number of Defendants (district court level)	Number of Defendants Sentenced to Imprisonment over 6 Months	Number of Suspended Sentences over 6 Months	Number of Defendants Actually Subject to Imprisonment	Incarceration Rate (%)	Incarcerations (per million people)
Copyright	1,209	222	143	79	6.5	3.4
Trademark	1,440	20	7	13	0.9	0.56
Patent	3	0	0	0	0	0
Total	2,652	242	150	92	3.5	4

Note: Discrepancies between the data reported in this table and the 2004 indictment/incarceration data reported in Table 6.8 are due to the different sources reporting the data – Table 6.8 is based on data from the Prosecutor's Office, which seems to have overcounted the number of cases; this table is based on data from the Judicial Yuan.

Source: Sifa tongji nianbao 2004.

China (0.17 incarcerations), the United States (0.2 incarcerations), the Czech Republic (0.5 incarcerations), and France (1.2. incarcerations).[71]

Taiwan-China Comparison

Taiwan and China have both experienced high levels of piracy and counterfeiting, yet one has been able to become a model enforcer of IPR laws, whereas the other remains the chief pirate in the world. How has this been possible? U.S. pressure on Taiwan to step up criminal enforcement and Taiwan's eagerness to comply are the key determinants of its success. Also important is the degree of coordination across the agencies involved in criminal IPR enforcement. Although both Taiwan and China have multiple enforcers with an IPR enforcement portfolio, this duplication has been an obstacle to effective enforcement only in China, not in Taiwan. The consequential difference here is that in Taiwan the laws are written in such a way that all enforcement activity culminates in criminal prosecution; civil and administrative enforcement are not widely used. Regardless of where right holders turn first, they are assured that the case will eventually reach a court of law for adjudication. In China, by contrast, the default is administrative enforcement, rather than criminal prosecution. Administrative enforcement in China is provided by a number of agencies, which operate in uncoordinated, unclear, and nontransparent ways. We should remember that the emergence of the Taiwanese courts as a dominant enforcer has been enabled by Taiwan's smaller size, which makes centralization and coordination easier than in China. Administrative enforcement in China is in part a response to the sheer volume of the problem. As a consequence of all these differences, the final enforcement outcome in China is less rational and less predictable than in Taiwan.

The Czech Republic

In the area of IPR, the Czech Republic is an exceptional case. Though it is a postsocialist country without a long tradition of IPR protection, its software piracy rate in 2005 was lower than that of France, which invented the very idea of copyright.[72] In no small measure, this achievement is due to a stepped-up criminal enforcement that is transparent and centralized.

Criminal enforcement is provided exclusively by the Ministry of the Interior. The procedure for accessing the police is straightforward. The right holder can apply for enforcement either at any local police station or at the Police Presidium

---

[71] No statistics on incarcerations are available for Russia. We do know that Russia had 1.3 guilty sentences per million people in 2003 (for copyright cases), so even if all of those found guilty were incarcerated, it would still have fewer incarcerations per million people than Taiwan.

[72] The Czech Republic had a software piracy rate of 40 percent in 2005, whereas France had a rate of 47 percent. *Third Annual BSA and IDC Global Software Piracy Study* (May 2006), 12–13, http://www.bsa.org/~/media/C9DA2873DCB84135957CB39B9FA2B666.ashx (accessed August 6, 2008).

in Prague.[73] Because the Ministry of the Interior has a highly centralized structure, the right holder is assured that regardless of where it is lodged, his or her complaint will be handled in a predictable way.[74] In addition to providing easy access, the criminal enforcement system has been made more efficient by the government's elimination of internal investigative organs within the police, which had the effect of slowing the movement of a case to the Prosecutor's Office and, eventually, the courts of law.[75] As we can see in Table 6.10, the Czech police have been very active in pursuing IPR violations. In fact, in terms of criminal investigations per million people in 2004, the Czech Republic was second only to Taiwan (88.3 cases in the Czech Republic versus 183 cases in Taiwan).

Is criminal enforcement in the Czech Republic deterrent? Table 6.11 contains data on the criminal caseload of the courts, the number of individuals sentenced, and the rate of incarceration. The Czech Republic, like Taiwan, has

TABLE 6.10. *Czech Criminal Enforcement Patterns, 2000–2005*

Year	Copyright Discovered	Copyright Punished	Trademark Discovered	Trademark Punished	Patent Discovered	Patent Punished
2000	847	390	1,048	700	5	4
2001	1,750	298	472	358	11	11
2002	975	285	325	254	16	8
2003	485	319	257	250	7	6
2004	462	300	418	228	3	3
2005	791	294	553	294	4	3

Sources: Policejní prezidium ČR (2001), *Statistický výkaz č. 1 – kriminalita za období od 1.1.2000 do 31.12.2000;* Policejní prezidium ČR (2002), *Statistický výkaz č. 1 – kriminalita za období od 1.1.2001 do 31.12.2001;* Policejní prezidium ČR (2003), *Statistický výkaz č. 1 – kriminalita za období od 1.1.2002 do 31.12.2002;* Policejní prezidium ČR (2004), *Statistický výkaz č. 1 – kriminalita za období od 1.1.2003 do 31.12.2003;* Policejní prezidium ČR (2005), *Statistický výkaz č. 1 – kriminalita za období od 1.1.2004 do 31.12.2004;* Policejní prezidium ČR (2006), *Statistický výkaz č. 1 – kriminalita za období od 1.1.2001 do 31.12.2005.* All of these Police Presidium statistical reports on crime and criminality are available at www.mvcr.cz (accessed August 3, 2006).

[73] Czech Interview 020704A, with an employee of the High Technology Crime Investigation Unit, Presidium of the Police of the Czech Republic (Prague); Czech Interview 020711A, with two employees of the IPR Crimes Unit, Police of the Czech Republic (Prague).

[74] Czech Interview 020706, with the president of a foreign copyright association (Prague).

[75] Czech Interview 020703B, with a foreign copyright association lawyer (Prague); Czech Interview 020704A, with an employee of the High Technology Crime Investigation Unit, Presidium of the Police of the Czech Republic (Prague). The governing idea is that the internal investigative units within the police serve as "quality control" mechanisms that transmit to the Procuratorate only those cases that meet the criminal liability threshold. In practice, however, these units simply add unnecessary weight to the criminal justice system, slowing the expeditious handling of criminal cases and making it less likely that alleged violators will be tried. This system of investigative bodies within the police still exists in socialist countries such as China, and in former socialist countries such as Russia and Bulgaria.

TABLE 6.11. *Number of Persons Sentenced for Copyright, Trademark, and Patent Infringement in the Czech Republic, 1992–2004*

Year	Persons Prosecuted for Copyright Crimes	Persons Sentenced for Copyright Crimes	People Imprisoned (incarceration rate as % of those sentenced for copyright crimes)	Persons Prosecuted for Trademark Crimes	Persons Sentenced for Trademark Crimes	People Imprisoned (incarceration rate as % of those sentenced for trademark crimes)
1992	382	236		20	1	
1993	154	125		28	2	
1994	166	132	3 (2.3)	96	44	
1995	181	121	3 (2.5)	511	245	1 (0.4)
1996	159	82	1 (1.2)	440	303	1 (0.3)
1997	256	132	4 (3)	363	248	1 (0.4)
1998	281	62	7 (11.3)	498	137	0 (0)
1999	325	148	7 (4.7)	888	481	3 (0.6)
2000	402	176	9 (5.1)	754	612	6 (1)
2001	350	137	7 (5.1)	373	346	8 (2.3)
2002	302	166	3 (1.8)	251	200	4 (2)
2003	350	126	2 (1.6)	245	144	2 (1.4)
2004	372	186	3 (1.6)	221	153	2 (1.3)

Note: Inconsistencies between Tables 6.10 and 6.11 are due to differences in the statistics reported by the Interior Ministry (Table 6.10) and the Ministry of Justice (Table 6.11).

Sources: Czech Ministry of Justice, *Statistická ročenka kriminality* (Crime Yearbook) (Praha: Ministerstvo spravedlnosti České republiky), 1995, 24–25; 1996, 26, 142, 151; 1997, 26–29; 1998, 26–29; 1999, 28–31; 2000, 28–31; 2001, 28–31, 171, 179; 2002, 28–31; 2003, 28–31; 2004, 28–31; 2005, 28–31, 173, 181.

a relatively high conviction rate, but a very low incarceration rate. The general trend since the mid-1990s has been downward. In 2004, only 1.5 percent of those sentenced for IPR violations were incarcerated. When we adjust for population, the Czech Republic has an even lower incarceration rate – in 2004, it stood at 0.5 incarcerations pmp, which was higher than the Chinese and U.S. and lower than the French and Taiwanese incarceration rates in the same year (see Table 6.6). As Figure 6.1 demonstrates, the incarceration rate for IPR crimes in the Czech Republic is considerably lower than the overall incarceration rate for all crimes committed in the country.

Given the low piracy rate in the Czech Republic, the relatively low incarceration rate is somewhat puzzling and suggests that the severity of criminal punishment is not on its own a good predictor of deterrence. The Czech case highlights that the frequency of police raids may have an equally significant deterrent effect on piracy. Ancillary enforcement by Customs and administrative agencies is also very strong in the Czech Republic. The Czech case emphasizes, yet again, that no single enforcement mode (civil, Customs, administrative, or criminal) should be examined in isolation from the other modes of enforcement in a given country.

France

The French Police
There are three types of police in France: the National Police (Police nationale), the Gendarmerie, and the Municipal Police (Police municipale), each of which is overseen by a different administrative superior: the Interior Ministry is responsible for the Police nationale, the Ministry of Defense for the Gendarmerie, and the local mayors for the Police municipale. The Police nationale is numerically the largest (146,000 employees), followed by the Gendarmerie (98,500 employees) and the Police municipale (13,000 employees).[76] I have not encountered any mention of the Police municipale as having an IPR enforcement mandate, either in printed sources or in interviews. What is the reach of the other two enforcers? Although the Gendarmerie has a smaller workforce than the Police nationale, it has jurisdiction over 95 percent of French territory and 48.5 percent of the French population and is present mostly in villages and cities with fewer than 20,000 inhabitants.[77] The Police nationale, in contrast, is effectively limited to the large urban centers. Historically, the smaller Gendarmerie has provided more enforcement than the Police nationale for both trademarks and copyrights.[78]

---

[76] Émile Pérez, "Polices d'Europe," *Pouvoirs*, no. 102 (2002), 71–76.
[77] *Aspects de la criminalité et de la délinquance constatées en France en 2000*, tome 2 (Paris: La Documentation française, 2001), 21.
[78] For specific annual Police nationale and Gendarmerie enforcement data, see *Aspects de la criminalité et de la délinquance constatées en France* (Paris: La Documentation française, all years from 1988 to 2005).

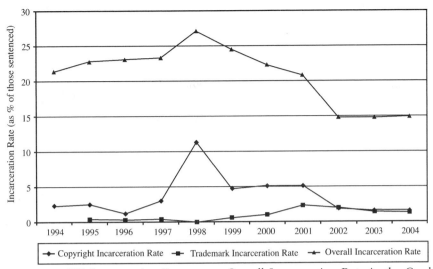

FIGURE 6.1. IPR Incarceration Rate versus Overall Incarceration Rate in the Czech Republic, 1994–2004. *Source:* Computed from data contained in *Statistická ročenka kriminality* (all years between 1994 and 2005).

The different structures of the Police nationale and the Gendarmerie help explain why the Gendarmerie has dominated enforcement, even though both agencies have similar mandates. The Gendarmerie is centralized, with clear lines of command from the center to the localities. The Police nationale, in contrast, has multiple subdivisions with overlapping jurisdictions. For example, at least three main divisions of the Police nationale share enforcement responsibility in the area of IPR: the DCPJ (Direction centrale de la police judiciaire, an internal security judicial police), the DCSP (Direction centrale de la sécurité publique, which is the ordinary police), and the DCPAF (Direction centrale de la police aux frontières, which is the border police).[79] These three enforcers are further subdivided into territorial divisions: the DCPJ has 19 *services régionaux*, whereas the DCSP and the DCPAF each have several hundred subdivisions. The complexity of the Police nationale has led to a predictable result. As one right holder put it:

It is much easier to work with the Gendarmerie, since there is only one Gendarmerie. The multiple subdivisions of the police are complex, each having its own territorial

---

[79] In addition to the DCPJ, the DCSP, and the DCPAF, at least two other subdivisions of the Police nationale can enforce in the area of IPR: Police scientifique et technique (Scientific and Technical Police) and Renseignements généraux (the French FBI). In practice, however, these two bodies rarely exercise their enforcement mandate.

jurisdiction. In practice, the territorial jurisdiction of each subdivision makes it difficult for them to coordinate investigative activities, especially when the criminal network extends beyond a single territorial subdivision.[80]

This finding is suggestive for the Chinese case, where case-transfer ambiguities and jurisdictional overlap within the PSB have prevented the emergence of robust criminal enforcement. Interestingly, however, the historical pattern in France is changing. In recent years, the gap between enforcement provided by the centralized Gendarmerie and enforcement provided by the decentralized Police nationale has begun to close rapidly.[81] The reasons for this are not yet clear. Certainly, IPR crimes are more likely to be concentrated in the large cities, where the Police nationale has jurisdiction. It is also likely that the Police nationale has become more effective by coordinating its different units. The French case suggests that a well-coordinated, decentralized enforcer can overtake a centralized enforcer.

The French Courts

Criminal enforcement of IPR in France is hindered by the relative incapacity of the prosecutors and courts to take on the cases brought to them by the Gendarmerie and the Police nationale. An existing backlog of both civil and criminal cases seriously hampers court effectiveness. As one right holder put it:

Delays of 7–8 years between the beginning of the criminal investigation and the final judgment are not unusual. The difficulty lies in the nature of the criminal process in France: it takes 2–3 years for the case to reach court and for the judge to issue a verdict; then, there can be an appeal of the sentence, followed by a second appeal (*cassation*); by the end of the appeals process, 7–8 years have passed and the right holder no longer cares what the outcome of the case is.[82]

Court delays are compounded by the fact that "judges are simply not interested in IPR cases."[83] This may help explain why the incarceration rate in France is as low as 1–3 percent (see Table 6.12). Another reason may be the botched anti-piracy campaign that the French chapter of the Business Software Alliance (BSA) carried out in 1995–1996, which was seen as too adversarial by the French authorities and made them unwilling to invest scarce police

---

[80] France Interview 020417B, with a controller, Department of Reproduction Rights, SACEM/ SDRM (French copyright association) (Paris).

[81] In 1999, the Gendarmerie-to-Police nationale IPR enforcement ratio was 5.89:1. By 2004, the ratio had shrunk to 1.1:1. See *Aspects de la criminalité et de la délinquance constatées en France en 1999*, tome 2 (Paris: La Documentation française, 2001), 24, 26; and *Aspects de la criminalité et de la délinquance constatées en France en 2004*, tome 2 (Paris: La Documentation française, 2005), 26, 28.

[82] France Interview 020418A, with the spokesperson of Union des Fabricants (trademark association) (Paris).

[83] France Interview 020416B, with the president of Syndicat national de l'édition phonographique (SNEP) (copyright association) (Paris).

TABLE 6.12. *French Criminal IPR Enforcement Statistics (selected years)*

	1988	1996	2004
Copyright crimes discovered by the police	3,755	421	463
Suspects charged for copyright crimes by the Procuratorate	727	224	239
Criminals incarcerated in copyright cases	48	12	14
Incarceration rate (incarcerations as % of criminals charged)	1.3	3.3	3
Trademark crimes discovered by the police	4,950	3,048	1,625
Suspects charged for trademark crimes by the Procuratorate	1,704	1,462	1,285
Criminals incarcerated in trademark cases	60	48	58
Incarceration rate (sentences as % of crimes discovered)	1.2	1.5	3.6

Source: Aspects de la criminalité et de la délinquance constatées en France (all years between 1988 and 2005). The complete 1988–2004 time-series data are on file with the author but are not presented here.

resources in pursuing software piracy.[84] On balance, although France has a healthy rate of police enforcement in cases of IPR violations, its low incarceration rate may be limiting the deterrence of the criminal enforcement it provides.

The United States

Like all countries analyzed in this book (except the Czech Republic), the United States has multiple police forces (at the federal and state levels) with jurisdiction over IPR enforcement. In practice, however, most criminal IPR matters are handled by the FBI, which works with the district attorneys, who in turn concentrate on getting cases accepted by the courts. Both the FBI and the U.S. attorneys assign a low priority to IPR crimes, as reflected in the enforcement statistics reported in Table 6.13. The table demonstrates that very few cases are referred by the police to U.S. attorneys, with only a portion of these cases reaching the courts. It is therefore not surprising that the United States has a very low incarceration rate per million people (0.2 incarcerations pmp), a figure comparable only to that of China (0.17 incarcerations pmp), where the volume of criminal enforcement is low overall. In the United States, the strategy seems to be to compensate for the low certainty of punishment by increasing its severity. Thus, although there are very few incarcerations per million people in the United States, the incarceration rate is very high: 44.8

---

[84] France Interview 020418A, with the spokesperson of Union des Fabricants (trademark association) (Paris); France Interview 020419B, with the spokesperson of the Business Software Alliance (Paris).

TABLE 6.13. *Persons Incarcerated for IPR Crimes in the United States, 2001–2005*

Year	2001	2002	2003	2004	2005
Criminal matters referred to U.S. attorneys	191	169	229	269	361
Criminal cases filed in court	84	78	100	101	147
Number of criminal defendants (total)	121	149	165	141	323
Number of guilty defendants	86	106	92	122	123
Number of defendants imprisoned	40	48	42	60	46
Incarceration rate (%)	46.5	45.3	45.6	49.2	37.4
Incarcerations (per million people)	0.14	0.17	0.14	0.2	0.15

Source: Intellectual Property Report, United States Attorney's Office, FY 2005, Appendix C.

percent of those found guilty between 2001 and 2005 were incarcerated. The experience of the United States suggests that countries that have achieved a low level of piracy need not strive to produce a high volume of criminal IPR enforcement. In China and other countries with high rates of piracy and counterfeiting, criminal enforcement should still be seen as a powerful tool for reducing IPR violations.

CONCLUSION

The very low volume of criminal enforcement in China in comparison with other countries can be attributed indirectly to a lack of foreign and domestic pressure for police participation in IPR enforcement. The absence of pressure allows entrenched bureaucratic patterns to persist, whereby agencies transfer to the police only a small percentage of the cases meeting the criminal liability threshold, and the police accept only a portion of the cases forwarded to them. The systematic culling of cases by the administrative agencies, police, and Procuratorare has led to a low aggregate volume of criminal enforcement. For understanding this pattern, it is important to recognize that the low volume of enforcement is accompanied by a very high rate of guilty sentences and imprisonment: the overall probability of criminal prosecution is low, but the severity of criminal punishment is high. Because of the courts' dismal record in areas such as human rights, the low volume of criminal enforcement in the relatively apolitical area of IPR has only recently become a target of foreign pressure. Should that pressure for increased criminal enforcement continue, the various actors in the case-transfer chain will need to have better incentives to coordinate with one another to generate consistent and transparent criminal enforcement across a range of cases, and not only, as now, in the most serious and "rock solid" ones. High evidentiary standards cannot be used to restrict court supervision only to IPR cases where the guilt of the accused will certainly be proven. A higher volume of criminal enforcement may be desirable, with a consequent lowering of the sentencing and incarceration rates.

TABLE 6.14. *Cross-National IPR Enforcement Efforts in 2004 (per million people)*

Country	Piracy Rate	Civil Court Cases (first instance)	Customs Enforcement	Administrative Enforcement	Criminal Enforcement
China	High	7.2	0.8	939	0.8
Russia	High	5.2	1.1	10	13.4
Taiwan	Medium	16.5	14.7	63.2	183
Czech Republic	Medium	ND	51.9	201.5	88.3
France	Medium	ND	106.6	45.2	36.9
U.S.	Low	32.5	24.8	0.1	1.2

Source: Yearbooks.

Is criminal enforcement in China rationalized? Despite some promising signs, numerous problems still plague criminal enforcement. Although incomplete data prevent us from making definitive assessments about consistency, transparency, and fairness, the future of criminal enforcement certainly depends on the introduction of clearer procedural regulations, as well as the greater coordination of all actors in advancing more cases forward to the courts for adjudication.

Before we move to Part III of this study, we should recapitulate the main findings of Part II, in terms of the state's role in supplying IPR enforcement. Table 6.14 presents the main findings about the IPR enforcement efforts of individual countries reported in Chapters 3–6.

In China, the state has provided enforcement in response to both foreign and domestic pressure. Contrary to popular perception, among the six countries analyzed in this book China is the uncontested leader in terms of the volume of administrative enforcement it supplies. But in areas where there has been no pressure to enforce, as in Customs, civil, or criminal IPR protection, there is a low volume of enforcement. The bias toward administrative enforcement suggests the importance of pressure for the development of a robust IPR regime, but also the dangers of equating the quantity and quality of enforcement. When foreign or domestic groups put pressure on the government to enforce, volume rather than quality is the default criterion by which the response is measured. In reaction to pressure, the central government has created an enforcement system that supplies a high volume of administrative enforcement for trademarks and copyrights. As we will see in the case studies in Chapters 7–8, however, this enforcement is not rationalized. In contrast, patents have been free of enforcement pressures, and as Chapter 9 reveals, although the volume of enforcement in that area is low, its quality is high. Policy implementation generated under pressure by the central government is not the only route to consistent and transparent enforcement; nor on its own is it adequate as a measure of state involvement in the development of improved IPR enforcement.

PART III

THE STATE IN ACTION

The Politics of IPR Enforcement in China

7

Trademarks

Capricious Enforcement

We never give bribes to the authorities – only shampoo samples.[1]

Imagine that you are a chocolate manufacturer operating in China. One morning you go to the office and you are told that perfect copies of the candy bars produced by your company have appeared on the market. They even bear your justly famed Chocoloco brand name.[2] Where do you turn for help? This is a trademark counterfeiting case, so according to official Chinese sources, you will have three options: enforcement through the civil courts, administrative enforcement through the State Administration for Industry and Commerce, or criminal enforcement through the police.[3] Yet Chapter 5 lists not one, but six different agencies sharing the trademark administrative enforcement portfolio – the State Administration for Industry and Commerce (SAIC), the Administration of Quality Supervision, Inspection, and Quarantine (AQSIQ), the State Food and Drug Administration (SFDA), the Ministry of Health (MOH), the State Tobacco Monopoly Administration (STMA), and the Ministry of Agriculture (MOA).[4] At least four of these agencies (the SAIC, the AQSIQ, the SFDA, and the MOH) can provide enforcement in this case. In addition, Customs may help as well, should you discover that the counterfeits were either manufactured abroad and shipped into China or produced in China

---

[1] China Interview 010622B, with a private investigator focusing on cosmetics counterfeiting (Beijing).

[2] This is a fictitious example. As far as I know, there is no Chocoloco brand chocolate being produced in China or elsewhere in the world, but there is a British chocolate fountain caterer called Chocoloco.

[3] See, for example, *Zhongguo zhishi chanquan nianjian 2000* (China IPR Yearbook 2000) (Beijing: Zhishi chanquan chubanshe, 2001), or www.cninaipr.com.

[4] The Administration of Quality Supervision, Inspection, and Quarantine is also known as the Technical Supervision Bureau (TSB) at the provincial level and below. Thus, the AQSIQ and the TSB are the same entity.

for export to another country. In short, there are numerous options for enforcement in cases of trademark counterfeiting. Yet instead of making it easier to protect the integrity of the Chocoloco brand, the abundance of choices may be the source of many problems.

The presence of multiple enforcers can lead to two radically different outcomes: one is the shirking of enforcement responsibilities, and the other is the provision of duplicative, uncoordinated enforcement. Although it is impossible to estimate how often agencies shirk, such behavior does occur with a certain frequency. Sometimes an agency (say, the SAIC) will directly refuse to enforce, claiming that another agency (say, the AQSIQ) is better suited to handle a given case. Other times, agencies will shirk strategically: they will suggest to right holders that they might be willing to enforce, but only in exchange for a small case-handling fee, which is just a thinly disguised bribe.

What explains shirking? Shirking is a result of the conflicts of interest that characterize the work of every administrative agency with a trademark or copyright enforcement portfolio in China.[5] The major conflict is between the licensing and the enforcement (supervisory) functions of the agency. Chinese bureaucracies grant a dizzying range of permits, approvals, and licenses to the firms that they regulate. Sometimes, properly licensed firms engage in illegal behavior, such as counterfeiting or piracy. Pursuing the firms with the full force of the law may drive them out of business, thus risking potential harm to the economic well-being of the locality; it may also eliminate the lucrative fees that the agencies collect through licensing. In such situations, the agencies may refuse to enforce in order to protect the guilty firm. In other cases, when the counterfeiters are not duly licensed, the agencies may strategically shirk until the right holder offers a bribe. Of course, as economic opportunists, agencies will try to extract bribes from the counterfeiters as well. For enforcement to take place, the right holder (or her agent) will have to offer a larger bribe than that which the agency can collect from the counterfeiter for "failure" to enforce. In the process, agency sympathies lie with the counterfeiters rather than with the right holders. The reason is simple: right holders may be here today and gone tomorrow, whereas counterfeiters are part of the local economy and therefore provide a more stable long-term source of rents for the enforcement agencies.[6]

Naturally, agencies in China do enforce, and at a very high rate. However, the incentives outlined earlier determine when and how often they will enforce. Agencies enforce when they have to, typically in response to either foreign or domestic pressure. The central government organizes periodic "concentrated

---

[5] These conflicts of interest do not apply to Customs and the police, who shirk IPR enforcement because it is a low-priority area conflicting with other more important tasks on which the two bureaucracies have to concentrate.

[6] This logic does not hold when right holders either have invested in a locality or hold a nationally famous trademark (*chiming shangbiao*) or a locally (provincially) famous trademark (*zhuming shangbiao*).

enforcement" campaigns (*jizhong zhifa xingdong*), when agencies at all levels of government from the center down to the county must register some enforcement. Enforcement campaigns focus on market sweeps; the result is that the source of the problem (e.g., the facilities used to produce counterfeits) is carefully skirted. In addition, public relations scandals (e.g., infants dying after consuming fake formula) also necessitate some enforcement effort. Finally, agencies may enforce at the request of the right holders, but this enforcement is selective, focusing on "easy" cases, such as checking whether stores sell counterfeits, rather than dealing with the hard task of detecting and closing down the enterprises that actually produce the counterfeits.

The cumulative effect of jurisdictional overlap among the various agencies is a high volume of enforcement. However, this enforcement is inefficient, ineffective, and of a low quality. Inefficiency is a product of uncoordinated enforcement. Most of the time the agencies work against one another instead of cooperating on enforcement. This situation leads to duplication and waste of administrative effort, for example, when the same stores are repeatedly checked, whereas others are repeatedly ignored. Uncoordinated enforcement prevents agencies from realizing the economies of scale that can be achieved when enforcement resources are pooled into a well-planned large-scale enforcement action. Ineffectiveness is also linked to the unwillingness of the police to support the administrative agencies during their enforcement activities. The resulting enforcement is toothless and lacks deterrent force. It is difficult to ensure consistency, transparency, and procedural fairness even when there is a single agency in charge of enforcement. The problem is exacerbated by an order of magnitude when we add the effect of jurisdictional overlap. In practice, low-quality enforcement means that raids are organized, but the infringing goods are rarely seized or destroyed, and that the right holder is usually kept in the dark as to the outcome of the enforcement action.

What implications does this have for the owners of the Chocoloco brand? They may need to approach several different agencies before they find one that is willing to enforce on their behalf. Furthermore, enforcement may only be possible after a bribe is paid. And, worst of all, enforcement may not resolve the problem of counterfeiting because it probably will not target the production facilities of the counterfeiter and thus will not lead to the destruction of the counterfeit Chocolocos. Finding high-quality enforcement in cases of trademark counterfeiting is far from easy.

Instead of further discussing the instructive but fictitious Chocoloco example, this chapter provides specific details on trademark protection in China through a focused case study of cigarette anticounterfeiting enforcement. Case studies are useful for two reasons. First, it is only by focusing on specific products that one begins to appreciate the complexity of the trademark enforcement framework. For example, unless one decides to study pharmaceuticals, the State Food and Drug Administration and the Ministry of Health would appear not to play a role in anticounterfeiting; similarly, the importance of the State Tobacco Monopoly Administration can only be appreciated by focusing on fake cigarettes. Nevertheless, regardless of which specific product we examine, the basic setup does not vary – there will be at least several administrative agencies with overlapping enforcement jurisdictions in each domain. It bears stressing that each agency can approach a counterfeiting case from a different standpoint: the SAIC will handle it as a trademark infringement case, the AQSIQ will handle it as a product quality case, and the SFDA or the MOH will handle it as a public health issue. This multiplicity of enforcers and enforcement mandates creates a fluid and uncertain environment for right holders who seek enforcement.

A second, more important reason for focusing on discrete product groups is that this allows us to gather concrete data on enforcement activities targeted at these specific products. We can go beyond the generality of earlier studies and confront the question of who enforces, when, and with whom. In other words, a study focusing on specific products will reveal the patterns of inter- and intraagency cooperation during policy implementation, an issue that until now has not received any systematic scholarly attention.[7]

The chapter starts with a brief background discussion on national trends in trademark enforcement in China. After highlighting the limited utility of national-level data for a nuanced understanding of enforcement, the chapter presents an extensive case study of cigarette anticounterfeiting activity in China and a short case study of cigarette anticounterfeiting in Russia and concludes with reflections about the quality of trademark anticounterfeiting enforcement in China today.

Trademark Administrative and Court Enforcement in China

Who enforces trademark laws in China – administrative agencies or courts? Data compiled from Chinese sources show that the amount of administrative enforcement by only one of the multiple agencies that can provide redress to foreign right holders is many times greater than the number of all trademark cases handled by the court system. Table 7.1 presents data on administrative enforcement cases handled by the SAIC in China, as well as statistics on the total number of first-instance trademark cases handled by Chinese courts. As we can see, between 1996 and 2005, the number of administrative cases was at least twenty-eight times greater than the number of court cases. The picture

---

[7] Two studies examine enforcement in cases of counterfeiting of specific product groups in China. For luxury goods, see Simon P. Cheetham, "Protection of Intellectual Property Rights in Luxury Goods," in *Chinese Intellectual Property Law and Practice*, ed. Mark A. Cohen, A. Elizabeth Bang, and Stephanie J. Mitchell (The Hague: Kluwer Law International, 1999), 385–398. For fast-moving consumer goods, see Daniel C. K. Chow, *A Primer on Foreign Investment Enterprises and Protection of Intellectual Property Rights in China* (The Hague and New York: Kluwer Law International, 2002). However, neither of these studies provides any systematic empirical evidence concerning the circumstances under which different bureaucracies enforce or about the patterns of cooperation within and among enforcement agencies.

TABLE 7.1. *Administrative versus Court Enforcement of Trademarks in China,* *1996–2005*

Year	Trademark Cases Concluded by the SAIC	Trademark Cases Concluded by the Courts (first-instance cases only)	SAIC–Court Case Ratio
1996	14,000	306	45.7
1997	ND	325	ND
1998	28,952	456	63.4
1999	32,298	487	66.3
2000	37,073	401	92.4
2001	39,777	445	89.3
2002	38,192	611	62.5
2003	36,881	906	40.7
2004	51,851 (accepted)	1,144	45.3
2005	49,412 (accepted)	1,782 (accepted)	27.7

Sources: 1996 nian Zhongguo zhishi chanquan zhifa zhuangkuang baogao (Status Report of the Enforcement of IPR Laws in China in 1996) (Beijing: Guowuyuan zhishi chanquan bangong huiyi bangongshi, 1997); *1998 nian Zhongguo zhishi chanquan zhifa zhuangkuang baogao* (Status Report of the Enforcement of IPR Laws in China in 1998) (Beijing: Zhishi chanquan ju, 1999); *1999 nian Zhongguo zhishi chanquan zhifa zhuangkuang baogao* (Status Report of the Enforcement of IPR Laws in China in 1999) (Beijing: Zhishi chanquan ju, 2000); *Zhongguo zhishi chanquan nianjian 2000* (China IPR Yearbook 2000) (Beijing: Zhishi chanquan chubanshe, 2001), 238–239, 249; *Zhongguo zhishi chanquan nianjian 2001–2002* (China IPR Yearbook 2001–2002) (Beijing: Zhishi chanquan chubanshe, 2002), 258–259, 266; *Zhongguo zhishi chanquan nianjian 2003* (China IPR Yearbook 2003) (Beijing: Zhishi chanquan chubanshe, 2003), 249–250, 278; *Zhongguo zhishi chanquan nianjian 2004* (China IPR Yearbook 2004) (Beijing: Zhishi chanquan chubanshe, 2004), 315–317, 336–337; *Zhongguo zhishi chanquan nianjian 2005* (China IPR Yearbook 2005) (Beijing: Zhishi chanquan chubanshe, 2005), 297–298, 305–310; *Zhongguo zhishi chanquan nianjian 2006* (China IPR Yearbook 2006) (Beijing: Zhishi chanquan chubanshe, 2006), 391–392, 405.

becomes even more complicated when we factor in the presence of multiple bureaucracies, all of which can provide enforcement, thus further increasing the administrative to court enforcement ratio (see Chapter 5).

What explains these statistical patterns? The chief reason for the empirically observed low court usage is the oversupply of administrative enforcement, which discourages right holders from seeking court enforcement. My research suggests that right holders prefer the cheapest and fastest method of obtaining redress, no matter whether it is provided by administrative agencies or by courts of law. Unless they are forced to go to court (e.g., when administrative enforcement options are limited or nonexistent), right holders will shun the slow and expensive court proceedings in favor of receiving rapid administrative relief. However, though it may appear to be optimal for right holders, a preference for administrative enforcement has negative consequences both for administrative efficiency and for the rise of the rule of law.

Regional Variation in Trademark Enforcement

We possess provincial-level statistics of trademark enforcement only by the SAIC, and not by any of the other bureaucracies with trademark enforcement portfolios. With this caveat, we can still learn something from the SAIC data. The SAIC publishes separate statistics on its enforcement activities in cases of foreign and domestic trademark infringement and counterfeiting. Because of severe fluctuations in enforcement activity in some poor inland provinces from year to year, the analysis that follows is based on a dataset of pooled enforcement statistics for the four-year period between 2000 and 2004.[8] This pooling of the enforcement data represents more accurately subnational enforcement activity in China in the early 2000s.

Enforcement in cases of domestic trademark counterfeiting was unevenly distributed among Chinese provinces (see GIS Map 7.1). Aggregate data for the period from 2000 to 2004, normalized after dividing by the population of each province, indicate that the variable had a minimal value of 31.3 enforcements per million people (Ningxia) and a maximal value of 610.6 enforcements per million people (Zhejiang), with a mean of 157.7 and a standard deviation of 128.7. Only seven provinces registered more than 200 enforcement cases per million people: Tianjin, Fujian, Shanghai, Liaoning, Beijing, Shanxi, and Zhejiang.[9] Although clustered, enforcement in cases of domestic trademark counterfeiting is more evenly distributed among Chinese provinces than enforcement in cases of foreign trademark counterfeiting (see GIS Map 7.2), which ranged from 0 (Gansu and Ningxia) to 92.7 cases per million people (Beijing), with a mean of 13.8 and a standard deviation of 26.2 in 2000–2004. Most provinces had fewer than 10 enforcement cases per million people during this period. Only Shanxi, Guangdong, Fujian, Zhejiang, Shanghai, and Beijing registered more than 10 cases. Overall, domestic and foreign trademark enforcement were correlated at 0.52, a finding that is suggestive of important differences between these two types of enforcement.

What factors explain these enforcement patterns? The protection of foreign trademarks was positively correlated with FDI (both net inflows and stock) and gross provincial product. Not surprisingly, increases in gross provincial product were linked to higher enforcement in cases of domestic trademark counterfeiting as well, but, as expected, FDI had no statistically significant effect. Understandably, domestic trademark anticounterfeiting actions were also very highly correlated with the number of locally famous trademarks in the province

---

[8] Dataset compiled by the author based on *Zhongguo zhishi chanquan nianjian* (all years between 2000 and 2005); *Zhongguo tongji nianjian* (China Statistical Yearbook) (Beijing: Zhongguo tongji chubanshe, all years between 2000 and 2005); and *China Commerce Yearbook* (Beijing: China Commerce Press, all years between 2000 and 2006).

[9] As of 2004, these provinces were also the most successful among China's thirty-one provinces in securing trademark application approvals. See *Zhongguo zhishi chanquan nianjian 2005*, 286.

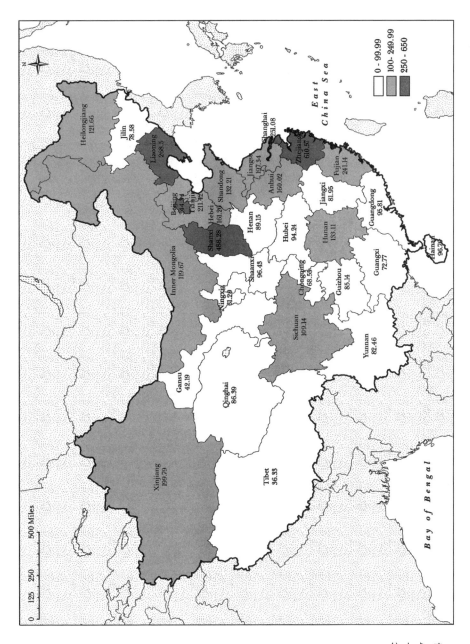

MAP 7.1. Domestic Trademark Cases Handled by the SAIC by Province, 2000–2004 (per million people)

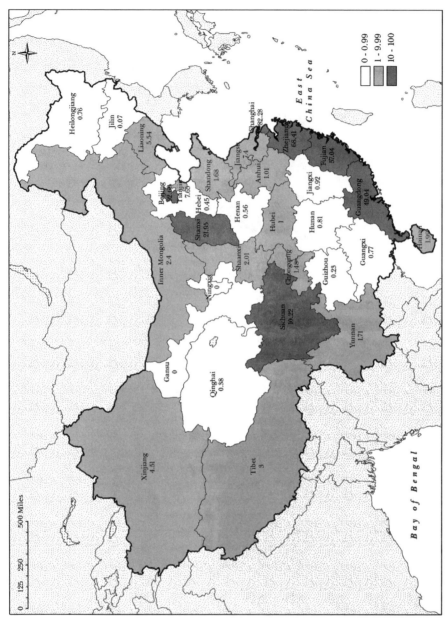

MAP 7.2. Foreign Trade-
mark Cases Handled
by the SAIC by Prov-
ince, 2000–2004 (per
million people)

(t value of 6.21 in a bivariate regression), but not with pure increases in the number of domestic trademark applications granted.[10] Also, the enforcement of foreign trademarks was positively correlated with the number of IPR cases handled by the courts, but there is no statistically significant relationship between court cases and domestic trademark enforcement.[11] In general, the data reveal the staggering disparities among Chinese regions in terms of their trademark enforcement records: trademark enforcement is distributed extremely unevenly across China, with the rich coastal provinces receiving the bulk of enforcement.

Data Limitations

Aggregate national-level enforcement statistics suffer from several shortcomings. First, they do not tell us how often agencies shirk their enforcement responsibilities. Second, we have no way of knowing how often agencies enforce in exchange for a bribe. Third, it is difficult to ascertain when agencies enforce on their own and when they cooperate with other agencies. Finally, we do not know whether enforcement is consistent, transparent, and fair. Many of these data limitations can be overcome by conducting a case study of trademark anticounterfeiting focused on a specific product.

CASE STUDY ONE: CIGARETTE ANTICOUNTERFEITING ACTIVITIES IN CHINA

Why study enforcement in cases of cigarette counterfeiting? Trademarks protect two broad categories of goods: luxury goods (e.g., Gucci shoes) and consumer goods (e.g., Hongtashan cigarettes, Head & Shoulders shampoo, or Gillette razors and batteries). We can reach different conclusions about enforcement depending on the category of goods we examine. For example, the protection of luxury goods is not a priority for either the central government or consumers. Thus, there is underinvestment in enforcement, with only two bureaucracies protecting luxury goods (the SAIC and the AQSIQ). If we were

---

[10] Each provincial AIC can award the status of a "locally famous trademark." This status is different from that of a "nationally famous mark," which is awarded by the SAIC. We only possess provincial-level data on locally famous trademarks for 2001. In that year some provinces, such as Tibet, Hainan, and Yunnan, had no locally famous trademarks, whereas Zhejiang had as many as 465. The mean of this variable was 165.2, and the standard deviation was 108.3. See *Zhongguo zhishi chanquan nianjian 2001–2002*, 506–619.

[11] This result is somewhat puzzling. We know that trademark cases constituted only 14.2 percent of the IPR court cases in 2004 and that foreign cases constituted 5 percent of the IPR court cases in the same year, but we do not know how these foreign cases were distributed among copyrights, patents, and trademarks. The statistical results presented here may indicate that most foreign cases were trademark cases.

to focus exclusively on luxury goods, we might fail to recognize that a much higher priority is placed on the protection of consumer goods. Both the government and consumers have an interest in limiting the amount of counterfeit consumer goods in the market. Consumers are motivated primarily by product safety, whereas the government acts out of both safety and tax evasion concerns. Thus, instead of underinvestment in enforcement, multiple bureaucracies with overlapping jurisdictions dedicate extensive resources to providing a high volume of enforcement for consumer goods.

Background: Economic Impact of the Tobacco Industry in China

Before we proceed with a discussion of the modalities of cigarette anticounterfeiting efforts, we need to have some background on the Chinese tobacco industry. China is the top producer and consumer of tobacco and tobacco products worldwide. In 2002, it produced 1,531,000 tons of tobacco leaf (27.1 percent of the world total)[12] and 1.72 trillion cigarettes.[13] Tobacco taxes have been the biggest single source of revenue in the consolidated annual budget of the PRC since the early 1990s. In 2002, tobacco tax revenues (excluding the special agricultural tax and the enterprise income tax) amounted to 105 billion yuan (US$13 billion).[14] Both the central and the local governments stand to benefit from tobacco production. The central government collects the tobacco consumption tax (*yanlei xiaofei shui*), the enterprise income tax (*qiye suode shui*), and 75 percent of the VAT (*zengzhi shui*) remitted by the tobacco procurement companies, cigarette factories, cigarette distribution companies, and cigarette wholesale companies (cigarette retail companies only pay a retail tax and are exempt from the VAT). Local governments collect the special crop tax (*yanye nongye techan shui*), imposed whenever growers sell tobacco to a procurement company or an allocation station, as well as 25 percent of the VAT.[15] In addition, the localities have historically imposed various special local taxes and fees on tobacco-producing enterprises, such as a municipal preservation and construction tax (*chengshi weihu jianshe shui*), real estate tax (*fangchan shui*), transportation vehicle tax (*chechuan shiyong shui*),

[12] STMA Tobacco Economic Research Institute Report No. 28, *Shijie yancao 2002 nian fazhan baogao* (World Tobacco 2002 Development Report) (April 8, 2003), www.tobacco.gov.cn/yjs/zeya028.htm (accessed July 24, 2003).

[13] STMA Tobacco Economic Research Institute Report No. 30, *Zhongguo yancao 2002 nian fazhan baogao* (China Tobacco 2002 Development Report) (April 18, 2003), www.tobacco.gov.cn/yjs/zeya030.htm (accessed July 24, 2003).

[14] In the same year, the total tax revenue in China's consolidated budget was 1.76 trillion yuan. See STMA, *Zhongguo yancao: 2002 nian fazhan baogao* and *Zhongguo tongji nianjian 2007* (China Statistical Yearbook 2007) (Beijing: Zhongguo tongji chubanshe, 2007), 279.

[15] Although the agricultural tax was officially abolished in 2005, the tobacco special tax was preserved.

stamp tax (*yinhua shui*), and educational surcharge (*jiaoyu fujia shui*).[16] Some poor and underdeveloped regions have become so dependent on the tobacco taxes, surcharges, and fees that their local public finance is called "tobacco finance" (*yan caizheng*).[17]

In some localities, government officials use the threat of force to make peasants plant and grow tobacco. When tobacco is harvested, county governments erect roadblocks and patrol mountain paths in order to discourage peasants from attempting to sell their tobacco in other counties, thus depriving the county government of the opportunity to collect the lucrative special crop tax.[18] Currently, of China's thirty-one provinces, only Zhejiang, Qinghai, Tibet, Hainan, Beijing, Tianjin, and Shanghai do not produce tobacco leaf.

Although tobacco growing is profitable, operating a tobacco factory is even more lucrative from the perspective of local governments. Driven by pecuniary interests, every Chinese province with the exception of Tibet has opened at least one cigarette factory.[19] In 2000, there were 146 cigarette factories, 121 of which were "within-plan" factories (*jihuanei yanchang*) and 25 of which were "local" factories (*difang yanchang*) opened by the localities without the approval of the STMA. In 2000, the production capacities of these cigarette factories varied a great deal, with the smallest factory having a capacity of 2,823 cases a year, and the largest (Yuxi Hongta Group) having the ability to produce 2.2 million cases annually.

Even though the number of cigarette factories was reduced by 50 percent from 1991 to 2000, the Chinese tobacco market is still extremely fragmented: there are 1,317 different brands (2,100 brands when we include line extensions), most of which are known only within a limited locale.[20] As Table 7.2 shows, the tobacco market concentration rate for the four leading brands in China is much lower than comparable indicators for the United States, the United Kingdom, or Japan. The large number of cigarette brands is directly

[16] Most of these taxes are illegal and were supposed to have been abolished, but they persist in at least some localities. For a rich account of illegal taxation in China in the 1990s, see Thomas Bernstein and Xiaobo Lü, *Taxation without Representation in Contemporary Rural China* (New York: Cambridge University Press, 2003).

[17] STMA, *Zhongguo yancao fazhan baogao 1949–1999* (Report on the Development of the Tobacco Industry in China 1949–1999) (Beijing: Gongshang chubanshe, 1999), 88. On tobacco taxes, see also Xiaolin Guo, "The Role of the Local Government in Creating Property Rights: The Case of Two Townships in Northwest Yunnan," in *Property Rights and Economic Development in China*, ed. Jean C. Oi and Andrew G. Walder (Stanford CA: Stanford University Press, 1999), 71–94.

[18] Yali Peng, "The Politics of Tobacco: Relations between Farmers and Local Governments in China's Southwest," *The China Journal*, no. 36 (1996), 67–82.

[19] STMA, *Zhongguo yancao fazhan baogao 1949–1999*, 618.

[20] STMA Tobacco Economic Research Institute Report No. 19, *Guanyu peiyu juanyan youshi pinpai yu shichang yingxiao dingwei de tantao* (An Inquiry into the Cultivation of Quality Cigarette Brands and Market Orientation) (July 29, 2002), www.tobacco.gov.cn/yjs/ zeya019.htm (accessed July 24, 2003).

TABLE 7.2. *Tobacco Market Concentration Rates in Four Countries*

Country	Market Share of Four Biggest Companies (%)	Market Share of Four Biggest Brands (%)	Market Share of Leading Company (%)	Market Share of Leading Brand (%)
U.S.	97.5	52.5	49.5	33.9
UK	91.5	33	39.5	11.8
Japan	99	47.5	75	35
China	17.5	8.3	6.5	2.7

Note: Table based on 1999 data.
Source: STMA Tobacco Economic Research Institute Report No. 5, *Zhongguo yancao hangye fazhan de beijing touxi ji zhanlüe silu* (Background Analysis and Strategic Planning for the Development of the Chinese Tobacco Industry) (May 18, 2001), www.tobacco.gov.cn/yjs/zeya05.htm (accessed July 24, 2003).

tied to the rise of regional trade barriers.[21] Driven by the profit motive, local governments established veritable "tobacco dukedoms" by erecting protectionist barriers impeding the entry of nonlocal brands. Regional trade barriers not only hindered the creation of a unified national market, but, by limiting the supply of specific brands of genuine cigarettes, also fueled counterfeiting as a response to unmet demand.[22] When a locality produces low-quality cigarettes that cannot compete with superior brands manufactured elsewhere, the local branch of the STMA has an incentive to establish quotas for the amount of non–locally produced cigarettes that can be sold in any given locality. Because the local tobacco administration manages both the cigarette production factories and the commercial cigarette distribution companies, it has the ability to enforce these quotas and to limit the inflow of nonlocal cigarettes to localities that produce inferior brands. As we will see later, this suggests that the STMA may be directly or indirectly implicated in counterfeiting.

The Economics of Cigarette Counterfeiting

Given the huge profits that can be reaped by cultivating tobacco and producing cigarettes, certain cash-strapped localities have either actively encouraged or passively tolerated the counterfeiting of both foreign and domestic cigarette brands. Since foreign brands cannot be legally produced in China, all localities have incentives to counterfeit them and counterfeiters are rarely targeted during enforcement. The counterfeiting calculus for domestic brands is more complicated, because localities may have nationally or provincially famous cigarette

---

[21] *China Tobacco Online*, "Imperativeness for China's Tobacco Industry to Form Enterprise Groups" (February 6, 2002), http://english.tobaccochinaonline.com/news.asp?id=2835 (accessed June 28, 2003).

[22] Fragmented markets and regional trade blockades can be identified in many areas. For valuable historical background, see Andrew Wedeman, *From Mao to Market: Rent-Seeking, Local Protectionism, and Marketization in China* (New York: Cambridge University Press, 2003).

brands. Local producers who counterfeit local brands that are famous nationally or provincially run a correspondingly greater risk of being targeted during enforcement. However, local protectionist concerns are less intense or even absent when nonlocal domestic brands are counterfeited: the authorities target local counterfeiters of nonlocal domestic brands less often. In sum, local interests trump regularized enforcement.

Two kinds of businesses engage in counterfeiting. The first are enterprises that are legitimate producers of low-end cigarette brands, which are less profitable than high-end domestic or foreign brands. Such duly licensed enterprises may be tempted to counterfeit brands with a higher profit potential. They acquire the know-how needed to produce such brands and then find ways to market them locally. The second kind of counterfeiting operation exists fully underground. Tobacco leaf is cut, cigarettes are rolled, packaging is printed, and cigarettes are packed and boxed mechanically or by hand – and all of this is done underground, sometimes in caves or in remote mountain villages, which are not easily accessible to employees of enforcement agencies. Right holders find it exceedingly difficult to motivate agencies to enforce against licensed enterprises. Therefore, most enforcement actions target underground cigarette production facilities.

It is important to stress that the growing and processing of tobacco leaf, as well as cigarette production, transportation, and trade, are a state monopoly in China. The STMA manages the entire tobacco sector on behalf of the state. Therefore, even underground counterfeiters have some connection with the STMA – otherwise, they would not have been able to procure the tobacco and other necessary production inputs, or to purchase the equipment required to engage in counterfeiting, such as a printing press and cigarette production and packaging machines.

How does counterfeiting benefit the locality? Underground counterfeiters create employment; they also channel bribes to local government agencies to avoid being targeted for enforcement. Licensed factories that produce counterfeits similarly create employment, and they pay taxes to the local government, as well as bribes to cover up their counterfeiting activity. In effect, as long as the counterfeiters are not counterfeiting famous local brands, there is an incentive to enforce superficially, without the threat of permanently closing down the offending enterprise. The profits from counterfeiting are so high that the odds are decidedly against effective enforcement. This is a stable equilibrium, benefiting both the local government and the counterfeiters.

The Modalities of Cigarette Anticounterfeiting Enforcement: The Data Problem

Even though it is widespread and highly lucrative, cigarette counterfeiting has not been the subject of scholarly analysis. This gap reflects the difficulty of gathering meaningful information on cigarette counterfeiting and on government measures to address the problem. In the early stages of my research,

I noticed that the businesspeople, lawyers, and private investigators I interviewed about counterfeiting and piracy consistently avoided two topics: pharmaceuticals and cigarettes. When asked to say more, they would simply answer that they did not know anything about counterfeiting in these areas. Private investigators, in particular, told me the same thing over and over: "Cigarette and pharmaceutical anticounterfeiting is very dangerous work, and we don't do it." I had almost lost hope of finding out more about either cigarettes or pharmaceuticals, when a series of serendipitous circumstances allowed me to gain access to the case files of Surefire, a private investigation firm in mainland China, which specializes in, among other areas, cigarette anticounterfeiting.[23]

We may wonder how (and why) private investigation firms are involved with IPR protection in China. In principle, a right holder should be able to approach a government agency directly and receive enforcement for his grievance. However, in practice, right holders often lack the knowledge necessary to navigate the administrative labyrinth that arises when so many agencies have jurisdiction over IPR enforcement. In addition, administrative agencies are often unwilling to take on directly cases presented to them by right holders. The niche that has emerged has been filled by private investigation companies, which act as intermediaries between right holders and administrative agencies. Right holders, administrative agencies, and private investigators all benefit from the current enforcement situation. Right holders like working with private investigators, because they possess specialized knowledge about the available enforcement options. Administrative agencies also like private investigators, because they do some of their work (investigation) and because they often channel bribes to them. Private investigators themselves like counterfeiting, because it allows them to charge right holders hefty fees for their services and to turn a handsome profit. Private investigation has emerged as a booming business in China.

The records of private investigators proved to be an important source of information for this project: Surefire allowed me access to 107 case files, which constituted its entire cigarette anticounterfeiting activity between the end of 1999 and early 2001. Although 107 raids had been organized, 7 had been canceled, thus leaving us with 100 completed raids. As only foreign companies can afford Surefire's hefty fees, all 107 files dealt with cases of counterfeiting of foreign cigarette brands. The files contained detailed reports on how Surefire identified the counterfeiters, verified that they were in fact engaging in the counterfeiting of foreign cigarette brands, and approached the relevant authorities to organize and conduct a raid. The case files frequently contained abundant photographic evidence of the counterfeiting location and of the tobacco products seized. Occasionally, a copy of the punishment decision issued by the enforcement agency was present in the case file as well. Finally, an itemized bill

---

[23] For reasons of confidentiality, I have changed the name of the investigation firm from which I obtained the case files.

for each raid allowed me to see what services clients were billed for, including the ubiquitous but illegal "case-handling fees," which will be discussed later in this chapter.

As the majority of Surefire's raids were conducted in Guangdong province,[24] I wanted to compile additional datasets that would allow me to compare how agency involvement in the protection of domestic brands might differ from foreign-brand anticounterfeiting efforts. Thus, with the help of a research assistant, I collected 99 newspaper articles on domestic-brand enforcement in Guangdong province from 2000 to 2002. I then coded the newspaper accounts for agency involvement and tabulated the results. In order to control for the special status of Guangdong as a developed coastal province, I also collected 108 newspaper reports of cigarette anticounterfeiting during the 2000–2002 period in provinces other than Guangdong. Despite my efforts to assemble as broad a geographical sample as possible, some provinces and autonomous areas were not represented in my non-Guangdong sample, whereas others were overrepresented.[25] However, given that the overrepresented provinces were targeted by the STMA as priority enforcement areas,[26] I am inclined to believe that the two newspaper datasets reflect relatively accurately the provincial-level distribution of cigarette anticounterfeiting activity in China.

The following analysis is based on the Surefire dataset, the two newspaper datasets, interviews with private investigators (who eventually were willing to talk), interviews with bureaucrats, official yearbooks, and a two-week research stint in the library of a private investigation firm in Hong Kong.

Agencies Involved in Cigarette Anticounterfeiting Work

Who enforces in cases of cigarette counterfeiting? Knowing that China has a specialized administrative agency with a monopoly over the production, distribution, sale, importation, and exportation of tobacco and tobacco products,

---

[24] Of the 107 Surefire raids, 97 were conducted in Guangdong province (90.65 percent of the total). The remaining raids were carried out in Fujian province (5 raids) and Henan province (5 raids).

[25] The non-Guangdong domestic brands newspaper dataset does not include data from Hunan, Inner Mongolia, Jilin, Ningxia, Qinghai, Shanxi, Tibet, and Xinjiang. It represents 18 provinces and 4 provincial-level municipalities. The number of cases for each represented region is as follows: Beijing: 2, Tianjin: 3, Hebei: 7, Liaoning: 4, Heilongjiang: 2, Shanghai: 10, Jiangsu: 5, Zhejiang: 4, Anhui: 4, Fujian: 7, Jiangxi: 1, Shandong: 7, Henan: 6, Hubei: 6, Guangxi: 2, Hainan: 1, Chongqing: 2, Sichuan: 19, Guizhou: 5, Yunnan: 8, Shaanxi: 2, and Gansu: 1. The overrepresentation of Sichuan in the sample is no accident: official statistics indicate that Sichuan produces a very small amount of cigarettes, even though it plants a large amount of tobacco (STMA, *Zhongguo yancao fazhan baogao 1949–1999*, 618). This leads us to believe that the excess tobacco is either sold to other provinces or used to produce counterfeit cigarettes, thus creating a significant need for enforcement.

[26] See Notice 680 of the STMA (1999), which designates Guangdong, Fujian, Guangxi, Henan, Hubei, and Hebei as priority areas for enforcement.

we might expect that it would be the main enforcer in cases of cigarette counter-feiting. The State Tobacco Monopoly Administration is, indeed, designated as the lead enforcer in the area of cigarette anticounterfeiting according to central-level laws and regulations. However, in practice, it is just one of many agencies with enforcement responsibility in this issue area. My three datasets reveal that at least fifteen agencies other than the STMA have actually participated in cigarette anticounterfeiting enforcement activities (see later discussion). In addition to these sixteen agencies included in the three datasets, several other agencies have enforcement jurisdiction as well. Customs can handle cases of counterfeit cigarettes smuggled into or out of China. The Finance Ministry and the Tax Administration have an interest in counterfeiting cases that involve tax evasion, and the now-defunct Planning Commission had the power to limit the procurement and production plans of locales with persistent counterfeiting problems. Finally, the City Management Administrative Enforcement Bureau (Chengshi guanli xingzheng zhifa ju) has a mandate to enforce in marketpla-ces.[27] Thus, altogether, over twenty ministries, agencies, and bureaus have primary or secondary enforcement responsibility in cases of cigarette counter-feiting.

The multiplicity of enforcement options gives rise to several questions. First, when do these agencies enforce? Do they shirk? Do they enforce in exchange for a bribe? Do they enforce alone or in cooperation with other agencies? Second, and more important, do these agencies provide high-quality enforcement?

An additional question is whether there are important differences between enforcement in cases of domestic-brand and foreign-brand counterfeiting. As Figures 7.1, 7.2, and 7.3 indicate, agency participation in cases of domestic-brand counterfeiting is virtually identical, no matter whether the enforcement occurs in Guangdong province or elsewhere in China. However, domestic-brand enforcement is significantly different from enforcement in cases of for-eign-brand counterfeiting: although the local tobacco administrations and the police are key enforcers in cases of domestic-brand counterfeiting, they are much less important when foreign brands are subject to counterfeiting. What explains the unwillingness of the tobacco administration and the police to become involved in foreign-brand cases?

The State Tobacco Monopoly Administration

The State Tobacco Monopoly Administration is legally designated as the lead agency responsible for fighting cigarette counterfeiting. However, as one inter-viewee put it, the STMA "sees itself more as a chamber of commerce for the tobacco industry rather than as an enforcement bureaucracy."[28] In the words of

---

[27] On the activities of this agency in one Chinese county, see *Zouping nianjian 1999–2003* (Zou-ping Yearbook 1999–2003) (Ji'nan: Shandong xinhua yinshuachang, 2004), 336–340.
[28] China Interview 020119, with a Hong Kong lawyer specializing in cigarette anticounterfeiting (by phone from Beijing).

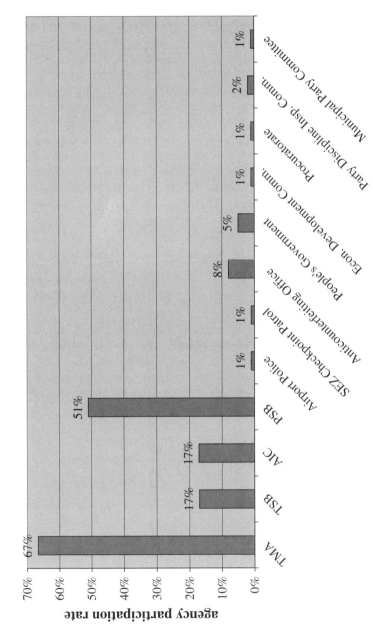

FIGURE 7.1. Agency Participation Rates in Raids against Counterfeiters of Domestic Cigarette Brands in Guangdong Province (raids N = 99). *Source:* Guangdong newspaper database.

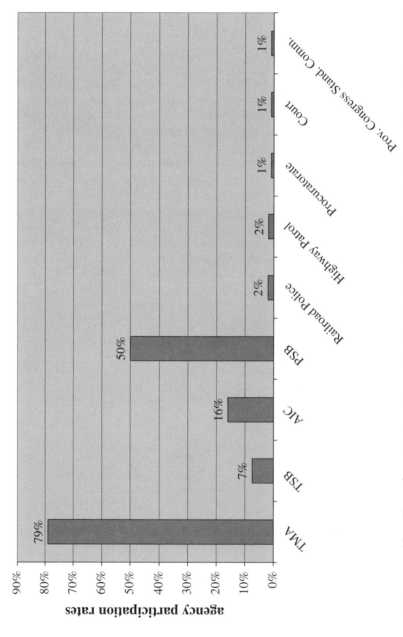

FIGURE 7.2. Non-Guangdong Province Agency Participation Rates in Raids against Counterfeiters of Domestic Cigarette Brands (raids N = 108). *Source:* Non-Guangdong newspaper database.

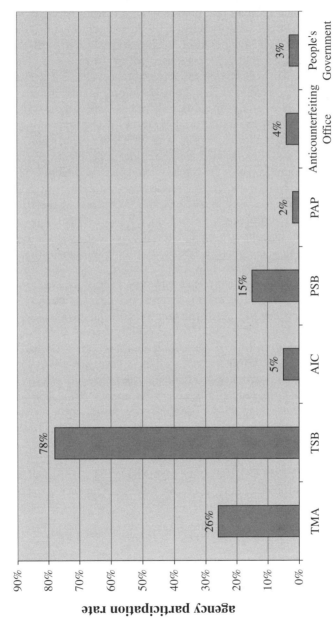

FIGURE 7.3. Agency Participation Rates in Raids against Counterfeiters of Foreign Cigarette Brands (raids N = 100). *Source:* Surefire case files.

a STMA bureaucrat, "We are highly trained specialists, so we cannot spend our time focusing on mundane enforcement issues."[29] Historically, the STMA avoided becoming directly involved in anticounterfeiting raids and preferred to disburse funds to other agencies that engaged in anticounterfeiting enforcement activities, such as the Public Security Bureau, the Administration for Industry and Commerce, and the Technical Supervision Bureau. In the early 1990s, the STMA established a special fund that was to be used to award prizes to enforcement officers. As a Shanghai Tobacco Monopoly Administration official told me, "Each year there are at least five criminal prosecutions against counterfeiters of our cigarette brands. However, at most we only initiate one of these prosecutions. The rest are carried out by the PSB, Administration for Industry and Commerce (AIC), and TSB. We actually like it this way."[30] Outsourcing enforcement to other bureaucracies did not resolve the counterfeiting problem, so in the early 1990s the STMA adopted a hands-on approach and became directly involved in a greater proportion of the raids. As mentioned in Chapter 5, the STMA was handling more than 200,000 counterfeiting cases by the end of the 1990s.

Despite this spike in enforcement activity, the STMA is strikingly unwilling to target foreign-brand counterfeiters. The enforcement datasets reveal that while the STMA and its local-level tobacco monopoly administrations participated in only 26 percent of the foreign-brand raids, their participation rate was 66.7 percent in the Guangdong sample and 78.7 percent in the non-Guangdong sample. This rather sharp difference is interest-driven. The counterfeiting of domestic brands hurts the STMA, as the factories producing genuine domestic brands belong to the China National Tobacco Corporation (CNTC), a mammoth conglomerate within the STMA *xitong* (bureaucratic system).[31] In contrast, genuine foreign-brand cigarettes sold in China are always produced abroad. Therefore, counterfeits of foreign cigarette brands do not hurt domestic producers. Since foreign-brand counterfeits are sometimes produced by licensed cigarette factories within China, STMA enforcement in such cases may expose complicity within its own ranks and would be rare indeed.[32]

Police Forces

As demonstrated in Chapter 6, the police forces have the potential of providing the most deterrent enforcement of IPR laws. Unlike other agencies, the police can

---

[29] China Interview 020108, with an employee of the Monopoly Supervision and Management Department, STMA (Beijing).

[30] China Interview 010723B, with an employee in the Legal Department of the Shanghai Tobacco Monopoly Administration (Shanghai).

[31] Under the Maoist system, ministries and central-level bureaucracies had to take care of the key industrial enterprises assigned to them (see, for example, Andrew G. Walder, *Communist Neo-Traditionalism: Work and Authority in Chinese Industry* [Berkeley: University of California Press, 1986]). This system has virtually disappeared with the privatization and restructuring of the major industrial enterprises but was preserved in the area of cigarette production and electricity generation into the late 2000s.

[32] China Interview 010810, with a private investigator (Hong Kong).

arrest suspected criminals and initiate the lengthy process of imprisoning them. Even if they do not arrest a suspect, the mere presence of the police has a positive effect on the quality of a raid, making it less likely that suspects will escape or assault enforcement officers. As a PSB employee said, "The SAIC uniform doesn't have the prestige of a PSB uniform. There are frequent cases of violence against SAIC officers, but if you hit a policeman, you can be sued criminally."[33] This statement would apply fully to the STMA as well. In the words of another knowledgeable observer, "The PSB is used as a bodyguard by the STMA."[34] Cooperation with the PSB "makes it less threatening for enforcement agencies to enter the premises of counterfeiting operations."[35] Thus, police assistance is often crucial in the risky enterprise of raiding cigarette counterfeiters.

A marked difference exists between PSB participation in raids against counterfeiters of domestic brands and counterfeiters of foreign brands. The PSB was involved in fifteen raids (15 percent of the total) in the Surefire dataset, whereas it participated in 51 percent of the Guangdong domestic raids and 50 percent of the non-Guangdong domestic raids. The reluctance of the PSB to initiate raids against counterfeiters of foreign brands bespeaks the inability of foreign companies to approach the PSB directly and to make their concerns heard.

The Technical Supervision Bureau and the Administration for Industry and Commerce

One notable feature of the data is that we cannot find any examples of AIC cooperation with the TSB. At the grass roots, those two agencies with very similar mandates are in fierce competition with each other to attract "clients" for their services (and to collect bribes). Thus, they may participate in multi-agency raids organized by the People's Government or the local Tobacco Monopoly Administration (TMA), but they never cooperate with each other. TSB involvement in raids against counterfeiters of foreign brands differs radically from its participation in raids against counterfeiters of domestic brands. According to my datasets, the TSB is the main enforcer for foreign brands, participating in 78 percent of these cases. In the area of domestic brands, the TSB was only involved in 7.4 percent of the cases in the non-Guangdong sample and in 17.2 percent of the cases in the Guangdong sample. The AIC was involved in very few raids in cases of foreign-brand counterfeiting (5 percent of the total). In cases of domestic-brand counterfeiting, the AIC took part in 17.2 percent of the Guangdong raids and 15.7 percent of the non-Guangdong raids. Thus, while the TSB and AIC participation in domestic raids was relatively similar, the TSB was a much more active participant in enforcement in

[33] Remarks by Mr. Yuan Zhongbo, deputy director, Public Order Department of the Ministry of Public Security, at the China-EU IPR Training Seminar, People's University, November 15, 2001 (Beijing).

[34] China Interview 010825, with a Hong Kong lawyer specializing in cigarette anticounterfeiting (Hong Kong).

[35] China Interview 020108, with an employee of the Monopoly Supervision and Management Department, STMA (Beijing).

cases of foreign-brand counterfeiting than the AIC. National-level data presented in Chapter 5 indicate that over time, the TSB has also emerged as the main enforcer in cases of domestic trademark counterfeiting, most likely as a result of its designation as the chief enforcer in the 2000–2001 National Anticounterfeiting and Product Quality Campaign.

What explains Surefire's decision to work with the TSB? The case files contain abundant evidence that Surefire's preferred enforcers were the STMA and the PSB, because they have direct competence over the administrative and criminal handling of cigarette counterfeiting cases. However, because these agencies were reluctant to work with Surefire, the private investigators had to capitalize on their existing relationship with the TSB and use it as the primary enforcer in cigarette counterfeiting cases.

Anticounterfeiting Office (Dajia Bangongshi)
The anticounterfeiting offices were created in the wake of the October 27, 2000, State Council circular calling for the establishment of a National Anticounterfeiting Office with provincial and subprovincial branches. As mentioned in Chapter 5, the original idea was that these offices would coordinate the activities of all agencies involved in anticounterfeiting. Since the 2000–2001 national anticounterfeiting campaign was initially led by the AQSIQ, the anticounterfeiting office was supposed to be housed within the AQSIQ/TSB system, both at the central and at the subnational level, under the tried and true Chinese bureaucratic practice of creating two agencies within the same bureaucracy ("one organization, two name plates," *yige jigou, liangkuai paizi*). Thus, in most places, the anticounterfeiting office was part of the TSB. The anticounterfeiting office participated in four Surefire raids, all of which were conducted jointly with the TSB. However, occasionally the anticounterfeiting office was established as part of the local government, and sometimes it was a fully independent entity. For example, the Guangdong domestic brands dataset contains two cases of raids conducted single-handedly by the anticounterfeiting office. In the early 2000s, the anticounterfeiting offices were gradually transformed into market order rectification offices. By 2004, responsibility for these offices was transferred to the Ministry of Commerce.

Other Agencies with Episodic Involvement in Cigarette Anticounterfeiting
The three datasets document the involvement of seven additional agencies in cases of cigarette counterfeiting: the Mayor's Office (People's Government), the Economic Development Commission, the Party Discipline and Inspection Commission, the provincial People's Congress, the Procuratorate, the People's Court, and the Special Economic Zone checkpoint patrol. In addition, five specialized police forces took part in anticounterfeiting enforcement: the People's Armed Police (Wujing), the Railroad Police (Tielu jingcha or Tiegong'an), the Airport Police (Jichang anjian), the Highway Patrol (Gaosu xunjing or Gaosu jiaojing), and the Traffic Police (Gongjiaojing). The frequencies of participation by each agency in enforcement are presented in Figures 7.1–7.3. As

TABLE 7.3. *Number of Agencies Participating in Raids in China*

	Guangdong Domestic Brands (N = 99) (%)	Non-Guangdong Domestic Brands (N = 108) (%)	Foreign Brands (N = 100) (%)
1	50.5	57.4	76
2	35.3	33.3	17
3	9.1	5.6	5
4	4	2.8	2
5	1	0	0
6	0	0.9	0

Sources: Surefire and newspaper enforcement datasets.

these agencies have episodic involvement in anticounterfeiting, I will not discuss them at length. We should note, however, that the very fact of their participation in enforcement complicates an already crowded enforcement domain and creates uncertainty regarding where right holders should turn for assistance when faced with a counterfeiting problem. In turn, the uncertainty can be exploited by bureaucrats who can either refuse to enforce or else only enforce in exchange for a bribe.

Patterns of Interagency Cooperation

Do agencies enforce alone or in cooperation with others? As Table 7.3 demonstrates, patterns of interagency cooperation differ substantially between domestic and foreign brands. Multiagency raids are relatively infrequent in the Surefire dataset (24 percent), whereas the Guangdong and non-Guangdong datasets show a much higher level of multiagency raids (49.5 percent and 42.6 percent, respectively). The dominant mode of operation for both domestic and foreign cigarette brands is the single-agency raid. As a Western diplomat who had worked in Beijing for a long time told me, "Chinese bureaucracies don't like sharing information with each other."[36] This preference is easily understood: agencies want to focus on the course of action that is the quickest and that has the lowest transaction costs. In addition, conducting a raid alone ensures that the agency receives all the proceeds from the fines (and bribes) imposed on the infringer.

If single-agency raids are the preferred outcome, why do we observe any two-agency and multiagency raids? One drawback of single-agency raids is that unless they are conducted by the PSB, enforcement officers may encounter violence or sabotage from the counterfeiters. Therefore, cooperation with the PSB is a top priority for enforcers, especially in dangerous cases. Table 7.4 reveals that the PSB rarely enforces alone; typically, it acts as a supporting

[36] China Interview 010611, with a U.S. diplomat (Beijing).

TABLE 7.4. *PSB Participation Rate in Foreign- and Domestic-Brands Raids*

Number of Agencies	Foreign Brands	Guangdong	Non-Guangdong
PSB alone	0 raids (0%)	7 raids (14.3%)	10 raids (18.5%)
PSB with another agency	9 raids (60%)	30 raids (61.2%)	34 raids (63%)
PSB in multiagency raids	6 raids (40%)	12 raids (24.5%)	10 raids (18.5%)
PSB total raids	15	49	54

Sources: Surefire and newspaper enforcement datasets.

(*peihe*) unit for the STMA or another administrative agency conducting enforcement. In fact, some tobacco monopoly bureaus have permanent PSB officers on staff and include them in most enforcement actions.[37] PSB support allows STMA agents to feel more secure during enforcement. In 2007, the PSB supported other departments in 10,870 enforcement cases; however, these cases were not processed as criminal cases; rather, they were concluded with administrative punishments imposed by the police or by the administrative agencies that were assisted by the police.[38]

Another reason for multiagency raids is the complexity of some cases. As an officer at the Shanghai AIC told me, "Sometimes we have difficult cases. We can't refuse to take such cases without a reason – otherwise we might be sued. So, what we do is either investigate and find a reason not to take the case, or we ask another agency to cooperate with us – this way we do it together."[39] A third reason for multiagency raids is campaign-style enforcement. As outlined in previous chapters, there is a difference between enforcement in response to a complaint (*tousu*) and proactive enforcement (*zhudong chachu*). Surefire's files reveal that enforcement in cases of foreign-brand counterfeiting was never proactive – a complaint had to be filed prior to enforcement. In contrast, proactive enforcement was quite common in domestic cases. Oftentimes, this enforcement was conducted campaign-style, with multiple agencies engaging in concentrated enforcement over a two-week or month-long period. Thus, the presence of campaign enforcement in domestic cases explains the high level of multiagency raids. Surefire, for example, would only invite a second agency to participate when absolutely necessary (e.g., the PSB was sometimes used for backup). As a business entity, Surefire had to keep its costs down. It thus avoided multiagency raids because they required paying higher case-handling fees or outright bribes to the authorities.

[37] China Interview 080108A, with employees of the Tobacco Monopoly Bureau (Zouping).
[38] Ministry of Commerce, "China's Intellectual Property Protection in 2007," http://english.ipr. gov.cn/ipr/en/info/Article.jsp?a_no=198450&col_no=102&;dir=200804"(accessed October 29, 2008). The cases with PSB involvement constituted less than 1 percent of total IPR enforcement in China in 2007.
[39] China Interview 020130C, with the chief of the AIC Inspection Team (Shanghai).

Intraagency Cooperation

Multiple levels of a single agency may also be involved in a raid when complicated enforcement actions necessitate the participation of the central, provincial, prefectural, or county level of a certain government bureaucracy. The patterns of intraagency cooperation allow us to understand to what extent the higher levels of an agency have an impact on the behavior of the lower levels of the same agency. Overall, we see less intraagency cooperation in the area of domestic-brands enforcement (8.7 percent) than in the area of foreign-brands enforcement (20 percent). This suggests that enforcement requests of foreign right holders meet resistance at the grassroots level, so foreigners must appeal to higher levels of the agency in order to obtain redress.[40] Involvement of a higher-up can be considered an indication of fighting local protectionism. However, given the small size of the samples, the differences may also be the result of chance and should therefore be interpreted with caution.

Negative Side Effects of Administrative Enforcement

Official newspaper reports ignore the negative side of enforcement. However, the Surefire dataset allows us to explore three negative externalities created by the current enforcement framework: canceled raids (which are sometimes due to shirking), no-seizure raids, and enforcement in exchange for a bribe. All of these phenomena are linked to bureaucratic corruption and local protectionism.

Canceled Raids

Some planned raids are canceled. The Surefire dataset contains information about seven such incidents, constituting 6.5 percent of all raids. In general, the case files provide scant information about the reasons for canceling a raid. In two cases, no specific information is given; in one case, Surefire "failed in seeking support from the local authorities"; in another, "the target was moved"; and in the final three raids, the "machinery was moved." Why are raids canceled? Surefire prides itself on verifying the location of counterfeiting operations through meticulous fact checking:

> Our usual mode of operating is to initially interview the informants (usually over the telephone) and then to dispatch personnel to meet the informants and check out the locations before making a final judgment on whether to carry out a raid.[41]

Thus, canceled raids are not the result of shoddy investigative work. The following description of a failed raid extracted from Surefire's case files reveals how enforcement authorities may be responsible for a canceled raid:

---

[40] China Interview 010601, with a private investigator (Beijing).
[41] Private communication between Surefire and one of its clients, April 20, 2000 (copy on file with the author).

On October 12 we received a report from our informant that there was a counterfeiting site in X town. When we arrived at X town, and before we had gone to meet with the TSB, the informant called us to say that 30 minutes earlier the production line had been moved, as reported by the contact working at the site. We quickly went to the site, which was located in a citizen's house in X town. It was approximately 100 sq. m. in size. All of the windows and doors were open. The house had a very strong smell of tobacco, but there was no cigarette production machinery inside. A worker told us that the boss had suddenly moved away the machine and sent all the workers out of the factory. The boss also told the workers that once he set up a new factory, he would contact them to work for him again. Hence, we asked the informant to trace this lead. Then we contacted the TSB to cancel the raid.[42]

Pending further investigation, two days later Surefire reported to its client that "our informant indicated that news of the TSB's planned raid had been leaked."[43]

When a planned raid is canceled, Surefire suffers a loss, because it can only bill its clients for preraid investigative services, rather than for a full-fledged raid. Surefire would only cancel a raid when agencies refuse to enforce (bureaucrats shirk) or when agencies leak information about the upcoming raid and the counterfeiters quickly relocate their operations. Either way, a canceled raid is indicative of local protectionism. As one interviewee put it, "All enforcement agencies are corrupt. Their employees always have a cousin or another relative working in the factory that they are supposed to raid."[44]

No-Seizure Raids

Enforcement agents may sometimes conduct a raid but go away empty-handed. Unfortunately, the statistical yearbooks and newspaper articles only focus on successful raids, which feature seizures of tobacco products, cigarette production materials, or machinery. Thus, if we were solely to rely on the official reports, we would have no way of estimating the proportion of raids that result in no seizures. However, the Surefire dataset indicates that such no-seizure raids are quite common. The dataset reveals that twenty-four raids (24 percent of the 100 raids that were actually carried out) resulted in no seizures.

The most likely reason for raids that produce no seizures is that the enforcement authority has tipped off the infringers about the upcoming raid. The following account of a no-seizure raid is extracted from Surefire's case files:

On October 14, after confirming information on this target without an informant, we decided to take action. The TSB of X town arranged an inspection team to take action against the site, which was located in Y town. It was a 300 sq. m. factory building. When the raid party entered, we found that the cigarette machinery had already been moved away. There were only about 300 bags of cut tobacco inside the factory. Judging from

---

[42] Surefire multiple raid report dated October 12–14, 2000 (copy on file with the author).
[43] Private communication between Surefire and one of its clients, October 16, 2000 (copy on file with the author).
[44] China Interview 010704C, with a private investigator (Shanghai).

the spot, we believed the machine had been moved no more than four hours earlier. The TSB of X town had confiscated the cut tobacco and other materials.[45]

Surprisingly, no-seizure raids are usually conducted by agencies that some may regard as "captured" by right holders. For example, 53 of the 100 raids in the Surefire dataset were conducted by one TSB located in X town of Guangdong province. The high number of raids indicates that there were intensive contacts between Surefire and the administrative agency. Some might be misled into thinking that given such frequent interaction, the local TSB might have been "captured" by Surefire. However, 16 of the 24 no-seizure raids in the Surefire dataset were conducted by that very same TSB. Thus, even when regularized exchanges exist between a bureaucracy and right holders, these exchanges do not unfold along the lines that theories of state capture would predict.[46] The functioning of Chinese bureaucracies can be better understood by a dynamic model that sees them as having multiple clients, all of whom bid for their services. In the end, the bureaucracies will sell enforcement to the highest bidder rather than indiscriminately catering to the needs of their putative "captors."

Case-Handling Fees (Ban'an fei) *and Bribes* (Hongbao)

Right holders frequently have to pay a "case-handling fee" in order to grease the wheels of the administrative enforcement machine. Unlike the court case-acceptance fees (*shou'an fei*), which are specified by law, the prevalence and average amount of case-handling fees vary a great deal across China, with some localities shunning the practice and others assessing hefty fees. Case-handling fees are extrabudgetary funds, which should be reported to the upper levels within the agency or to the Finance Bureau but are usually retained in the "small treasuries" (*xiao jinku*) of the grassroots agencies that collected them.[47] If and when receipts are issued for the acceptance of case-handling fees, they are informal receipts (*shouju*), rather than official receipts (*fapiao*) subject to auditing.[48] Case-handling fees are an accepted cost of doing business in China, with clients often paying "disbursements" of between US$500 and US$1,000 per raid to the private investigation firms, which then channel the fees to the administrative agencies conducting the raid. As one private investigator told me, "The incentive for paying the case-handling fee is that it helps maintain good relations with the authorities."[49]

---

[45] Surefire multiple raid report dated October 12–14, 2000 (copy on file with the author).

[46] Studies of state capture have been developed to understand how powerful business groups can "capture" the central state and purchase favorable legislation from it. The paradigmatic case is Russia under Yeltsin. See Joel Hellman, Geraint Jones, and Daniel Kaufmann, *Seize the State, Seize the Day: State Capture, Corruption, and Influence in Transition*, World Bank Policy Research Paper, no. 2444 (September 2000).

[47] On "small treasuries," see Xiaobo Lü, "Booty Socialism, Bureau-preneurs, and the State in Transition: Organizational Corruption in China," *Comparative Politics* 32:3 (2000), 273–294.

[48] China Interview 010601, with a private investigator (Beijing).

[49] China Interview 010601, with a private investigator (Beijing).

Other types of semilegal and illegal practices necessary to induce agencies to perform their duties involve routine postraid banquets and less frequent entertainment in karaoke bars and "massage parlors."[50] Occasionally, as a way of building or maintaining good relationships with government officials, right holders will "sponsor" foreign "study trips" for top bureaucrats.

Payment may be made directly to an official in the form of a bribe (*hongbao*), for which no receipt is provided. In this case, the official can simply pocket the money.[51]

Local Protectionism

Trademark anticounterfeiting can be dangerous work. In 1994, the Yuxi Tobacco Monopoly Authority received a letter of complaint (*jubao xin*) about a cigarette counterfeiting operation in the town of Zhaoping in Yunnan province. After confiscating a certain amount of counterfeit cigarettes and apprehending some of the counterfeiters, a joint STMA/PSB team prepared to destroy the counterfeit cigarettes. However, angry locals armed with knives and guns surrounded the inspection team and threatened its members. The local law enforcement authorities made no effort to help the STMA/PSB team. As a result, the counterfeiters dispersed, the peasants squirreled away the counterfeit cigarettes, the car of the inspectors was destroyed, and the inspection team hastily left Zhaoping, where the party, government, and law enforcement authorities were all implicated in the counterfeiting operation.[52] Similarly, in a case in which counterfeit cigarettes worth 600,000 yuan (an amount that meets the criminal liability threshold) were discovered in a location in northern Jiangsu, the town mayor, county head, and head of the Finance Bureau interceded on behalf of the traffickers. In the end, only a fine was imposed.[53]

In another counterfeiting case, which took place near Kunming in Yunnan province, an undercover police officer was blindfolded and abandoned in a mountain cave, while four police officers were surrounded by a crowd of three hundred angry peasants, who were unhappy that the police officers were destroying the village's "life and blood."[54] Official government publications admit such problems exist and report that "twenty law enforcement officers were sacrificed in the frontline of enforcing the tobacco monopoly system."[55] The stakes are often so high that huge enforcement teams have to be dispatched to resolve what seem like small problems.

---

[50] China Interview 010601, with a private investigator (Beijing).
[51] China Interview 020117, with consumer rights advocate Wang Hai (Beijing).
[52] Wang Yinsheng, *Zhongguo yancao de lishi zhuangkuang yu weilai* (The Past and Future of China's Tobacco) (Hefei: Anhui daxue chubanshe, 2000), 302.
[53] Ibid., 303.
[54] "Jiayanshang zuoda qi sheng taoshui 200 yi" (Tobacco Counterfeiting Expanding in Seven Provinces: 20 Billion Yuan in Taxes Avoided), *Dongfang ribao* (Oriental Daily), January 11, 2000.
[55] STMA, *Zhongguo yancao fazhan baogao 1949–1999*, 7.

Localities are subject to perverse incentives to frustrate the implementation of centrally formulated anticounterfeiting policies and to nurture the current enforcement framework, which focuses on small-scale, ineffective raids against relatively minor counterfeiting operations. Local protectionism allows counterfeiters to operate with impunity under the protection (*baohu san*) of the local authorities.

The Quality of Cigarette Anticounterfeiting Enforcement in China

Is cigarette anticounterfeiting enforcement consistent? The newspaper datasets do not allow us to answer this question, but the Surefire case files suggest that enforcement is plagued by canceled raids and no-seizure raids and thus cannot be deemed consistent.

How about transparency? In the 107 Surefire case files I consulted, I found only five punishment decisions (*xingzheng chufa jueding shu*). By law, punishment decisions have to be issued for every case that is accepted for investigation (*li'an chachu*). We know that at least two-thirds of the caseloads of the major agencies with an IPR portfolio consist of cases accepted for investigation.[56] Therefore, all of these cases should end in punishment decisions. In practice, however, this rule is broken, and only cases that have been accepted after a complaint from the right holder (*tousu*) are concluded with a written punishment decision. As mentioned in Chapter 1, statistics from the SAIC indicate the proportion of *tousu* cases has never exceeded 5 percent of the total SAIC caseload. This greatly restricts the number of cases in which the actions of the SAIC are subject to public accountability through written punishment decisions. Be that as it may, all of Surefire's cases were initiated after a complaint from the right holder and, in principle, should have been concluded with punishment decisions. Without a punishment decision, the right holder has no way of verifying that the counterfeiter was punished and that the goods were destroyed. In fact, oftentimes a raid is nothing more than a slap on the wrist of the infringer, who is never fined and who can "purchase" his fakes back from the enforcement authorities after the departure of the right holder from the scene of the raid. Overall, then, administrative enforcement in China is far from transparent.

Is cigarette anticounterfeiting enforcement fair? Surefire did not appeal a single enforcement action through either administrative reconsideration or administrative litigation. Time and financial considerations (and, above all,

---

[56] In addition to *li'an* cases, there are also cases in which punishments are imposed on the spot (*dangchang chufa*). In 2005, three-quarters of the cases handled by the SAIC were accepted for investigation (calculations based on *Zhongguo zhishi chanquan nianjian 2006*, 391–392). In the same year, 64 percent of the AQSIQ counterfeiting cases were accepted for investigation (see *Zhongguo zhiliang jiandu jianyan jianyi nianjian 2006* [China AQSIQ Yearbook 2006] [Beijing: Zhongguo biaozhun chubanshe, 2006], 226).

the possibility that Surefire might be forced to seek the assistance of the corrupt agency in the future) precluded the lodging of appeals. This suggests that enforcement is unfair. We should note that Surefire's experience with appeals is typical of trademark enforcement in China. Published statistics allow us to reconstruct how often individuals appeal the decisions of administrative agencies. In 2000, the SAIC accepted nine cases for administrative reconsideration (which was equivalent to 0.03 percent of its total trademark enforcement caseload). In the same year, the SAIC was a defendant in seven cases of administrative litigation brought against it in the courts (which was equivalent to 0.02 percent of the total number of trademark cases handled by the SAIC).[57] What is striking is the difference between trademark and nontrademark enforcement. In nontrademark cases, the rate of administrative reconsideration at the SAIC was 3.5 percent (100 times higher than the rate for trademark cases), whereas the rate of administrative litigation was 1.5 percent (about 80 times higher than the rate of administrative litigation for trademark cases).[58] How can we explain these differences between trademark cases and nontrademark cases handled by the SAIC? One possibility is that the quality of enforcement in the area of trademarks is vastly superior to the quality of enforcement in other domains; another, more likely possibility is that the Trademark Division of the SAIC is more adept than other SAIC departments at using intimidation to limit the lodging of administrative reconsideration and administrative litigation complaints.

The resulting enforcement situation is best described as a vicious circle: right holders pay a bribe for small-scale enforcement; administrative agencies impose a small fine on the infringer that is insufficient to put him out of business; that in turn leads to the right holders paying another bribe to organize a second raid against the same infringer; and so on. As one interviewee put it, "Producers of counterfeits have set up deals with the PSB or the SAIC to tip them off so that they have less stock on hand than the criminal threshold (50,000 yuan). This does three things: the PSB or the SAIC collects its fine (2,000–50,000 yuan – up to the total value of the goods); the infringer gets slapped on the wrist; and the investigative firm gets its fees."[59] The implication is that in the end it is the right holders who stand to lose from such "piecemeal, expensive, and ineffective actions."[60] One can only hope that over time, right holders will change their strategy to focus on large-scale raids coordinating the activities of multiple bureaucracies and thus will have a better chance of reducing counterfeiting.

[57] Calculated from *Zhongguo zhishi chanquan nianjian 2000*, 238–239.

[58] *Zhongguo gongshang xingzheng guanli nianjian 2002* (China AIC Yearbook 2002) (Beijing: Gongshang chubanshe, 2002), 604. This yearbook reports 2001 data. No comparable data are reported for 2000. I assume that the rates of administrative litigation and administrative reconsideration remained relatively constant in 2000 and 2001.

[59] China Interview 010704C, with a private investigator (Shanghai).

[60] China Interview 010618B, with a private investigator (Beijing).

Another strategy would be to seek redress through the courts; if implemented, this strategy would have the additional benefit of effecting high-quality enforcement in an area of IPR where rationalization has been absent.[61]

CASE STUDY TWO: CIGARETTE ANTICOUNTERFEITING EFFORTS IN RUSSIA

Background Information on the Russian Tobacco Industry

The main difference between the Chinese and the Russian tobacco industries concerns their relative importance as a source of tax revenue. In China, taxes levied on tobacco and cigarettes have been the single largest source of budget revenue, but in Russia tobacco and cigarette taxes account for only 2 percent of the consolidated budget revenues, whereas alcohol is the chief source of taxes, accounting for about 10 percent of the consolidated budget revenue.[62] Despite its lesser significance for the consolidated budget, cigarette production is very important for the Russian localities, since they retain the lucrative cigarette excise tax.[63] This explains why, as of 2003, there were as many as 157 officially licensed cigarette factories in Russia (only 89 of which were actually working), producing 1,200 brands of cigarettes (only 134 of which were officially registered as trademarks with Rospatent, the Russian Patent and Trademark Agency).[64] When it comes to the level of cigarette production, Russia surpassed China by making 2,600 cigarettes per capita in 2002, whereas China produced about 1,300 cigarettes per capita in the same year.[65]

Available statistics suggest that the level of counterfeiting in the two countries is similar. In the early 2000s, Russian industry estimated the level of counterfeiting to be 5–10 percent,[66] whereas consumers responding to a survey claimed to have encountered counterfeit cigarettes 23 percent of the

---

[61] IPR specialists based in China have already begun to advise right holders to pursue civil litigation. See Rebecca Ordish and Alan Adcock, *China Intellectual Property Challenges and Solutions: An Essential Business Guide* (Singapore: John Wiley, 2008), 181–198.

[62] "Kommentarii nedeli: Kuri – ne khochu!" (Weekly Commentary: I Don't Want to Smoke!), *Rossiiskaia gazeta* (RGA No. 183), September 22, 2000, 4, http://dlib.eastview.com/sources/article.jsp?id=1817919 (accessed July 10, 2003); "Praktika: Nalogi – kak gaika s boltom" (Practice: Taxes – like a Nut and Bolt), *Rossiiskaia gazeta* (RGA No. 065), April 11, 2000, 10, http://dlib.eastview.com/sources/article.jsp?id=4043930 (accessed July 10, 2003).

[63] "Tabachnyi rynok: Chto kurili, kuriat, i budut kurit' v Rossii" (The Cigarette Market: What Was Smoked, What Is Being Smoked, and What Will Be Smoked in Russia), *Moskovskaia pravda* (MPR No. 193), October 22, 2002, 3, http://dlib.eastview.com/sources/article.jsp?id=4438601 (accessed July 10, 2003).

[64] "Tovary dlia naroda: Gosdume dali prikurit'" (Consumer Products: The State Duma Was Allowed to Light Up), *Trud* (TRD No. 097), May 29, 2003, http://dlib.eastview.com/sources/article.jsp?id=4763899 (accessed July 10, 2003).

[65] "Tovary dlia naroda: Gosdume dali prikurit'"; STMA, *Zhongguo yancao: 2002 nian fazhan baogao*.

[66] "New Ways of Distribution in Russia," *Tobacco Journal International* (June 2000), 75–77.

time, a proportion that is roughly equivalent to the counterfeiting rate in China.[67]

Description of the Russian Data

I used the Russian and Newly Independent States newspaper database to locate relevant articles about cigarette counterfeiting published in central and regional Russian newspapers between 1999 and 2003. The newspaper enforcement dataset I compiled is comparable to the ones compiled for China. I conducted several searches for cognates related to tobacco (*tabak*) and counterfeiting (*kontrafakt* and *poddel'ka*). These searches produced more than 500 articles. In compiling the final list, I used only articles that contained a detailed description of a raid and explicitly mentioned the agency or agencies involved in the raid. (My selection of Chinese articles used identical criteria.) In the end, only thirty-four Russian articles (describing thirty-nine separate raids) met my selection criteria. As a result of the small number of cases, I did not have two separate datasets for domestic and foreign cigarette brands. However, the distinction between foreign brands and domestic brands is nebulous in Russia. In the early 2000s, two-thirds of the market was controlled by four foreign companies (Japan Tobacco International, Philip Morris, British American Tobacco, and Gallaher), which owned Russian factories producing both foreign and Russian cigarette brands.[68]

Agency Participation in Raids against Cigarette Counterfeiters

As we see in Table 7.5, the police (MVD) was the most active individual enforcer in cases of cigarette counterfeiting. The police participated in twenty-three raids (constituting 59 percent of the total). Unlike in China, where the police tended to cooperate with other agencies most of the time, the Russian police displayed a strong preference for noncooperative enforcement: they conducted nineteen of the twenty-three raids in which they participated on their own.

The second most important enforcer was the now-defunct Russian Tax Police, which participated in nine raids (23.1 percent of the total).[69] This entity was formed after the dissolution of the Soviet Union, in part to address the challenge of effective tax collection in a transitional economy. Thus, the Tax

---

[67] "Top-poddelki" (Top Counterfeits), *Vremia novostei* (VRN No. 049), March 20, 2003, 8, http:// dlib.eastview.com/sources/article.jsp?id=4783715 (accessed July 10, 2003).

[68] Russia Interviews 020518A and 020518B, with employees of major tobacco companies (Moscow); Russia Interview 020520, with the president of a tobacco manufacturers' association (Moscow).

[69] The Tax Police was abolished during the 2004 round of government restructuring and its functions were assumed by the Ministry of Internal Affairs and the Federal Tax Service.

TABLE 7.5. *Individual Agency Participation in Raids in Russia*

Agency	Number of Raids	Percentage (Total = 39)
Police	23	59
Tax Police	9	23.1
Customs	8	20.5
Trade Inspectorate	7	17.9
State Standardization and Certification Committee	1	2.6
Sanitary-Epidemiological Inspectorate	1	2.6
Moscow City Department of Consumer Products	1	2.6

Note: Some raids were conducted by more than one agency.
Source: Russian newspaper enforcement dataset.

Police had characteristics of both a fiscal and a security agency.[70] The participation of the Tax Police in cigarette anticounterfeiting reflects the legal requirement that cigarettes sold in Russia bear a genuine excise tax banderole. Counterfeit banderoles can be found on both genuine and counterfeit cigarettes. Also, cigarettes are often sold without any (even counterfeit) tax banderole. The Tax Police could become involved in cases when the banderoles are counterfeit or missing.

The third most important enforcer was Customs, which participated in eight raids (20.5 percent of the total). Overall, Customs became involved in anti-counterfeiting raids under unusual circumstances. Some of the raids took place in politically unstable regions of the Russian Federation (the Northern Caucasus), some in border regions (Kaliningrad), and some on the Trans-Siberian Railway, while trains were entering or leaving Russia.

The fourth most significant enforcer was the now-defunct Russian State Trade Inspectorate (Gostorginspektsiia), which was the Russian equivalent of the SAIC in China.[71] The Trade Inspectorate participated in seven raids (17.9 percent of the total). The Trade Inspectorate was responsible for monitoring whether goods sold in Russian retail outlets and restaurants conformed to labeling and quality standards. As mislabeled and substandard goods are also often counterfeit, the Trade Inspectorate could, if it so desired, become involved in cases of counterfeiting; however, it was under no obligation to enforce. This legal ambiguity was easily exploited to extract bribes.

[70] Gerald Easter, "The Russian Tax Police," *Post-Soviet Affairs* 18:4 (2002), 332–349.
[71] As mentioned in Chapter 5, Gostorginspektsiia was dissolved in 2004.

TABLE 7.6. *Dependence on Police Assistance during Raids in China and Russia*

Datasets	Raids Conducted with the Participation of the Police Forces or Customs (%)	Raids Conducted Exclusively by the Police Forces or Customs (%)
Guangdong Domestic	54.5	9.1
Non-Guangdong Domestic	52.8	12
China Foreign	15	0
Russia	87.2	79.5

Sources: Surefire and newspaper enforcement datasets.

Other agencies with episodic involvement in enforcement included the State Standardization and Metrology Committee (Gosstandart), the Sanitary-Epidemiological Inspectorate (Gossanepidnadzor), and the Moscow City Department of Consumer Products and Services. Specific statistics on their involvement are provided in Table 7.5. It should be noted that the Federal Antimonopoly Service, discussed in Chapter 5, was not mentioned in any of the enforcement reports included in the database. Over time, all of the other agencies with episodic involvement in enforcement also stopped participating in anticounterfeiting activities. Today, all trademark enforcement is provided by the police and by Customs. These streamlined enforcement arrangements create a more predictable IPR protection environment.

How Does Russia Differ from China?

As shown in Table 7.6, the police have emerged as a much more active enforcer in Russia than in China. Similarly, Russia has had a much higher percentage of raids conducted exclusively by police forces or Customs (the so-called *siloviki*, or employees of the power ministries). This reflects a conscious choice by the Russian state to emphasize the use of deterrent enforcement. The police forces have the power to put criminals behind bars and, unlike in China, do not need to take a reactive position in which they are fed cases in a piecemeal fashion by administrative agencies. In the long run, police enforcement may have a greater potential to establish compliance with the law than administrative enforcement.

CONCLUSION

The chapter grew from the idea that there often exists a divergence between official designations of enforcement responsibility and actual enforcement practice on the ground. In the case of cigarette anticounterfeiting, although the STMA should be the only administrative enforcer, in practice, it shares its enforcement responsibilities with several other administrative agencies, as well as with the civil courts, Customs, and the police. The effects of this oversupply of administrative enforcement options are negative. Jurisdictional overlap creates uncertainty as to which agency has primary enforcement responsibility. One possible consequence is the emergence of campaign-style enforcement. Another consequence is for agencies to shirk their ill-defined enforcement responsibilities, unless they are motivated by bribes. The Surefire data presented in this chapter allow us to analyze enforcement in the latter case. No matter which of the two scenarios ensues, they both lead to inconsistent, nontransparent, and unfair enforcement. This chapter has shown that the Chinese state can provide a high volume of trademark enforcement. However, this enforcement is of a low quality.

The next chapter analyzes the enforcement of copyright laws in China, where several dynamics may unfold. In one, multiple enforcers with overlapping jurisdictions provide unpredictable campaign-style enforcement, whereas in the other the same enforcers are unwilling to organize enforcement raids even when they are offered a bribe. In contrast to trademark enforcement, copyrights also feature a small volume of quasi-judicial enforcement that is relatively predictable and transparent. Most interesting is that over time the courts have begun to handle more copyright cases, demonstrating that the prospects for the rise of rationalized enforcement in the area of copyrights are not as dim as in the area of trademarks. But it is Chapter 9 that presents the most hopeful scenario, where a single administrative agency (the State Intellectual Property Office [SIPO]) has exclusive and clearly defined jurisdiction over the administrative enforcement of patents. The SIPO also has a staff of highly professional employees. These two variables contribute to producing administrative enforcement that is consistent, transparent, and fair. In addition, the courts of law have emerged as very active players in patent protection in China, thus providing even greater procedural guarantees for the rise of rationalized enforcement. In short, China is not destined always to have arbitrary enforcement of laws and regulations. When certain institutional arrangements are put in place, rationalized enforcement may emerge even in a neuralgic area such as IPR protection.

This then raises the question about the role of the state in IPR enforcement. Why has the state been unable to create rationalization in trademark enforcement but made partial progress in rationalizing copyright enforcement and, especially, patent enforcement? There are two main reasons. The first is that pressure for enforcement in trademarks has been exerted by both domestic and foreign sources, whereas pressure for enforcement in copyrights has been purely foreign. This created a greater sense of urgency in trademarks than in copyrights. The central government allowed a larger number of enforcers to enter the trademark enforcement domain and urged them to provide quick campaign-style enforcement in order to respond to aggrieved domestic and foreign constituencies. In contrast, the mobilization of fewer agencies resulted in the establishment of a more predictable enforcement environment in copyrights. Most importantly, patent enforcement has been subject to neither domestic nor foreign pressures, and the enforcement framework the state has created in this area has evolved toward rationalization. The second reason is historical. Trademark and consumer protection bureaucracies have existed for a long time and have become entrenched. In sharp contrast, copyrights and, especially, patents are both relatively new regulatory areas, in which it is easier to establish a rationalized enforcement system from scratch.

8

Copyrights

Beyond Campaign-Style Enforcement

Anyone visiting China will immediately be struck by the presence of pirated copyrighted materials and by the speed and efficiency of their manufacture. For eight to fifteen yuan (one or two U.S. dollars), DVDs of the most recent Chinese and foreign movies can be obtained simultaneously with their studio release. The same holds for music CDs. The latest versions of business software (e.g., Microsoft Office) and entertainment software (video games) are similarly sold at a fraction of the official retail price. Although in recent years stores that trade in legitimate products have sprung up, piracy has not disappeared. If anything, hawkers of pirated media seem to be even more visible than in the past, sometimes in the unlikeliest of places – on street overpasses in Guangzhou, in upscale foreign restaurants in Beijing, and outside ticket booths at the Badaling section of the Great Wall. Book piracy is thriving as well. When Bill Clinton's autobiography was published in Chinese in 2004, an unauthorized translation also hit the streets, complete with two hundred pages of additional text that promised to give the full details of the president's private life.

Why is the level of copyright piracy so high in China? The fundamental reason for the persistence of piracy is, of course, that it is favored by two strong domestic constituencies: counterfeiters and consumers. If counterfeiters are in favor of piracy because it yields them handsome profits, consumers obviously benefit from access to cheap copyrighted goods. What about the government? Since pirated products are not dangerous to consumers, the government has no incentive to enforce either on health or on safety grounds. Nor does the government have an interest in stemming the tax evasion that results from copyright piracy: even if the market were flooded with legitimate (and expensive) copies of Windows, end-user sales would not increase tremendously, for reasons of cost. At the present time, the potential tax gains from ending piracy and taxing all retailers of legitimate software are limited.[1]

---

[1] Tax evasion is a more serious concern in areas where there is a small differential between the

In terms of the enforcement that does take place, a major factor facilitating piracy is the absence of a well-organized domestic copyright industry in China. Ultimately, this means that the main advocates of stronger copyright protection are foreign right holders. The majority of these, especially in the software and audiovisual product industry, are based in the United States. Unsurprisingly, the government response to foreign right holders is complex. In reaction to constant pressure to step up the enforcement of its copyright laws, the government does supply campaign-style enforcement. That said, because enforcement is against the wishes of important domestic constituencies, government agencies usually provide it reluctantly. Even though the volume of copyright enforcement is high, the quality is low. The reason for the low quality of campaign-style enforcement is the same as in the area of trademarks: multiple agencies have overlapping responsibilities for copyright enforcement.

However, copyright enforcement differs from trademark enforcement in important ways. One difference is that copyright agencies are unwilling to provide enforcement raids in response to complaints from right holders. The only type of routine copyright enforcement in China is quasi-judicial enforcement, and the National Copyright Administration of China (NCAC) is the only agency that provides this type of enforcement. This enforcement framework has produced a streamlined and predictable enforcement environment. In addition, the limited administrative enforcement options have had an unexpected positive side effect, namely, a steady increase in the number of copyright cases adjudicated through courts of law. In the area of copyright protection, relative to trademark protection, there is therefore greater potential for the emergence of rationalized enforcement.

ENFORCEMENT AND PIRACY

Copyright is the only IPR subtype for which we can consistently assess the rate of piracy. This is possible because copyrights cover only two types of goods: printed publications and digital media. Printed publications include books and periodicals. Digital media include audiovisual products, as well as business and entertainment software.[2] Assessments of the level of piracy are most easily produced for business software, where Microsoft dominates the market.[3] Knowing what percentage of the PCs in a country run on its software, Microsoft can make an educated guess about its expected sales volume in that particular national market. If Microsoft's estimates indicate that there are 1,000,000

---

price of the pirated version and the price of the legitimate product (for instance, books and domestic audiovisual media). Pirated products there displace genuine products and lead to losses. We see a greater volume of enforcement for these goods than for software or foreign audiovisual products.

[2] Because digital media are loaded onto optical disks, they are also known as optical media.

[3] Assessments of other types of copyright piracy exist as well. See www.iipa.com.

copies of Microsoft Office in use in a particular country, yet records show that it only sold 100,000 copies, it follows that 900,000 of the copies in use were not sold legitimately and thus were pirated (the piracy rate in this case would be estimated to be 90 percent). Even though there is potential measurement error in this methodology, it is much smaller than for other types of copyright piracy where there is no market monopolist like Microsoft. In general, estimating copyright piracy seems easy in comparison to the challenge of assessing the level of trademark and patent counterfeiting, since the great diversity of goods covered by those IPR subtypes makes it impossible even to arrive at rough estimates of the problem's scope.

From 1995 onward, the Business Software Alliance (BSA) has produced assessments of software piracy rates throughout the world.[4] Table 8.1 presents statistics on the business software piracy rates in ten countries in 1995 and 2005. I have provided data for the six countries analyzed in this book, as well as for four out-of-sample cases, which were chosen to represent different levels of piracy in 1995: three countries had high piracy (Bulgaria, Vietnam, and India) and one country a medium level of piracy (Japan). I have also provided data on the worldwide software piracy levels in 1995 and in 2005.

We can infer several trends from this table. First, most countries have experienced a drop in software piracy rates during the eleven-year period for

TABLE 8.1. *Business Software Piracy Rates in Selected Countries, 1995 and 2005 (%)*

Country	1995	2005	% Change
China	96	86	−10
Russia	94	83	−12
Taiwan	70	43	−38
Czech Republic	62	40	−35
France	51	47	−8
U.S.	26	21	−20
Japan	55	28	−48
Bulgaria	94	71	−24
Vietnam	99	90	−9
India	78	72	−8
WORLD	46	35	−24

Sources: Sixth Annual BSA Global Software Piracy Study (BSA, 2001); *Third Annual BSA and IDC Global Software Piracy Study* (May 2006), http://www.bsa.org/~/media/C9DA2873 DCB84135957CB39B9FA2B666.ashx (accessed August 6, 2008).

---

[4] In 2006, the BSA published data on software piracy levels in 97 countries. See *Third Annual BSA and IDC Global Software Piracy Study* (May 2006), http://www.bsa.org/~/media/ C9DA2873DCB84135957CB39B9FA2B666.ashx (accessed August 6, 2008).

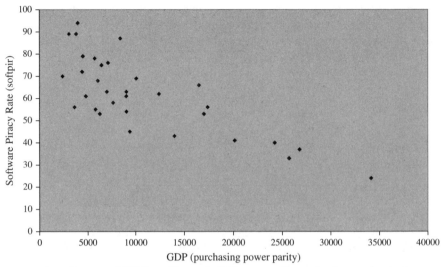

FIGURE 8.1. Impact of GDP on Piracy in Thirty-two Countries (2000 data). *Source:* Thirty-two-country copyright enforcement database.

which we have data. In 1995, the worldwide software piracy rate was 46 percent, but by 2005 it had declined to 35 percent (a 24 percent reduction). Second, some countries have registered higher reductions in piracy rates than the world average. Particularly noteworthy among the group of six countries examined in this volume are Taiwan (38 percent reduction) and the Czech Republic (35 percent reduction). Out-of-sample cases like Japan and Bulgaria can claim 48 percent and 24 percent declines in piracy, respectively. Third, some countries showed drops in piracy that were lower than the world average, for example, France, whose piracy rate declined by 8 percent and the United States, where piracy fell by 20 percent. The French case is surprising: even though its piracy rate was comparable to that of Japan in 1995, France did not come close to matching Japan's success in reduction thereafter. Finally, the 10 percent decline in China's piracy rate between 1995 and 2005 is twice lower than the world average.

What drives these drops in piracy? Per capita GDP (adjusted for purchasing power parity) is the best predictor, as demonstrated by Figure 8.1, which presents a scatterplot of purchasing power parity GDP and the software piracy rate in thirty-two countries in 2000.[5] A bivariate OLS regression using

---

[5] The thirty-two countries are the only countries for which I was able to compile a complete panel of data. The countries are Argentina, Australia, Brazil, Bulgaria, China, Colombia, the Czech Republic, the Dominican Republic, Egypt, El Salvador, Estonia, France, Greece, India, Indonesia, Israel, Japan, Lithuania, Mexico, Paraguay, Peru, Poland, Romania, Russia, South Africa, South Korea, Taiwan, Turkey, Ukraine, Uruguay, the United States, and Venezuela. Enforcement data compiled from numerous sources on file with the author. Population and GDP data from *World Development Indicators*, www.worldbank.org/data.

purchasing power parity GDP as a predictor of piracy has a whopping R^2 value of 0.61 (t = −6.8). This result is not surprising – as people become richer, they are more likely to be able to afford genuine copyrighted goods. There is a statistical literature on IPR protection that reaches similar conclusions.[6] Therefore, a skeptic looking at Table 8.1 might attribute China's 10 percent drop in piracy to dramatic increases in GDP between 1995 and 2005, rather than to vigorous enforcement of its IPR laws.[7] A similar story can be told about Russia, which underwent a transformation from a barter economy in the mid-1990s to an economic powerhouse in the 2000s.[8]

In fact, cross-national data reveal that enforcement volume does not have a clear effect on piracy rates. This is demonstrated by Figure 8.2, which displays a scatterplot of the criminal enforcement actions (per million people) and the software piracy rate in thirty-two countries (R^2 = 0.0005 in bivariate OLS regression). How do we make sense of the counterintuitive finding that the volume of enforcement has no statistically significant impact on piracy? Even more striking is that there is no statistically significant relationship between GDP and enforcement volume (R^2 = 0.009 in bivariate OLS regression). These results are fully consistent with the main argument of this study: what is important is not the volume of enforcement, but, rather, its quality. A large volume of low-quality enforcement either will have no effect on piracy or will even lead to increases in piracy, as pirates feel emboldened by ineffective enforcement.[9] This allows us to understand Table 8.1, which indicates that Russia, despite its modest enforcement efforts, experienced a reduction in piracy rates similar to that of China, which provided a significantly higher volume of enforcement on a per capita basis. High enforcement volume per se may not lower piracy rates, but if we had cross-national data taking into account the *quality* of enforcement, we should expect that they would indicate that

---

[6] Previous studies have produced a robust correlation between rising GDP and stronger IPR laws *on paper* (Walter G. Park and Carlos Ginarte, "Intellectual Property Rights and Economic Growth," *Contemporary Economic Policy* 15 [2000], 51–61; Keith Maskus, *Intellectual Property Rights in the World Economy* [Washington, DC: Institute for International Economics, 2000]). However, the strength of the laws on paper does not allow us to evaluate how the laws are enforced in practice. I use actual enforcement data rather than "perceived strength of IPR laws" in the results that I report in this book.

[7] China's per capita GDP (in comparable constant prices) increased 120 percent between 1995 and 2005. *Zhongguo tongji nianjian 2006* (China Statistical Yearbook 2006) (Beijing: Zhongguo tongji chubanshe, 2006), 60.

[8] On barter, see David Woodruff, *Money Unmade: Barter and the Fate of Russian Capitalism* (Ithaca, NY: Cornell University Press, 1999). Russian per capita GDP (purchasing power parity) rose 53 percent between 1995 (US\$6,354) and 2005 (US\$9,747), when measured in constant 2000 dollars. See WDI Online, at http://devdata.worldbank.org.ezp2.harvard.edu/dataonline/ (accessed December 24, 2006).

[9] An alternative hypothesis is that this result is driven by the poor quality of the data and that better data for a longer period would indicate that increases in enforcement have a statistically significant negative effect on piracy rates. My theory suggests that this alternative hypothesis will not be borne out by the data, should they become available.

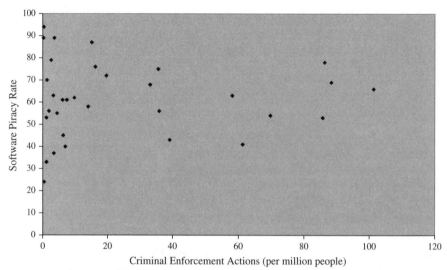

FIGURE 8.2. Impact of Enforcement on Piracy in Thirty-two Countries. *Source:* Thirty-two-country copyright enforcement database (2000 data).

countries with high-quality enforcement are also experiencing large drops in piracy.

HIGH-VOLUME ENFORCEMENT VERSUS RATIONALIZED ENFORCEMENT

When they are under pressure, Chinese government agencies can deliver a high volume of enforcement. Witness the Anti-Pornography and Anti-Piracy Campaign. Though the initial target was the elimination of politically subversive publications and pornography, as a result of U.S. pressure the goals of the campaign eventually also included the reduction of piracy. As detailed in Chapter 5, both the Ministry of Culture and the General Administration of Press and Publications (which also houses the National Copyright Administration of China) participated in this campaign and registered high levels of seizures. As I have argued throughout this book, however, campaign-style enforcement need not be rationalized. The very character of campaigns may encourage questions of consistency, transparency, and fairness to be abrogated in favor of delivering a high volume of high-profile enforcement.[10] William Alford, in assessing the copyright enforcement campaigns of the early 1990s, rightly

---

[10] Scholars of the "strike-hard" anticrime campaign of the 1980s and 1990s have noted similar patterns in criminal enforcement. See M. Scot Tanner, "State Coercion and the Balance of Awe: The 1983–1986 'Stern Blows' Anti-Crime Campaign," *The China Journal*, no. 44 (2000), 93–125; Melanie Manion, *Corruption by Design: Building Clean Government in Mainland China and Hong Kong* (Cambridge, MA: Harvard University Press, 2004).

stresses that some pirates were executed for mere misdemeanors, a punishment so far in excess of the crime as to question the campaign's commitment to procedural fairness.[11] In short, campaigns deliver high-quantity, though not necessarily high-quality, enforcement.

When copyright agencies are approached with requests to organize enforcement raids, they either refuse outright or engage in various bureaucratic delay tactics. Although both the Ministry of Culture (MOC) and the State Administration for Industry and Commerce (SAIC) can supply copyright protection, statistical evidence indicates that the NCAC has emerged as the dominant provider of routine administrative enforcement in this area. For all intents and purposes, the only kind of routine copyright enforcement in China is quasi-judicial enforcement, where requests from right holders are examined in-house at the NCAC and resolved through mediation or by the imposition of an administrative punishment. We know that in 2005 the NCAC accepted 9,644 such copyright infringement and piracy cases, a relatively modest volume.[12]

Not all news about copyright enforcement is bleak. If they are denied administrative enforcement, right holders are likely to turn directly to the specialized IPR chambers. Courts provide procedurally fair enforcement, because individuals can freely appeal their decisions. As this chapter will demonstrate, although in principle the decisions of administrative agencies may be appealed as well, the barriers that the agencies erect to those pursuing administrative reconsideration and administrative litigation raise the transaction costs for any individuals contemplating such moves.

The remainder of this chapter proceeds as follows. I will first focus on the evolution of the Anti-Pornography Campaign into primarily an anti-piracy campaign. For more specific data about enforcement on the ground, I then turn to a newspaper dataset that allows me to track agency participation in the ongoing Anti-Piracy Campaign. Third, I document the various difficulties that right holders face when trying to organize copyright enforcement raids. Fourth, I discuss the relation between quasi-judicial administrative enforcement of copyrights and the unexpected rise of the courts as important enforcers, a development that provides some hope for the eventual emergence of rationalization. Finally, I discuss copyright protection in Russia, in order to highlight the distinctive features of enforcement in China, as the chapter has described them.

THE ANTI-PORNOGRAPHY CAMPAIGN: ENFORCEMENT OF A HIGH-PRIORITY POLICY

The Anti-Pornography Campaign (*saohuang jizhong xingdong*) began in earnest around the time of the 1989 Tiananmen Square protests. Though an

---

[11] William Alford, *To Steal a Book Is an Elegant Offense: Intellectual Property Law in Chinese Civilization* (Stanford, CA: Stanford University Press, 1995), 90–91, 164 n. 179.

[12] See http://www.ncac.gov.cn (accessed November 28, 2006).

official in charge of the campaign denies that there was any link between the two events,[13] the timing of the establishment of the National Anti-Pornography Working Committee (Quanguo saohuang gongzuo xiaozu) suggests otherwise. In August 1989, Li Ruihuan, CCP Politburo Standing Committee member with the portfolio of propaganda and ideology, declared that

> counterrevolutionary books and periodicals that promote bourgeois liberalization and suffer from serious political mistakes are unworthily occupying prominent market positions, alongside a torrent of books, periodicals, and tapes of an obscene, pornographic, violent, and feudal-superstitious nature. If these publications aren't thoroughly suppressed they will produce serious spiritual pollution and social dangers. . . . Rectifying and cleaning up book, periodical, and tape markets is closely related to our country's efforts to achieve long-term stability.[14]

Li Ruihuan's speech identified the problems that the campaign had to address (spiritual pollution and social dangers) and its targets (counterrevolutionary and pornographic books, periodicals, and tapes). At first, the campaign eschewed copyright piracy and focused on illegal or unlicensed producers and distributors of pornographic materials. In particularly severe cases, offenders received the maximal penalty available under the law (life imprisonment). When targeting pornography, the government was careful to keep up with technological change. A case in point is a fabricated letter that appeared in the *People's Daily* in 1995.[15] The letter purportedly detailed the suffering of a mother whose son had been corrupted by watching pornographic VCDs, which at the time were the newest type of media available on the cultural market. The letter legitimated the VCD crackdowns that were already taking place. Soon after their appearance, DVDs were added to the plate of the anti-pornography enforcement agencies as well.

Government agencies considered participation in the *saohuang* campaign to be prestigious. On July 18, 1994, in his capacity as general secretary of the Central Committee of the CCP, Jiang Zemin spoke against pornographic and illegal publications, thereby showing his personal approval of the Anti-Pornography Campaign. As a consequence, the number of agencies officially involved in the campaign at the national level quickly mushroomed to fifteen. These were the General Office of the State Council; the Propaganda Department of the Central Committee of the CCP; the Political and Legal Committee of the Central Committee of the CCP; the Ministry of Public Security; the Ministry of Railways; the Ministry of Communications; the Ministry of Information Industry;

---

[13] China Interview 020123, with a senior employee of the Office of the National Anti-Pornography and Anti-Piracy Working Committee (Beijing).

[14] Daniel Lynch, *After the Propaganda State: Media, Politics, and "Thought Work" in Reformed China* (Stanford, CA: Stanford University Press, 1999), 199–200.

[15] Office of the National Anti-Pornography and Anti-Piracy Working Committee, *Saohuang dafei zai Zhongguo* (Anti-Pornography and Anti-Piracy in China) (June 2001), 6.

the Ministry of Culture; the General Administration of Customs; the Civil Aviation Administration of China; the State Administration of Radio, Film, and Television; the State Administration of Industry and Commerce; the General Administration of Press and Publications; the Propaganda Department of the General Political Department of the People's Liberation Army; and the People's Government of Beijing Municipality.[16] Agencies were eager to jump on the anti-pornography bandwagon as a way to demonstrate their general support of official government policies.

In order to coordinate the work of those fifteen bureaucracies, the Office of the National Anti-Pornography and Anti-Piracy Working Committee (NAPWC) was established as an umbrella entity. The Office of the NAPWC (which is known simply as the Anti-Pornography Office, or Saohuang ban) has a central and local presence. At the central level, it is housed at the General Administration of Press and Publications (GAPP). In addition to GAPP personnel, the Anti-Pornography Office includes representatives of four of the fifteen agencies formally under the NAPWC: the Publications Bureau of the Propaganda Department of the Central Committee of the CCP, the Social Order Department of the Ministry of Public Security, the Market Supervision Bureau of the Ministry of Culture, and the Social Affairs Management Bureau of the State Administration of Radio, Film, and Television.[17] These five agencies constitute the core group at the national level and meet regularly to discuss coordination of their activities. In different parts of China, the leading administrative agency can differ, but the crucial point is that the Anti-Pornography Office has a deep reach all the way down to the county level. At the county level, the office is typically housed at the Culture Bureau or the Culture and Sports Bureau.

An important change in the campaign occurred in the mid-1990s: previously individuals were usually charged with distributing pornography. Thereafter, additional counts of copyright infringement and profiteering were occasionally added to the charges. This move, which may have been necessary to justify the imposition of lengthier prison terms, had the effect of linking copyright protection with the Anti-Pornography Campaign. The campaign remained primarily focused on limiting pornography, but since pornographic publications were mostly pirated, the authorities could hit two birds with one stone. This coupling of the issues proved particularly useful to China during the diplomatic wars with the U.S. Trade Representative over China's inadequate protection of intellectual property rights in 1995–1996. The authorities were able to claim that the confiscation of offensive materials and the closure of distribution centers, unlicensed stalls and shops, illegal VCD showrooms, and both licensed and underground producers of unauthorized copies of optical media were all aimed

[16] Ibid., 1.
[17] Ibid., 3; China Interview 020931B, with the secretary of the Office of the NAPWC (Beijing).

specifically at reducing piracy.[18] In fact, though pirated materials were seized and destroyed, this was not done with the specific purpose of fighting piracy but emerged as a subsidiary outcome of the Anti-Pornography Campaign.

The intersection of pornography and copyright infringement allowed administrative agencies to present evidence of progress to the State Council and the Propaganda Department of the CCP and at the same time to show to the U.S. Trade Representative that China was making progress on the anti-piracy front. Unsurprisingly, in 1999, the Anti-Pornography Campaign was officially renamed the Anti-Pornography and Anti-Piracy Campaign (*saohuang dafei xingdong*).[19] The change in name reflected a change in emphasis that was already emerging. Although the spread of politically subversive and pornographic publications continued to be an important concern, pirated materials accounted for 88 percent of the 1.3 billion items seized in the campaign between 1989 and 2004.[20] To take another example, the General Administration of Press and Publications confiscated 107 million pirated optical disks during the 2005 *saohuang* campaign but seized only 1 million political publications, 4.6 million Falun Gong publications, and 5 million pornographic items.[21] These numbers unambiguously demonstrate that over time, piracy has emerged as the main focus of the Anti-Pornography Campaign.

WHO ENFORCES? FINDINGS FROM THE CHINA COPYRIGHT ENFORCEMENT DATASET

Who participates in the Anti-Pornography Campaign as it has evolved since 1999? Two main sources of data shed light on this question: official statistics and media reports on enforcement. Official statistics have certain shortcomings. For one, some bureaucracies (e.g., the Ministry of Public Security) do not release data on their involvement in *saohuang* enforcement. This makes it difficult to compile an aggregate dataset detailing the actual participation on the ground of all bureaucracies with a copyright enforcement portfolio. In the absence of such data, we cannot provide a definitive answer to the question of "who enforces."

As a partial substitute, I constructed a dataset of media reports on campaign-style copyright enforcement in China. The dataset was compiled by using

---

[18] For additional details, see the 1995 exchange of letters between State Councilor Wu Yi and Ambassador Mickey Cantor, reproduced in Andrew Mertha, "Pirates, Politics, and Trade Policy: Structuring the Negotiations and Enforcing the Outcomes of the Sino-U.S. Intellectual Property Dialogue, 1991–1999" (Ph.D. Dissertation, Department of Political Science, University of Michigan, 2001), 209–229.

[19] This is the currently accepted official translation. The literal translation is the "campaign to sweep away pornography and to strike down illegal goods."

[20] *Zhongguo zhishi chanquan nianjian 2005* (China IPR Yearbook 2005) (Beijing: Zhishi chanquan chubanshe, 2005), 88.

[21] *Zhongguo chuban nianjian 2006* (China Publishers' Yearbook 2006) (Beijing: Zhongguo chuban nianjian she, 2006), 45.

Chinese Internet search engines to locate newspaper accounts of campaign-style enforcement in cases of optical disk piracy, including CDs, VCDs, DVDs, computer games, and disk-loaded software. Although hundreds of articles were read, the only ones included in the final dataset were those containing clear references to the locality where the enforcement took place, the specific bureaucracies involved in the anti-piracy raid, and the volume of pirated goods seized. The final dataset comprises thirty-seven articles containing forty discrete reports of optical disk enforcement actions conducted between July 2003 and April 2006.[22]

Geographical Variation in Enforcement

The forty cases of copyright enforcement are spread out across seventeen Chinese provinces. No interprovincial raids were found among the cases included in the dataset. Beijing is represented in the dataset with ten raids, followed by Liaoning (five raids), Jiangxi (four raids), Guangdong (three raids), and Tianjin, Hebei, Shanxi, Jiangsu, and Guangxi (each with two raids). The other provinces in the dataset had a single raid each: Jilin, Heilongjiang, Shanghai, Zhejiang, Anhui, Fujian, Shandong, and Hainan. Although skewed, the distribution of the provinces in the dataset roughly reflects the overall distribution of enforcement efforts across China. The fourteen provinces that are absent from the dataset are located mostly in western China and in general tend to exert only minimal effort to enforce central government policies. The sole province that is clearly overrepresented is Beijing, a consequence of the tendency of the Chinese media to overexpose anti-piracy activities taking place in the capital.

Agency Participation in Enforcement

The dataset contains information about six different agencies participating in copyright enforcement activities: the Ministry of Public Security (which is known as the Public Security Bureau, or PSB, at the local level), the Ministry of Culture, the Office of the NAPWC, the General Administration of Press and Publications, the National Copyright Administration of China, and the General Administration of Customs. In terms of frequency of involvement in anticounterfeiting work, the PSB was well ahead of all other agencies, participating in 70 percent of the raids. The Ministry of Culture and its local-level Cultural Market Management Offices took part in 37.5 percent of the enforcement actions. The Anti-Pornography and Anti-Counterfeiting Office was involved in 17.5 percent of the actions. Most interestingly, the General Administration of Press and Publications and the National Copyright Administration of China were

---

[22] The specific breakdown of the enforcement actions by year is as follows: 2003: 2; 2004: 11; 2005: 14; and 2006: 13. The paucity of pre-2004 reports is consistent with other data pointing to the relatively anemic optical disk enforcement efforts prior to 2004.

relatively minor enforcers, each participating in 7.5 percent of the enforcement actions.[23] The marginal role of the NCAC is particularly noteworthy, since it has been designated by law as the lead anti-piracy enforcer. Finally, Customs participated in 10 percent of the enforcement cases recorded in the dataset. Here we should note that the dataset does not record a single case where the SAIC participated in enforcement. The SAIC is overburdened with trademark enforcement, and, though authorized to participate in anti-piracy actions, it has chosen to avoid entry into campaign-style enforcement.

The data presented here demonstrate that although the Ministry of Culture is a more important actor than the GAPP and the NCAC, it is overshadowed by the PSB, which emerges as the dominant copyright enforcer in China. This finding highlights an enforcement paradox: if the PSB participates in so many raids, how can we explain why so few of these raids result in criminal prosecutions and convictions? The answer lies in the absence of incentives for criminal enforcement. The police can participate in enforcement in one of two capacities: informally, by lending support to other enforcement agencies that lack its deterrent capability (*peihe bumen*), and, formally, on its own, as the unit in charge (*zhuguan bumen*). Cases of cooperative enforcement with other agencies are reported as police participation in the *saohuang* campaign, even though they are handled as administrative, not criminal, cases. The dataset lists thirteen such cooperative raids, none of which resulted in criminal detention or imprisonment. The dataset also reveals that the PSB conducted fifteen raids on its own. Although all of these raids met the criminal liability threshold, only six culminated in some sort of criminal punishment. In three cases, individuals were criminally detained. In another three cases, suspects were sentenced to imprisonment ranging from one year to five years. All individuals sentenced to imprisonment were also required to pay a fine, which was as high as 600,000 yuan (US$75,000) in one case.[24]

The dataset confirms what the national-level statistics presented in Chapter 6 have already suggested: enforcement actions usually result at most in administrative fines; criminal punishments are exceedingly rare, even when the relevant criminal liability thresholds have been met. The unwillingness of the police to open a criminal case means that campaign-style copyright enforcement is less deterrent and effective than it could be, since so few individuals are criminally prosecuted.

Data Limitations

This dataset is derived from media reports about enforcement in cases of optical disk piracy. Certain limitations are therefore present. First, the dataset allows us

---

[23] Although the GAPP is merged with the NCAC, only one raid report lists the joint participation of the two agencies. In the other cases, the GAPP or the NCAC is listed as participating in enforcement on its own.

[24] The levying of a fine instead of, or in addition to, detention or fixed-term imprisonment is sanctioned by Articles 213–220 of the 1997 Criminal Code.

to comment on only a portion of the IPR enforcement unfolding on the ground in China. Since pirated books are not produced and distributed in the same way as pirated disks, for example, we would expect enforcement patterns for books to be different from those for optical disks. Enforcement for Internet piracy will also differ. Second, the dataset includes no smaller-scale enforcements, but only high-profile cases of enforcement deemed newsworthy by the media. We should also note that a newspaper report of enforcement will always reflect the decision of a certain bureaucracy to go public and to invite journalists to attend an enforcement action. Such actions are more likely to be handled in accordance with the law than actions that are not reported. Third, the dataset reports only coercive enforcement actions, where pirates are raided by government agencies. However, copyright grievances in China sometimes are settled in other ways, including mediation and litigation, as well as through various administrative dispute resolution channels. Given these limitations, it is especially important to compare the enforcement patterns revealed in the dataset with routine copyright enforcement, in order to show the full complexity of copyright protection in China.

Is Campaign-Style Enforcement Rationalized?

It is difficult to provide a definitive assessment of the consistency of campaign-style copyright enforcement in China. To be sure, the campaign is a priority for the central government and has been conducted repeatedly at least once a year since the late 1980s. If there is certainty that the campaign will take place, its length, however, varies from year to year – in some years, it lasts a month, in other years three months, and in others six months.[25] Another source of variation is the location of the anti-pornography office, which is the local-level equivalent of the Office of the NAPWC. This is never an independent administrative actor but is always housed within some other administrative agency, so that the activities of the anti-pornography office may not be predictable across the territory of China. The location of this office varies from province to province. Data from 2003 indicate that in twenty-four provinces the office was hosted by Press and Publications; in three other provinces by the party Propaganda Department; and in another three by the Culture Bureau. Shanghai was the only Chinese province with a free-standing (*danshe*) office.[26] In sixteen provinces the leading anti-pornography small group was directed by the vice

---

[25] For example, in 2006 the campaign was initially held for 100 days (July–September), but a second round began in December ahead of the Sino-U.S. Strategic Dialogue. See "New Campaign to Fight Piracy," *Beijing Today*, December 15, 2006, 5.

[26] *Zhongguo chuban nianjian 2004* (China Publishers' Yearbook 2004) (Beijing: Zhongguo chuban nianjian she, 2004), 55.

secretary of the provincial party committee, in six provinces by the party standing committee head or the propaganda department chief, and in another four by the vice provincial governor.[27] Although the free-standing Shanghai office is apparently quite effective in fighting piracy,[28] existing data do not allow us to draw more definitive conclusions about the overall consistency of campaign-style enforcement in China.

What about the transparency of enforcement? Official statistics on the *sao-huang* campaign are sparse, already suggesting limited transparency. More significantly, the campaign has not adopted procedures that help ensure transparency. First, most cases are resolved with a punishment imposed on the spot (*dangchang chufa*), rather than being accepted for formal investigation (*li'an chachu*). Only cases accepted for investigation allow for open administrative hearings (*tingzheng hui*) and written punishment decisions (*xingzheng chufa jueding shu*). Obviously, in the absence of written punishment decisions, there can be no published punishment decisions.

The preference for imposing punishments on the spot also impacts the procedural fairness of enforcement, because it makes it impossible for both right holders and alleged pirates to exercise their right of appeal. The existing evidence gives no cause for optimism in this regard. For example, published statistics indicate that 31,862 administrative punishments were imposed during the Anti-Pornography Campaign in 2004. No data have been released about the percentage of these cases appealed through either administrative reconsideration or administrative litigation.[29] This suggests that appeals are actively discouraged, since no administrative enforcement agency, no matter how exemplary its enforcement of a law, could leave everyone satisfied with its decisions. Overall, on the basis of the existing data, we cannot make a positive assessment of the consistency, transparency, and fairness of campaign-style copyright enforcement.

COPYRIGHT ENFORCEMENT IN RESPONSE TO COMPLAINTS: BUREAUCRATIC DEFLECTION IN A LOW-PRIORITY AREA

Previous sections of this chapter noted that as many as fifteen agencies plus the NAPWC are involved in the Anti-Pornography Campaign. These agencies have managed to deliver a high volume of enforcement. In contrast, routine copyright enforcement is a low-priority area for the government and, consequently, remains a low-priority area for the administrative agencies responsible for enforcing the relevant laws and regulations. The National Copyright Administration of China formally takes the lead in the routine enforcement of

---

[27] Ibid. The yearbook does not contain data about the leadership of some of the anti-pornography offices.

[28] China Interview 020124, with an employee of the Shanghai Anti-Pornography Office (by phone).

[29] *Zhongguo zhishi chanquan nianjian 2005*, 88.

copyright laws. However, the Ministry of Culture, the State Administration for Industry and Commerce, and the General Administration of Customs, along with the Ministry of Public Security, all have, to varying degrees, responsibility for routine copyright enforcement. But because these agencies are not interested in enforcement, there has been a minimal amount of routine anti-piracy activity.

The NCAC, the main agency in charge of copyright protection, is weak and unable to coordinate and guide the activities of the other organizations with anti-piracy enforcement mandates. Its weakness reflects its low bureaucratic status (it is essentially a department of the GAPP) and its shallow reach (below the provincial level, it is typically subsumed under the Culture Bureau). Thus, even if it wanted to spearhead copyright protection, the NCAC would not be able to do so because of its circumscribed mandate. Furthermore, the NCAC has not traditionally been interested in copyright enforcement. As a result of its organizational culture, it thinks of its mission mainly in ideological terms. As an NCAC official told me, "We do not exist in order to punish the public; we exist in order to educate it as to why piracy is wrong."[30] In general, the NCAC sees its employees as an elite group of technocrats, who are not willing to become involved in the nitty-gritty of conducting market sweeps. Another NCAC employee said, "The NCAC will only work with registered legitimate enterprises; it does not go after pirates without a fixed address."[31] Overall, this attitude has resulted in unwillingness to organize raids in response to complaints from right holders.

The NCAC is especially unwilling to provide raids when foreign companies seek its assistance. Prior to the 2001 amendment of the Copyright Law, all cases involving foreign companies had to be handled by the NCAC in Beijing.[32] However, the NCAC typically refused to organize raids by arguing that the provincial copyright administrations should handle such matters. In turn, the provincial copyright administrations were unwilling to take on these cases, given that they were difficult and often politically charged. The absence of direct leadership relations (*chuizhi lingdao*) between Beijing and the provincial copyright administrations meant that the center could not force the provincial copyright administrations to take on requests for enforcement raids. This left foreign copyright holders in limbo and made it exceedingly difficult for them to find agencies willing to organize raids on their behalf. Although the 2001 amendment of the Copyright Law eliminated the requirement that foreign cases must be handled by Beijing, the provincial copyright administrations are still under no obligation to accept requests for raids.[33]

---

[30] China Interview 020125A, with NCAC official (Beijing).
[31] China Interview 020122, with a former NCAC employee (Beijing).
[32] Article 7 of the 1990 Copyright Law. The 2001 Copyright Law allows foreign right holders to bypass Beijing and approach the provincial copyright administrations directly.
[33] China Interview 020125A, with NCAC official (Beijing).

Additionally, the NCAC has exploited the overlapping mandates of the numerous law enforcement agencies to encourage foreign copyright holders to turn to other agencies for enforcement. As a former NCAC employee put it, "Whenever we had a foreign case, we would try to help the foreign company find another administrative agency that would be better suited to meet its needs."[34] Typically, even offers of case-handling fees (*ban'an fei*) and bribes (*hongbao*) would not motivate NCAC employees to become involved in enforcement raids, which carried the risk of alienating important domestic constituencies.

QUASI-JUDICIAL COPYRIGHT ENFORCEMENT

On the bright side, the NCAC does provide a limited volume of quasi-judicial enforcement. In contrast to raids, this enforcement is conducted in-house and features written punishment decisions, which introduce a certain degree of consistency and transparency.

We have national- and provincial-level statistics about the NCAC caseload. Aggregate enforcement data reveal that domestic and foreign copyright enforcement are quite distinct (they are correlated at 0.41).[35] Therefore, it is important to examine enforcement in cases of domestic and foreign copyright piracy separately.

What are the enforcement patterns when foreign copyrights are infringed? Pooled statistics for 2000–2005 demonstrate that the mean is 0.5 enforcement cases per million people, with a standard deviation of 1.48.[36] The maximal value in the dataset is 7.63 cases per million people, which was registered in Shanghai. Between 2000 and 2005, there were three distinct groups of provinces: fifteen western and rust-belt provinces provided absolutely no enforcement, thirteen provinces had between 0 and 1 case per million people, and three provinces (Guangdong, Beijing, and Shanghai) had more than 1 case per million people (see GIS Map 8.1). In short, not only is the volume of foreign copyright enforcement very low (it rarely surpasses 1 percent of the total NCAC caseload), but there is also significant variation across provinces in terms of their enforcement effort.[37] When we examine the specific independent variables that influence foreign copyright enforcement in any given year

---

[34] China Interview 020122, with a former NCAC employee (Beijing).

[35] Statistical results on copyright enforcement reported in this chapter are based on a dataset compiled by the author from *Zhongguo zhishi chanquan nianjian* (China IPR Yearbook) (Beijing: Zhishi chanquan chubanshe, various years); *Zhongguo tongji nianjian* (China Statistical Yearbook) (Beijing: Zhongguo tongji chubanshe, various years); and *China Commerce Yearbook* (Beijing: China Commercial Press, various years).

[36] Pooling is necessary because of the extreme variation in provincial-level enforcement activities from year to year.

[37] For example, in 2000 the NCAC handled 2,457 cases of copyright infringement, among which 24 involved a foreign party, accounting for 0.98 percent of the total cases. *Zhongguo zhishi chanquan nianjian 2000* (China IPR Yearbook 2000) (Beijing: Zhishi chanquan chubanshe, 2001), 220.

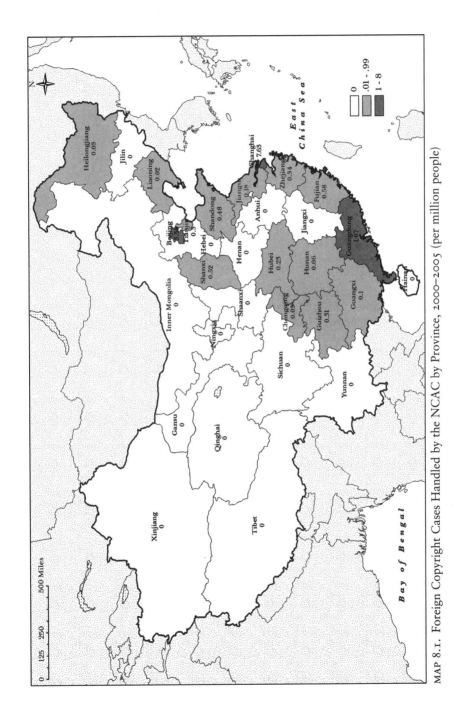

MAP 8.1. Foreign Copyright Cases Handled by the NCAC by Province, 2000–2005 (per million people)

between 2000 and 2005, only gross provincial product, FDI (both net inflows and stock), and the number of copyright export registrations in the province have a statistically significant effect at the 0.05 or 0.01 level. These results are not surprising. Richer provinces have more administrative resources, which can be directed toward copyright enforcement. Similarly, provinces with higher inflows of FDI have more to lose if foreign investors are dissatisfied with the level of copyright protection they provide. The effect of copyright export registrations is more difficult to interpret, though it probably means that provinces that produce more copyrights for export will be more sympathetic to foreign requests for enforcement.

When it comes to domestic enforcement, the variable takes a minimal value of 1.32 cases per million people (Qinghai) and a maximal value of 226.5 (Guangdong). The mean is 38.8, and the standard deviation is 49.6. Domestic copyright enforcement is also clustered, though not as heavily as foreign copyright enforcement (see GIS Map 8.2). The first cluster is formed by ten poor provinces that registered fewer than 10 cases per million people in 2000–2005.[38] Eighteen moderately rich provinces fall into an intermediate group with fewer than 100 cases per million people. Finally, there are three provinces that have over 100 cases per million people and constitute a "high" group: Guangxi, Tibet, and Guangdong. The presence of Guangxi and Tibet in this group is very surprising, as they are both poor provinces. According to the former NCAC commissioner Shen Ren'gan, whom I interviewed in 2004, the explanation for Guangxi's record is the personal activism of the leader of its Copyright Bureau, a man who has upheld a long-standing tradition of protecting IPR.[39] The case of Tibet, however, is extremely puzzling and most likely reflects data error.[40] Tibet aside, enforcement in cases of domestic copyright infringement seems to be quite erratic – regression analysis revealed that the only variable that was significant at the 0.05 level was gross provincial product, although its effect was lost as soon as other variables were introduced into the model.

Thus, overall, foreign copyright enforcement seems more rational (though we cannot say that it is rationalized) than enforcement in cases of piracy of domestic copyrights. Of course, the important question is whether this enforcement is consistent, transparent, and fair.

---

[38] Zhejiang is also in this group. Despite its very high gross provincial product and FDI inflows, in 2000–2005 Zhejiang had the second lowest enforcement record after Qinghai.

[39] China Interview 041230B, with former NCAC commissioner Shen Ren'gan (Beijing).

[40] In all years prior to and following 2004, Tibet has reported 0 cases of both domestic and foreign copyright enforcement. In 2004, however, the official statistics report 420 cases, which, given Tibet's small population, pushes the autonomous region to the position of second most active enforcer after Guangdong province for the entire 2000–2005 period. The suspicion that we are dealing with data error or manipulation is strengthened by the fact that although the *China IPR Yearbook 2005* discusses at length Tibet's modest achievements in patent and trademark protection in 2004, it does not even have a section on copyright work in the autonomous region. See *Zhongguo zhishi chanquan nianjian 2005*, 210–212.

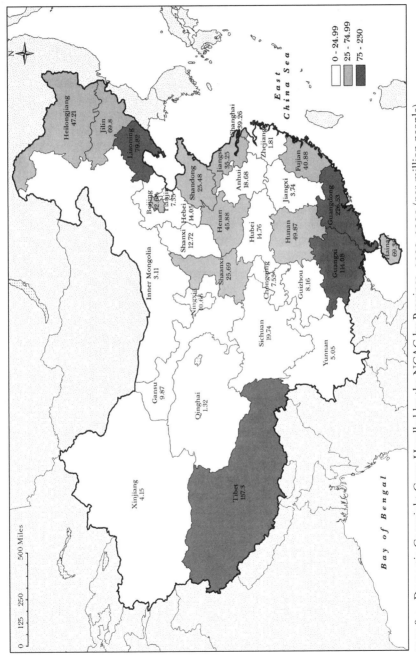

MAP 8.2. Domestic Copyright Cases Handled by the NCAC by Province, 2000–2005 (per million people)

Legend:
- 0 – 24.99
- 25 – 74.99
- 75 – 230

Heilongjiang 47.21
Jilin 69.8
Liaoning 79.82
Shanghai 39.26
Zhejiang 1.81
Fujian 40.88
Jiangsu 35.25
Anhui 18.68
Shandong 25.48
Beijing 32.64
Tianjin 7.35
Hebei 14.05
Shanxi 12.72
Henan 45.88
Shaanxi 25.69
Ningxia 10.62
Hubei 14.76
Jiangxi 3.74
Hunan 49.87
Guangdong 226.53
Guangxi 114.08
Hainan 69.34
Chongqing 7.53
Guizhou 8.16
Sichuan 19.74
Yunnan 5.05
Inner Mongolia 3.11
Gansu 9.87
Qinghai 1.32
Xinjiang 4.15
Tibet 157.3

East China Sea

Bay of Bengal

N

0   125   250   500 Miles

Consistency and Transparency of Quasi-Judicial Copyright Enforcement

Is the routine enforcement of copyright consistent and transparent? Despite some shortcomings, in comparison to trademark enforcement, copyright enforcement does show signs of hope. First, the rules about who should enforce are clearer in copyright cases than they are in trademark cases. Most important in terms of raising the quality of enforcement is that the NCAC does not organize raids, which are prone to produce substandard enforcement. Second, although both the trademark and copyright bureaucracies are decentralized, the NCAC penetrates only to the provincial level, whereas most trademark bureaucracies reach all the way down to the county. This difference has two implications. First, the shallow "reach" of the copyright bureaucracy makes it relatively easy to monitor. Second, the NCAC has better trained and more professional personnel than most trademark bureaucracies working at the grassroots level. Both the ease of monitoring and the high degree of professionalism increase the consistency of policy implementation.

Enforcement is more likely to be transparent when open administrative hearings are held and when administrative punishment decisions are published. The NCAC does have some open hearings and publishes some of its administrative punishment decisions. Similarly, there are hundreds of easily accessible books containing laws and administrative regulations applicable in cases of copyright enforcement. Making regulations publicly available raises transparency, as it allows both right holders and alleged pirates to ascertain the specific legal grounds on which a decision is based. Thus, we can say that in contrast to the SAIC, the NCAC has made more progress toward the establishment of both consistency and transparency.

Fairness of Quasi-Judicial Copyright Enforcement

Is routine copyright enforcement fair? The number of administrative reconsideration and administrative litigation cases brought against the NCAC is very small. As Table 8.2 indicates, between 1998 and 2006, the NCAC concluded over 67,000 copyright enforcement cases. During this period, in only 35 cases were NCAC decisions appealed through the administrative reconsideration process (0.05 percent of the total caseload of the NCAC). In 29 cases, the NCAC sustained the initial administrative decision, which means that the plaintiffs won in whole or in part in the remaining six cases. The 17 percent winning rate is reasonable. But the extreme rarity of cases reaching appeal is a powerful argument against there being a viable check on administrative discretion in place. Strikingly, only 1 in every 1,900 routine copyright enforcement cases was appealed internally within the NCAC through the reconsideration procedure.

The state of administrative litigation is even more alarming, with a total of only 26 cases between 1998 and 2006, meaning that 1 in every 2,550 NCAC cases was appealed through the courts (0.04 percent of the total NCAC

TABLE 8.2. *Copyright Administrative Enforcement, Administrative Reconsideration, and Administrative Litigation in China, 1998–2006*

Year	Copyright Administrative Enforcement Cases Concluded	Administrative Reconsideration Cases	Agency Decision Sustained	Administrative Litigation Cases	Agency Decision Sustained
1998	1,208 (accepted)	0	0	2	0
1999	1,504	1	0	9	2
2000	2,277	6	4	2	1
2001	4,306	4	3	2	2
2002	6,107	4	3	2	2
2003	22,429	4	4	4	2
2004	9,497	5	4	0	0
2005	9,380	5	5	2	2
2006	10,344	6	6	3	3
TOTAL	67,052	35	29	26	14

Sources: Zhongguo zhishi chanquan nianjian 2000, 206, 214, 220; *Zhongguo zhishi chanquan nianjian 2001–2002* (China IPR Yearbook 2001–2002) (Beijing: Zhishi chanquan chubanshe, 2002), 238; *Zhongguo zhishi chanquan nianjian 2003* (China IPR Yearbook 2003) (Beijing: Zhishi chanquan chubanshe, 2003), 255; *Zhongguo zhishi chanquan nianjian 2004* (China IPR Yearbook 2004) (Beijing: Zhishi chanquan chubanshe, 2004), 321; *Zhongguo zhishi chanquan nianjian 2005*, 276; *Zhongguo zhishi chanquan nianjian 2006* (China IPR Yearbook 2006) (Beijing: Zhishi chanquan chubanshe, 2006), 370; *Zhongguo zhishi chanquan nianjian 2007* (China IPR Yearbook 2007) (Beijing: Zhishi chanquan chubanshe, 2007), 509.

caseload). Although plaintiffs won in 46 percent of the cases (a very reasonable figure), the rate of administrative litigation overall is extremely low. These statistics suggest that the NCAC discourages plaintiffs from using either administrative reconsideration or administrative litigation to hold it accountable for its actions.

Has rationalized enforcement emerged in the area of routine copyright enforcement? Despite some signs of progress, the extreme difficulty of appealing NCAC administrative decisions prevents us from saying that there has been even incremental progress toward the establishment of fairness. Thus, routine copyright enforcement, though better than routine trademark enforcement, is not rationalized. In contrast, patent protection, to be discussed in Chapter 9, does show signs of rationalization.

POSITIVE EXTERNALITIES CREATED BY THE CURRENT COPYRIGHT ENFORCEMENT SYSTEM: AN INCREASED DEMAND FOR COURT ENFORCEMENT

Administrative enforcement does not exist in isolation. Copyright administrative agencies share their enforcement mandate with the courts, Customs, and the police. One of the main tasks of this study is to outline the conditions under which the courts become the dominant enforcers of laws and regulations. Chapter 4 showed that because the courts allow for appeal of judicial decisions and subscribe to higher standards of transparency and consistency than administrative agencies, their increased use is desirable for the emergence of rationalized enforcement and the eventual rise of the rule of law. Court use is especially important when administrative agencies operate with a high degree of opacity and without strong standards of accountability, as is the case in China.

The data presented in Table 8.3 show that although the number of both court cases and routine administrative cases has increased, administrative enforcement remains the preferred enforcement method in China. However, the situation in the area of copyrights is not at all similar to what we observe in the area of trademarks, where, as illustrated in Chapter 7, the total number of court trademark cases equaled less than 1 percent of the administrative trademark caseload. For most of the period between 1995 and 2005, court copyright cases corresponded to an impressive 40–50 percent of the administrative copyright cases handled by the NCAC.

TABLE 8.3. *Administrative versus Court Enforcement of Copyrights in China, 1995–2005*

Year	Total Routine Copyright Administrative Cases	Total Copyright Court Cases	Ratio of Administrative to Court Cases
1995	520	385	1.3
1996	673	463	1.4
1997	1,361	438	3.1
1998	1,082	546	2
1999	1,504	654	2.3
2000	2,277	989	2.3
2001	4,306	1,063	4
2002	6,107	1,776	3.4
2003	22,429	2,283	9.8
2004	9,497	3,608	2.6
2005	9,644	6,096	1.6

Note: The spike in the 2003 figures is explained by the decision of Guangdong province to adopt a controversial new way of counting cases (China Interview 041230B, with former NCAC commissioner Shen Ren'gan). Guangdong went from handling 318 cases in 2002 to 16,025 cases in 2003 – a fiftyfold increase. In 2004 Guangdong handled 632 cases, and in 2005 it handled 775 cases (www.ncac.gov.cn, accessed December 25, 2006).

Sources: Zhongguo zhishi chanquan nianjian 2000, 202–203, 206, 214, 220, 226, 249–250; *Zhongguo zhishi chanquan nianjian* 2001–2002, 238–239, 266; *Zhongguo zhishi chanquan nianjian* 2003, 255, 277–278; *Zhongguo zhishi chanquan nianjian* 2004, 329, 333, 336–337; *Zhongguo zhishi chanquan nianjian* 2005, 276, 307–309; *Zhongguo zhishi chanquan nianjian* 2006, 370, 405–406.

Time-series data indicate that the NCAC has succeeded in progressively alienating some of its "customers" and reducing demand for its services. This seems to have been a conscious strategy on the part of the enforcers. As a former NCAC employee put it, "As cases became progressively more difficult over the 1990s, we started imposing various types of fees. What we saw was that as a result more and more right holders started turning to the court system."[41] In effect, the NCAC deliberately began to price itself out of the market for the provision of copyright protection services. As an experienced IPR lawyer handling copyright cases in China estimated, pursuing administrative enforcement is now not necessarily less expensive than handling a case through the court system.[42]

Court cases are expensive. Right holders have to pay for the services of investigators, lawyers, and the notaries who procure the necessary paperwork (notarized powers of attorney, etc.). They also have to cover the court acceptance fee. Court proceedings do provide an opportunity to receive and collect a damage award, but a plaintiff who loses the case will have to bear the court costs, in addition to paying whatever damages are awarded the defendant. Court decisions are, of course, subject to appeal, but even when the case is strong, the process is costly and time-consuming, in comparison to the quick enforcement provided by administrative agencies. It is no surprise that right holders have tended to avoid the courts in favor of administrative protection, especially in the area of trademarks, where agencies are willing to organize raids after a request from the right holders.

This picture is changing. Though free in principle, administrative enforcement has become increasingly expensive in practice. Right holders have to pay various fees at the outset: fees for private investigative services necessary to discover evidence of the infringement, lawyers' fees, and official and unofficial fees assessed by the administrative agency (or agencies) responsible for enforcement. Frequently, there are significant additional costs associated with identifying an agency that is both able and, more importantly, willing to assist the right holder with his or her problem. Given that a search requires time and expert advice and often depends for its success on the connections of paid counsel and investigators, handling a case through administrative channels can turn out to be even more expensive than court litigation.[43]

The notion that administrative agencies continue to provide cheap enforcement is a myth. This change, combined with the difficulty of appealing administrative decisions, may explain why, over time, right holders have begun to turn to the courts of law in ever greater numbers. The preference for court enforcement has implications for our overall assessment of the quality of copyright enforcement in China. Even though campaign-style enforcement and routine

---

[41] China Interview 020122, with a former NCAC employee (Beijing).

[42] China Interview 010906B, with a Chinese IPR lawyer (Guangzhou).

[43] China Interviews 010605C, 010611, 010906B, and 020129E, with an intellectual property attorney (Beijing, Shanghai, Guangzhou, and Shanghai, respectively).

enforcement are problem-ridden, the growing importance of the courts suggests that a portion of copyright enforcement in China is already of a high caliber.

Why then is it that right holders do not turn to the courts for trademark cases in the same way they do for copyright cases? In 2005, the ratio of routine administrative copyright cases to court cases stood at 1.6:1.[44] In contrast, in the same year the ratio of routine trademark administrative enforcement (by the SAIC) to court enforcement was 28:1.[45] The most important difference between trademarks and copyrights is that a significantly greater number of administrative agencies are able and willing to provide routine administrative enforcement in cases of trademark counterfeiting than in cases of copyright piracy. In practice, if the SAIC rejects a request for enforcement by a candy-bar producer, he can go the Technical Supervision Bureau (TSB), then to the State Food and Drug Administration (SFDA), and subsequently to the Ministry of Health (MOH), and so on, until someone is willing to take his case, with or without a bribe. This oversupply of administrative enforcement has led to a very light trademark caseload for IPR tribunals. Clearly, administrative and civil enforcement are intertwined.

INTERNATIONAL COMPARISONS: COPYRIGHT ENFORCEMENT IN RUSSIA

The distinctive features of copyright enforcement in China can be highlighted through a paired comparison with Russia, another large country that has decentralized bureaucracies and suffers from a similarly high level of piracy. Who enforces copyright laws in Russia? Chapters 3, 4, 5, and 6 collectively described the different enforcement options right holders theoretically have in Russia (Customs enforcement, civil litigation, administrative enforcement, and criminal enforcement). A case study in Chapter 7 provided specific details of on-the-ground enforcement in cases of trademark counterfeiting. To date there have been no such empirical studies of the copyright situation on the ground. We lack knowledge even about why right holders seeking redress prefer a specific enforcement avenue.

In the absence of official statistics, I rely on a proprietary dataset of enforcement actions in cases of copyright counterfeiting. I obtained this dataset from the Russia office of the International Federation of the Phonographic Industry (IFPI) in January 2006. It consists of thirty-eight discrete cases of copyright enforcement that took place between December 2002 and December 2005, with 90 percent of the cases occurring between January 2004 and December 2005. Although this dataset is maintained by the IFPI, it does not focus

---

[44] *Zhongguo falü nianjian 2006* (China Law Yearbook 2006) (Beijing: Falü chubanshe, 2006), 117.

[45] Ibid., 117. The ratio would be skewed to as much as 500:1 in favor of administrative enforcement if we were to include data about the activities of all other agencies sharing the trademark enforcement portfolio (see Chapters 5 and 7).

exclusively on music piracy, and it includes cases of video- and computer-game piracy as well. Unfortunately, there are no software piracy cases in the dataset, as these are handled exclusively by Microsoft's Business Software Alliance. Nevertheless, there is no reason to believe that the government agencies that enforce in cases of software piracy will be radically different from those providing enforcement in other cases of optical disk piracy, given that all pirated optical disks have similar modes of production and distribution.[46]

The IFPI dataset allows us to make some observations about the geographical variation in copyright protection, about the participation of different agencies in anti-piracy activities, and, most importantly, about the preferred enforcement avenue of right holders. We can also gain some insights into the work of the Procuratorate and the sentencing patterns of Russian courts.

Geographical Variation in Enforcement

Russia's enormous landmass spans eleven time zones and is subdivided into eighty-three subjects of the federation, which are roughly equivalent to the individual states in the United States.[47] The IFPI dataset reveals that copyright enforcement was skewed in favor of Moscow and Moscow oblast, which jointly accounted for 55 percent of all enforcement actions. The remainder of the anti-piracy raids were distributed among seven other subjects of the federation: Tatarstan (18 percent), St. Petersburg (10 percent), Rostov-on-the-Don (5 percent), as well as Novosibirsk, Penza, Krasnodar, and Stavropol *krai* (2.6 percent each). Although enforcement was heavily skewed toward more affluent regions, it closely mirrored the distribution of optical disk production and mastering plants throughout the territory of Russia. In January 2005, there were forty-five such plants, 49 percent of which were in Moscow, 11 percent in St. Petersburg, and 9 percent in Kazan (the capital of Tatarstan). The remaining plants were distributed among ten other Russian cities and regions (Rostov-on-the-Don, Novosibirsk, Penza, Krasnodar, Stavropol *krai*, Tambov, Samara, Yekaterinburg, Kaluga oblast, and Lipetsk).[48] It is readily apparent that the mastering plants are located in the most economically developed regions of Russia, which also have markets where a high volume of pirated goods are sold. According to interviewees, most pirated disks are produced by officially

---

[46] Like the China enforcement dataset, the IFPI dataset does not include cases of Internet piracy or book piracy.

[47] Until 2003, there were eighty-nine subjects of the federation. Thereafter, Perm oblast in the Urals merged with the neighboring Komi-Permyak autonomous *okrug*, and several additional mergers followed. As of March 2008, the Russian Federation was composed of twenty-one republics, nine *krais*, forty-six oblasts, four autonomous *okrugs*, two cities of federal significance (Moscow and St. Petersburg), and one autonomous oblast. Russia has a system of asymmetrical federalism: the different designations reflect differences in status among the subjects of the federation.

[48] Data extracted from *List of Russian Optical Disk and Mastering Plants* (January 8, 2005), obtained by the author in January 2006 from IFPI Russia.

licensed factories that churn out both authorized and unauthorized optical media.[49] Therefore, with the exception of several Customs actions to stop the importation of unauthorized optical disks into Russia, virtually all enforcement activity in the IFPI dataset targets licensed factories producing unauthorized disks for domestic consumption.

Who Enforces?

The enforcement field in Russia is composed of five different government agencies: the police (MVD), the Federal Security Service (FSB), the Federal Customs Service (FTS), the Procuratorate, and the Cultural Protection Service (Rosokhrankul'tury). Most of the enforcement actions (74 percent) were conducted by a single agency. Interagency cooperation was relatively rare, with two-agency raids accounting for only 18 percent of all enforcement actions and three-agency raids making up the remaining 8 percent.

The dataset reveals that, in marked contrast to China, administrative enforcement in Russia is extremely rare. Rosokhrankul'tury, the administrative agency that distributes licenses for the operation of optical disk plants, was involved in just one raid, which was conducted in cooperation with the FSB and the Procuratorate. Customs enforcement in Russia is also very rare, with Customs participating in only two raids. Similarly, there was only one case of civil litigation, where, after a Customs seizure, a Moscow court imposed a fine of 180,000 rubles (about US$6,500) on an illegal importer of optical disks into Russia. The Procuratorate was a relatively minor enforcer, participating in only six raids.

The MVD and the FSB dominated enforcement, collectively participating in 95 percent of all enforcement activities. The role of the FSB in enforcement is especially noteworthy, because it is the only government agency that can easily enter the so-called restricted-access enterprises (*rezhimnye ob"ekty*), which are usually located on military property and strategically use their special status to turn away right holders attempting to conduct an inspection without FSB backing.[50] Needless to say, these enterprises are often the worst offenders in terms of producing pirated disks. Overall, criminal enforcement is the avenue of choice for right holders. This is not surprising, given interview evidence about the weakness of the civil courts and the ineffectiveness of administrative enforcement, as cited in the preceding chapters.

---

[49] Russia Interview 060116A, with Igor Pozhitkov, regional director for Russia and the CIS, IFPI (Moscow). Factories may be authorized to produce some CDs (say, Russian labels) but not others (say, foreign labels carried by BMG). Production of unauthorized CDs is technologically simple because the factories already possess all the necessary equipment.

[50] Russia Interview 060116A, with Igor Pozhitkov, regional director for Russia and the CIS, IFPI (Moscow).

Are Criminals Punished for Their Actions?

The deterrence of criminal enforcement is raised when enforcement results in the imprisonment of individuals who have violated the relevant laws and regulations. In Russia, a criminal case begins when the Procuratorate decides to initiate a criminal investigation. The Procuratorate can rely on evidence that it has collected on its own, or on evidence that has been transferred from the MVD or the FSB. According to the IFPI dataset, 37 percent of the enforcement actions (fourteen cases) eventually culminated in a criminal investigation. Sometimes the Procuratorate at first refused to initiate a criminal investigation but eventually acquiesced after the right holders appealed its decision and pressure from a higher-level Procuratorate was applied. A criminal investigation, however, need not result in a criminal case being lodged with the courts. After gathering all the necessary evidence, the Procuratorate decides whether it wants to pursue the matter further and charge a suspect with committing a crime. Once a suspect is charged, the case enters a court of law, which then determines whether the suspect is guilty. Of the cases in the dataset that were accepted by the Procuratorate, only 36 percent (five cases) resulted in criminal punishments, ranging from a one-year conditional sentence to four years imprisonment. Generally, the IFPI dataset produces rates of initiating a criminal investigation, of deciding to convict the alleged criminal, and of sentencing that are consistent with national-level data for Russia, as cited in Chapter 6.[51]

As outlined here, the most consequential difference between Russia and China is that Russian right holders have an understandable preference for criminal enforcement, which is more deterrent than administrative enforcement. In contrast, Chinese right holders prefer administrative enforcement, in no small measure because of the difficulty of initiating a criminal prosecution. In the end, these differences between the two countries mean that Russia has a higher number of criminal sentences per capita and a more deterrent enforcement environment than China. Unfortunately, available data do not allow us to make any claims about the consistency, transparency, and fairness of enforcement in Russia.

CONCLUSION

This chapter demonstrates that Chinese copyright agencies can deliver a high volume of campaign-style enforcement under pressure. However, the same agencies provide a relatively limited volume of quasi-judicial administrative enforcement. A counterintuitive result is that the limited provision of administrative enforcement has increased demand for the services of the courts of law. This is a positive trend, which should be encouraged. Courts of law provide

---

[51] *Metodika rassledovaniia prestuplenii predusmotrennykh st. 146 UK RF* (Methods of Investigating the Crimes Specified in Article 146 of the Russian Criminal Code) (Sankt Peterburg: Iuridicheskii tsentr press, 2004), 4.

better protection to right holders and can be held accountable for their decisions through the appeals process. More importantly, the increased use of the court system may indicate a general movement away from unpredictable enforcement in the direction of rationalized enforcement. We should also be heartened by the findings presented in this chapter about the consistency and transparency of quasi-judicial copyright enforcement. Though numerous difficulties remain (and procedural fairness is still lacking), routine copyright protection appears to be of a higher quality than routine trademark protection, thus indicating the potential for the future rise of rationalization in this area.

9

Patents

Creating Rationalized Enforcement

Patents are an unusual subtype of IPR in China because administrative agencies and courts of law both provide rationalized enforcement in this domain. Three factors explain this outcome. First and foremost, the administrative enforcement field is not crowded by the presence of multiple agencies with overlapping (and poorly defined) enforcement jurisdictions. A single agency – the State Intellectual Property Office (SIPO) – is charged with providing administrative enforcement. In contrast to copyrights and trademarks, the technical complexity of patents presents a barrier to the entry of multiple administrative enforcers. This has allowed simple and predictable enforcement arrangements to emerge and to become institutionalized. Second, the SIPO functions as a quasi-centralized bureaucracy, thus increasing the accountability of subnational enforcers to the center. Third, enforcement responsibility is clearly divided between the SIPO and the courts. The SIPO has exclusive jurisdiction over enforcement for some types of patents; for others, where the SIPO and the courts share enforcement responsibility, the Patent Law unambiguously delineates their respective mandates. Overall, patent enforcement is consistent, transparent, and fair.

Why has high-quality enforcement emerged for patents but not for trademarks or copyrights? First, patents are a priority for the central leadership. Ever since Deng Xiaoping included science and technology among the Four Modernizations, Chinese leaders have made a special effort to promote indigenous inventiveness. Second, and more importantly, prior to the early 2000s, there was little foreign or domestic pressure to increase the volume of patent enforcement. This allowed the central government to develop a patent protection regime that was more streamlined than the trademark and copyright regimes, where pressure to enforce has led to the launch of largely ineffective enforcement campaigns that featured the participation of multiple enforcers.

This chapter is organized as follows. After a brief definition of patents and a note on the history of their protection in China, the chapter focuses on national- and provincial-level trends in inventiveness since 1985. We then move to a discussion of the volume and quality of different kinds of patent enforcement. Thereafter, we present a brief case study of Viagra anticounterfeiting enforcement and then conclude with a discussion of the rationalization of patent enforcement in China.

What Are Patents?

Patents protect new, nonobvious, and useful inventions, such as blockbuster antidepressants or new types of computer chips. Inventors who hold a patent enjoy exclusive rights to reap the financial rewards from their inventions for a certain period, typically up to twenty years. Once a patent expires, it becomes part of the public domain and anyone can use the invention – it is due to this feature of patents that we now have access to generic drugs, for example.

There are three broad categories of patents: invention patents, utility model patents, and design patents. An invention patent can protect either a new product (e.g., the molecule of sildenafil citrate, the active ingredient in Viagra) or a new process (e.g., an innovative chemical process for producing sildenafil citrate). In China, invention patents are awarded for twenty years. Utility model patents protect simpler inventions that do not meet the stringent requirements for patentability that are applied to products and processes. Unlike invention patent applications, where a substantive examination for novelty, nonobviousness, and usefulness is required, utility model applications are subject only to a formal examination for novelty. Finally, design patents are awarded to unique shapes and forms, for example, the classic Coca-Cola bottle. Like utility models, design patents are relatively easy to obtain. In China, both utility model and design patents are awarded for ten years.

Patents in China: A Historical Overview

Patents are relatively new to the Chinese legal system. Imperial China had no provisions for the protection of industrial property. Although a proto–patent law ("Reward Regulations for Vitalizing Technologies and Crafts") was issued by the Guangxu Emperor in 1898, the first Patent Law was not adopted until 1912. The law was subsequently revised four times: in 1923, 1928, 1932, and, finally, 1939. However, none of the revisions of the act provided patent protection for foreigners. Furthermore, the protected subject matter excluded foodstuffs, beverages, and pharmaceuticals. Initially, only invention patents for products were allowed, but the 1923 law extended invention patents to cover processes as well. In addition, the 1939 law granted protection to utility models and design patents. Patents were issued after formal application and examination conducted by the Ministry of Industry and Commerce. Overall, given China's low level of technological development at the time, the patent system was underutilized: fewer than one thousand patents were granted between 1912 and 1944.[1] In 1944, a new Patent Law was adopted by the Kuomintang (KMT) government, but because of the political turmoil culminating in the KMT's final retreat to Taiwan in 1949, it was never implemented in mainland China.

When the Communists came to power in 1949, they repealed all KMT laws. The post-1949 period witnessed a gradual decline of patents and their eventual abolition. From 1950 to 1963, there was a system of invention certificates (for major inventions) and patent certificates (for minor inventions), patterned after that in the Soviet Union.[2] These certificates were abolished in 1963, however, and thereafter China had no patent system for two decades. A Patent Law was passed in 1984 and amended in 1992 and 2000. In less than two decades, China had moved from providing no patent protection to granting 190,238 patents in 2004 alone.[3] Between 1985 and 2004, a total of 1,255,499 patents were issued.[4] In 2005, China was among the top three countries in the world in terms of invention patent filings.[5] These are remarkable achievements by any standard.

Patent Activity in China after 1985

Because they provide the broadest scope of protection, invention patents (*faming zhuanli*) are the most useful patents, but they are also the hardest to obtain. Since the 1980s, foreign applications for invention patents have outnumbered domestic Chinese applications. However, in 2003 this trend was reversed, with domestic applications surpassing foreign applications for the first time. Between 1985 and 2006, as many as 565,147 domestic and 524,368 foreign applications for invention patents were accepted.[6] During the same period, 184,061 invention patents were granted to foreigners, whereas only 112,442 patents were granted to domestic inventors.[7] In contrast to invention

---

[1] This paragraph is based on Chung Jen Cheng, "The Role of the Patent System in the Development of Technology in Taiwan" (JSD Dissertation, Stanford University School of Law, 1993), 150–188.

[2] Xiang Wang, *Chinese Patent Law and Patent Litigation in China* (Baltimore: School of Law, University of Maryland, 1998), 7–8.

[3] For example, 23,191 patents were granted in Russia in 2004. When adjusted for population, China and Russia are now comparable in terms of their inventive activity, despite Russia's initial comparative advantage in science and technology. See *Analiticheskie materialy i statistika po nekotorym napravleniiam deiatel'nosti Rospatenta v 2005 g.* (Analysis and Statistics on Certain Aspects of the Activity of Rospatent in 2005) (Moscow: Rospatent, 2006), http://www.fips.ru/ruptoru/stat2005.rtf (accessed October 28, 2008).

[4] *Zhongguo zhishi chanquan nianjian 2005* (China IPR Yearbook 2005) (Beijing: Zhishi chanquan chubanshe, 2005), 266.

[5] *WIPO Patent Report: Statistics on Worldwide Patent Activity* (Geneva: WIPO, 2007), 12, http://www.wipo.int/ipstats/en/statistics/patents/patent_report_2007.html#P211_16003 (accessed August 12, 2008).

[6] *Zhongguo zhishi chanquan nianjian 2007* (China IPR Yearbook 2007) (Beijing: Zhishi chanquan chubanshe, 2007), 493.

[7] *Zhongguo zhishi chanquan nianjian 2007*, 499.

patents, Chinese citizens apply for and receive the lion's share of utility model patents (*shiyong xinxing*) and design patents (*waiguan sheji*). Altogether, foreigners accounted for 18 percent of the 3.3 million patent applications and received 14 percent of the 1.7 million patents granted in China prior to 2007.[8]

What is the regional distribution of inventive activity in China? We can answer this question by examining statistics on the number of patent applications in individual provinces. A dataset I compiled reveals that between 1985 and 2004, the top five provinces in terms of patent applications and patents granted (per million people) were Beijing, Shanghai, Guangdong, Tianjin, and Zhejiang. Not surprisingly, the least inventive province during this period was Tibet. Regression results indicate that regional inventiveness is strongly correlated with gross provincial product: controlling for population, richer provinces account for more patent applications and receive more patents than poorer provinces.[9]

Patent Protection in China

Patents are a valuable kind of intellectual property, and they require protection against infringement, counterfeiting, and passing off. Under the Chinese Patent Law, an infringement (*qinquan*) is an act of using, making, or selling a patented invention without authorization (e.g., a firm manufactures a screwdriver that is largely similar to a patented screwdriver).[10] Infringement is difficult to ascertain, because it frequently arises out of complicated contractual agreements between the original patent holder and the alleged infringer. In contrast, passing off an unpatented product as a patented invention (*maochong*) refers to activities such as printing a likeness of the name of the patent holder and patent number and affixing them to a product similar to the product embodying the invention for which the patent has been granted.[11] Patent counterfeiting (*jiamao*) involves counterfeiting the patent certificate or other patent document belonging to the legitimate holder of the patent.[12] Overall, establishing acts of patent counterfeiting and passing off is technically less challenging than determining whether patent infringement has taken place. Therefore, different

---

[8] The top four foreign countries in terms of patent applications and patents granted between 1985 and 2006 were Japan, the United States, Germany, and South Korea. Among the top ten companies that applied for Chinese patents in 2006, five were Japanese, two South Korean, one Dutch, one German, and one American (IBM). See *Zhongguo zhishi chanquan nianjian 2007*, 493, 495–499, 501–504, 507.

[9] Dataset compiled from *Zhongguo zhishi chanquan nianjian 2005*, 260–273, and other yearbooks.

[10] 2000 Patent Law, Article 57.

[11] 2000 Patent Law, Articles 58–59. For a passing-off case, see *Guo Li Wen et al. v. Gao Chun County Lighting Company et al.* (*Zuigao renmin fayuan gongbao* [PRC Supreme People's Court Gazette], no. 1 [1994], 43–45), also reported in Wang, *Chinese Patent Law*, 46–47.

[12] Implementing Regulations of the Patent Law of the People's Republic of China (2001), Articles 84–85.

structures have emerged for protecting patents against infringement, counterfeiting, and passing off.

What types of remedies are available when patent infringement disputes arise? One option is to handle the dispute through one of the regional intellectual property offices, which are the subnational equivalents of the SIPO. If the regional IPO finds that infringement has occurred, it can order the infringer to stop the infringing act immediately. This decision may subsequently be appealed in a court of law. A second option is to institute an invalidation proceeding at the SIPO's Patent Reexamination Board (PRB) in Beijing. This proceeding may culminate with a finding in favor of the plaintiff, but the decision is sometimes in favor of the defendant, when the PRB finds that the original patent is invalid because it does not meet one of the requirements for patentability, and, consequently, that no infringement has occurred. It is even possible for the plaintiff's patent to be found both invalid and infringing on the defendant's patent. The losing party may appeal the PRB's decision in court. The third option is for the parties to institute court proceedings directly at one of the courts authorized to hear patent disputes. In addition, Customs and the police may provide specialized enforcement in cases of patent infringement.

What options exist when a right holder has suffered from patent counterfeiting or patent passing off? In keeping with the provisions of the Patent Law, the courts play no role in such cases; the SIPO and its regional offices have exclusive jurisdiction over enforcement in this domain. This division of the enforcement portfolio reflects the complexity of patent infringement cases and the relative ease of handling counterfeiting and passing-off cases.

We should emphasize that in contrast to China, in other countries the patent and trademark offices handle only patent and trademark applications, oppositions, and invalidations and do not provide any administrative enforcement in cases of patent counterfeiting and passing off.[13] Nor do most countries have regional intellectual property offices that can hear patent infringement disputes. China is thus unique in terms of both the breadth and the depth of patent protection that it provides.

The State Intellectual Property Office

The State Intellectual Property Office has exclusive jurisdiction over the administrative protection of patents in China. The SIPO grew out of the State Patent Office (Zhongguo zhuanli ju), which was established in 1980. In theory, the State Patent Office was directly subordinate to the State Council, yet in practice it was officially managed (*daiguan*) by the Science and Technology Commission on behalf of the State Council. By 1982, the State Patent Office was merged into the State Economic Commission, but in 1988 its status changed again, when it was reclassified as an "office directly subordinate to the State Council but

---

[13] Most countries do not maintain separate trademark and patent offices. Rather, they are merged into a single office.

managed by the Science and Technology Commission" (*Guowuyuan zhishu juji, you kexue jishu weiyuanhui guikou guanli*). This higher rank allowed it to be listed on the official Chinese government organization chart for the first time. The next stage in its institutional evolution occurred in 1993, when it acquired the rank of "administrative unit directly subordinate to the State Council" (*Guowuyuan zhishu shiye danwei*), meaning that it had a direct reporting relationship with the State Council. Finally, in 1998 the State Patent Office was renamed the State Intellectual Property Office and it was simultaneously elevated to the vice-ministerial rank of an "organization directly subordinate to the State Council" (*Guowuyuan zhishu jigou*).[14]

In 1998 the SIPO was given an official personnel allocation (*bianzhi*) of eighty central-level staff positions in Beijing.[15] It is well known that Chinese bureaucracies often engage in various practices that allow them to exceed their official personnel allocations (*chaobian*). According to official data, in 2004 the SIPO and its various subordinate units (*xiashu danwei*) employed as many as 3,000 people at the central level.[16] In addition, in the early 2000s, the SIPO had at least fifty-four offices located in provincial capitals and large cities throughout the country.[17] The SIPO maintains only professional relations with its subordinate units, leaving the personnel and budgeting decisions to the local governments at the level where these units operate. For example, the personnel allocation of the Shanghai Intellectual Property Office (IPO) is determined by the Shanghai people's government. Although the SIPO administrative hierarchy is not formally centralized, some IPOs in places like Beijing municipality, Shanghai, and Guangdong maintain close relations with the SIPO, which has a certain measure of control over them.[18] These offices are very important, as they handle a disproportionate share of the patent work in China. We should also stress that the activity of examining, reexamining, and invalidating patents is centralized and handled exclusively by the SIPO in Beijing. Thus, the SIPO effectively has a quasi-centralized bureaucratic structure.

---

[14] *Zhonghua renmin gongheguo zhengfu jigou wushi nian* (Government Organizations of the PRC over Fifty Years) (Beijing: Dangjian duwu chubanshe and Guojia xingzheng xueyuan chubanshe, 2000), 156–157.

[15] *Zhongyang zhengfu zuzhi jigou 1998* (Central Government Organs 1998) (Beijing: Gaige chubanshe, 1998), 435.

[16] Zhu Jingwen, ed., *Zhongguo falü fazhan baogao: Shujuku he zhibiao tixi* (Report on China Law Development: Database and Indicators) (Beijing: Zhongguo renmin daxue chubanshe, 2007), 435.

[17] China Interview 010613, with an employee of the Foreign Affairs Department of the SIPO (Beijing). In recent years, many localities have established IPR offices, but the SIPO does not recognize most of them as part of its official hierarchy. An example is the IPR office of Zouping county in Shandong province, which is not recognized as an IPR office by the SIPO. China Interview 080110, with two employees of the Zouping Technology Office (Zouping IPR Office) (Zouping).

[18] China Interview 041227, with the director general of the Beijing IPO (Beijing); China Interview 010718A and China Interview 020129D, with the director general of the Shanghai IPO (Shanghai).

Patent Infringement in China: The Administrative Agency/Court Nexus

Like all other types of IPR in China, both administrative agencies and courts of law can provide patent enforcement. A commentator on patent litigation in China claims that

the court system is used as a last resort, reflecting a long history of strong executive power by the central government with a weak judiciary system, often exemplified by better equipped administrative authorities with more staff, more operating expenses, and organizational connections.[19]

This statement is misleading, because it implies that courts are inconsequential actors in patent disputes. In practice, the interplay between administrative and judicial enforcement is more nuanced. As the statistics in Table 9.1 demonstrate, the courts have emerged as the dominant enforcers in patent infringement disputes. Importantly, rationalized enforcement can exist both for cases resolved through the courts and for cases handled by the administrative agencies, provided there are laws that clearly specify the respective jurisdictions of the administrative agencies and the courts. An administrative agency with a clearly specified mandate is able to enforce laws as consistently, transparently, and fairly as the courts do. In addition, clear mandates make it easier to hold the agencies accountable for failing to enforce the law.

Table 9.1 contains time-series data on the ratio of patent infringement cases handled through the courts to patent infringement cases handled by the SIPO from 1996 to 2006. As should be apparent, court cases outnumbered administrative cases in each of the eleven years for which we have data. On average, the ratio of court cases to administrative cases during this period was 1.82:1. Thus, the preference for court enforcement in the area of patent infringement disputes is clear. This enforcement arrangement is consistent with the provisions of Article 57 of the 2000 Patent Law, which specifies that in cases of patent infringement, individual patent owners have the option of either going to a court of law or submitting to administrative proceedings. When asked to comment on the increasingly more modest role that their agency plays in resolving patent infringement disputes, a SIPO employee curtly replied that "these matters should be handled by the courts; I wish we had nothing to do with them."[20]

Is Administrative Patent Enforcement Rationalized?

When we assess the extent to which administrative enforcement is rationalized, we should take care to differentiate among the three main activities of the SIPO and its regional offices: patent examination, reexamination, and invalidation; resolving patent infringement disputes; and providing enforcement in cases of patent counterfeiting and passing off. The first two activities are examples of

[19] Wang, *Chinese Patent Law*, 23.
[20] China Interview 020111, with an employee of the Foreign Affairs Department of the SIPO (Beijing).

TABLE 9.1. *Administrative versus Court Enforcement of Patent Infringement Disputes in China, 1996–2006*

Year	SIPO Patent Infringement Cases	Court Patent Infringement Cases	Ratio of Court Cases to SIPO Cases
1996	546	1,091	2
1997	591	1,024	1.73
1998	612	1,114	1.82
1999	791	1,420	1.79
2000	802	1,562	1.95
2001	977	1,567	1.6
2002	1,399	1,796	1.28
2003	1,448	2,212	1.53
2004	1,414	2,387	1.69
2005	1,360	2,947	2.17
2006	1,227	3,196	2.6

Sources: Zhongguo zhishi chanquan zhuangkuang 1997 (Report on IPR Protection in China in 1997) (Beijing: SIPO, 1998); *Zhongguo zhishi chanquan zhuangkuang 1999* (Report on IPR Protection in China in 1999) (Beijing: SIPO, 2000); *Zhonghua renmin gongheguo guojia zhishi chanquan ju nianbao 1999* (SIPO Annual Report 1999) (Beijing: SIPO, 2000); *Zhongguo zhishi chanquan nianjian 2000* (China IPR Yearbook 2000) (Beijing: Zhishi chanquan chubanshe, 2001), 249–250; *Zhongguo zhishi chanquan nianjian 2001–2002* (China IPR Yearbook 2001–2002) (Beijing: Zhishi chanquan chubanshe, 2002), 266; *Zhongguo zhishi chanquan nianjian 2003* (China IPR Yearbook 2003) (Beijing: Zhishi chanquan chubanshe, 2003), 236–237; *Zhongguo zhishi chanquan nianjian 2004* (China IPR Yearbook 2004) (Beijing: Zhishi chanquan chubanshe, 2004), 333–337; *Zhongguo zhishi chanquan nianjian 2005*, 260–310; *Zhongguo zhishi chanquan nianjian 2006* (China IPR Yearbook 2006) (Beijing: Zhishi chanquan chubanshe, 2006), 366–367, 405–406; *Zhongguo zhishi chanquan nianjian 2007*, 97, 504–506.

quasi-judicial enforcement, whereas the third is an example of campaign-style enforcement. We should note that the SIPO, in contrast to the bureaucracies engaged in trademark administrative protection, does not organize enforcement raids in response to complaints from right holders.

Unambiguously, patent examination, reexamination, and invalidation are rationalized. These activities are conducted in-house by the SIPO in Beijing and therefore benefit from centralization and from a very high level of specialization. The SIPO has as many as 1,700 patent examiners in Beijing, who handle patent applications with care and expertise matched by few other patent offices around the world.[21] Patent examination decisions are public, and their outcomes are published in the *SIPO Gazette*. Those who are dissatisfied with the decisions of the SIPO have several options. If a patent application is denied, inventors can appeal the decision internally through administrative reconsideration proceedings or can launch an administrative litigation lawsuit in a people's court; in addition, they can request that reexamination (*fushen*) of the patent application

[21] Zhu Jingwen, ed., *Zhongguo falü fazhan baogao*, 435.

be performed by the Patent Reexamination Board.[22] Anyone who wants to oppose the validity of a patent can make a request for invalidation (*wuxiao*) to the PRB. In turn, these invalidation decisions can be appealed in court. From 2004 to 2006, the rate of appeal for invalidation decisions by the PRB was 23.3 percent, suggesting that the SIPO does not unduly constrain right holders from appealing its decisions.[23] Appeals are heard at the Beijing No. 1 Intermediate People's Court, the Beijing High People's Court, and, occasionally, the Supreme People's Court. These courts are staffed by highly competent judges, who are unlikely to be corrupt or to suffer from political interference, in contrast to judges in lower-level courts.[24] Thus, the activity of patent examination, reexamination, and invalidation seems to be consistent, transparent, and fair.

Are patent infringement disputes resolved in consistent, transparent, and fair ways as well? All of these disputes are handled by the regional offices of the SIPO and therefore cannot benefit from the same level of specialization that characterizes examination, reexamination, and invalidation conducted in Beijing. However, pooled data for the 1985–2004 period indicate that more than 50 percent of the patent infringement disputes were handled by Guangdong, Zhejiang, Shandong, Shanghai, and Beijing (see GIS Map 9.1). These are rich coastal provinces with high levels of inventive activity. As such, their IPOs are more likely than the IPOs of poor provinces to have specialized personnel who can provide consistent adjudication of patent disputes.

Consistency is also enhanced by the existence of clear rules for resolving patent infringement disputes. For the most part, administrative infringement cases are resolved in a quasi-judicial manner. First, an official complaint (*tousu*) must be made. This complaint is then examined both for formal compliance with procedural requirements (e.g., whether the plaintiff has a patent registration license and a production certificate) and for evidence of infringement (e.g., whether the plaintiff has supplied a copy of the infringing product and an address for the infringer). If infringement is found to have taken place, the complaint will be accepted by one of the regional IPOs. The IPO then organizes an administrative mediation (*xingzheng tiaochu*), which will culminate with the issuance of an administrative decision (*xingzheng jueding shu*) specifying the final decision in the case, including the damage awards.[25]

Most patent infringement disputes feature administrative hearings (*tingzheng hui*) that are open to the public. Similarly, many of the decisions in

---

[22] Between 1985 and 2006, the SIPO accepted 14,882 requests for reexamination. *Zhongguo zhishi chanquan nianjian 2007*, 79.

[23] From 2004 to 2006, the PRB made 6,459 invalidation decisions, 1,506 of which were appealed. Calculated from *Zhongguo zhishi chanquan nianjian 2005*, 76–77; *Zhongguo zhishi chanquan nianjian 2006*, 89–90; and *Zhongguo zhishi chanquan nianjian 2007*, 79–80.

[24] Mei Y. Gechlik, *Protecting Intellectual Property Rights in Chinese Courts: An Analysis of Recent Patent Judgments*, Carnegie Paper No. 78 (Washington, DC: Carnegie Endowment for International Peace, 2007).

[25] China Interview 010718A and China Interview 020129D, with the director general of the Shanghai IPO (Shanghai).

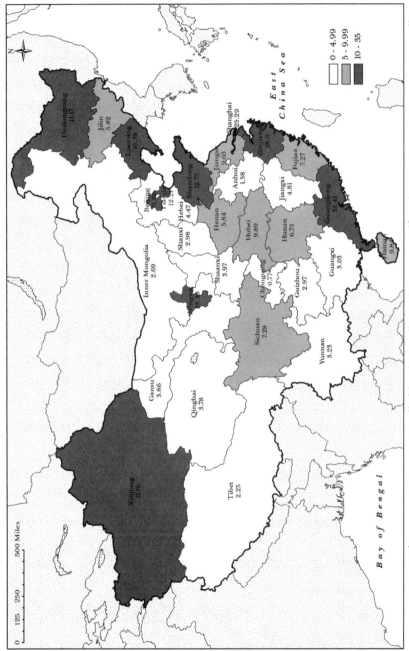

East
China Sea

☐ 0 - 4.99
▨ 5 - 9.99
■ 10 - 35

Heilongjiang
11.17

Jilin
5.82

Liaoning
10.33

Shanghai
25.29

Jiangsu
9.63

Zhejiang
28.9

Beijing
Tianjin
12.2

Shandong
12.73

Anhui
1.58

Fujian
7.27

Hebei
4.47

Henan
5.84

Jiangxi
4.81

Inner Mongolia
2.69

Shanxi
2.98

Hubei
9.89

Hunan
6.73

Guangdong
31.41

Shaanxi
3.97

Ningxia
3.58

Chongqing
0.77

Guizhou
2.97

Guangxi
3.03

Taiwan
9.8

Gansu
3.86

Sichuan
7.28

Yunnan
3.23

Qinghai
3.78

Xinjiang
11.76

Tibet
2.25

Bay of Bengal

N

500 Miles

0   125   250

MAP 9.1. Patent Infringement Disputes Handled by the Intellectual Property Offices by Province, 1985–2004 (per million people)

these disputes are publicly available on the Web sites of the regional IPOs or in various legal compendia. Although the SIPO does not publish data on the frequency of appeal of patent infringement decisions, the high level of patent-related litigation in China should reassure us that right holders do not face undue difficulties in appealing the outcomes of patent infringement disputes. Thus, on the basis of the existing evidence we can conclude that patent infringement disputes are characterized by rationalized enforcement, similar to that in patent examination, reexamination, and invalidation.

What about enforcement in cases of patent counterfeiting and passing off? In contrast to the quasi-judicial enforcement in cases of patent infringement disputes, which is initiated after a formal complaint, local IPOs usually proactively investigate counterfeiting and passing off (*zhudong chachu*) or provide campaign-style enforcement. Typically IPO officers visit the large markets and conduct spot-checks of the patent numbers printed on numerous patented goods. The numbers are cross-checked against a database. When discrepancies are found (i.e., the patent number is not registered to the person selling the goods or the patent has already expired), violations are deemed to have occurred. As interviewees told me, most cases of passing off involve patents that have expired and therefore should have entered the public domain, rather than allowing the original patent holders to continue to reap the benefits that accrue from an extended period of patent exclusivity.[26] Overall, the task of identifying cases of passing off patents is far less demanding than that of resolving patent infringement disputes and is thus shunned by employees in the local IPOs, who see themselves as technocrats rather than as bureaucrats engaged in mundane law enforcement. A similarly disinterested attitude exists toward counterfeiting cases, which account for less than 1 percent of the enforcement activity of the local IPOs.[27]

We can gain some additional insights into patent counterfeiting and patent passing off by examining pooled enforcement data for the 1985–2004 period. Regression analysis reveals that (controlling for population) investigations of patent passing off and patent counterfeiting are not sensitive to the inventiveness of a province (as measured by the number of patents granted by the SIPO to inventors from the province) and are only weakly correlated with the level of wealth of a province (as measured by gross provincial product). This is in sharp contrast to regression results for patent infringement disputes during the 1985–2004 period, where the correlations with inventiveness and wealth are extremely high (t values of 13.15 and 8.29, respectively).[28] Even though they

---

[26] China Interview 041227, with the director general of the Beijing IPO (Beijing); China Interview 010718A and China Interview 020129D, with the director general of the Shanghai IPO (Shanghai).

[27] *Zhongguo zhishi chanquan nianjian 2007*, 504–506.

[28] These results are from bivariate regressions. The total number of patents granted to each province and gross provincial product are correlated at 0.84, thus not allowing us to run multivariate regressions including both variables as predictors of the number of patent infringement disputes handled in the individual provinces.

are conducted by the same agency, the two types of enforcement are substantially different (they are correlated only at 0.4) and display different patterns of geographical variation (see GIS Maps 9.1 and 9.2). The weakness of the statistical models for passing off and counterfeiting highlights that in contrast to enforcement in patent infringement disputes, enforcement in cases of patent passing off and patent counterfeiting is somewhat random and unpredictable. This is not surprising when we keep in mind that we are dealing with campaign-style enforcement.

Is this enforcement transparent and fair? We have no statistics on the proportion of decisions in passing off and counterfeiting cases that are made publicly available. We should not expect a high volume of public hearings in this area, as these cases are usually decided on the spot and are not subject to lengthy formal administrative proceedings. Similarly, we do not have statistics on the proportion of these cases that culminate in administrative reconsideration and administrative litigation. Given doubts about the consistency and transparency with which such cases are handled, we cannot definitively conclude that enforcement in cases of patent counterfeiting and patent passing off is procedurally fair.

In sum, we have evidence that two of the three main activities of the SIPO are rationalized. Why is it that rationalization exists for enforcement in patent examination, reexamination, and invalidation, as well as for enforcement in patent infringement disputes, but enforcement in patent counterfeiting and passing off does not seem to be rationalized? The key difference is that in the first two areas, the SIPO shares its enforcement jurisdiction with the courts. This presents right holders with an additional patent protection avenue and incentivizes SIPO bureaucrats to resolve grievances to the satisfaction of right holders and thus to avoid being subject to oversight by the courts. This system of checks and balances increases the quality of enforcement provided by the SIPO. In addition, both areas are technically complex, thus raising the evidentiary demands and making written decisions de rigueur. It is more difficult to engage in arbitrary enforcement when a written document (that later can be appealed) exists. Finally, enforcement of patent examination, reexamination, and invalidation is centralized in Beijing, and enforcement of patent infringement disputes tends to be concentrated in the rich coastal provinces. This means that these two activities benefit from the expertise of employees at the highest rungs of the administrative ladder.

In contrast, patent passing off and patent counterfeiting cases are technically simple, tend to be subject to campaign-style enforcement, and are not concentrated in the coastal provinces. Furthermore, the SIPO has exclusive jurisdiction over enforcement in this domain, with the courts playing no role at all. On the basis of the available data, we cannot conclude that enforcement in this domain is rationalized. This suggests that clear legal mandates and an exclusive administrative jurisdiction over an issue area are only a step in the right direction. For enforcement to be rationalized, it seems that the administrative agencies should share their enforcement jurisdiction with the courts and should also be

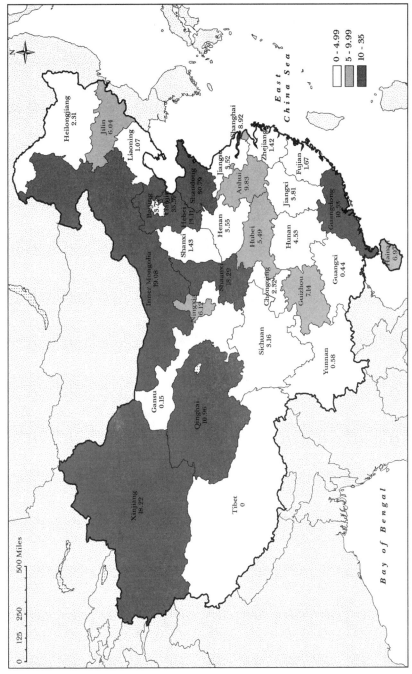

MAP 9.2. Patent Passing Off and Counterfeiting Cases Handled by the Intellectual Property Offices by Province, 1985–2004 (per million people)

centralized (or quasi-centralized, as in the case of the SIPO). The case of Customs is also instructive in this regard. Although Customs is centralized and has exclusive jurisdiction over the border protection of IPR, the absence of supervision by the courts or the police has lowered the quality of enforcement it provides.

Police and Customs Enforcement

In China, both Customs and criminal enforcement are rare for patent cases. For example, in 2005 the General Administration of Customs handled thirty-seven patent cases (3 percent of its total caseload), whereas just one patent case reached the criminal courts in 2004, constituting 0.2 percent of the criminal IPR caseload.[29] The unwillingness of Customs to handle such cases can be attributed to the complexity of ascertaining patent infringement. For similar reasons, the police are mainly a reactive enforcer in the area of patents. The low volume of criminal cases also reflects the fact that the SIPO transferred only fifteen cases for criminal prosecution to the Ministry of Public Security in 2005, thus making it unlikely that there would be many criminal patent cases in that year.[30] Fundamentally, neither Customs nor the police have an interest in increasing the level of enforcement they currently supply in this area. For all intents and purposes, patent enforcement is provided by the civil courts and by one administrative agency, both of which are at least partially rationalized.

CASE STUDY: VIAGRA ANTICOUNTERFEITING ACTIVITY

Chapters 7 and 8 presented case studies of trademark and copyright protection based on datasets of actual enforcement on the ground for two specific product groups: cigarettes (Chapter 7) and digital media (Chapter 8). Without these case studies, we might have concluded that the State Administration for Industry and Commerce (SAIC) and the National Copyright Administration of China (NCAC) were the only agencies with jurisdiction over the enforcement of trademarks and copyrights. The case studies reveal that the enforcement dynamics on the ground are much more complex, with multiple agencies sharing the trademark and copyright enforcement portfolios. Does the same situation exist in patents? Can it be that the State Intellectual Property Office, though a provider of rationalized enforcement, is only one of many agencies with jurisdiction over patent protection? In order to test this possibility, with the help of a research assistant, I compiled a newspaper article dataset on pharmaceuticals counterfeiting. As many pharmaceuticals are counterfeited in China, I chose to focus on one particular brand – the erectile dysfunction drug Viagra.

Viagra is a blockbuster drug owned by Pfizer, a U.S. pharmaceutical manufacturer. In 2001, Pfizer successfully obtained a product patent in China for

---

[29] *Statistics for China Customs IPR Seizures (1996–2005),* http://english.customs.gov.cn (accessed October 28, 2008) and *Zhongguo zhishi chanquan nianjian 2005,* 306.

[30] *China's Intellectual Property Rights in 2005,* http://www.ipr.gov.cn (accessed June 26, 2006).

Viagra's active ingredient, sildenafil citrate (patent CN 94192386.X). More than a dozen Chinese companies that already held process patents for sildenafil citrate immediately challenged Pfizer's patent on the grounds of insufficient disclosure.[31] The PRB invalidated the patent in 2004, leading Pfizer to lodge a complaint against the SIPO at the No. 1 Intermediate People's Court in Beijing. Under heavy foreign pressure, Pfizer won the case in 2006, but the Chinese manufacturers of sildenafil citrate appealed the court decision. In 2007 the Beijing High People's Court upheld the decision of the intermediate court and reaffirmed Pfizer's patent over sildenafil citrate.

Nevertheless, this may not be the end of Pfizer's troubles in China. As of October 2007, local manufacturers were still planning to launch another attack on Pfizer's patent.[32] This time, the main challenge was the lack of an inventive step.[33] What is ultimately at stake here is who will be able to produce sildenafil citrate in China. If the Pfizer patent is successfully invalidated (as happened in the United Kingdom, for example), then anyone with a process patent will be able to produce the active ingredient in Viagra but will not be able to market the drug using the Viagra brand name, which is a registered trademark of Pfizer. Regardless of whether Pfizer keeps its patent, it will still be able to stop other companies from using the valuable Viagra trademark, over which it maintains full control.

Drugs are complex products, which are simultaneously protected by trademarks (in this case, Viagra), design patents (for the special shape of the Viagra pill, and for its specific packaging), process patents (for the method of producing the active ingredient, sildenafil citrate), and, finally, product patents (for the use of sildenafil citrate to treat erectile dysfunction). It is important to stress that counterfeit Viagra sold in China in the early 2000s did not infringe on any patents. Pfizer had no design patent on Viagra, and its product patent was in dispute. Under these circumstances, counterfeiters could use a variety of channels to obtain sildenafil citrate legitimately from one of Pfizer's local Chinese competitors who had process patents for its production. Of course, although they were not infringing on Pfizer's sildenafil citrate patent, these counterfeiters were infringing on the Viagra trademark, since even if a drug contained legitimately sourced sildenafil citrate, no company apart from Pfizer had the right to market the drug under the Viagra name. Sometimes, counterfeit pills that did not even contain sildenafil citrate were still marketed as Viagra, thus infringing both trademark and product safety laws. What should be stressed is that technically the SIPO had no grounds to become involved in enforcement in cases of

---

[31] Article 26 of the Chinese Patent Law specifies that a patent application must disclose sufficient information so that someone "skilled in the art" can reproduce the invention. This is a standard provision in the patent legislation of most countries.

[32] Emma Barraclough, "Pfizer Victorious over Viagra in China," *Managing Intellectual Property*, no. 173 (October 2007), 10.

[33] Sildenafil citrate was first developed to treat heart disease, rather than erectile dysfunction. Some jurisdictions may not consider the new use of an already existing chemical compound to be as inventive (and thus worthy of a product patent) as the synthesis of a new molecule.

Viagra counterfeiting, which was a trademark counterfeiting and a product safety issue, rather than a patent infringement problem. Viagra anticounterfeiting is thus a good test of the degree to which the SIPO respects the letter of the law and does not enter areas that are beyond its jurisdiction. The specially compiled Viagra enforcement dataset allows us to track SIPO's involvement in this issue.

The Viagra Enforcement Dataset

The Viagra enforcement dataset was constructed from newspaper reports on enforcement in cases of production and sale of counterfeit drugs bearing the Viagra brand name. Hundreds of newspaper articles were read in order eventually to identify forty-one reports containing information on forty-two specific enforcement actions conducted in China between August 1999 and November 2005.[34] The final dataset allows us to make observations about the geographical distribution of enforcement, agency participation in enforcement, patterns of interagency cooperation, and the likelihood of criminals' receiving appropriate punishment for their misdemeanors.

Geographical Distribution of Enforcement

The forty-two enforcement cases in the dataset were spread out across seventeen Chinese provinces. Most of the raids took place in Guangdong (eight raids), Jiangsu (seven raids), Zhejiang (six raids), and Shanghai (three raids). Beijing, Hubei, and Hainan each had two raids, while Shanxi, Liaoning, Anhui, Shandong, Henan, Guangxi, Chongqing, Yunnan, and Xinjiang each had one raid. Three raids were interprovincial, taking place in Tianjin/Jiangsu, Henan/Tianjin, and Shanghai/Zhejiang. The absence of published provincial-level data on pharmaceuticals anticounterfeiting enforcement by the different agencies with jurisdiction over this domain prevents us from drawing conclusions regarding the representativeness of our sample. However, it is readily apparent that provinces that in general provide low levels of IPR enforcement are missing from this dataset as well (Gansu, Guizhou, Inner Mongolia, Qinghai, Shaanxi, and Tibet). Similarly, it is not surprising that Guangdong comes out on top, as it is often one of the most vigorous enforcers of IPR laws nationwide. Therefore, we have no reason to believe that the geographical distribution of the enforcement actions represented in the dataset is radically different from the actual distribution of Viagra anticounterfeiting enforcement.

---

[34] One of the reports describes two enforcement actions. Therefore, the dataset contains descriptions of 42 discrete enforcement actions. The specific breakdown of enforcement actions by year is as follows: 1999: 1, 2000: 1, 2001: 8, 2002: 3, 2003: 6, 2004: 11, 2005: 12. This pattern is consistent with the stepping up of the anticounterfeiting campaign in 2001, its subsequent relaxation in 2002–2003, and the renewed enforcement zeal in 2004–2005.

Agency Participation in Enforcement

The dataset reveals that nine different agencies participated in Viagra anti-counterfeiting enforcement: the State Food and Drug Administration (SFDA), the Ministry of Health, the Public Security Bureau (PSB), the SAIC, the Technical Supervision Bureau (TSB), the Anticounterfeiting Office, the Comprehensive Pharmaceuticals Anticounterfeiting Office, Customs, and Airport Security. In terms of specific enforcement activity, the SFDA, although legally designated as the lead enforcer for cases of pharmaceutical counterfeiting, was involved in only 50 percent of the raids. Quite surprisingly, the PSB participated in 62 percent of all raids, thus enforcing more actively than the SFDA. The Ministry of Health, though not supposed to handle pharmaceuticals counterfeiting after the creation of the State Drug Administration in 1998, still participated in three raids. The involvement of other agencies in enforcement was episodic: Customs, the Anticounterfeiting Office, and the SAIC participated in three raids each; the TSB took part in two; and Airport Security and Shenzhen's Futian District Comprehensive Pharmaceuticals Anticounterfeiting Office each initiated one enforcement action. As expected, the SIPO was not involved in enforcement in cases of counterfeit Viagra, thus following the letter of the law. We should emphasize that had the Viagra cases involved patent counterfeiting or patent passing off, we would expect the SIPO to have been involved, as required by law.

Patterns of Interagency Cooperation

Did agencies enforce alone or in cooperation with others? Twenty-five raids were single-agency raids, most of which were conducted by the PSB and the SFDA. In two of these single-agency raids, the agency was represented by an upper and a lower level: one involved cooperation between a provincial- and a city-level PSB, whereas the other one was carried out by a city- and a district-level Food and Drug Bureau. Seventeen raids were conducted by multiple agencies: eleven involved two agencies, three involved three agencies, two involved four agencies, and one raid was conducted by five agencies. The PSB was involved in sixteen of the seventeen multiagency raids. Usually, the PSB was located at the same level as the other agencies participating in enforcement (e.g., the provincial PSB cooperated with the provincial Food and Drug Administration). Unfortunately, the dataset does not provide information whether the PSB initiated the multiagency raids or rather was invited to join by the other agencies. However, on the basis of evidence presented in previous chapters, we can surmise that the PSB participated in enforcement as a supporting unit (*peihe bumen*), rather than as the unit in charge (*zhuguan bumen*). We can only conclude that most of the time, when confronted with cases of pharmaceuticals counterfeiting, agencies enforce alone rather than in concert with others.

Frequency of Criminal Punishment

As outlined in Chapter 6, pharmaceutical counterfeiting can be a criminal offense when it endangers the health of consumers or leads to their death. Although the dataset contains information on the monetary value of twenty-two seizures (twenty of which met the criminal liability threshold), there are only four reports of individuals who were sentenced to imprisonment (ranging from one to ten years). In addition to incarceration, criminal fines ranging from 10,000 yuan to 700,000 yuan were imposed on some defendants. All in all, criminal punishment seems to be unusual among the cases reported in the dataset.

In short, as many as nine different agencies enforce in this domain. However, the SIPO is not one of them. The SIPO eschews enforcement because the relevant laws do not allow it to participate in Viagra trademark anticounterfeiting activities. Unlike administrative agencies enforcing in copyrights and trademarks, the SIPO seems to respect the letter of the law.

CONCLUSION: BUREAUCRATIC RATIONALIZATION IN PATENT
ENFORCEMENT IN CHINA

China's post-1978 reform period has been guided by the idea of the Four Modernizations (*sige xiandaihua*): modernization of agriculture, industry, science and technology, and national defense. Modernization depends in large part on cutting-edge technology. Although China, much like Japan in the 1950s and 1960s, was initially involved in copying foreign technology, as the reform era progressed, the top leadership attached more importance to developing indigenous Chinese inventions. As demonstrated in this chapter, most of the patents that are currently issued in China are awarded to Chinese inventors rather than to foreigners. More tellingly, China is now second only to the United States in terms of spending on research and development (R&D).[35] This highlights the importance that the country attaches to R&D in general, and to patent protection in particular. Top leaders like Presidents Jiang Zemin and Hu Jintao make regular visits to the SIPO in order to demonstrate their support of patent activity. In this vein, in 2006 President Hu Jintao pledged to transform China into an "innovative country" by 2020.[36]

Strategic leadership concerns over China's future course of development only partially account for its exemplary patent protection record. This study has argued that the main explanation for differences in IPR enforcement patterns lies elsewhere: namely, unlike trademarks and copyrights, patents have been free of both domestic and foreign pressures for enforcement. Despite recent attempts by the U.S. pharmaceutical and automobile industries to put

[35] Geoff Dyer, "China Overtakes Japan on R&D," *The Financial Times*, December 3, 2006, http://www.ft.com/cms/s/da4ed9f2–82fa-11db-a38a-0000779e2340.html (accessed December 18, 2006).
[36] As cited in Gechlik, *Protecting Intellectual Property Rights*, 20.

pressure on the SIPO in connection with specific patentability decisions,[37] patents have never been subject to crisis-mode enforcement as copyrights and trademarks have. Crisis-mode enforcement makes it easier for multiple bureaucracies to provide duplicative, inconsistent, unfair, and nontransparent IPR protection. The absence of pressure has allowed patent enforcement to move in the direction of rationalization.

Patent enforcement is unusual in three additional regards. First, the SIPO has evolved into a competent bureaucracy, staffed with highly trained employees who provide consistent, transparent, and fair enforcement. Second, over time the IPR tribunals have come to play a dominant role in patent infringement disputes, thus presenting an important blueprint for transferring the main responsibility for enforcement in a specific domain from an administrative agency to the courts. Third, the SIPO is much more open to administrative reconsideration and administrative litigation than either the trademark or the copyright bureaucracies.

Patent enforcement provides us with two additional general insights, which are important for this study. First, exclusive jurisdictions and clear mandates may not be sufficient for rationalization to emerge. While the SIPO has a clearly defined exclusive jurisdiction over patent counterfeiting and patent passing off, enforcement in this area is not rationalized. What seems to be necessary is for an administrative agency to share its enforcement mandate with the courts, as is the case for patent infringement disputes, as well as for patent application, reexamination, and invalidation. Second, the state is a key actor in setting up the proper regulatory framework within which rationalized enforcement can emerge. Agencies cannot simply enter an enforcement domain without the encouragement of the state, which delineates the scope of their permissible activity and polices them when they overstep their bounds. Trademarks and patents lie at the two ends of the spectrum of effective regulation: in trademarks, the state has actively encouraged multiple agencies to step in and supply high-volume crisis-mode enforcement, whereas in patents a single agency alongside the courts was entrusted to provide a small volume of rationalized enforcement.

---

[37] In addition to the Viagra case, the Chery QQ/Spark GM minicar case has been the source of a major controversy. See "GM Charges Chery for Alleged Mini-Car Piracy," *China Daily*, December 18, 2004, http://www.chinadaily.com.cn/english/doc/2004-12/18/content_401235. htm (accessed August 12, 2008).

PART IV

CONCLUSION

10

State Capacity and IPR

We cannot understand state capacity unless we know what the state *does*, and whether it does it *well*. The Chinese state is an enormous machinery of bureaucracies, courts, and police that enforces hundreds of laws and regulations. To date, we know surprisingly little about how this machinery is organized and actually operates. It is often difficult to find answers even to basic questions, such as which Chinese agencies enforce a given law or policy. A more important question, and one whose answer is even less well understood, is whether the machinery of the state is able to supply high-quality enforcement. This study answers these questions for the area of IPR. Although the main findings are derived from IPR, they have broad implications for our understanding of the Chinese state. First, the study develops a methodology for measuring the volume and quality of enforcement, one that can be used to assess state capacity in areas outside IPR. Second, the study presents general theoretical arguments about the conditions under which rationalized enforcement, and, by extension, the rule of law, may arise.

Several findings about state capacity emerge from this study. The key finding is that the presence of multiple bureaucracies with poorly defined and overlapping jurisdictions is a serious obstacle to the emergence of rationalized enforcement. A second, related finding is that, although a high volume of IPR enforcement already exists in China, in general this enforcement is uncoordinated, duplicative, inefficient, and unaccountable. The central state is aware of this problem, but it has allowed duplication to persist, not least because it depends on the different agencies to provide quick campaign-style enforcement when crises arise. Attempts to reform this system through centralization and coordination have been unsuccessful. So rationalization has emerged in areas where the center has been able to establish *new* enforcement bodies with clearly specified enforcement mandates. Progress toward rationalization in these admittedly delimited areas occurred without pressure from either foreign or domestic groups.

Bureaucratic complexity means that the Chinese state is primarily reactive. It can provide a high volume of enforcement of IPR laws when it is forced to do so by a domestic crisis or by foreign pressure. However, there are limits to the center's control over the quality of enforcement. The existing bureaucracies resist change, especially when change involves restricting or fundamentally altering their mandates. So in areas where there are complex enforcement arrangements already in place, the quality of protection tends to remain low. To the extent that the central government has chosen to be proactive and design clear rules for the emergence of rationalized enforcement, it has been easier to create rationalization in new areas (and to regulate from scratch) than in ones governed by already entrenched bureaucratic interests.

FINDINGS

Although this book focuses on China, it is also a comparative study of the state's capacity to protect IPR beyond the Chinese context. A basic finding is that the Customs, civil, and criminal IPR protection options tend to be similar across the countries analyzed. In all six countries, the Customs administration has exclusive jurisdiction over the border protection of IPR, and the courts of law provide civil IPR protection. Criminal IPR protection is also largely similar across countries: the police, the Procuratorate (the district attorney's office), and the criminal courts all have enforcement responsibility in this domain.[1] By and large, the enforcement responsibilities of Customs and the civil courts are clearly defined. Even in the area of criminal protection, where multiple enforcers exist, the police, the Procuratorate, and the criminal courts tend to have discrete enforcement mandates. In stark contrast, administrative IPR protection arrangements are much more variable across the six countries considered in this book. The United States has a single administrative enforcer, France two, the Czech Republic three, Taiwan four, and Russia five. In China, the administrative arrangements are extremely complex, with at least twelve different administrative agencies sharing the IPR portfolio.

Table 10.1 presents aggregate statistics for the amount of IPR enforcement provided by each of the countries examined in this study. The data are for 2004 and have been normalized by dividing the raw enforcement indicators by the population of each country. China provides the highest level of per capita administrative enforcement among the countries analyzed here. The dominance of administrative enforcement reflects the influence of domestic and foreign pressure groups seeking a high volume of enforcement. However, the allotment of so many resources to administrative enforcement has led to very low levels of enforcement through other channels. As administrative agencies in China are least likely to provide rationalized enforcement, the marginalization of Customs, civil, and criminal enforcement has negative implications for the eventual rationalization of IPR enforcement.

The key findings of this study concern the possibility of rationalized enforcement in China. We should stress that enforcement varies. As defined in Chapter 1,

---

[1] China, Russia, Taiwan, and France have multiple police forces, as detailed in Chapter 6.

TABLE 10.1. *Cross-National IPR Enforcement Efforts in 2004 (per million people)*

Country	Piracy Rate	Civil Court Cases (first instance)	Customs Enforcement	Administrative Enforcement	Criminal Enforcement
China	High	7.2	0.8	939	0.8
Russia	High	5.2	1.1	10	13.4
Taiwan	Medium	16.5	14.7	63.2	183
Czech Republic	Medium	ND	51.9	201.5	88.3
France	Medium	ND	106.6	45.2	36.9
U.S.	Low	32.5	24.8	0.1	1.2

Source: Yearbooks.

there are five kinds: judicial enforcement, quasi-judicial administrative enforcement, proactive administrative enforcement, administrative enforcement (raids) in response to complaints, and campaign-style administrative enforcement. Proactive administrative enforcement and raids organized in response to complaints are provided mainly by the bureaucracies engaged in trademark enforcement, whereas campaign-style enforcement exists for all three IPR subtypes, but it is especially prominent for trademarks and copyrights.[2] In the area of IPR, only the judicial enforcement provided by the IPR tribunals of the civil courts and the quasi-judicial administrative enforcement provided by the State Intellectual Property Office (SIPO) (and, to a certain extent, by the National Copyright Administration of China [NCAC]) come close to satisfying the requirements for consistency, transparency, and procedural fairness. The three other kinds of enforcement suffer from various inefficiencies.

On the basis of an examination of the five kinds of enforcement, we can derive some insights about the conditions that facilitate the rise of rationalized enforcement in China. In terms of judicial enforcement, the sole requirement is that enforcement should be provided by the IPR tribunals of the civil courts: these tribunals operate consistently, transparently, and fairly. In the area of quasi-judicial administrative enforcement, the parameters for rationalization are more stringent, since the administrative agencies doing this work are unlikely on their own to embrace the principles of rationalized enforcement. It is especially important that the responsibilities of the administrative agencies should be clearly defined and right holders should also have unimpeded access to the courts, which can then be used to hold the agencies accountable. In practice, it is easiest to meet these requirements when a single agency is charged with providing administrative enforcement in a certain domain. According to these criteria, rationalization exists for patent examination, reexamination, and

[2] The General Administration of Customs and the Public Security Bureau (PSB) may also provide proactive administrative enforcement, but only rarely.

invalidation, as well as for patent infringement disputes. The SIPO handles these cases professionally and does not limit appeals through the courts. However, cases of patent counterfeiting and patent passing off fall within the exclusive jurisdictional domain of the SIPO. The courts are not involved in these cases, and quality is affected. Some oversight by the courts may therefore be necessary for the institutionalization of rationalized quasi-judicial enforcement.

Proactive administrative enforcement, raids organized in response to complaints, and campaign-style enforcement are not rationalized. These kinds of enforcement are typically performed by agencies that exploit their poorly defined mandates to shirk or to provide a minimal level of enforcement. Furthermore, these agencies are unaccountable to those they serve, since right holders face undue difficulties if they attempt to challenge the agencies in court. Lack of accountability makes this enforcement unpredictable, nontransparent, and, at least sometimes, corrupt. Customs enforcement in China is a good case in point. Although the General Administration of Customs is a centralized agency with exclusive jurisdiction over the border protection of IPR, it provides a low volume of enforcement, which, although consistent, does not appear to be transparent and fair.

Enforcement may be complicated further by two additional factors: jurisdictional overlap and decentralization. The administrative enforcement of trademarks illustrates the negative effects of the presence of multiple enforcers with poorly defined and overlapping jurisdictions. These enforcement agencies are also decentralized and operate under conditions of poor accountability. The resulting enforcement is uncertain, wasteful, and ineffective. Campaign-style copyright enforcement is similarly affected by poorly defined mandates, overlapping jurisdictions, and low accountability. Nevertheless, copyright campaigns show a somewhat higher quality than campaign-style trademark enforcement, proactive trademark enforcement, or trademark enforcement in response to complaints. This reflects the fact that fewer bureaucracies actively participate in copyright campaigns than in trademark enforcement. The quality of enforcement is also improved because the NCAC, one of the main copyright enforcers, has a shallow reach, thus facilitating central monitoring of provincial-level bureaucrats. Campaign-style enforcement in patent counterfeiting and patent passing off also has a higher quality than trademark enforcement. This kind of patent enforcement is conducted exclusively by the SIPO, which, like the NCAC, has a shallow reach and is thus relatively immune to the endemic perversions of campaign-style enforcement.

International comparisons illustrate that overlap on its own need not affect the quality of enforcement. Overlap exists in France, Taiwan, and the Czech Republic, but it does not present enforcement problems there. Three significant differences between China and these countries account for this outcome. First, in contrast to China, the enforcement mandates in these countries are clearly defined. Second, the bureaucracies are not decentralized. Third, the bureaucracies are subject to strict accountability standards. This suggests that overlap in China must be compounded by other problems, cumulatively lowering the quality of enforcement.

The central state in China is aware of the staggering complexities and inefficiencies that characterize most IPR enforcement. The government has tried to raise the quality of enforcement by selectively centralizing some agencies, and by coordinating the activities of others. These measures have improved monitoring and have increased the accountability of bureaucrats. However, to date no agency apart from the State Tobacco Monopoly Administration (STMA) is fully centralized from the national level down. Some agencies, like the NCAC and the SIPO, are quasi-centralized, because they penetrate only down to the provincial and major-city levels: although the national-level agency has no control over the budgets of the provincial-level agencies, it is still capable of monitoring them with relative ease. Since 1998, several agencies with a sub-provincial reach have been subject to centralization from the province down (*sheng yixia chuizhi*): the State Administration of Industry and Commerce (SAIC), the General Administration of Quality Supervision, Inspection, and Quarantine (AQSIC), the State Food and Drug Administration (SFDA), and the General Administration of Customs. This type of partial centralization allows the provincial level to determine the budget and personnel of lower-level agencies. Despite these attempts at centralization, however, a number of the IPR enforcement agencies remain fully decentralized: the ministries of culture, health, agriculture, and public security are all decentralized. As laudable as the attempts at centralization have been, the quality of enforcement will improve only if such efforts are accompanied by the successful coordination of the activities of the various enforcement agencies. Such coordination has been attempted since 1998, when the respective mandates of the SAIC and the Administration for Technical Supervision (precursor to the AQSIQ) were clarified; however, this initiative was unsuccessful.

After several rounds of government restructuring, and the eruption of a dozen major IPR and product-quality standards, enforcement remains almost as chaotic as it was in the mid-1990s. Why? The central government cannot successfully coordinate the work of the IPR agencies because it often needs them to provide enforcement quickly in response to crisis situations. When babies die after consuming counterfeit or substandard formula (as they did in two separate high-profile scandals in 2004 and 2008), the central government must take swift measures to step up enforcement as a way to restore confidence among consumers. Even though the scandals are rooted partly in the poor oversight of the various uncoordinated agencies that share the trademark protection portfolio, these same agencies are the only ones capable of delivering a fast response in times of crisis. The government therefore has repeatedly postponed the tricky but necessary task of clarifying their mandates and coordinating their work. In the end, the central government cannot escape its own bureaucracies, on which it depends to implement laws and regulations. Bureaucracies *are* the state, and they dislike change. Not surprisingly, progress toward rationalization of IPR enforcement has emerged only in new areas where the central government can establish new rules, not in areas where the government would have to reform already existing bureaucracies.

EMPIRICAL IMPLICATIONS

Casting a Wider Net: Jurisdictional Overlap beyond IPR

Far from being a phenomenon limited only to IPR, jurisdictional overlap exists in many other policy areas. We do not yet know precisely what these are, since students of Chinese politics have not produced a complete map of the organization of the state across issue areas. There are at least two areas beyond IPR where such overlap causes problems: environmental protection and mine safety.[3] We also know that there is at least one area in which the problem of jurisdictional overlap was acknowledged and successfully resolved: securities regulation. I will briefly examine environmental protection and securities regulation to illustrate two divergent approaches taken by the central government toward overlap.

Existing research on environmental protection inevitably focuses on the activities of the State Environmental Protection Agency (SEPA) and therefore creates the mistaken impression that the SEPA is the only agency charged with enforcement in this area.[4] However, research I conducted in 2004–2005 indicates that the environmental protection domain is as cluttered as trademark protection.[5] The SEPA shares the environmental protection portfolio with at least eleven other agencies.[6] To readers of this book on IPR protection, the resulting problems will seem familiar. The agencies have poorly defined enforcement mandates that allow them to shirk when faced with difficult cases and to engage in unnecessary, duplicative enforcement when dealing with easy ones. Overlap also hampers successful interagency coordination. Until 2008, an

---

[3] On mine safety, see Fubing Su, "Centralization and Decentralization: Agency Problem and Institutional Change in China's Coal Mining," paper presented at the conference *Reconfiguring the Party-State: The Shifting Locus of Power in Reform-Era China*, Fairbank Center for East Asian Research, Harvard University, May 19–20, 2006, and Tim Wright, "State Capacity in Contemporary China: 'Closing the Pits and Reducing Coal Production,'" *Journal of Contemporary China*, no. 51 (2007), 173–194.

[4] Barbara Sinkule and Leonard Ortolano, *Implementing Environmental Policy in China* (Westport, CT: Praeger, 1995); Xiaoying Ma and Leonard Ortolano, *Environmental Regulation in China: Institutions, Enforcement, and Compliance* (Lanham, MD: Rowman & Littlefield, 2000); Mara Warwick, "Environmental Information Collection and Enforcement at Small-Scale Enterprises in Shanghai: The Role of Bureaucracy, Legislatures and Citizens" (Ph.D. Dissertation, Department of Civil and Environmental Engineering, Stanford University, 2003); and Elizabeth Economy, *The River Runs Black: The Environmental Challenge to China's Future* (Ithaca, NY: Cornell University Press, 2004). See Andrew Mertha, *China's Water Warriors: Citizen Action and Policy Change* (Ithaca, NY: Cornell University Press, 2008), for a list of several bureaucracies regulating the environmental impact of dams.

[5] In 2004–2005, I conduced over fifty interviews with bureaucrats, lawyers, and NGOs engaged in environmental protection in China. The interviews took place in Beijing, Shanghai, Guangzhou, Haikou, and Dalian.

[6] These agencies are the State Development Reform Commission, the Ministry of Construction, the SAIC, the AQSIQ, the Ministry of Land and Resources, the Ministry of Water Resources, the State Oceanographic Administration, the State Forestry Agency, the Ministry of Agriculture (MOA), the Ministry of Health (MOH), and the Ministry of Commerce.

additional complicating factor existed: the SEPA was decentralized. Local environmental protection bureaus (EPBs) were subject to dual leadership (*shuangchong lingdao*) by their SEPA administrative superiors and by local governments, with the local governments having primary responsibility for personnel and budgets.[7] This arrangement has been a breeding ground for local protectionism, whereby local governments and local EPBs shielded heavily polluting enterprises from enforcement. In short, decentralization allowed economic development goals to be privileged over effective environmental protection.

As in the area of IPR, scandals have prompted the central government to attempt to improve environmental protection through centralization and coordination. A series of environmental disasters in the early 2000s eventually led to the decision to transform the SEPA into a cabinet-level ministry, to rename it the Ministry of Environmental Protection (MEP) (Huanjing baohu bu), and to centralize it. However, at this time, the budgets and personnel allocations of the local EPBs continue to be determined by the local governments rather than by the MEP.[8] Therefore, one must remain cautious about the possibility of change, especially considering that the State Council has not adjusted (*tiaozheng*) the points of jurisdictional overlap between the MEP and other agencies. Centralization cannot improve environmental protection unless budgetary control is taken away from the local governments and the activities of the various agencies sharing the environmental protection portfolio are successfully coordinated.

Securities regulation offers a different story. Here, in contrast to environmental protection, centralization and coordination were implemented with success. The securities market in China has undergone very significant changes over the last two decades. It has moved from a heavily decentralized structure with multiple regulators to a centralized system with a single regulator.[9] In 1998, the China Securities Regulatory Commission (CSRC) was elevated to ministerial rank and the Securities Law was passed, establishing the CSRC as the single (and centralized) regulator of the securities market.[10] Though

---

[7] *Zhongguo huanjing nianjian 2003* (China Environment Yearbook 2003) (Beijing: Zhongguo huanjing kexue chubanshe, 2003), 218.

[8] "China's Environment Ministry 'Lacks Local Powers,'" Reuters, March 13, 2008.

[9] This paragraph is based primarily on Carl E. Walter and Fraser J. T. Howie, *Privatizing China: The Stock Markets and Their Role in Corporate Reform* (Singapore: Wiley, 2003); Stephen Green, *China's Stockmarket: A Guide to Its Progress, Players, and Prospects* (London: The Economist, 2003); Stephen Green, *The Development of China's Stock Market, 1984–2002: Equity Politics and Market Institutions* (New York: RoutledgeCurzon, 2004); and Dali Yang, *Remaking the Chinese Leviathan: Market Transition and the Politics of Governance in China* (Stanford, CA: Stanford University Press, 2004), 91–94.

[10] The People's Bank of China, the State Development and Reform Commission, the State Administration of Foreign Exchange, and the State-Owned Assets Supervision and Administration Commission retain some regulatory functions in the securities domain, but the division of responsibility between the CSRC and these agencies has been clarified. See *China Country Finance 2004* (London: The Economist Intelligence Unit, 2004), 68–69.

problems remain, initial post-1998 assessments indicate that centralization and interagency bureaucratic coordination have led to the rise of transparent and regularized management of the stock market. Power has reverted to the center, and local governments have been forced to play according to uniform rules.[11] In sum, the example of securities rationalization in China shows that decentralization, the presence of multiple regulatory bodies, and ambiguous mandates all must be dealt with in order to establish a transparent, rule-based system of regulation. Securities regulation also indicates that centralization and coordination are simpler to achieve when there are fewer agencies involved, and when the issues are relatively new, thus making it less likely that deeply entrenched bureaucratic interests will oppose rationalization.

THEORETICAL IMPLICATIONS

This study has two sets of broad implications: the first concerns state capacity and crisis politics in China, and the second concerns the accountability of the state to its citizens.

State Capacity and Crisis

The China field is divided in its assessments of the strength of the Chinese state, with some arguing that the state is weak, and others that it is strong.[12] This study suggests that more nuance is needed: the Chinese state is weak in certain areas and strong in others. If we accept that a strong state is capable of providing rationalized enforcement, IPR teaches us some general lessons about state capacity in China. In the area of IPR, crises have not been conducive to rationalization. As in other areas, crises in IPR have led to a high volume of enforcement, and they have prompted the government to attempt to rationalize enforcement. But these attempts have been unsuccessful. This finding contrasts with that of Dali Yang, who reports that crisis has been a motor for rationalization in antismuggling activities undertaken by Customs and in tax collection.[13] Two differences between IPR and these other areas may be relevant. First, IPR suffers from both decentralization and excessive jurisdictional overlap, whereas tax collection and antismuggling activities were subject only to decentralization: the absence of jurisdictional overlap made the reforms that Yang describes somewhat easier to implement. Second, IPR is not a priority area for the central government in the same way that taxation and

---

[11] Some scholars argue that local governments retained their leverage vis-à-vis the stock market after 1998. See, for example, Mary Comerford Cooper, "Returning Shares to the People? The Politics of the Stock Market in China" (Ph.D. Dissertation, Department of Political Science, Yale University, 2002).

[12] The argument about weakness is most notably associated with Minxin Pei, *China's Trapped Transition: The Limits of Developmental Autocracy* (Cambridge, MA: Harvard University Press, 2006). See Yang, *Remaking the Chinese Leviathan* for an argument about state strength.

[13] Yang, *Remaking the Chinese Leviathan*.

antismuggling are; given limited resources and the multiplicity of issues competing for the attention of top policymakers, the central government will address priority areas first and make a special effort to rationalize them.

At a more general level, this study offers a method for assessing state capacity that can be applied to studying a range of issue areas in contemporary Chinese politics. The central premise of this study is that state strength cannot be assessed unless we have identified *all* agencies that can provide enforcement in a certain domain. The next step is to measure the volume of enforcement these agencies provide. We can then turn to an assessment of the quality of enforcement. These sequential steps in the evaluation of state strength cannot be completed until we have more detailed information about state activity in a wide range of policy issue areas. Political scientists need a more detailed map of the Chinese state, similar to the map of IPR enforcers presented in Chapters 3–6. It is only when this complete map across a wide range of issue areas has been constructed that we can actually perform an overall assessment of state strength in reform-era China.

Accountability: Citizens versus the State

The second general implication of this study concerns the degree to which the Chinese state is accountable to its citizens. In the area of IPR, individuals have been largely unable to hold bureaucrats accountable for their actions through administrative litigation and administrative reconsideration. However, groups of individuals within China have indeed been successful in forcing the state to respond to their demands for enforcement, especially in relation to protecting consumers from shoddy and counterfeit goods. The media have also helped raise accountability by publishing stories that eventually give rise to high-profile scandals and force the government to provide some type of enforcement. As imperfect as enforcement provided in response to pressure might be, its existence is evidence that the Chinese state is responsive to the public. Even though China is not a democracy, the attention the top leadership pays to public opinion is considerable. In fact, precisely because China is not democratic, China's leadership may be even more sensitive and responsive to public opinion than the leaders of certain democracies are: after all, public opinion is virtually the only channel through which the government can find out what people want; willingness to respond to demands from the public is perhaps a practical way for the central government to demonstrate to its citizens that it is accountable to them.[14] The problem, of course, is that by the time public demands are deemed serious enough for the government to respond, a crisis is already under way. As noted, crisis-mode enforcement has not been conducive to rationalization and the rise of the rule of law in the area of IPR.

---

[14] For an argument about the importance of public pressure in the area of Chinese foreign policy, see Susan Shirk, *China: Fragile Superpower* (New York: Oxford University Press, 2007).

A FINAL REFLECTION: IS CHINA MOVING TOWARD THE RULE
OF LAW?

Although this study is focused on the rationalization of enforcement rather
than on the rule of law, it has implications for one of the most important questions in comparative politics, namely, whether China is moving
closer to the rule of law as part of its trajectory of economic and political
development.

There is a large literature about countries at one or the other end of the
continuum from lawlessness to the rule of law. Scholarly agreement seems to
exist on what constitutes lawlessness – there is a total absence of law or an only
arbitrary enforcement of existing laws, often accompanied by high levels of
corruption and criminality, as exemplified by post-Soviet Russia for most of the
1990s.[15] When it comes to the rule of law, there is significantly less agreement on
a suitable definition and measurement, leading some of the most prominent legal
scholars to conclude that the term is "an essentially contested concept."[16] Nonetheless, it is possible to derive a minimal definition of the rule of law acceptable to
most legal theorists who have written about this issue: there is rule of law when
laws are general, clear, prospective, capable of being followed, promulgated by
disinterested lawmakers, and enforced by unbiased judges.[17] In addition, no
person should be above the law, and those who are accused of violating the
law should be allowed to use legal remedies to defend themselves.[18] Although
critics have pointed out certain flaws or limits in the promotion of the rule of

[15] The literature on lawlessness in post-Soviet Russia and Eastern Europe is immense. Some of
the key works on corruption include Janine Wedel, *Collision and Collusion: The Strange Case
of Western Aid to Eastern Europe, 1989–1998* (New York: St. Martin's Press, 1998);
Marshall Goldman, *The Piratization of Russia: Russian Reform Goes Awry* (New York:
Routledge, 2003); and Alena Ledeneva, *How Russia Really Works: The Informal Practices
That Shaped Post-Soviet Politics and Business* (Ithaca, NY: Cornell University Press, 2006).
On crime, see Federico Varese, *The Russian Mafia: Private Protection in a New Market
Economy* (Oxford: Oxford University Press, 2001), and Vadim Volkov, *Violent Entrepre-
neurs: The Use of Force in the Making of Russian Capitalism* (Ithaca, NY: Cornell University
Press, 2002).

[16] See, for example, Margaret Jane Radin, "Reconsidering the Rule of Law," *Boston University
Law Review* 69:4 (1989), 781–819, and Jeremy Waldron, "Is the Rule of Law an Essentially
Contested Concept (in Florida)?" *Law & Philosophy* 21:2 (2002), 137–164.

[17] Albert Venn Dicey, *Lectures Introductory to the Study of the Law of the Constitution* (London:
Macmillan, 1885); Friedrich August von Hayek, *The Road to Serfdom* (Chicago: University of
Chicago Press, 1944); Lon Fuller, *The Morality of Law* (New Haven, CT: Yale University Press,
1964); Joseph Raz, *The Authority of Law: Essays on Law and Morality* (Oxford: Clarendon
Press, 1979); and Judith Shklar, "Political Theory and the Rule of Law," in *The Rule of Law:
Ideal or Ideology*, ed. Allan C. Hutchinson and Patrick Monahan (Toronto: Carswell, 1987),
1–16.

[18] John Rawls, *A Theory of Justice* (Cambridge, MA: Belknap Press of Harvard University Press,
1971); Raz, *The Authority of Law.*

law, it is clear that a society is better off approximating some version of the rule-of-law ideal than remaining in a state of lawlessness.[19] Where is China in relation to this ideal?

Thin and Thick Conceptions of the Rule of Law

The rule of law is best understood as a continuous variable that ranges from thin to thick. Rule by law is a version of thin rule of law, where the law is used as an instrument of government action, but where those who govern are not constrained by the law. Individuals in a rule-by-law regime have some basic rights, such as the right to property, contract, privacy, and autonomy. An intermediate category is formal legality, where laws are general, prospective, clear, certain, and (to some degree) binding on government officials. Individuals have the right to dignity and (under some circumstances) to justice. One thick version of the rule of law is the liberal-democratic ideal, where consent determines the content of the law and where individuals can expect not just procedural, but also substantive equality, as well as welfare and the preservation of communitarian values.[20] When political scientists discuss the rule of law, they usually are referring to the liberal-democratic ideal.[21] Where does China fit on this continuum? Most theorists would say that China today has a rule-by-law system.[22] A minority of scholars believe that China has moved away from rule by law and currently meets the threshold requirements for formal legality.[23] No one argues that China has (or will necessarily develop) a liberal democratic version of the rule of law.

How does a study of rationalized enforcement fit within this discussion of the rule of law? I agree with those who see China as having moved beyond rule

---

[19] Critics point out that the benefits of the rule of law flow disproportionately to those with money and influence and that the rule of law is an abstract ideal that even the United States has not yet reached. See Frank Upham, "Mythmaking in the Rule-of-Law Orthodoxy," in *Promoting the Rule of Law Abroad: In Search of Knowledge*, ed. Thomas Carothers (Washington, DC: Carnegie Endowment for International Peace, 2006), 75–104.

[20] Thin and thick definitions and examples are based on Randall Peerenboom, *China's Long March toward Rule of Law* (New York: Cambridge University Press, 2002), and Brian Tamanaha, *On the Rule of Law: History, Politics, Theory* (New York: Cambridge University Press, 2004).

[21] See, for example, Barry R. Weingast, "Political Foundations of Democracy and the Rule of Law," *American Political Science Review* 91:2 (1997), 245–263; Michael David Sabados, "The Influence of the Judiciary upon the Development of the Rule of Law in Post-Communist Poland" (Ph.D. Dissertation, Department of Political Science, Ohio State University, 1998); Mark Ungar, *Elusive Reform: Democracy and the Rule of Law in Latin America* (Boulder, CO: Lynne Rienner, 2002); and Rebecca Bill Chavez, "The Construction of the Rule of Law in Argentina: A Tale of Two Provinces," *Comparative Politics* 35:4 (2002), 417–437.

[22] Yongnian Zheng, *From Rule of Law to Rule by Law? A Realistic View of China's Legal Development*, EAI Working Paper no. 1 (Singapore: East Asian Institute, National University of Singapore, 1998); Yongnian Zheng, *Globalization and State Transformation in China* (New York: Cambridge University Press, 2004), 187–202.

[23] Peerenboom, *China's Long March toward Rule of Law*.

by law, at least in certain domains. This last qualification is central. My conception of the rule of law is that it emerges incrementally. Therefore, identifying areas where rationalized enforcement has already arisen may actually be pointing us to the areas precisely in which rule of law is more likely to develop later. More importantly, analyzing the conditions under which rationalization emerges may also help us understand the factors that facilitate the rise of the rule of law. In the area of Chinese IPR, the rule of law is unlikely to emerge soon in trademark protection, but it may emerge in patent protection, as well as in copyrights.

Patchy Rule of Law

Political science prizes generalizability. Yet when we investigate the emergence of the rule of law, we cannot make blanket statements about its presence or absence in a country as a whole. We need to be aware of three dividing lines that can create "patchy" rule of law: geographical, political/economic, and issue area. First, although sometimes the rule of law exists countrywide, it may also be geographically limited, developing only in certain provinces or regions, as the experience of China's special economic zones demonstrates.[24] Democratization theorists have long been aware that the spread of democracy can be uneven across a country's territory,[25] yet this fundamental insight has not been applied to studying the spatial variations in the presence of the rule of law.[26] Second, the rule of law need not emerge in the political and economic spheres simultaneously. Especially in nondemocratic states, the rule of law may arise first in the economic sphere and only then, potentially, spill over to the political sphere. Historical examples of this sequencing pattern include Franco's Spain, Chile under Pinochet, and Greece during the reign of the junta.[27] Third, we need to distinguish between issue-specific and universal rule of law. It is often

---

[24] Rebecca Bill Chavez, *The Rule of Law in Nascent Democracies: Judicial Politics in Argentina* (Stanford CA: Stanford University Press, 2004), argues that there are spatial differences in the presence of the rule of law in the Argentine provinces of San Luis and Mendoza.

[25] On Italy, see Robert D. Putnam, with Robert Leonardi and Raffaella Y. Nanetti, *Making Democracy Work: Civic Traditions in Modern Italy* (Princeton, NJ: Princeton University Press, 1993). On Russia, see Nicolai N. Petro, *Crafting Democracy: How Novgorod Has Coped With Rapid Social Change* (Ithaca, NY: Cornell University Press, 2004), and Gulnaz Sharafutdinova, "When Do Elites Compete? The Determinants of Political Competition in Russian Regions," *Comparative Politics* 38:3 (2006), 273–293.

[26] For an exception, see Phyllis Dininio and Robert Orttung, "Explaining Patterns of Corruption in the Russian Regions," *World Politics* 57:4 (2005), 500–529.

[27] On Chile, see Robert Barros, "Dictatorship and the Rule of Law: Rules and Military Power in Pinochet's Chile," in *Democracy and the Rule of Law*, ed. José María Maravall and Adam Przeworski (New York: Cambridge University Press, 2003), 188–219. On Spain, see José J. Toharia, "Judicial Independence in an Authoritarian Regime: The Case of Contemporary Spain," *Law and Society Review* 9:3 (1975), 475–496. On the consequences of undergoing a political transition in Eastern Europe without first building the institutions of the rule of law, see Richard Rose and Doh Chull Shin, "Democratization Backwards: The Problem of Third-Wave Democracies," *British Journal of Political Science* 31:2 (2001), 331–354.

the case that some political or economic issue areas develop the rule of law (e.g., small business contract enforcement in China), even when others do not (e.g., land-use rights in China). Thinking of the rule of law as a binary variable that is either present or absent on the entire territory of a country can blind us to its emergence, which is often limited by geography, or by issue area, or by exclusivity to the economic realm.

Courts and the Rule of Law

We usually focus on the strength of a country's court system as the chief indicator of progress toward the institutionalization of the rule of law. Research on the rule of law cannot ignore the operation of the courts. But laws are rarely enforced only by courts of law, especially in a transitional economy like China, where, depending on the issue area, administrative agencies are either the dominant enforcers of the law or the second most important enforcers after the courts. In such economies, an assessment of progress toward the rule of law based solely on an analysis of the operation of the courts is at best incomplete and at worst misleading. A final implication of this study is that to understand the role that law plays in postcommunist economies, we need to observe the interactions among civil, criminal, and administrative enforcers within sharply defined issue areas. The bureaucratic details matter. It may be that the areas where we find that rationalized enforcement is being nurtured are those in which the rule of law will first take root.

Glossary of Selected Chinese Terms

Note on Characters and Transliteration: Terms used in the People's Republic of China are rendered in simplified Chinese characters, whereas terms used in Taiwan are rendered in traditional Chinese characters. Transliterations are all rendered in pinyin.

Pinyin	Character	English Translation
ban'an fei	办案费	case-handling fee
Banquan guanli si	版权管理司	Copyright Management Department
baohu san	保护伞	protection, cover (lit., umbrella)
Baohu zhihui caichanquan jingcha dadui	保護智慧財產權警察大隊	Specialized IPR Police (IPRP) (Taiwan)
bei'an	备案	recordation
bianzhi	编制	personnel allocation
buji	部级	ministerial rank (government agency)
Caizheng bu	财政部	Ministry of Finance
Caizhengbu guanshui zongju	財政部關稅總局	Ministry of Finance Directorate General of Customs (Taiwan)
Chajin fangmao shangpin xiaozu	查禁仿冒商品小組	Anticounterfeiting Committee (ACC) (Taiwan)
chaobian	超编	to exceed the personnel allocation
Chengshi guanli xingzheng zhifa ju	城市管理行政执法局	City Management Administrative Enforcement Bureau
chiming shangbiao	驰名商标	nationally famous trademark
chuizhi jigou	垂直机构	vertical bureaucratic structure

Pinyin	Character	English Translation
da'an yao'an	大案要案	big and important case
daiguan	代管	to manage on behalf of somebody else
Dajia bangongshi	打假办公室	anticounterfeiting office
danbaojin	担保金	bond (financial)
dangchang chufa	当场处罚	impose a punishment on the spot
danshe	单设	independent (office or agency)
daoban	盗版	pirated copy of copyrighted material
dazhuan	大专	two-year college
difang fayuan	地方法院	district court (in Taiwan)
duzhi zui	渎职罪	(crime of) dereliction of duty
Faji jiancha ting	法纪检查厅	Prosecutorial Department for Dereliction of Duty and Infringement of Citizens' Rights
faming zhuanli	发明专利	invention patent
Fan tanwu huilu zongju	反贪污贿赂总局	General Administration for Combating Embezzlement and Bribery (GACEB)
fapiao	发票	official receipt
feifa jingying shu'e	非法经营数额	illegal business volume
feifa jingying zui	非法经营罪	crime of illegal business activity
fenju	分局	branch
fu buji	副部级	vice-ministerial rank (government agency)
fushen	复审	(patent) reexamination
fushengji chengshi	副省级城市	subprovincial-level city
fuzeren	負責人	responsible person (Taiwan)
ganbu kaohe	干部考核	cadre evaluation
gangwei mubiao zerenzhi	岗位目标责任制	target responsibility system
Gangwu jingcha ju	港務警察局	coast guard police (Taiwan)
Gaoji renmin fayuan	高级人民法院	high people's court
Gaosu nailun	告訴乃論	doctrine of prosecution upon complaint (Taiwan)
Gaosu xunjing (or gaosu jiaojing)	高速巡警 or 高速交警	highway patrol
ge'an jiandu	个案监督	individual case supervision
geren	个人	individual
Gong'an bu	公安部	Ministry of Public Security (MPS)
gonggao	公告	notice
Gongjiaojing	公交警	traffic police

Pinyin	Character	English Translation
gongsu zui	公訴罪	public crime prosecuted without complaint (Taiwan)
guangdie zu	光跌組	Optical Disk Department (Taiwan)
Guojia churujing jianyan jianyi ju	国家出入境检验检疫局	Administration for Entry-Exit Inspection and Quarantine
Guojia gongshang xingzheng guanli ju	国家工商行政管理局	State Administration for Industry and Commerce (SAIC)
Guojia guangbo dianying dianshi zongju	国家广播电影电视总局	State Administration on Radio, Film, and Television (SARFT)
guojia peichang fa	国家赔偿法	State Compensation Law
Guojia shipin yaopin jiandu guanli ju	国家食品药品监督管理局	State Food and Drug Administration (SFDA)
Guojia yancao zhuanmai ju	国家烟草专卖局	State Tobacco Monopoly Administration (STMA)
Guojia zhiliang jiandu jianyan jianyi zongju = Jishu jiandu ju	国家质量监督检验检疫总局 = 技术监督局	Administration for Quality Supervision, Inspection, and Quarantine (AQSIQ) = Technical Supervision Bureau (TSB)
Guojia zhishi chanquan ju	国家知识产权局	State Intellectual Property Office (SIPO)
Guojia zhongyiyao guanli ju	国家中医药管理局	State Administration for Traditional Chinese Medicine
Guowuyuan zhishu jigou	国务院直属机构	vice-ministerial-level agency (directly under the State Council)
Guowuyuan zhishu shiye danwei	国务院直属事业单位	administrative unit directly subordinate to the State Council
Guowuyuan zucheng buwei	国务院组成部委	ministerial-level agency or commission
Haiguan zongshu	海关总署	General Administration of Customs (GAC)
Hangkong jingcha ju	航空警察局	air police (Taiwan)
heyi ting	合议庭	collegiate bench (in a court of law)
Huanjing baohu bu	环境保护部	Ministry of Environmental Protection (MEP)
jia	假	fake
jiamao	假冒	counterfeit
jiamao weilie	假冒伪劣	fake and substandard (goods)
Jiancha bu	监察部	Ministry of Supervision
Jiancha yuan	检察院	Procuratorate

Pinyin	Character	English Translation
Jiaotong bu	交通部	Ministry of Communications
jiaoyu fujia fei	教育附加费	educational surcharge
jiceng renmin fayuan	基层人民法院	basic people's court
Jichang anjian	机场安检	airport police
jigou	机构	organ
jingcha fenju	警察分局	police branch station (Taiwan)
jizhong xingdong	集中行动	enforcement campaign (lit., concentrated enforcement)
jubao xin	举报信	letter of complaint
kaiting shenli	开庭审理	to hold an open court hearing
kangsu	抗诉	protest by the Procuratorate
ke	科	department or section in an administrative agency
lanyong zhiquan	滥用职权	abuse of power
li'an chachu	立案查处	investigation after accepting a case
lingdao guanxi	领导关系	leadership relationship
maochong	冒充	passing off
Nongye bu	农业部	Ministry of Agriculture (MOA)
po'an	破案	solve (lit., break) a case
pohuo	破获	uncover
qinfan zhishi chanquan	侵犯知识产权	crime of IPR infringement
qinquan	侵权	infringement
qiye suode shui	企业所得税	enterprise income tax
Quanguo saohuang dafei gongzuo xiaozu bangongshi = Saohuang ban	全国扫黄打非工作小组办公室 = 扫黄办	Office of the National Anti-Pornography and Anti-Piracy Working Committee (Anti-Piracy Office subnationally)
quanguo saohuang dafei jizhong xingdong = saohuang dafei xingdong	全国扫黄打非集中行动 = 扫黄打非行动	Anti-Piracy and Anti-Pornography Campaign
raoluan shichang chengxu zui	扰乱市场程序罪	crime of upsetting market order
renmin fating	人民法庭	people's tribunal
Renshi bu	人事部	Ministry of Personnel
shangbiao	商标	trademark
shengchan xiaoshou weilie shangpin zui	生产销售伪劣商品罪	crime of manufacturing and marketing of fake and substandard commodities
sheng yixia chuizhi	省一下垂直	centralized (having a vertical bureaucratic structure) from the province down

Pinyin	Character	English Translation
shiye danwei	事业单位	administrative unit
shiyong xinxing	实用新型	utility model
shou'an fei	受案费	acceptance fee for a court case
shouju	收据	informal receipt
shuangchong lingdao	双重领导	dual bureaucratic subordination
shudi jigou	属地机构	decentralized ("local") bureaucratic structure
Taiwan gaodeng fayuan	臺灣高等法院	Taiwan High Court
tiaozheng	调整	adjust
tidaiyi	替代役	military recruits doing alternative military service (Taiwan)
Tielu jingcha or tiegong'an	铁路警察 or 铁公安	railroad police
tingzheng hui	听政会	administrative hearing
tongzhi	通知	circular or notice
tousu	投诉	make an official complaint or request
waiguan sheji	外观设计	design patent
weifa suode shu'e	违法所得数额	illegal profit
Weisheng bu	卫生部	Ministry of Health (MOH)
Weisheng shu	衛生署	Department of Health (DOH) (Taiwan)
Wenhua bu	文化部	Ministry of Culture (MOC)
Wenhua shichang si	文化市场司	Cultural Market Department
Wenhua tiyu ju	文化体育局	Culture and Sports Bureau
Wujing	武警	People's Armed Police (PAP)
wuxiao	无效	(patent) invalidation
xiashu danwei	下属单位	subordinate unit
Xingshi jingcha ju	刑事警察局	criminal investigation police (Taiwan)
xingshi juliu	刑事拘留	criminal detention
xingzheng fuyi	行政复议	administrative reconsideration
xingzheng jueding shu	行政决定书	administrative decision
xingzheng susong	行政诉讼	administrative litigation
xingzheng ting	行政庭	administrative tribunal (within a court of law)
Xingzhengyuan gongping jiaoyi weiyuanhui	行政院公平交易委員會	Fair Trade Commission (FTC) (Taiwan)
Xinwen chuban zongshu	新闻出版总署	General Administration of Press and Publications (GAPP)
yan caizheng	烟财政	"tobacco finance"

Pinyin	Character	English Translation
yanli daji = yanda	严厉打击 = 严打	"strike hard" (against crime)
yanye nongye techan shui	烟叶农业特产税	tobacco leaf special crop tax
yewu guanxi	业务关系	professional relationship
yige jigou, liangkuai paizi	一个机构两块牌子	one system (of government offices), two nameplates
zaishen	再审	retrial
zengzhi shui	增值税	VAT
zhengdun he guifan shichang jingji chengxu xingdong	整顿和规范市场经济程序行动	Campaign to Rectify and Standardize Market Order
zhihui caichanquan	智慧財產權	IPR (Taiwan)
zhiju	支局	suboffice
zhishi chanquan	知识产权	IPR
zhishi chanquan fating	知识产权法庭	IPR tribunals (at the people's courts)
zhishi chanquan jubao tousu zhongxin	知识产权举报投诉中心	IPR complaint center
zhiwu mingcheng biao	职务名称表	*nomenklatura*
Zhonggong zhongyang jilü jiancha weiyuanhui (abbreviated as Zhongjiwei)	中共中央纪律监察委员会 (中纪委)	Central Discipline Inspection Commission of the Central Committee of the Chinese Communist Party (CC CCP)
zhongji renmin fayuan	中级人民法院	intermediate people's court
zhuanli	专利	patent
zhudong chachu	主动查处	investigate proactively
zhuming shangbiao	著名商标	locally famous trademark
zhuzuoquan = banquan	著作权 = 版权	copyright
zisu anjian	自诉案件	private prosecution case
zonghe zhifa dui	综合执法队	comprehensive enforcement team
Zuigao fayuan	最高法院	Supreme Court (in Taiwan)
Zuigao jiancha yuan	最高检察院	Supreme People's Procuratorate (SPP)
Zuigao renmin fayuan	最高人民法院	Supreme People's Court (SPC)

Index

Abnett, William, 17, 97
accountability, 36–46, 68, 274, 278, 279;
    administrative, 36, 38, 44; from citizens,
    36–39, 279; and clarity of mandate, 28, 35;
    and enforcement, 24–25, 28, 274;
    horizontal, 40, 41–44; and jurisdiction, 28,
    36; and letters and visits system, 40; and
    media, 37, 279; and pressure, 53
Adcock, Alan, 12, 27, 163, 215
Administration for Entry-Exit Inspection and
    Quarantine (China), 120
Administration for Industry and Commerce
    (AIC; China), 62, 204, 205–206. See also
    SAIC
administrative agencies, 6, 10, 17, 25, 115–
    142; and Anti-Pornography and Anti-Piracy
    Campaign, 60, 228–229; in campaign-style
    enforcement, 230–234; centralization of,
    144–145, 275; and cigarette counterfeiting,
    199–200, 207–208, 218; competition
    between, 22–23; conflicts of interest within,
    134; cooperation of, 134, 207–209, 246;
    coordination of, 164, 187, 276, 277,
    278; and copyright enforcement, 227, 231–
    232, 234–235; corruption in, 214–215,
    274; vs. criminal enforcement, 146–147,
    246; cross-national comparisons of, 116,
    181, 272; Czech, 116, 140–142, 144, 176;
    and environmental protection, 276; French,
    116, 142–143, 144; jurisdictional overlap
    in, 116, 144–145, 187, 218–219; for
    patents, 219, 250, 255; and police, 115,
    147–148, 207–208, 241; and quality of
    enforcement, 130, 141–142; rank system
    in, 51–52; and rate of appeals, 11–12;
    regional variation in, 81, 158; Russian, 116,
    130–134, 135, 144–145, 218, 246, 247;

shirking by, 274, 276; Taiwanese, 116, 135–
    140, 144; for trademarks, 118–126, 185,
    189; U.S., 116, 143–144; and volume of
    enforcement, 142, 144. See also
    bureaucracies
administrative enforcement, 22, 115–142; of
    copyrights, 126–130, 222, 227, 241, 242,
    245, 247; vs. criminal enforcement, 135,
    140, 146–147, 152–153, 173, 204–205,
    217–218, 246; cross-national comparison
    of, 115–116; Czech, 116, 140–142, 144,
    176, 272; defined, 115; French, 272; vs.
    judicial enforcement, 23, 65, 107, 188–189,
    222, 241–244, 247–248, 256, 283; of
    patents, 256; proactive, 13, 14, 23, 273,
    274; quality vs. volume in, 145, 181; in
    response to complaints, 273, 274; Russian,
    216–218, 244, 245, 272; Taiwanese, 136,
    140, 272; of trademarks, 206–207, 214–
    215, 274; U.S., 113, 115, 272; volume of,
    145, 181. See also campaign-style
    enforcement; quasi-judicial enforcement
administrative litigation (xingzheng susong),
    37–38, 40; and Anti-Pornography and Anti-
    Piracy Campaign, 234; and copyright
    enforcement, 227, 240–241; fairness of, 38–
    39; and patent enforcement, 256, 260, 268;
    vs. reconsideration, 38, 39; in Russia, 37–
    38; and state accountability, 279; and State
    Compensation Law, 40; and trademark
    enforcement, 214
administrative reconsideration (xingzheng
    fuyi), 37–38, 40; vs. administrative
    litigation, 38, 39; and Anti-Pornography
    and Anti-Piracy Campaign, 234; and
    copyright enforcement, 227, 240, 241;
    and patent enforcement, 40, 256, 260,